Lionel is the registered trademark of Lionel L.L.C.

Books by Tom McComas and James Tuohy

Lionel: A Collectors Guide & History
Vol. I: Prewar O Gauge
Vol. II: Postwar
Vol. III: Standard Gauge
Vol. IV: 1970-1980
Vol. V: The Archives
Vol. VI: Advertising & Art
Great Toy Train Layouts of America
Collecting Toy Trains

Videos by Tom McComas

1991 Lionel Video Catalog
1992 Lionel Video Catalog
23rd Annual LCCA Convention
Atlas 21st Century Track System
A Lionel Christmas
Fun & Thrills With American Flyer
Great Lionel Layouts, Parts 1 and 2
Great Toy Train Layouts of America, Parts 1-6
Holiday Music
How To Build A Toy Train Layout
I Love Big Machines
I Love Cat Machines, Parts 1 and 2
I Love Christmas
I Love Toy Trains, Parts 1-7
I Love Toy Trains Special 90-minute Edition
Lionel: The Movie 1-3
No Game Today
The Great Montana Train Ride
The History of Lionel Trains
The Magic of Lionel, Parts 1-4
The Making of the New Lionel Showroom Layout
The Making of the Scale Hudson
The Re-Making of the Lionel 1949 Showroom Layout
Toy Train Accessories, Parts 1 and 2
Toy Train Revue Video Magazine, 1-12
Toy Trains & Christmas, Parts 1-3
Toys of the Past
YogaKids

Price and Rarity Guides

Lionel Prewar: 1900-1943 No. 1
Lionel Postwar: 1945-1969 No. 1
Lionel Postwar: 1945-1969 No. 2
Lionel: 1970-1989
Lionel: 1970-1992
Lionel: 1901-1995
Lionel: 1901-1996
Lionel: 1901-1997
Lionel: 1901-1998
Lionel: 1901-1969 (1999 Edition)
Lionel Illustrated: 1970-1999
Lionel Illustrated: 1970-2000
3-Rail Guide, No. 1 (1996 edition)
M.T.H. Guide, No. 1 (1999 edition)

Magazines

Toy Train Revue Journal

Webzine

wwwtoytrainrevue.com

DVD

I Love Toy Trains, Parts 1-3

LIONEL
Price & Rarity Guide
Volume 1
1901 - 1969
2000 Edition

ISBN: 0-937522-91-0
Published by TM Books & Video, Inc.
Box 279
New Buffalo, Michigan 49117
1-219-879-2822

Copyright © 2000 by TM Books and Video, Inc., Tom McComas, President. All rights reserved. No part of this book may be reproduced without the prior written permission of TM Books & Video, excepting brief quotes used in connection with reviews written specifically for inclusion in a magazine or newspaper.

Printed in the United States of America
First printing January, 2000

Lionel
Price & Rarity Guide
Volume 1
1901 - 1969
2000 Edition

by
Tom McComas
and
Charles Krone

For Emily Elizabeth Shreve,
CK's first granddaughter.

Page

Introduction
About the Guide   3

Prewar, 1901-1942
Accessories   9
Track & Transformers   22
O Gauge   35
OO Gauge   59
Standard Gauge   61
2 7/8-Inch Gauge   79

Postwar, 1945-1969
Diesels   80
Electrics   88
Powered Units   90
Steamers   92
Passenger Cars   100
Rolling Stock   104
Accessories   143
Sets   159
Boxes   172
HO   184
Plasticville   198

Index   220

Quick Reference   232

Introduction

Lionel trains started in 1900 and are still going strong in 2000. Few companies (and no toy makers) can make that claim. Along the way, Lionel has weathered World Wars, recessions, depressions, fads, dramatic changes in technology and weak management. Lionel came close to bankruptcy at least twice and, in the early 1950s, enjoyed huge profitability as it became the largest toy maker in the world. Lionel has ridden the hectic roller coaster ride of 20th Century America and survived – a tribute to old-fashioned innovation, resilience and enterprise.

This two-volume set is in celebration of that accomplishment. Every train item ever produced by Lionel is listed. And not only do we list the item, but we describe the item, indicate the collectible variations, assign a rarity rating and print a current market price. No small undertaking, but with computers, hard work, and the help of our friends, we did it.

Our vision was to make these special editions, well...special. After all, it's the 100th Anniversary of Lionel and we wanted to produce guides commensurate with that event. We also wanted to appeal to both the serious collector and the casual observer, because with all the hoopla concerning Lionel's 100th Anniversary, these books will be read by a wider-than-normal audience. To accomplish that, we added color pictures and a new history section that combines the story of the company with quotes from the Lionel catalog, reminiscences, catalog illustrations and photographs. To provide a historical backdrop, we included interesting events of the 20th Century, because, in many ways, the story of Lionel is also the story of America. We are happy with the results and feel our new history provides readers with a fun-to-read story of a company that has been enchanting both children and grown-ups for 100 years.

But this is a price guide first and recent changes in our hobby have dictated changes in our approach to pricing. First, we dropped the *Mint* price in our Postwar section. In this edition, we print only the price for an item in *Like New* condition, without the box.

We began printing *Mint* prices in 1997 because many actual *Mint* items were turning up for sale (aging collectors were selling their collections) and no price guide accurately reported on *Mint* prices. While we attempted (in the "How to Use" section of the book) to make it clear that the price to the right of the slash was for legitimate *Mint/Boxed* items only, many readers applied it to items in less-than-*Mint* condition. The result was a general feeling that TM prices were too high. To change that perception, we have eliminated *Mint* prices.

Prices for Postwar items in *Like New* or better are strong. Prices for items in *Excellent* or below are falling and the gap between the two is growing wider. Collectors will still pay top prices for *LN* and better (with crisp, complete boxes) but demand for the lesser grades has fallen drastically because there are so many new trains on the market. Why would an operator pay $600/$700 for a Postwar Lionel engine in *Very Good* when he can buy a new engine for less and get the latest technology?

Boxes, auctions and the Internet are generating the most buzz. As collectors continually seek to upgrade, boxes are still in big demand. In fact, some boxes are bringing more than the hardware that came inside the box. There seems to be a new "crazy-price-paid-at-auction" story every day. The latest was the $68,000 paid for an uncataloged Lionel Sears set. High prices are also being generated on the Internet, but all auction and Internet prices are not abnormally high. Those are just the prices you hear about. There are bargains too. We picked up a 156 Station in *LN* for $65 on e-Bay and lots of trains are sold for below book at auctions after the high-rollers go home. So we receive conflicting reports – crazy high there, ridiculously low here. Prices are a mixed bag.

When Lionel is mentioned, one thinks of Christmas mornings, happy times with dad, irresistible catalog illustrations and toys so impressive and heavy, they were difficult for a six-year-old to lift. When Joshua Lionel Cowen, Lionel's founder, died in 1968, the *New York Times* noted that Cowen had established Lionel trains as the third wing of Christmas, right up there with Santa Claus and the Christmas tree – quite an accomplishment for a young tinkerer who designed his first train as an attention-getting device in a store window.

Lionel trains enter our consciousness when we are young, and never really leave. Oh, they are put on the back shelf for awhile, but all it takes is a chance meeting, a serendipitous glance in a store window, to have all those memories come flooding back. "I loved Lionel trains as a kid," recalls collector Phil Baragne of New Jersey. "But as I grew older I forgot about them. Then one day, I happened to see a set in an antique store and I fell in love all over again. I became fanatical.

Bought all the catalogs, bought all the stuff I dreamed about but never was able to wangle out of my parents, and now we have a huge layout. I'm doing everything with my kids that my dad did with me and his dad did with him. It made me realize you never really own Lionel trains. You are just the caretaker until you pass them on to the next generation."

Few products inspire such loyalty, passion and zeal. Thousands attend weekend toy train meets in cities all over the country. Attendees span all social and economic boundaries. Some are operators. Some are collectors. Some rich. Some poor. But all are connected by a mutual fascination with a toy. New electronics are dramatically changing the way toy trains sound and the way you control them. The Internet is dramatically changing the way toy trains are bought and sold. But the basic appeal remains unchanged – a toy train chugging around a track is as irresistible in 2000 as it was in 1900. Lionel, it would seem, is forever.

Acknowledgments

We are grateful to the many collectors and experts who helped us establish prices and rarity ratings for this book. The method we use to determine prices is quite simple. We send copies of the book to experienced collectors all over the country and ask that they indicate any changes in price in the categories they feel knowledgeable in. We also ask them to indicate any changes in how difficult an item is to find (Rarity Rating) and if they detect any discernible trend (Trend Arrow). We also check the Internet, the LCCA and TCA newsletters, and we observe asking prices at meets.

We then analyze the data and come up with a consensus price, Rarity Rating and trend. It's not a perfect system. None exists. But it does provide our reader with a guide to what items are selling for.

Dave Garrigues helped with the facts, but had nothing to do with the pricing (as he feels strongly that prices should not be been printed). Dave is a dedicated researcher and very knowedgable about all manufacturers of toy trains. We are honored to have Dave's help.

A special thanks to Charles Sommer, who makes a mighty effort each year to expand and improve his HO section. Also thanks to John LaLima, David Dansky, John Caron, John Potter, Fritz Von Tagen, Fred Stribey, Bill Tardy, Tom and Tony Rotunda, Joe Pehringer, Lou Palumbo, Mike Moore, Tom Shanahan, Denis Foster, Floyd Kenlay, John Keene Kelly, Scott Bloomquist, Matt Towne, Rodney Windham, Richie Kohn, Rod and Tammy La Gard, Annie Clauder, Gayle Orvis and Dan Bengert.

Thanks to Jim Herron of the Houston Tinplate Operators Society for sending their Aquarium car. We know that acknowledgement belongs in the other book, but we didn't have the space.

Once again, the lovely Charyl McComas and Joseph Stachler combined their talents to produce fine photographs for the cover of this and our Modern Era Guide. On the homefront, Stew, Karen, Connie, Sharon, Ben, Judy, James and Seymore continue to thrill and delight.

Our sincere thanks to Christopher for obtaining gainful employment and to Tom for volunteering to do Toy Fair gratis as partial payment for previous kindnesses extended on his behalf. Congratulations to Jack Lane for making high honors and discovering the rewards of hard work. Also to Jeffrey for still trying hard even after going 0 for 11.

Researching trains is an ongoing process and we ask our readers to help. Call, write or e-mail us with information you do not find in this book. With your help, each edition will become more accurate and informative. Thanks for participating and thanks for buying this book.

Condition	Add or subtract to listed price
Prewar 1901-1929	
Mint Boxed	+60% or more
Mint (without box)	+50%
Like New	+40%
Excellent	20% to 25%
Very Good	**Price Listed**
Good	-15%
Fair	-30%
Prewar 1930-1943	
Mint Boxed	+50% or more
Mint (without box)	+40%
Like New	+25%
Excellent	**Price Listed**
Very Good	-20%
Good	-30%
Fair	-40%
Postwar 1945-1969	
Mint Boxed	+50-100% plus
Like New (with box)	+25-50%
Like New (no box)	**Price Listed**
Excellent	-30%
Very Good	-45%
Good	-60%
Fair	-75%+

About the Current Market

In real estate, it's location, location, location. In the current train market, it's boxes, boxes, boxes. Boxes are so much in demand, in fact, it is impossible to accurately indicate the difference in value for an item with and without the box. We have tried, but the zeal with which some collectors go after boxes is impossible to gauge. Just know that if you have an item with the original box in *Like New* or *Mint* condition, you can expect to get a significant premium over the same item without the box.

Postwar items in average condition without a box have dropped dramatically in value. For example, you could expect to get $3000-$3500 for a Western Pacific in *LN* with the box in similar condition. For a *LN* 2345 without the box, the price drops to $1500. In *Ex* (no box), one would be lucky to get $800-$1000 and in *VG*, $500 or less. In the past, items in average condition were snapped up by operators, who don't share the same fanatical concern for condition that collectors do. Today, operators can buy new and get mint condition plus the latest technology. All these new trains have hurt the market for Postwar Lionel in average condition. Prewar Lionel is up significantly – across the board – Standard gauge and O gauge – boxes or no boxes. Of course, Prewar boxes are in great demand too, but most Prewar collectors are still looking to upgrade on condition. They view boxes with less urgency than their Postwar counterpart. Lionel HO is up as is OO. In general, the hobby is healthy. More new trains are being manufactured then ever and interest in both operating and collecting is on the rise.

A note to a non-collector selling trains to a collector: The prices printed in this book are retail asking prices for trains sold at train shows by train collectors to train collectors. If you are selling an assortment of trains to a collector, expect to receive forty to fifty percent less than the prices in this guide.

TCA and TTOS Grading Standards

Mint	Brand new. Unmarred, all original and unused with original box and all appropriate contents.
Like New	Free of any blemishes, nicks or scratches; original condition throughout, very little sign of use.
Excellent	Minute nicks or scratches. No dents or rust.
Very Good	Few scratches, exceptionally clean; no dents.
Good	Scratches, small dents, dirty.
Fair	Well-scratched, chipped, dented, rusted or warped.
Poor	Beat-up, junk condition, some useable parts.

About This Guide

Getting Started

Take time to read this section. Our format is easy but you have to understand it. Items are listed in the text by category, F-3s under Diesels, etc. Within their category, the catalog number for each item is listed in numerical order. Items are also listed by numerical order in the index.

Sample entry:
1234   **Roadname** 54-56
    1. Gray-red/blue   (3)   900
    2. Gray-red/yellow   (4)   700▲

The number on the left in boldface type is the catalog number. Next is the road name of the item followed by the years in the catalog. The number in parenthesis is the Rarity Rating based on a 1 to 5 scale. 5 is rare. 1 is common.

Prices

The number in boldface on the right is the asking price based on grading standards established by the TCA and TTOS (see page 2).

Postwar Prices - Postwar prices are based on *Like New* condition, no box. We discontinued printing a price for *Mint* as readers were applying our *Mint* prices to items in less-than-*Mint* condition. This resulted in the perception that Postwar prices were higher than they really were.

Prewar Prices are based on *Excellent* for items made after 1930 and *Very Good* for items made in 1930 and before.

We chose these grades for the various eras because we feel it is possible for a collector to assemble a collection of items from the various eras in the condition we selected. If you have an item in a grade different than the one printed, check the chart on page 2 to see how much to add or subtract from the printed price.

How to Find an Item

If you know the catalog number – go to the index, find the catalog number listed in numerical order, the page the item is on is printed to the right.

If you don't know the catalog number – check the contents page to find the category.

Variations

We list all collectible variations (those worth more than the normal production version).

Colors

The dominant exterior color is to the left of the slash. The color of the type is to the right of the slash. Two exterior colors are separated with a hyphen. Example: white body, red roof and red type would be white-red/red.

Trend Arrows

▲ Indicates item is in demand and the price is going up. ▼ Indicates demand is down and the price is falling. No Trend Arrow indicates no discernible trend, one way or another.

* Indicates less than normal sampling used in determining price.

Abbreviations and Symbols:

*	Insufficient sales reported to arrive at a price. An * after a price indicates the price listed was arrived at using less than usual reported sales.	T&W	Indicates tender comes with or without whistle
		U	Uncataloged
		VAD	Value Added Dealer
		W	Whistle
alum	Aluminum	WL	Warning Light
ASF (trucks)	Strong-Arm truck	X	Indicates different from normal production-higher couplers, different trim, color, etc.
blk	Black		
bj	Black journals		
bnt org	Burnt Orange	YED	Year-end deal
brn	Brown	yell	Yellow
crm	Cream	2PR	Two-position reverse
D	Dummy	3PR	Three-position reverse
D-C	Distance Control	4W	Four-wheel trucks
DD	Double Door	4WPT	Four-wheel plastic trucks
DG	Door guides	4WT	Four-wheel die-cast trucks
dk	Dark	5+	Indicates a pre-production mock-up, paint sample or special item of which less than 100 were made.
DL	Directional lights		
DSS	Department Store Special		
E	Automatic Reverse Unit	5P	Indicates a prototype.
EC	Electrocouplers	6W	Six-wheel trucks
ECP	Electrocouplers Plus	6WT	Six-wheel die-cast trucks
EH	Electronic horn		
ERU	Electronic reverse unit		**Road Name Abbreviations**
ESOS	Electronic Sound of Steam	ACL	Atlantic Coast Line
fc	Fixed couplers	ACY	Akron, Canton & Youngstown
FG	Fire-box glow	AT&SF	Atcheson, Topeka & Santa Fe
FM	Factory mistake	B&A	Boston & Albany
grn	Green	BAR	Boston & Aroostook
HL	Headlight	BN	Burlington Northern
hs	Heat stamped	B&LE	Bessimer & Lake Erie
LH	Left hand switch	B&M	Boston & Maine
litho	Lithographed	B&O	Baltimore & Ohio
lt	Light	CCC&STL	Cleveland, Chicago, Cincinnati & St. Louis
mar	Maroon		
MB	1955 Door	C&IM	Chicago & Illinois Midland
MR	Manual reverse	C&NW	Chicago & North Western
MT	Magne-Traction	C&O	Chesapeake & Ohio
MSOS	Mechanical Sound of Steam	CIRR	Chatahoochie Industrial Railroad
N-D	Non-derailing switch	CN	Canadian National
NDV	No difference in value	CN&L	Columbia, Newberry & Laurens
NIB	No individual box. Item came in set box.	CP & CP Rail	Canadian Pacific
		CPR	Canadian Pacific Railroad
nj	Nickel journals	D&H	Delaware & Hudson
NM	Announced but never made	D&RGW	Denver and Rio Grande West
ob	Original box	DT&I	Detroit, Toledo & Ironton
Obvs	Observation	DT&S	Detroit, Toledo & Shoreline
oc	Operating Couplers	EMD	Electro Motive Division of GM
op	Operating	FEC	Florida East Coast
org	Orange	GM&O	Gulf, Mobile & Ohio
PDM	Pullmor Direct Motor	GN	Great Northern
PF	Possible fake	GTW	Grand Trunk Western
PM	Pullmor Motor	IC	Illinois Central
U	Uncataloged	ICG	Illinois Central Gulf
rd	Red	L&C	Lancaster & Chester
RH	Right-hand switch	LL	Lionel Lines
rs	Rubber stamped	L&N	Louisville & Nashville
RT	Rubber Tire	LV	Lehigh Valley
SB	1953 Door	MKT	Missouri, Kansas & Topeka
SG grn	Stephen Girard Green	MP	Missouri Pacific
SM	Service Manual	MPA	Maryland and Pennsylvania
SMT	Sprung Metal Trucks	NKP	Nickel Plate Road
SS	Service Station	NJZ	New Jersey Zinc
SSS	Service Station Special	NP	Northern Pacific
TL	Tail Lights	N&W	Norfolk & Western
TT	Traction Tire	NYC	New York Central
Tus	Tuscan	NY,NH&H	New York, New Haven & Hartford

Determining Rarity

In addition to value, we also ask our experts to list an indication of how hard an item is to find. Rarity is an important element of collecting and we feel our Rarity Ratings add greatly to the usefulness of this guide. While it is generally true that the higher the price, the rarer the item, it is by no means an inflexible truth. There are items that turn up with regularity but are in such great demand that they cost dearly (GG-1s for example). Conversely, some items are hard-to-find, but have a low price tag because collectors are not that interested in them.

Our system goes from 1, the most common, through 5, the rarest and most desirable. The rarity of an item is affected by quantity produced and desirability. Some Prewar and Postwar items were produced for a short time and in low quantity, which explains their rarity today.

No prices are listed for 5X or 5P items because when so few items exist, sometimes only one, it is impossible to get a consensus.

5P Prototypes of which there were one, or two made.
Examples: 213 Lift Bridge, brown Burro Crane.

5X Pre-production mock-ups, factory mistakes, paint samples, or special items of which less than 100 were made. *Examples: 6464-100 1954, 14 Harmony Creamery reefer.*

5 Items that are high-priced, very difficult to find, and in great demand. Such as:
517 caboose with black roof, 2023 with gray nose, 2332 GG-1 in black.

4 A regular production item, but produced in lower numbers than normal. Good chance it will turn up at a large meet. *Examples: 2341 Jersey Central FM, 225E in gunmetal, 6517 Erie.*

3 Items that are gaining in collector popularity and are getting hard to find.
Examples: Dark green 253, 3360 Burro crane

2 Medium-priced rolling stock and small steam engines that are easy-to-find and lack the appeal and collector value of the more glamorous, higher-priced items.
Examples: 603 orange passenger cars, 2055 steamer, 2023 UP Alco.

1 Low-priced, common items that are usually made of plastic and have little collector or intrinsic value. *Examples: 152 crossing gate, 6465 Sunoco tank car.*

Note: A Rarity Rating with a plus sign (+), as in 3+, is an indication of a rarity that is more than a 3 but less than a 4.

Abbrevations & Symbols continued

ON	Ontario Northland
PC	Penn Central
P&E	Peoria & Eastern
PFE	Pacific Fruit Express
PL&E	Pittsburgh & Lake Erie
PRR	Pennsylvania Railroad
RF&P	Richland, Fredericksburg & Potomac
RI	Rock Island
SCL	Seaboard Coast Lines
SP	Southern Pacific
SP&S	Spokane, Portland & Seattle
TAG	Tennessee, Alabama & Georgia
TP&W	Toledo, Peoria & Western
UP	Union Pacific
WM	Western Maryland
WP	Western Pacific

Organization Name Abbreviations

ADTCA	Atlantic Division of TCA
CLRC	Chicagoland Lionel Railroader Club
D-TTCA	Detroit-Toledo Chapter of TCA
EDTCA	Eastern Division of TCA
FPTCA	Fort Pitt Division of TCA
GLTCA	Great Lakes Division of TCA
GTCA	Gateway Chapter of TCA
IETCA	Inland Empire Train Collectors Association
LCOL	Lionel Central Operating Lines
LCCA	Lionel Collectors Club of America
LCAC	Lionel Collectors Association of Canada
LOTS	Lionel Operating Train Society
LRRC	Lionel Railroaders Club
LSDTCA	Lone Star Division of TCA
MDTCA	Midwest Division of TCA
METCA	Metropolitan New York Div. of TCA
NLOE	Nassau Lionel Operating Engineers
NETCA	New England Division of TCA
PNWTCA	Pacific Northwest Division of TCA
RMTCA	Rocky Mountain Division of TCA
SDTCA	Southern Division of TCA
S-STCA	Sacramento-Sierra Chapter of TCA
TCA	Train Collectors Association
TTOM	Toy Train Operating Museum
TRTCA	Three Rivers Chapter of TCA
TTOS	Toy Train Operating Society
VTC	Virginia Train Collectors
WMTCA	Western Michigan Chapter of TCA

Method Used in Determining Prices

Lionel collectors and experts are selected from all parts of the country. They are sent our list and asked to assign an asking price and rarity rating for each item within the limits of their expertise. We also observe prices at meets, auctions, "buy-sell" sections in club magazines and hobby stores. The prices and rarity ratings that appear in this book are a consensus of all those factors.

We urge the reader to remember that this is a guide and the actual selling price will always depend on a number of factors, including how motivated the buyer and seller are, the location, and the economic climate. The skills of the buyer at bargaining and the seller at promoting also affects the price. It is impossible to combine all these factors and arrive at one definitive price. That is why we call this book a *guide*. It gets you in the ball park, even takes you to your section, but you have to find your own seat.

Variations

We list only major variations that are worth more than the normal production version. Major variations are those which can be readily seen, exist in sufficient numbers so as to be attainable, and are accepted as legitimate collectable variations by the majority of experienced collectors. Major variations usually have to do with body type, exterior color and the size, color or placement of graphics. An example would be the 6464 Rutland boxcar with a solid shield.

We do not list minor variations. Minor variations are not worth more than the normal production version. They are not easily recognizable and are ignored by the majority of experienced collectors. Examples would be slight changes of color, different body molds, or different types of doors, trucks, frames or couplers – all of which can be easily changed.

Prewar Trim and Colors

In most cases, we use the color names established by the TCA in their fine book on Prewar Lionel (available through the TCA, Strasburg, PA.). In general, Lionel used dull colors (maroon, gray, mojave) up to 1924, and bright colors (orange, cream, green) from 1924 to 1936. After 1936, the trend was to more realistic appearing trains, and colors became subdued again.

Trim refers to handrails, journals, number plates, brakewheels, window inserts and other small decorative pieces added to the item. Brass plates were used until 1935, when a combination of brass and nickel was used. In 1938, plates changed to nickel. Nickel journals were used until 1929 or 1930, when they changed to copper. Copper was used until 1934 or 1935, when the journals changed back to nickel. From 1939 through 1942, journals were both nickel and black oxidized.

Warning: Trim can easily be switched. So can trucks, couplers, roofs, door guides and bases of accessories. Example: 813 cattle cars exist with the orange roof from a 814 boxcar. It is unlikely a major variation is going to surface in the mid-90's that has gone undetected by 1000s of collectors for over 60 years. Best to have a healthy skepticism about unusual color schemes and odd combinations of trim.

Many fine reproductions and repaints have been created of the more desirable locos and cars. Some are not identified as reproductions. If you have doubt, seek the help of an experienced collector.

Toy Train Revue

Issue Number 15
Fall, 1999

For Collectors and Operators | The Collectors Journal | Toy Trains Forever

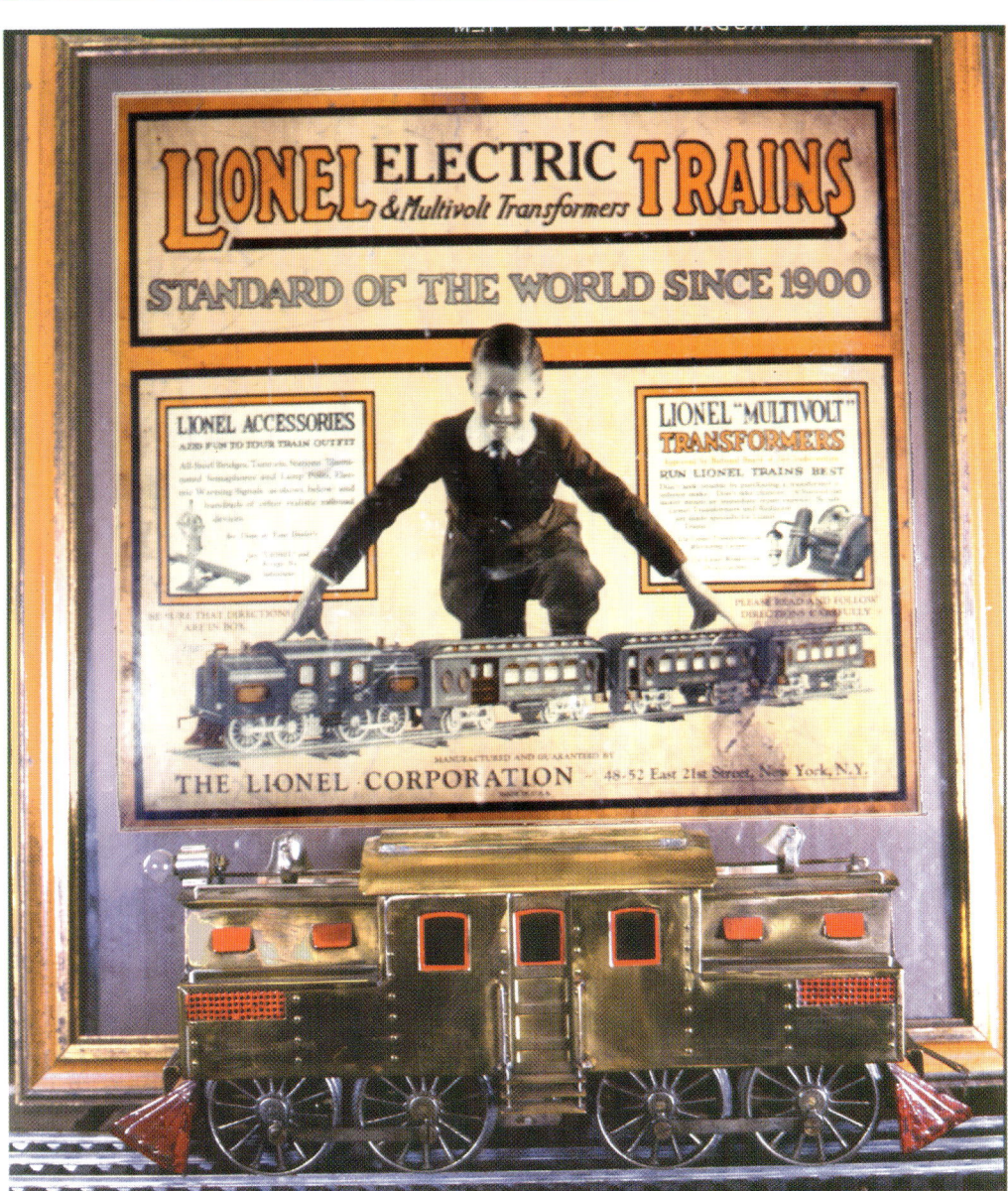

Lionel® Electric Trains
A History, Part 1, 1900-1969

In the early 1800s, the first model trains were crude wooden, cast iron or tin toys which were just pulled or pushed along the floor. Wind-up motors were added in the 1850s and some live-steam trains were produced around 1870. Carlisle & Finch of Cincinnati offered the first battery-powered electric train in 1885. By the end of the century, an energetic 23-year-old man with a curious mind was developing a small electric motor that would provide fun and happy memories for countless sons and fathers over the next century. The young man's name was Joshua Lionel Cowen.

(continued on page 201)

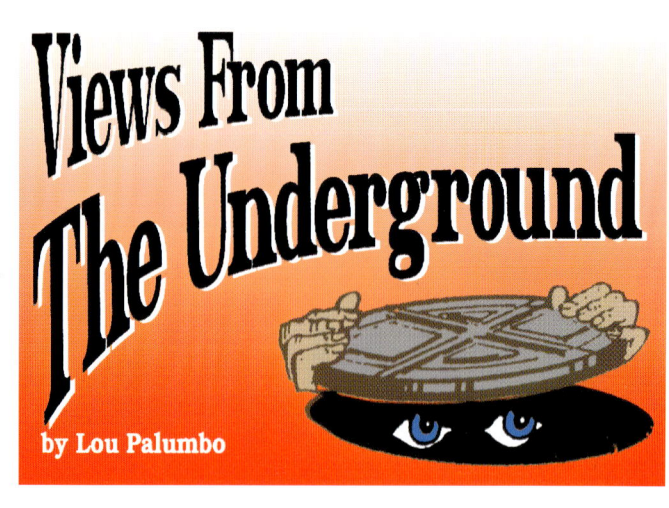

Views From The Underground

by Lou Palumbo

Compared to the '80s, Postwar prices are down, unless you have LN or Mint boxed, then prices are way up. Take a Lackawanna FM, LN without box. $650-700 would be a dream price (used to bring $800-$1000). Ex no box $300-$350. VG no box – the price of the parts - maybe $200. If you operate, why not buy a Williams Lackawanna FM? Great puller, same detail, great paint job, and a lifetime warranty, for $179. Don't start with Magne Traction. Williams' two motors with rubber tires pulls better than Lionel with Magne Traction.

Williams is doing a great job of offering a nice selection of engines and sets for under $200. And his step-up line is in the $300 to $450 range. He's doing to MTH what MTH did to Lionel. It's a case of the teacher teaching the pupil again. Williams seems to be offering the best value in trains today. The gap between LN and Mint and the rest is wide and getting wider, particularly with the more desirable pieces. I have a Milwaukee Road F-3 with a cracked nose. In LN it might bring $2500. With a cracked nose, who knows? Collectors only want LN or Mint and operators won't pay a premium because they can buy new for less. So what can I get for my cracked nose?

Today, condition means more than ever. The operator market for Ex and below has dried up because operators would rather buy new. So Lionel Postwar in below Excellent is biting the dust. About the only market left for those trains is the restoration market, which is also being hurt because of all the new trains. Restored items cost more than new, so why pay more and get stuck with the old technology?

The crowds at York seem to get bigger every year. I saw a Williams Niagara with sound go for $850. An MTH N&W J with sound went for $975. A LN Airplane car with the reversed yellow plane with box sold for $295. A three-car O-27 Livingston set of passenger cars, *Ex*, no boxes, went for $250, which is higher than book. The green O-27 cars are also still up. Both these series are hanging in there because they haven't been reproduced.

The catalog business has taken a nose-dive. Used to be a 1950 Lionel catalog would bring $100. Now they sit at $50. Everyone who wanted them has them and the new guys don't care. And today's catalogs, forget about them. There are just too many to interest collectors. Between Lionel, MTH, K-Line and the rest, there are about 50 catalogs a year. You need a catalog to keep track of the catalogs.

Seems like Lionel and MTH are producing short runs on their better engines. You just don't see many Lionel Alleghenies or MTH Challengers for sale. I don't know how a company like Lionel can make money producing such low numbers, but maybe they want to create a demand so when they announce another high-priced engine, everyone will pre-order. Also, they probably want people to forget all the blow-outs they have released lately.

Wouldn't it be nice if things were available when they were announced? I'm getting tired of looking at stuff, then more stuff, then still more stuff, when I still haven't received the original stuff I ordered three or four catalogs ago. I get confused.

This is not the Golden Age of Toy Trains, it's the Platinum Age of Toy Trains. O gauge is hot, hot, hot and it's going to get hotter because Lionel is gearing up for a big push. MTH has everyone talking about their gold this and gold that, K-Line has that beautifully detailed caboose, Williams has a Hudson for $450 that looks almost as good as Lionel's 700E, Atlas has solid T-rail track and a great line of freight cars, 3rd Rail has some nice scale engines and Weaver just brought out authentically styled Hiawatha cars. What's going on? I don't know, but I love it.

Lionel finally booted out those amateurs and they now have a pro running things. Lionel will always survive just like baseball will always survive. Baseball survives dumb owners and greedy players because the game is great. Lionel survives because a toy train running around a track is irresistible. Will they last another 100 years? Who cares? By that time I'll be in that big layout in the sky where trains run forever, the milk man never misses and there's no such thing as a short.

Prewar 1900-1942
Accessories

Note: "O" designates item made for O Gauge. "N" designates Standard Gauge.

76 Bell Shack, 124 City Station tan/red

2	**Figure Set** (seated) 10-18					(5)	**300**
023	**Bumper** 15-33 1. Black 15-26	(2)	**30**	2. Red 27-33		(3)	**30**
23-65N	**Bumper** 15-33					(3)	**65**▲
025	**Illuminated Bumper** 29-42 1. Cream/red stripes 29-32	(4)	**50**	2. Black 33-42		(1)	**25**
25-50N	**Illuminated Bumper** Black/yellow-red 27-42					(3)	**50**▲
27N	**Lighting Set** for early cars 11-23					(4)	**30**
35	**Boulevard Lamp** 40-42 and Postwar 1. Aluminum	(2)	**40**	2. 92 Gray		(3)	**60**
43	**Bild-A-Motor Gear Set** Std Gauge 29					(4)	**150**
043	**Bild-A-Motor Gear Set** 29					(4)	**150**
43	**Pleasure Boat** White/vermilion/cream top, with display stand 33-36					(4)	**925**
44	**Racing Boat** White/green/dark brown top, with display stand 35,36					(5)	**1500**
45 045	**Gateman** Green/ivory/vermilion roof 35,36 1. Blue gateman	(2)	**70**▲	2. Brown gateman		(5)	**90**▲
45N	**Gateman** (Same as 45/045) 37-42 1. Silver crossing post 37-40	(1)	**70**▲	2. Gray crossing post 41,42		(4)	**90**▲
46	**Single Arm Crossing Gate** (add $50 for original latern) 38-42 1. Green/aluminum gate	(2)	**95**	2. Green/gray gate		(4)	**150**
47	**Double Arm Crossing Gate** (add $100 for 2 original laterns) 38-42 1. Green/aluminum gate	(2)	**175**	2. Green/92 gray gate		(4)	**275**
48W	**Whistling Station** lithograph 37-42					(2)	**50**
49	**Airport** 58" diameter cardboard base w/color lithograph 37-39					(5)	**600**
50	**Airplane** with pylon and controls 36					(3)	**1000**
50	**Paper Train** Price listed is for complete set unassembled in box 43,44					(4)	**600**

Top row: 56 gray Park Lamp, 56 green Park Lamp, 58 green Small Gooseneck Lamp, 57 orange Broadway Lamp Post, 58 pea green Small Gooseneck Lamp. Bottom row: 54 maroon Double Gooseneck Lamp, 61 dark green Large Gooseneck Lamp, 67 dark green large Twin Gooseneck Lamp

57 orange Broadway Lamp Post

PREWAR

51	**Airport** Square cardboard airport, color lithograph 36,38				(5)	**500**
52	**Street Lamp** Aluminum 33-41				(4)	**175▲**
53	**Street Lamp** 31-42					
	1. Light mojave	(3)	**50▼**	2. Light ivory	(3)	**65▼**
	3. Aluminum	(4)	**100▼**			
54	**Small Double Gooseneck Lamp** 29-35					
	1. Pea green	(3)	**80▲**	2. State brown	(5)	**100▲**
	3. Green	(4)	**80▲**	4. Maroon	(5)	**80▲**
55	**Airplane** with pylon and controls 37-39				(4)	**1000**
56	**Park Lamp Post** 24-42 and Postwar					
	1. Dark gray	(3)	**50**	2. Gray	(3)	**50**
	3. Mojave	(3)	**65**	4. Green	(1)	**50**
	5. Pea green	(2)	**50**	6. Copper	(5)	**150**
	7. Aluminum	(5)	**100▲**			
57	**Broadway Lamp Post** 22-42					
	1. Gray	(3)	**75▼**	2. Yellow	(4)	**150▼**
	3. Orange	(3)	**100▼**			

Note: All three colors exist with the following celluloid printed lamp shades in either silver or black lettering. Silver lettering is harder to find:

	a. Broadway & Main	(1)	b. Broadway & 21st Street	(4)
	c. Fifth Avenue & 21st Street	(5)	d. Fifth Avenue & 42nd Street	(4)
	e. Broadway & Fifth Avenue	(2)	f. Broadway & 42nd Street	(2)

58	**Small Gooseneck Lamp** 22-42, 46-50 (Postwar carry-over)					
	1. Maroon	(3)	**40**	2. Green	(3)	**40**
	3. Pea green	(3)	**50**	4. Aluminum	(4)	**70**
	5. Cream	(3)	**70**			
59	**Gooseneck Lamp** 20-36					
	1. Dark green	(2)	**35▲**	2. Olive green	(2)	**30▲**
	3. State brown	(5)	**100▲**	4. Pea green	(2)	**35▲**
	5. Mojave	(5)	**60▲**	6. Maroon	(5)	**60▲**
	7. Red	(5)	**100▲**			
60N	**Telegraph Post** 20-35					
	1. Gray/maroon	(2)	**45**	2. Peacock/red	(3)	**50▼**
	3. Apple green/maroon	(3)	**40**			
060	**Telegraph Pole** O gauge w/track extension arm 29-42					
	1. Orange/maroon	(2)	**3**	2. Peacock/red	(3)	**40**
	3. Gray/light red	(4)	**45**			
61	**Large Gooseneck Lamp** 14-32, 34-36					
	1. Black	(5)	**95▲**	2. Dark green	(3)	**60▲**
	3. Olive green	(3)	**60▲**	4. Maroon	(2)	**55▲**
	5. Mojave	(4)	**60▲**			

85 Telegraph Poles orange, green, 69 Warning Bells olive, maroon *Red Car from 80 Race Car Set*

62	**Semaphore** single arm 20-32				
	1. Dark green/yellow	(3)	**50▲**	2. Pea green (2)	**45▲**
	3. Apple green	(4)	**55▲**		
63	**Semaphore** single arm Black/orange/dark green 15-20			(4)	**45▲**
63	**Twin Street Lamp** Aluminum 33-42			(4)	**300▲**
64	**Semaphore** double arm Black/orange/dark green 15-21			(4)	**50▲**
64	**Highway Lamp** Green 40-42 and Postwar			(3)	**60▲**
65	**Semaphore** single arm, illuminated Black/cream/orange 15-26				
	1. Notched arm	(4)	**50▲**	2. Unnotched arm (5)	**55▲**
66	**Semaphore** double arm Black/orange/dark green 15-28			(5)	**55▲**
67	**Large Twin Gooseneck** 15-32				
	1. Dark green/large shade	(5)	**100▲**	2. Dark green/small shade (3)	**50▲**
	3. State brown	(4)	**75▲**		
68	**Warning Signal** 20-39			(1)	**10**
068	**Warning Signal** 25-42			(1)	**10**
69	**Warning Bell** (Also in white, dk green, orange & red NDV) 21-35				
069	1. Maroon/brass/black	(3)	**75▲**	2. Olive green/black/brass (2)	**70▲**
69N	**Warning Bell** Red or aluminum. NDV 36-42			(3)	**100▲**
70	**Accessory Set** O & Standard gauge w/box 21-25			(5)	**725**
	1-59 Lamp Post, 2-62 Semaphores, 1-68 Warning Signal				
71N	**Set of Six 60 Telegraph Poles** w/box 21-31				
	1. Gray/maroon	(2)	**300**	2. Peacock/red (3)	**350**
	3. Apple green/maroon	(3)	**300**		
071	**Set of Six 060 TelegraphPoles** w/box 29-42				
	1. Orange/maroon	(3)	**350**	2. Green/red (3)	**375**
	3. Gray/light red	(4)	**450**		
76	**Block Signal** illuminated 23-29				
076	1. Mojave	(2)	**80**	2. White (3)	**100**
76	**Watchman's Shack** with Ringing Bell, 39-42				
	1. Red/white/orange	(4)	**375▲**	2. Same with gray post (4)	**425**
77	**Crossing Gate** 23-35				
077	1. Black/black-white/unlit	(4)	**60**	2. Black/red-white/unlit (3)	**50▲**
	3. Dark gray/black-white/lit	(3)	**50▲**	4. Dark green/green-white/lit (3)	**50▲**
	5. Pea green/black-white/lit	(3)	**50▲**		
77N	**Crossing Gate** Black/red, lighted 36-39			(3)	**60**
78	**Block Signal** 24-32				
078	1. Maroon base/mojave	(4)	**150**	2. Orange base/cream (3)	**125**

PREWAR

11

87 Crossing Signal, 82 Semaphore, 87 Crossing Signal, 78 Block Signal, 83 Traffic Control Signal, 78 Block Signal, 79 Crossing Signal, 83 Traffic Control Signal, 80 Semaphore

79	**Railroad Crossing Signal** 28-40					
	1. Cream 28-34	(3) **125▲**	2. Aluminum 36-40		(4)	**150▲**
80	**Racing Car Set** One orange or red car, 12-16				(5)	**3500***
	two figures, 36" diameter track circle with starting post					
80	**Operating Semaphore** 26-35					
080	1. Black/mojave	(3)	**75**	2. Terra cotta/mojave	(4)	**80**
80N	**Operating Semaphore** Red/alum/orange 36-42				(3)	**125**
81	Same as **Racing Car Set** 80 w/30" diameter track circle					
82	**Operating Semaphore** 27-35					
082	1. Peacock/cream/number plate				(4)	**175**
	2. Peacock/cream/no number plate				(4)	**150**
	3. Green/aluminum/no number plate				(3)	**125**
82N	**Operating Semaphore** Green/aluminum/black 36-42				(2)	**125**
83	**Traffic Control Signal** 27-42					
	1. Mojave/cream/white	(4) **200▲**	2. Red/cream/flesh		(3)	**125▲**
	3. Light red/cream/white	(3) **150▲**				
84	**Two Race Sets** 12-16					*****
84 & 084	**Operating Semaphore** manual Dark green/cream/orange 27-32				(4)	**150▲**
85	**Racing Car Set** one 80 and one 81 racing car 12-16					*****
85	**Telegraph Post** with extension arm 29-42					
	1. Orange/orange/maroon	(2)	**45**	2. Aluminum/aluminum/red	(4)	**50**
	3. Gray/gray/red	(4)	**60**			
86	**Set of Six 85 Telegraph Poles** 29-42					
	1. Orange/orange/maroon	(2)	**350**	2. Aluminum/aluminum/red	(4)	**400**
	3. Gray/gray/red	(4)	**400**			
87	**Railroad Crossing Signal** 27-42					
	1. Mojave/orange	(4) **140▲**	2. Dark green/pea green		(5)	**300▲**
	3. Dark green/yellow	(4) **250▲**				
89	**Flag Pole** Ivory 23-34				(2)	**160**

438 Signal Tower, 840 Power Station 25 Bumper

90	**Flag Staff and Flag** 27-42				(3)	**150**
092	**Signal Tower** 23-28					
	1. White/red/mojave	(3)	**150**	2. Terra cotta/red/mojave	(4)	**150**
	3. Lt. Terra cotta/pea/ivory	(3)	**150**	4. Terra cotta/pea/mustard	(3)	**150**
92	**Floodlight Tower** 31-42					
	1. Terra cotta base/pea green tower 31-34				(3)	**175**
	2. Red base/aluminum tower 35-40				(2)	**165**
	3. Red base/gray tower 40-42				(4)	**250**▼
93	**Water Tower** 31-42 and Postwar					
	1. Terra cotta/pea green tank				(3)	**125**
	2. Aluminum/aluminum tank /decal				(2)	**75**
	3. Gray/aluminum tank/decal				(4)	**150**
	4. Gray/gray tank/decal				(5)	**300**▲
94	**High Tension Tower** 32-42					
	1. Terra cotta base, dark gray tower 32-34				(4)	**500**▼
	2. Red/aluminum tower 35-40				(3)	**300**
	3. Red/gray tower 41,42				(5)	**500**▲
96	**Manual Coal Elevator** Aluminum/yellow/red roof 38-40				(4)	**250**▲
97	**Remote Control Coal Elevator** w/controller 38-42					
	1. Alum/yellow/red roof	(3)	**300**▲	2. Gray/yellow/red roof	(4)	**375**▲
097	**Telegraph Post Set** with 6 Pea green/pea green-red 096 poles 34, 35				(3)	**350**▲
98	**Elevated Coal Storage Bunker** Aluminum/yellow/red roof 39,40				(4)	**375**▲
99	**Train Control Block Signal** 32-35					
099	1. Black/ivory/black	(2)	**100**▲	2. Red/ivory/black	(2)	**100**▲
	3. Black/light mojave/red	(2)	**100**▲			
99N	**Train Control Block Signal** Red/aluminum/red 36-42				(2)	**125**▲
100-104	**Bridge Center Span & Approaches** 20-31					
	Std. Gauge, Pea green/cream and olive green/cream. NDV					
100	Two Approaches				(2)	**40**
101	Two Approaches, one Center Span				(3)	**200**
102	Two Approaches, two Center Spans				(3)	**225**
103	Two Approaches, three Center Spans				(4)	**250**
104	Center Span				(2)	**50**

105-110	**Bridge Center Span and Approaches** O-Gauge, Pea green/cream 20-31		
105	Two Approaches	(3)	30
106	Two Approaches, Center Span	(3)	125
108	Two Approaches, two Center Spans	(3)	150
109	Two Approaches, three Center Spans	(3)	175
110	Center Span	(3)	50
111	**Lamp Assortment** (complete) 20-31		
	1. Wooden lamp boxes (5) **500**▲ 2. Cardboard lamp boxes (4)		**400**▲
112	**Single Window Station** Cream/green no outside lights 31-35	(3)	300

115 Single Window Station   *113 Single Window Station*

113	**Single Window Station** Cream/green outside lights 31-34	(4)	**650**▲
114	**Double Window Station** Cream/green no *Automatic Train Control* 31-34	(4)	**1700**
115	**Single Window Station** Ivory/red outside lights *Auto Train Control* 36-42	(4)	**700**▲
116	**Double Window Station** *Automatic Train Control*		
	1. Cream/green 35,36 (4) **2000** 2. Ivory/red 36-42 (4)		**1800**
117	**Single Window Station** Ivory/red 36-42	(3)	300
	No outside lights, *Automatic Train Control*		
118	**Tunnel** metal no light 20-32	(1)	50
118L	**Tunnel** illuminated 27	(5)	100
119	**Tunnel** no light 20-42	(1)	60
119L	**Tunnel** illuminated 27-33	(5)	125
120	**Tunnel** 20-27	(3)	125
120L	**Tunnel** illuminated 27-42	(1)	125
121	**Lionel City Station** Salmon/pea green no lights 20-26	(3)	250
	Note: Lionel City Stations come with or without departure board. NDV		
122	**Lionel City Station** interior light 20-31		
	1. Salmon/pea green (3) **300** 2. Terra cotta/pea green (3)		300
123	**Lionel City Station** Salmon/pea green interior light 20-23	(3)	250
123	**Tunnel** 90 degree curve O gauge 33-42	(3)	450
124	**Lionel City Station** interior light 1920-30, 1933-36		
	plus two exterior corner lights		
	1. Brown/pea green (3) **375** 2. Burnt orange/pea green (3)		375
	3. Salmon/pea green (3) **375** 4. Terra cotta/pea green (3)		375
	5. Tan/red (4) **450**		
125	**Track Template** 38	(5)	5
125	**Lionelville Station** Brick lithograph/pea green no lights 23-25	(3)	**225**▲

126	**Lionelville Station** w/inside light 23-36			
	1. Crackle red/maroon/mojave		(3)	**250**
	2. Crackle red/pea green/mojave		(3)	**200**
	3. Brick litho/pea green/flat light gray		(3)	**200**
	4. Mustard/light red/green		(4)	**350**
127	**Lioneltown Station** w/interior light 23-36			
	1. Ivory/red/mojave (2) **150**	2. White/light red/mojave	(3)	**200**
	3. White/light red/mustard (3) **225**	4. Mustard/maroon/gray	(4)	**250**
128	**Lionel City Station & Terrace Platform** 28-42			
	129 Platform in combination with:			
	1. Lionel City Stations 121, 122 & 124, 28-30		(4)	**1900**
	2. Single Window Stations 112 & 113, 31-36		(4)	**2000**
	3. 115 Single Window Station 37-42		(4)	**2000**
129	**Terrace Station Platform** 28-33, 35-42			
	1. Light mojave/pea grn lattice gold light posts 28-33		(4)	**1500**
	2. Cream/cream, aluminum light posts 35-42		(5)	**3000**
130	**Tunnel** 90 degree curve O gauge 24-26 90		(5)	**550**
130L	**Tunnel** Same as 130 but illuminated 27-33		(5)	**800**
131	**Corner Display Platform** Part of set 198 24-28		(4)	**450▲**
132	**Corner Display Platform** Part of set 198 24-28		(4)	**450▲**
133	**Heart Shaped Display Platform** Part of set 198, 24-28		(4)	**450▲**
134	**Oval Shaped Display Platform** Part of set 198, 24-28		(4)	**450▲**
134	**Lionel City Station** 124 Tan/red with *Automatic Train Control* 37-42		(4)	**500**
135	**Circular Platform** Part of set 199, 24-28		(4)	**375▲**
136	**Large Elevation** Part of set 199, 24-28		(4)	**375▲**
136	**Lionelville Station** w/interior light *Automatic Train Control* 37-42			
	1. Mustard/red/green (4) **200**	2. Cream/red/green	(3)	**175**
	3. Yellow/red/green (4) **250▲**			
137	**Lioneltown Station** w/interior light *Automatic Train Control* 37-42			
	1. White/red/mustard (3) **250**	2. White/red/light mojave	(3)	**225**
	3. White/red/92 gray (5) **300**			

PREWAR

140L	**Tunnel** O or Standard gauge 90 degree curve 27-32		(4)	**1500**
152	**Crossing Gate** 40-42 and Postwar			
	1. Red base/aluminum gates (1) **50▲**	2. Red base/gray gates	(3)	**75▲**
	3. Red base/white gates (5) **100▲**			
153	**Block Signal** 40-42 and Postwar			
	1. Green/alum post/orange (1) **45**	2. Green/gray post/orange	(3)	**75**
154	**Highway Crossing Signal** 40-42 and Postwar			
	1. Red or orange base/silver post 40		(5)	**200**
	2. Black/aluminum 40 and Postwar		(2)	**35**
	3. Black/gray 41,42		(3)	**45**

155	**Freight Shed** 30-42 illuminated			
	1. Terra cotta/maroon 30-42 (3) **450**	2. Red/gray 40-42	(4)	**500**
156	**Illuminated Station Platform** 39-42			
	1. Green base/vermilion roof/silver posts		(3)	**175▲**
	2. Green base/vermilion roof/gray posts		(4)	**225▲**

162 Dump Truck green bin, 162 Dump Truck peacock bin, 161 pea green Baggage Truck, 161 green Baggage Truck.

157	**Hand Truck** 30-32					
	1. Dark red	(2)	**25**	2. Red	(3)	**30**
158	**Station Platform** Set Two 156 Platforms, one 136 Station in set box 40-42				(5)	**900▲**
161	**Baggage Truck** 30-32					
	1. Pea green RS *Lionel Lines* (3)		**75**	2. Pea green no RS	(3)	**75**
	3. Green no RS	(2)	**50**			
162	**Dump Truck** Note: Bins can be switched 30-32					
	1. Yellow/green bin	(4)	**75**	2. Orange/blue bin	(3)	**60**
	3. Orange/peacock bin	(2)	**50**			
163	**Freight Station Set** 30-42					
	2-157 Handtrucks, 1-161 Baggage Truck, 1-162 Dump Truck					
	1. Large box illustrated display insert				(4)	**475**
	2. Small box no insert				(3)	**400**
164	**Remote Control Log Loader** 40-42					
	1. Green/cream/aluminum/light red				(3)	**350▲**
	2. Green/cream/92 gray/light red				(4)	**450▲**
165	**Magnetic Crane** 40-42					
	1. Aluminum superstructure	(3)	**425▲**	2. Gray superstructure	(4)	**600**
184	**Bungalow** Illuminated 23-32					
	1. Ivory/dark green/gray	(5)	**175**	2. Flesh/orange/gray	(4)	**175**
	3. Cream/red/gray	(4)	**175**	4. White/apple green/gray	(4)	**175**
	5. Yellow/red/gray	(4)	**175**	6. Lithograph	(3)	**125**
185	**Bungalow** not Illuminated 23,24					
	1. Ivory/dark green/gray	(5)	**200▼**	2. Flesh/orange/gray	(4)	**200▼**
	3. Cream/red/gray	(4)	**200▼**	4. White/apple green/gray	(4)	**200▼**
	5. Yellow/red/gray	(4)	**200▼**	6. Lithograph	(2)	**125▼**
186	**Bungalow Set** Five 184 Bungalows 23-32					
	1. Large box illustrated display insert				(4)	**2000***
	2. Small box no insert				(4)	**2000***
187	**Bungalow Set** Five 185 Bungalows w/box and insert 23,24				(4)	**2000***
189	**Villa** 23-32					
	1. Ivory/dark gray/pea green (4)		**400**	2. Ivory/maroon/pea green	(3)	**350**
	3. Sand/peacock/terra cotta (4)		**500**	4. Lt mustard/apple grn/gray	(4)	**425**
191	**Villa** 23-32					
	1. Brick litho/ pea green/mojave				(4)	**425**
	2. Terra cotta/pea green/mojave				(3)	**375**
	3. Red crackle/pea green/mojave				(3)	**425**
	4. Cream/red/Hiawatha gray				(4)	**450**
	Note: 184,185,189, and 191 come in many different variations. For a complete list refer to the TCA's book on prewar Lionel.					
192	**Villa and Bungalow Set** w/box and insert 23-32				(4)	**4000**
	Two 184, one 189 villa, and one 191 villa in assorted colors					
193	**Accessory Set** w/box and insert 27-29				(5)	**950***
	1 each: 069 Warning Bell, 076 Block Signal, 077 Automatic Crossing Gate, 078 Automatic Train Control Signal, 080 Semaphore					
194	**Box Set** (Contains 1 each 69, 76, 77, 78, 80) w/box and insert 27-29				(4)	**1000***

195	**Illuminated Terrace** 27-30 Contains 90 flag, 184 bungalow, two 56 lamp posts, 189 villa, and 191 villa		(5)	**2000**
196	**Accessory Set** O & Standard gauge 27 Two 58 Lamp Posts, six 60 Telegraph Poles, 62 Semaphore, 68 Warning Signal, 127 Station		(5)	**1000***
198	**Large Platform Set** 24-28		(4)	**1750**
199	**Small Platform Set** 24-28		(4)	*
200	**Manual Turntable** 28-36 1. Pea green/red center/brass (3) **250**▼ 2. Black/red center/brass		(4)	**600**▼
205	**LCL Containers** (set of three) Hinged doors, brass trim, dark green 30-38		(4)	**400**
208	**Tool Set** 34-42 1. Dark gray painted chest (3) **300** 2. 92 gray 3. Silver painted chest, w/hoe, sledge hammer, pick, shovel, axe, and rake		(4) (3)	**400** **300**
209	**Set of 4 Barrels** Std. Gauge 30-42 1. No box (3) **100** 2. With box		(4)	**250**
0209	**Set of 6 Barrels** O gauge 30-42 1. No box (2) **75** 2. With box		(4)	**150**▼
270	**Girder Bridge** O-Gauge, Dk red, red NDV 31-42 1. Brass plate (3) **50** 2. Nickel plate 3. Decal (4) **150**		(3) (3)	**50** **50**
271	**Girder Bridge** Two of 270 31-42		(4)	**300**
272	**Girder Bridge** Three of 270 31-42		(5)	**600**
280	**Steel Girder Bridge** Std. Gauge Red, pea grn, olive grn, grn. NDV 31-33		(3)	**125**
280X	**280 Bridge** modified to fit O gauge track 36-42		(4)	**150**▲
281	**280 Bridge Span** Std. Gauge, set of 2 31-33		(4)	**350**
282	**280 Bridge Span** Std. Gauge, set of 3 31-33		(4)	**600**

300	**Hellgate** O or Standard gauge 28-42 1. Pea green/cream/orange (4) **1600** 2. Aluminum/ivory/red		(5)	**1900**
308	**Set of Yard Signs** w/box 40-42 and Postwar		(2)	**100**▲
313	**Bascule Bridge** O-Gauge 40-42 and Postwar 1. Aluminum bridge (3) **500** 2. Gray bridge		(4)	**700**
314	**Girder Bridge** O-Gauge U40-42 and Postwar 1. Aluminum (1) **35** 2. Gray		(3)	**50**

313 Bascule Bridge, gray variation 2   *200 Manual Turntable, rare black variation 2*

315	**Trestle Bridge** w/red warning light O-Gauge 40-42						
	1. Aluminum	(3)	**150**	2. Gray		(4)	**250**
316	**Trestle Bridge** O-Gauge U42						
	1. Aluminum	(3)	**75**	2. Gray		(4)	**90**
435	**Power Station** 26-38						
	1. Mustard/mojave/gray	(3)	**450**	2. Cream/terra cotta/gray		(4)	**450**
	3. Mustard/terra cotta/gray	(3)	**450**	4. Cream/light mojave/green		(4)	**450**
436	**Power Station** 26-37						
	1. Terra cotta/mustard					(3)	**700**
	2. Same as 1 with *Edison Service* sign over door rather than the common *Power Station*					(5)	**1500**▲
	3. Cream/terra cotta	(3)	**500**	4. Cream/light mojave		(4)	**700**
437	**Switch Signal Tower** 26-37						
	1. Burnt orange/mustard/peacock roof					(3)	**750**
	2. Terra cotta/cream/pea green roof					(4)	**850**
	3. Cream/orange roof					(5)	**4000***

438	**Signal Tower** 27-39						
	1. Orange/red/pea green, no switches 27					(4)	**500**
	2. Same with knife switches 28-35					(3)	**450**
	3. Orange/maroon/pea green	(3)	**450**	4. White/red/silver 36-39		(3)	**900**▲

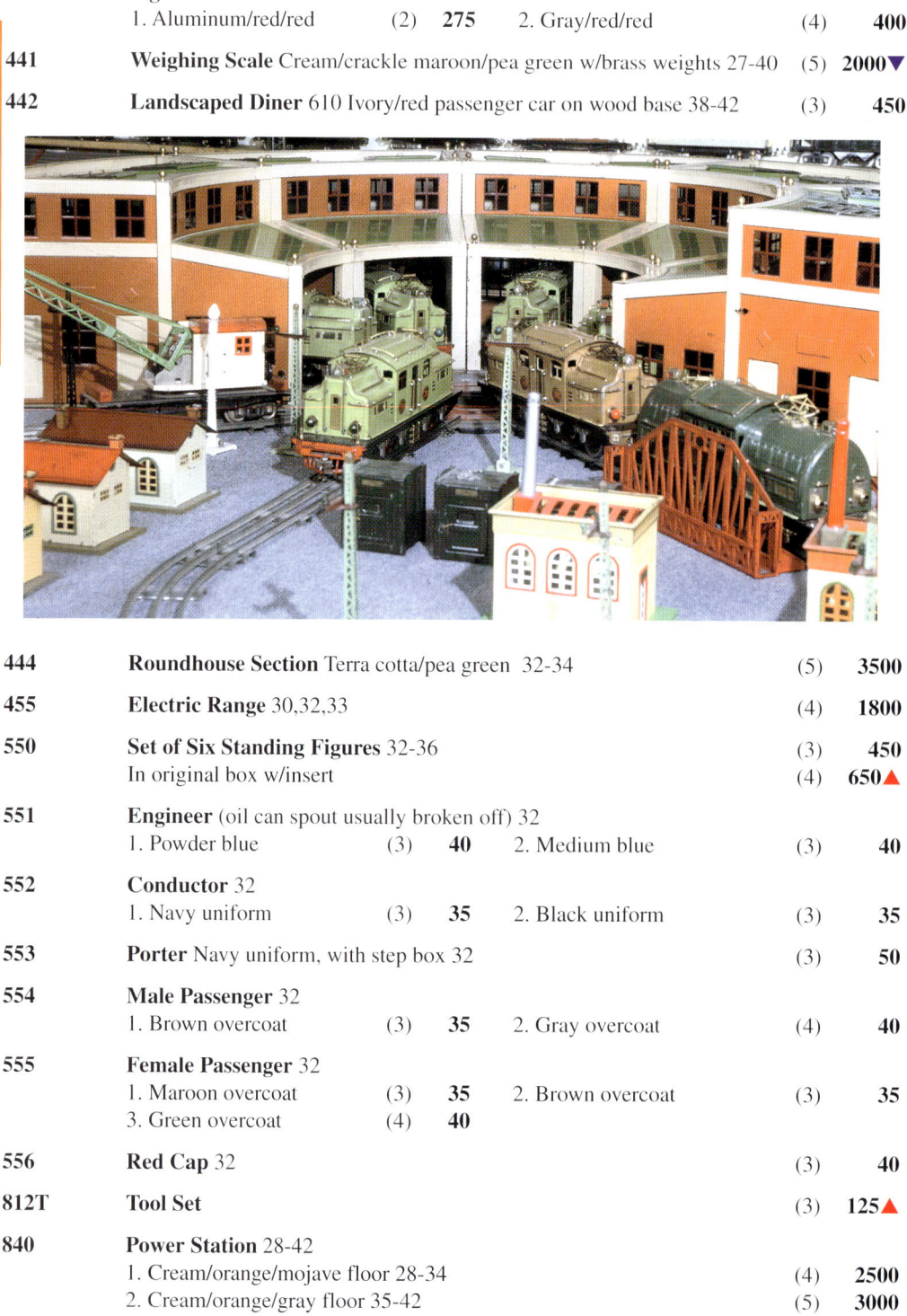

439	**Panel Board** 28-42					
	1. Crackle maroon/white	(3)	**200**	2. Maroon/black panel	(3)	**175**
	3. Red/black	(3)	**175**	4. Aluminum/white	(4)	**225**
440	**Signal Bridge** 32-35					
0440	1. Gray/maroon/terra cotta 32-34				(2)	**350**
	2. Aluminum/red/red 35				(4)	**475**
440C	**Panelboard** for 440 or O440 32-35				(4)	**200**
	Mentioned in catalog but number never listed					
440N	**Signal** 36-42					
	1. Aluminum/red/red	(2)	**275**	2. Gray/red/red	(4)	**400**
441	**Weighing Scale** Cream/crackle maroon/pea green w/brass weights 27-40				(5)	**2000▼**
442	**Landscaped Diner** 610 Ivory/red passenger car on wood base 38-42				(3)	**450**
444	**Roundhouse Section** Terra cotta/pea green 32-34				(5)	**3500**
455	**Electric Range** 30,32,33				(4)	**1800**
550	**Set of Six Standing Figures** 32-36				(3)	**450**
	In original box w/insert				(4)	**650▲**
551	**Engineer** (oil can spout usually broken off) 32					
	1. Powder blue	(3)	**40**	2. Medium blue	(3)	**40**
552	**Conductor** 32					
	1. Navy uniform	(3)	**35**	2. Black uniform	(3)	**35**
553	**Porter** Navy uniform, with step box 32				(3)	**50**
554	**Male Passenger** 32					
	1. Brown overcoat	(3)	**35**	2. Gray overcoat	(4)	**40**
555	**Female Passenger** 32					
	1. Maroon overcoat	(3)	**35**	2. Brown overcoat	(3)	**35**
	3. Green overcoat	(4)	**40**			
556	**Red Cap** 32				(3)	**40**
812T	**Tool Set**				(3)	**125▲**
840	**Power Station** 28-42					
	1. Cream/orange/mojave floor 28-34				(4)	**2500**
	2. Cream/orange/gray floor 35-42				(5)	**3000**
910	**Grove of Trees** 32-42				(4)	**550▲**

PREWAR

840 Power Station, 113 Single Window Station, 116 Double Window Station

911	**Illuminated Country Estate** 32-42		
	Wood base covered with shrubbery and trees around 191 villa, many variations. NDV		
	1. Terra cotta/pea green/mojave	(3)	**1400▲**
	2. Crackle red/pea green/mojave	(4)	**1500▲**
	3. Yellow/red/gray	(3)	**1400▲**
912	**Illuminated Suburban Home** 32-42		
	Wood base covered with shrubbery and trees around 189 villa, many variations. NDV		
	1. Mojave/white/dark gray (3) **1200** 2. Gray/ivory/apple green	(4)	**1300**
	3. Terra cotta/white/pea grn (3) **1200** 4. Ivory/cream/mojave	(5)	**1400▲**
	5. Light mustard/apple green/gray	(4)	**1300**
913	**Illuminated Landscaped Bungalow** 32-42		
	Wood base w/shrubbery and trees around 184 bungalow		
	1. Lithographed (3) **700** 2. Cream/red/mojave	(3)	**700**
	3. Ivory/red/gray (3) **700** 4. Ivory/apple green/gray	(3)	**700**
	5. Yellow/red/gray (4) **700**		
914	**Park Landscape** 32-36	(3)	**550**
	Wood base with trees, shrubbery, and garden urn with flowers		
915	**Tunnel** 90 degree curve Standard gauge 32-34	(5)	**750**
915	**Tunnel** 90 degree curve 1935	(5)	**400**
	O gauge, slightly smaller than previous 915		
916	**Tunnel** 90 degree curve O gauge, handpainted 1932	(4)	**350**
916	**Tunnel** 90 degree curve. Slightly smaller than previous 916, 33-42	(4)	**300**
917	**Mountain** O or Standard gauge. Handpainted scenic hillside 32-36	(5)	**1250▲**
918	**Mountain** O or Standard gauge. Handpainted scenic hillside 32-36	(5)	**1250▲**
919	**Sack of Grass** 32-42	(3)	**40**
920	**Illuminated Scenic Park** 32,33	(5)	**3000**
	Two sections, two 189 villas, two 191 villas, and two 184 bungalows		
921	**Illuminated Scenic Park** 32,33	(5)	**4500**
	Three sections, two 920 end sections, and one 921C center section		
921C	**Illuminated Center Section** 32,33	(5)	**2500**
	Contains one 189 villa, 191 villa, 184 bungalow, 910 grove of trees, 914 park landscape, or 922 illuminated lamp terrace.		
922	**Lamp Terrace** (56 lamp/copper) 32-36	(5)	**325**
923	**Tunnel** O or Standard gauge 33-42	(4)	**1000**

924	**Tunnel** 90 degree turn 072 gauge 35-42	(4)	**180**
925	**Lubricant** 35-42	(1)	**10**
927	**Ornamental Flag Plot** 37-42	(3)	**450▲**
1022	**Tunnel** 90 degree turn Lionel Jr. and small O gauge 35-42	(2)	**100**
1023	**Tunnel** Lionel Jr. and small O gauge. Handpainted 34-42	(3)	**25**
1045	**Operating Watchman** 38-42 and Postwar		
	1. Black uniform (4) **75** 2. Brown uniform	(3)	**60**
	3. Blue uniform/silver post (2) **50** 4. Blue uniform/gray post	(3)	**60**
1500	**Locoscope** 39	(4)	**400▲**
	Viewer in the shape of a steam locomotive with thirty-nine black & white pictures on 16mm film		
1560	**Station** Lithograph Clockwork Sets 33-37		
	1. Terra cotta base (3) **40** 2. Dark green base	(4)	**50**
1569	**Accessory Set** 34-37	(4)	**175**
	Four 1571 Telegraph Poles, 1572 Semaphore, 1573 Warning Signal, 1574 Clock, 1575 Gate		

Track, Transformers & Switches
Miscellaneous Track Accessories

OTC	**Lockon** 23-36	(1)	**2**
RCS	**Remote Control Track** 38-42	(1)	**15**
UTC	**Universal Lockon** 36-42	(1)	**5**
030	**Curved Silent Track Bed** 31-39	(4)	**20**
031	**Straight Silent Track Bed** 31-39	(4)	**20**
032	**90 Degree Silent Track Bed** 31-39	(4)	**20**
033	**45 Degree Silent Track Bed** 31-39	(4)	**20**
034	**Switch Silent Track Bed** (Pair) 31-39	(4)	**20**
41	**Accessory Contactor** 37-42	(2)	**10**
153C	**Track Contactor** 41-42	(1)	**10**
159	**Block Control Actuator** with box 40-42	(4)	**100**

O Gauge Track, Crossings & Switches

1/2 0C	**One-Half Section Curved Track** 34-42	(4)	**5**
0C	**Curved Track** 15-19	(1)	**2**
0C	**Curved Track** 20-42	(1)	**2**
1/2 OS	**One-Half Section Straight Track** 32-42	(2)	**5**
0S	**Straight Track** 15-42	(1)	**2**
0SS	**Straight Track** w/2 insulated rails 22-42	(4)	**5**
011	**N-D Distant Control Switches** (Pair) 33-37		
	1. Pea green 33 (4) **50** 2. Black 34-37	(2)	**50**
011L	**N-D Distant Control LH Switch** 33-37		
	1. Pea green 33 (4) **25** 2. Black 34-37	(2)	**25**
011R	**N-D Distant Control RH Switch** 33-37		
	1. Pea green 33 (4) **25** 2. Black 34-37	(2)	**25**
012	**Distant Control Switches** (Pair) 27-33	(2)	**30**
012L	**Distant Control LH Switch** 31-33	(2)	**15**
012R	**Distant Control RH Switch** 31-33	(2)	**15**

013	**Switch and Panel Board** 29-31 One pair 012 switches and 439 illuminated panel board		(5)	**150**
020	**90 Degree Crossing** 30-42 1. Pea green 30-33 (2) **5** 2. Black 34-42		(1)	**5**
020X	**45 Degree Crossing** 30-42 1. Pea green 30-33 (3) **7** 2. Black 34-42		(1)	**7**
021	**Illuminated Manual Switches** (Pair) 22-37 1. Unpainted w/o insulated frogs 22 2. Unpainted with insulated frogs 23-26 3. Pea green 27-33 (2) **25** 4. Black 34-37		(5) (3) (1)	**50** **25** **25**
021L	**Illuminated Manual LH Switch** 15-21,31-37 1. Unpainted w/o insulated frog 15-21 2. Pea green 31-33 (3) **10** 3. Black 34-37		(5) (1)	**25** **10**
021R	**Illuminated Manual RH Switch** 15-21,31-37 1. Unpainted w/o insulated frog 15-21 2. Pea green 31-33 (3) **10** 3. Black 34-37		(5) (1)	**25** **10**
022	**Unlighted Manual Switches** (Pair) 22-26 1. Unpainted w/o insulated frogs 22 2. Unpainted with insulated frogs 23-26		(5) (5)	**40** **40**
022L	**Unlighted Manual LH Switch** Unpainted without insulated frog 15-21		(5)	**20**
022R	**Unlighted Manual RH Switch** Unpainted without insulated frog 15-21		(5)	**20**
022L	**Remote Control LH Switch** 38-42		(1)	**25**
022R	**Remote Control RH Switch** 38-42		(1)	**25**
042	**Manual Switches** (Pair) 38-42		(1)	**50**
042L	**Manual LH Switch** 38-42		(1)	**25**
042R	**Manual RH Switch** 38-42		(1)	**25**

O-27 Track, Crossings & Switches

1013	**Curved Track** 33-42		(1)	**1**
1018	**Straight Track** 33-42		(1)	**1**
1019	**Remote Control Track** 38-42		(1)	**10**
1021	**Remote Control Track** 38-42		(1)	**10**
1024	**Manual Switches** (Pair) 36-42		(1)	**20**
1024L	**Manual LH Switch** 37-42		(1)	**10**
1024R	**Manual RH Switch** 37-42		(1)	**10**
1025	**Illuminated Bumper** 40-42		(1)	**20**
1121	**Remote Control Switches** (Pair) 37-42		(1)	**25**

O-72 Track, Crossings & Switches

711	**Remote Control Switches** (Pair) 35-42		(3)	**200▲**
711L	**Remote Control LH Switch** 35-42		(3)	**100▲**
711R	**Remote Control RH Switch** 35-42		(3)	**100▲**
720	**90 Degree Crossing** 35-42		(3)	**20▲**
721	**Manual Switches** (Pair) 35-42		(4)	**150▲**
721L	**Manual LH Switch** 35-42		(4)	**75▲**
721R	**Manual RH Switch** 35-42		(4)	**75▲**
760	**16 pcs of 761** (72" circle) 35-42		(4)	**75**
761	**Curve Track** 35-42			

762	**Straight Track** 35-42		
762S	**Insulated Straight Track** w/lockon and wires 35-42		

O-72 T-Rail Track, Crossings & Switches

730	**90 Degree Crossing** 35-42	(4)	40▲
731	**Remote Control Switches** (Pair) 35-42	(4)	300▲
731L	**Remote Control LH Switch** 35-42	(4)	150▲
731R	**Remote Control RH Switch** 35-42	(4)	150▲
771	**Curved Track** U35-42	(4)	15▲
772	**Straight Track** U35-42	(4)	20▲
772S	**Straight Track** Two rails insulated for operating accessories 40-42	(4)	75▲
773	**T-Rail Fish Plate Set** 100 screws, 100 nuts, 50 plates, wrench 36-42	(5)	75▲

OO Gauge Track, Crossings & Switches

OO-31	**Curved Track** 2-rail 39-42	(4)	15
OO-32	**Straight Track** 2-rail 39-42	(5)	25
OO-34	**Curved Track** 2-rail 39-42	(4)	15
OO-51	**Curved Track** 3-rail 39-42	(3)	10
OO-52	**Straight Track** 3-rail 39-42	(4)	20
OO-54	**Curved Track** 3-rail with electrical connections 39-42	(3)	15
OO-61	**Curved Track** 3-rail 38	(3)	10
OO-62	**Straight Track** 3-rail 38	(4)	20
OO-63	**Curved Track** 3-rail 1/2 section 38-42	(5)	10
OO-64	**Curved Track** with electrical connections 38	(3)	15
OO-65	**Straight Track** 3-rail 1/2 section 38-42	(5)	15
OO-66	**Straight Track** 3-rail 5/6 section 38-42	(5)	25
OO-70	**90 Degree Crossing** 38-42	(3)	5
OO-72	**Switches** 3-rail pair 38-42	(4)	125
OO-72L	**Switch** 3-rail 38-42	(4)	60
OO-72R	**Switch** 3-rail 38-42	(4)	60

Standard Gauge Track & Switches

S	**12" Straight Track** 3 ties 07,08	(5)	10
S	**14" Straight Track** 3 ties 08-30	(3)	4
S	**14" Straight Track** 4 ties 31-42	(2)	2
SC	**14" Straight Track** with electrical connections, 3 ties 15-22	(4)	10
20	**90 Degree Crossing** 09-42		
	1. Depressed center	(4)	5
	2. Fibre center and solid metal base	(2)	5
	3. Bakelite center and solid metal base	(2)	5
20X	**45 Degree Crossing** 28-32	(3)	10
21	**90 Degree Crossing** 1906	(4)	10
21	**Manual Switch** Illuminated		
	1. No fibre rails 15-22 (3) **20** 2. Fibre rails 23-25	(4)	25

22	**Manual Switch** 06-22					
	1. Cast iron switch stand 06-15			(3)		20
	2. Stamped steel switch stand 16-22			(2)		20
22	**Manual Switch** with fibre rails 23-25			(3)		20
23-65	**Bumper** 15-33			(3)		65▲
25-50	**Bumper** Black/yellow-red 27-42			(3)		50▲
210	**Pair of Switches** Right and left hand 26-42					
	1. Green base 26-33	(3)	30	2. Black base 34-42	(2)	30
210L	**Manual Switch** Left hand 26-42			(2)		20
210R	**Manual Switch** Right hand 26-42			(2)		20
220	**Pair of Manual Switches** Not Illuminated 26			(2)		15
222	**Pair of Distance Control Switches** w/controllers Illuminated 26-32			(3)		100
222L	**Left-Hand Distance Control Switch** Illuminated 26-32			(2)		45
222R	**Right-Hand Distance Control Switch** Illuminated 26-32			(2)		45
223	**Pair of N-D Switches** Illuminated 32-42					
	1. Green base	(4)	175	2. Black base	(4)	175
223L	**Left-Hand N-D Switch** Illuminated 32-42			(4)		75
223R	**Right-Hand N-D Switch** Illuminated 32-42			(4)		75
225	**439 Control Panel** w/222 switches 29-32			(4)		400▲

PREWAR

Transformers and Controllers

Note: All transformers are for 110 volt, 60 cycle current, unless otherwise noted.

A	**Transformer** 22-37					
	1. 40 Watts 22-31	(3)	5	2. 60 Watts 32-37	(1)	10
B	**Transformer** 17-38					
	1. 50 Watts 17	(4)	5	2. 75 Watts 18-38	(1)	7
C	**Transformer** 75 Watts 25-40 cycle 22-37			(5)		5
F	**Transformer** 40 Watts 25-40 cycle 30-37			(5)		5
H	**Transformer** 75 Watts 25-40 cycle 38-39			(5)		5
J	**Transformer** 100 Watts 4 current U36 selection: 90-250 volt/40-133 cycle			(5)		5
K	**Transformer** 15-38					
	1. 200 Watts cast iron case slate top 15-19			(3)		45
	2. 150 Watts sheet-metal case & top 20-38			(1)		20
L	**Transformer** 14,35-38					
	1. 75 Watts brass case slate top 14			(4)		8
	2. 50 Watts black sheet-metal case & top 35-38			(1)		5
	3. 50 Watts red sheet-metal case & top			(4)		5
N	**Transformer** 50 Watts 42			(3)		5
Q	**Transformer** 75 Watts 39-42			(2)		5
R	**Transformer** 100 Watts 39-42			(1)		5
T	**Transformer** 15-38					
	1. 75 Watts 15-17	(4)	5	2. 150 Watts 18-21	(5)	5
	3. 110 Watts 22	(5)	8	4. 100 Watts 23-38	(1)	5
U	**Transformer** 50 Watts 33			(3)		40
V	**Transformer** 150 Watts 39-41			(2)		125
W	**Transformer** 75 Watts 39-42			(3)		10
Z	**Transformer** 250 Watts 39-42			(4)		250▲

25

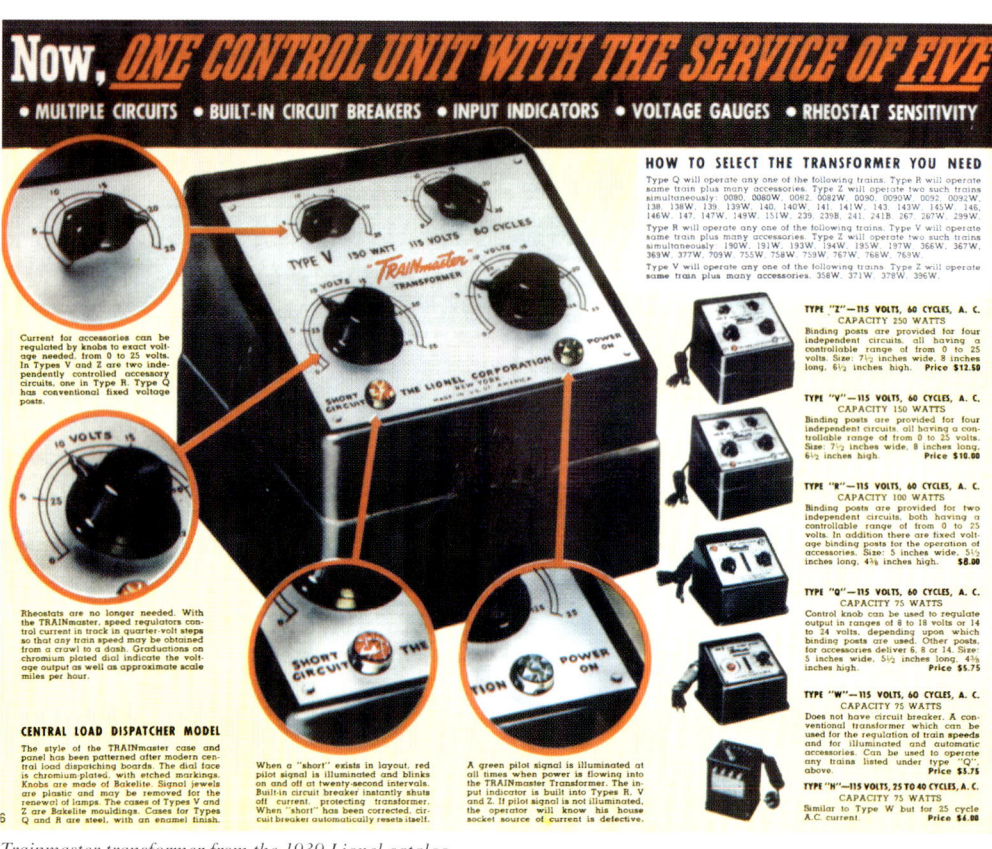

Trainmaster transformer from the 1939 Lionel catalog

65	Whistle Controller 35	(4)	10
66	Whistle Controller 36-39	(1)	5
67	Whistle Controller 36-39	(1)	5
81	Controlling Rheostat 27-33	(2)	5
88	Battery Rheostat 15-28	(3)	50
91	Circuit Breaker 30-42	(1)	5
95	Controlling Rheostat 34-42	(2)	5
96C	Control Button 38-42	(1)	15
167	Whistle Controller 40-42	(1)	10
167X	Whistle Controller OO 40-42	(3)	25
168	Magic-Electrol Controller 40-42	(3)	50▲
169	Teledyne Controller 40-42	(3)	50▲
170	Direct Current Reducer 220 Volt 14-38	(5)	100
171	Direct Current Inverter 115 Volt 36-42	(3)	100
172	Direct Current Inverter 220 Volt 37-42	(5)	100
1012	Station Transformer 30-32	(4)	50

Winner Lines Transformers

1017	Station Transformer 33	(3)	70▲
1027	Station Transformer 34	(2)	70▲
1028	Transformer 25 Watts 35	(3)	25
1029	Transformer 25 Watts 36-37	(1)	5
1030	Transformer 50 Watts 36-37	(1)	5
1037	Transformer 40 Watts 41-42	(1)	4

1038	**Transformer** 30 Watts U37	(3)	4
1039	**Transformer** 35 Watts 38-40	(1)	3
1040	**Transformer** 60 Watts 39	(1)	15
1041	**Transformer** 60 Watts 40-42	(1)	15
1229	**Transformer** 25 Watts 220 volt U36	(5)	25
1230	**Transformer** 50 Watts 220 volt U36	(5)	25
1239	**Transformer** 30 Watts 220 volt U38	(5)	25

Clockwork Trains

1536   **Mickey Mouse Circus Train Outfit** 35   (5)   **3500**
1508 Commodore Vanderbilt engine and 1509 stoker tender with diner, animal car, and band car all numbered 1536. Complete set includes cardboard Mickey Mouse barker, circus tickets, auto, gas station, sign, and circus tent. Price is for set in original box.

1107 Donald Duck Rail Car

1105 Santa Claus Handcar

1100	**Mickey Mouse Handcar** 35-37				
	1. Red base	(4)**1000**▲	2. Maroon base	(5)	**1500**▲
	3. Apple green base	(4)**1200**▲	4. Orange base	(5)	**1500**▲
1103	**Peter Rabbit Chickmobile Handcar** U35-37				
	1. Yellow with flanges (track version)			(5)	**850**▲
	2. Same no flanges (floor version)			(5)	**1200**▲
1105	**Santa Claus Handcar** 35,36				
	1. Green base	(5)**1800**▲	2. Red base	(4)	**1500**▲
1107	**Donald Duck Rail Car** 36,37				
	1. White house/red roof	(4) **900**▲	2. White house/green roof	(4)	**800**▲
	3. Orange house/green roof	(5)**1300**▲			

27

Locomotives

1506	**0-4-0** Black/red 35		(4)	**600**
	1509 Mickey Mouse stoker tender, 1515 tank, 1517 caboose, set no. 1532			
1506L	**0-4-0** Black/red 33,34		(3)	**125**
	Same as 1506 with 4-wheel 1502 tender			
	3 1811 Pullman cars, set no. 1525			
1508	**0-4-0 Mickey Mouse** Red 1509T *(see Mickey Mouse Circus Train)* 35		(5)	**1000**▲
1511	**0-4-0** 1516T 36,37			
	1. Black (3) **125**	2. Red	(4)	**150**

1588	**0-4-0** Torpedo-type 1588T 36,37		(4)	**150**

The Gray Years 1941, 1942

During the years 1941-42, Lionel began to eliminate the use of aluminum paint on various parts of their accessories and rolling stock, and started to use gray paint instead. Commonly called 92 gray, this paint is a high gloss medium gray, and is very distinctive. The prevailing theory is that the aluminum used in the pigment was needed for the war effort in Europe. This may also explain the replacement of gunmetal paint with black on their steam engines at approximately the same time. The following is a list of the accessories and rolling stock which came in gray.

Accessories

35	**Boulevard Lamp**		(3)	**60**
45N	**Operating Gateman**		(4)	**90**▲
46	**Single Arm Crossing Gate**		(4)	**150**
47	**Double Arm Crossing Gate**		(4)	**300**
060	**Telegraph Pole**		(4)	**45**
071	**Telegraph Pole Set** w/box		(4)	**450**
76	**Watchmans Shack** w/gray posts		(4)	**375**
085	**Telegraph Pole** w/track connector		(4)	**50**
086	**Telegraph Pole Set** w/box		(4)	**400**
92	**Floodlight Tower**		(4)	**250**
93	**Water Tower**		(5)	**300**▲
94	**High Tension Tower**		(5)	**500**▲
97	**Coal Loader**		(4)	**375**▲
137	**Lioneltown Station**		(5)	**300**
152	**Crossing Gate**		(3)	**75**
153	**Block Signal**		(3)	**75**
154	**Highway Crossing Signal**		(3)	**45**
156	**Station Platform**		(4)	**225**▲
164	**Log Loader**		(4)	**450**▲

165	Gantry Crane	(4)	500
208	Tool Set Box	(3)	400
313	Bascule Bridge	(4)	700▲
314	Girder Bridge	(3)	50
315	Trestle Bridge	(4)	175
316	Trestle Bridge	(4)	90
440N	Signal Bridge	(4)	400
1045	Operating Watchman	(3)	60

Rolling Stock

620	Floodlight Car	(3)	85
654	Tank	(3)	60
1630	Passenger	(4)	60▲
1631	Passenger	(4)	60
2620	Floodlight Car	(3)	125
2630	Passenger	(4)	125
2631	Passenger	(4)	125
2642	Passenger	(4)	125
2643	Observation	(4)	125
2654	Tank	(3)	85
2755	Tank	(4)	175

Lithographed Cars

Note: Early versions have latch couplers, brass or nickel journals. Late versions have box couplers, black journals. Numbers changed in 1938 when couplers changed from manual to automatic.

4-Wheel, 6-inch Freight Series

1512	**Gondola** 31-33,36,37		
	1. Dark blue *Winner Lines* 31,32	(4)	20
	2. Dark blue no *Winner Lines* 31-33	(4)	20
	3. Light blue *Winner Lines* 31,32	(3)	20
	4. Light blue no *Winner Lines* 31-33	(3)	20
	5. Light blue/red 36,37	(3)	20
	6. Light blue/red and yellow 37	(4)	20
1514	**Box Erie** 31-37		
	1. Yellow/dark blue 31-33	(3)	25
	2. Yellow/dark blue *Lionel Lines* 33	(3)	25
	3. Yellow/light blue *Lionel Lines* 34	(2)	25
	4. Yellow/light blue *Lionel & Baby Ruth* 35	(2)	25
	5. Yellow/light blue/red *Lionel & Baby Ruth* 36,37	(4)	30
	6. Yellow/light blue/red and yellow *Lionel & Baby Ruth* 37	(4)	30
1515	**Tank** 31-37		
	1. Aluminum *Winner Sunoco* 31,32	(4)	25
	2. Aluminum *Sunoco* 31,32	(2)	25
	3. Aluminum *Union Tank Lines* 33	(5)	75
	4. Aluminum *Lionel Lines & Sunoco* 34,35	(2)	25
	5. Aluminum/red *Lionel Lines & Sunoco* 36,37	(3)	25
	6. Aluminum/red & yellow *Lionel Lines & Sunoco* 37	(4)	25

1517 **Caboose** 31-37
    1. Dark red/brown *Winner Lines* 31,32 (3) 20
    2. Dark red/brown no *Winner Lines* 33 (2) 20
    3. Red/black no *Lionel Lines* 34 (4) 20
    4. Red/black *Lionel* 35 (2) 20
    5. Red/red/yellow cupola stripe *Lionel* 36,37 (3) 20
    6. Red/red & yellow/yellow stripe *Lionel* 37 (4) 20

8-Wheel, 8-inch 1600-2600 Freight Series

Note: X designates no journals

1677 **Gondola** either latch or box couplers 33-35, 39-42
    1. Peacock/copper or nickel journals 33-35 (4) 50
    2. Red/nickel journals 39 (3) 30
    3. Red/black journals 40-42 (4) 50

1679 **Baby Ruth Box** 33-42
    Either orange or brown doors and guides. NDV
    1. Yellow/dark blue 33-35 (3) 35 2. Yellow/medium blue 36-39 (2) 25
    3. Yellow/turquoise 37,38 (2) 25 4. Yellow/light blue 38,39 (2) 25
    5. Yellow/maroon 39-42 (2) 25 6. Yellow/brown 39-40 (5) 35

1679X **Baby Ruth Box** U36-42
    1. Yellow/medium blue 36,37 (4) 25 2. Yellow/turquoise 37 (4) 25
    3. Yellow/light blue 38,39 (4) 25 4. Yellow/maroon 39-42 (3) 25

1680 **Tank** 33-42
    1. Aluminum 33,34 (4) 25
    2. Aluminum *Sunoco* 33,34 (3) 25
    3. Aluminum *Sunoco & Lionel Lines* 35-38 (2) 20
    4. Orange *Shell*, copper or nickel journals NDV 39-40 (3) 30
    5. Aluminum *Lionel Lines* 40 (3) 20
    6. Silver *SUNX* X *Sunoco & Lionel Lines* 41,42 (3) 25
       Nickel or black journals NDV
    7. Gray *SUNX* nickel or black domes, nickel or black journals NDV42 (4) 20

1680X **Tank** U36,39,41,42
    1. Aluminum *Sunoco & Lionel Lines* no journals 36-39 (3) 20
    2. Orange *Shell* dummy box coupler 39,40 (4) 30
    3. Silver *SUNX* dummy box coupler 41 (4) 20
    4. Gray *SUNX* nickel domes dummy box coupler 42 (3) 25

1682 **Caboose** 33-42
    1. Red/brown 33-35 (3) 20 2. Red/yellow/yellow stripe 36 (3) 20
    3. Red/yellow/no stripe 39-42 (3) 20 4. Dark brown/brown (2) 15

1682X **Caboose** no journals U36-42
    1. Red/yellow/yell stripe 36 (5) 30 2. Red/yellow/no stripe 37-40 (3) 20
    3. Dark/brown/brown 41,42 (3) 15

2677 **Gondola** Red 40-42 (2) 75▲

2679 **Baby Ruth Box** nj bj 38-42
    1. Yellow/medium blue 37,38 (2) 45 2. Yellow/turquoise 39,40 (3) 45
    3. Yellow/light blue 39,40 (2) 45 4. Yellow/maroon 39-42 (2) 35

1680 Tank variation 7 (top), variation 3 (bottom)

2680   **Tank** 38-42
         1. Aluminum *Sunoco & Lionel Lines* 38,39   (2)   **30▲**
         2. Orange *Shell* 39,40   (2)   **35▲**   3. Silver *SUNX* 41   (3)   **30▲**

         4. Gray *SUNX* nickel or black domes NDV 42   (4)   **35▲**

2682   **Caboose** front coupler only 38-42
         1. Red/yellow/no stripe 38-40 (2)   **20**   2. Dark brown/brown 41,42   (3)   **20**

2682X   **Caboose t**wo couplers 40-42
         1. Red/yellow/no stripe 40   (3)   **30▲**   2. Dark brown/brown 41,42   (4)   **30▲**

1700-2700, 9 1/2-inch Freight Series

1717   **Gondola** U33-40
         1. Tan/orange U33,34   (4)   **35**   2. Tan/cream U35   (4)   **25**
         3. Tan/orange U35-40   (2)   **25**   4. Tan/orange U41,42   (4)   **35**

1717X   **Gondola** Tan/orange U41,42   (4)   **35**

1719   **Box** Peacock/blue U33-42
         1. Copper journals U33,34 (3)   **35**   2. Nickel journals U35-40   (3)   **35**
         3. Black journals U41,42   (4)   **40**

PREWAR

1719X	**Box** Peacock/blue U41,42		(4)	**40**
1722	**Caboose**			
	1. Orange/maroon U33,34 (3) **25**	2. Red/maroon U35	(4)	**45**
	3. Orange-red/maroon U36-40 (2) **25**	4. Orange-red/maroon U41,42	(3)	**25**
1722X	**Caboose** Orange-red/maroon U41,42		(4)	**25**
2717	**Gondola** Tan/orange U38-42			
	1. Nickel journals U38,39 (3) **35▲**	2. Black journals U41,42	(3)	**30▲**
2719	**Box** Peacock/blue U38,39,U41,42			
	1. Nickel journals U38,39 (3) **35**	2. Black journals U41,42	(3)	**30**
2722	**Caboose** Orange-red/maroon U38,39,U41,42			
	1. Nickel journals U38,39 (2) **30**	2. Black journals U41,42	(3)	**30**

Lionel-Ives

1017	**Transformer Station** 32,33	(2)	**35**
1053E	**Complete Electric Railroad** 43 1/2" X 29 1/2" 33	(5)	*****
	Includes set 1052E, mountain, 913 country estate and decorated platform		
1651	**Electric 0-4-0** Red litho/brown/black, Sets only 33	(3)	**150**
	Set no.1050E w/ 2 1690 Pullmans and 1 1691 Observation	(3)	**350**
1661E	**Steam 2-4-0** 4-wheel 1661 lithograph tender. Sets only 33	(3)	**250**
	Set no. 1051E with 1679 box car, 1680 tank car, and 1682 caboose	(3)	**650▲**
	Set no. 1052E with 2 1690 Pullmans and 1 1691 Observation	(4)	**175**
1677	**Gondola** Peacock sold separately 33-35	(4)	**50**
1678	**Cattle** Green/orange lithograph sold separately, 33	(5)	**400**

Lionel Jr.

1057E	**Distant Control Railroad** 34	(5)	*****
	43 1/4" X 29 1/2" Includes set no. 1056E, mountains, 913 bungalow		
1066E	**Distant Control Railroad** 43 1/4" X 29 1/2" 35,36	(5)	*****
	Includes set no. 1065E, 913 bungalow, transformer, rheostat, and curved tunnel		
1681	**Steam 2-4-0** 4-wheel 1661 lithograph tender. Sets only 34,35		
	1. Black/red frame 34 (3) **85** 2. Red/red frame 35	(4)	**100**

Set 1055E

1681E	**Steam 2-4-0** Sets only 34,35		
	4-wheel 1661 litho tender (same as 1681 with reversing E-unit)		
	1. Black/red frame 34	(3)	75
	2. Red/red frame 35	(4)	100
	Set no. 1056E w/ 2 1690 Pullmans and 1 1691 Observation	(4)	200
	Set no. 1055E w/ 1679, 1680, 1682	(3)	175
1700	**Articulated Streamline Power Car** U35-37		*
	Same as 1700E but no reverse. Used in uncataloged sets.		

PREWAR

1700E	**Articulated Streamline Power Car** 35-37		
	Set 1065E 1701 Coach, 1702 Observation		
	1. Aluminum/light red 35 (3) **275** 2. Chrome/red 35	(2)	225
	3. *Hiawatha Orange* and gray, Set 1071E, 2 1701 Coaches, 1702 Obs. 36	(4)	1000▲
	4. Chrome/red sides come both smooth and fluted. NDV 36,37	(3)	200

Passenger Cars

2 1690 Pullmans 1691 Observation 8-wheel 8" 33-40		
1. Dark red/brown/yellow brass handrails 33-35	(2)	35
2. Red/cream 36-39 underbellies nickel handrails	(3)	35
3. Red/cream 40 no underbellies nickel handrails	(4)	40

1692 Pullman 1693 Observation 8" Peacock cream inserts U37,38 (4) **40**

1811 **Pullman** 4-wheel Lionel Lines 6" 33-37
 1. Peacock/orange/cream 33,34 (3) **25** 2. Gray/red/ivory 35 (3) **30**
 3. Red/cream 36,37 (3) **35**

1812 **Observation**
 1. Peacock/orange/cream 33,34 (4) **50** 2. Gray/red/ivory 35 (4) **50**
 3. Red/cream 36,37 (4) **50**

1813 **Baggage**
 1. Peacock/orange/cream 33,34 (5)**100** 2. Gray/red/ivory 35 (5) **100**

Winner Lines 30-32

1010 **Electric** 0-4-0, Sets only 31-32
 1. Orange/green/cream (Engine only) (3) **75**
 2. Tan/green/cream (Engine only) (3) **75**
 3. Either w/2 matching 1011 Pullmans (4) **200**

1011 Pullman, 1019 Observation, 1020 Baggage Litho *Winner Lines* 31,32
 1. Orange/green/cream (3) **30** 2. Dark orange/green/cream (3) **30▲**

1015 **Steam** 0-4-0. Sets only 31,32 (3) **100**
 Black/orange/copper trim, 4-wheel 1016 black/orange tender

1030 **Electric** 0-4-0 Dark orange/green/cream. Sets only 32 (3) **100**

1035 **Steam** 0-4-0. Sets only 32
 1. Black/red (3) **100** 2. Black/orange (4) **100**

1512 **Gondola** lithograph. Sets only 31,32
 1. Light blue (2) **25** 2. Dark blue (2) **25**

1514 **Boxcar** lithograph Yellow/dark blue *Erie* markings. Sets only 31,32 (2) **30**

1517 **Caboose** lithograph Dark red/brown/yellow. Sets only 31,32 (2) **25**

2682 Caboose variation 1

O Gauge
Electrics

Note: Cab color/trim/frame color if other than black

4	0-4-0 9 1/4" 28-32				
	1. Orange	(4) **1000**	2. Gray/apple green stripe	(5)	**1200**▲

Note: Hand reverse slot in cab. Exists with or without weights in frame. NDV

PREWAR

4U	0-4-0 *Bild-A-Loco* **4** in kit form Orange 9 1/4" 28-32 with 8 sections of track. Price based on complete kit with original box	(5)	**2000**
150	0-4-0 Early *NYC* in oval, Dark green same body as 700 electric 1917	(5)	**200**

150 late 0-4-4 variation 3 (top), 152 0-4-0 variation 1 (bottom)

150	**0-4-0** Later *NYC* in oval 18-25					
	1. Dark green	(3)	**125**	2. Brown	(4)	**200**
	3. Maroon	(3)	**125**	4. Dark olive green	(3)	**125**
	5. Mojave	(5)	**300**	6. Peacock	(5)	**300**
	7. Gray	(4)	**175**	8. Olive green	(3)	**125**
152	**0-4-0** *NYC* in oval 17-27					
	1. Dark green	(3)	**100**	2. Dark olive green	(3)	**100**
	3. Dark gray	(3)	**100**	4. Gray	(4)	**125**
	5. Peacock	(5)	**375**	6. Mojave	(5)	**350**
	7. Pea green	(4)	**125**			
153	**0-4-0** *NYC* in oval Same as late 152 but with reverse 24,25					
	1. Dark green	(3)	**125**	2. Dark olive green	(4)	**150**
	3. Gray	(4)	**150**	4. Mojave	(5)	**350**
	5. Dark gray	(4)	**125**	6. Peacock	(4)	**125**
	7. Olive green	(4)	**125**	8. Glossy maroon	(4)	**125**
154	**0-4-0** *NYC* in oval 17-23					
	1. Dark green	(4)	**150**	2. Dark olive green	(5)	**250**
156	**4-4-4** *NYC* in oval 17-23					
	1. Dark green	(5)	**600**	2. Maroon	(5)	**700**
	3. Olive green	(5)	**800**	4. Mojave	(5)	**900**
	5. Apple green	(5)	**800**	6. Gray	(5)	**800**
156	**0-4-0** *NYC* in oval Dark green 22				(4)	**500**
156X	**0-4-0** *NYC* in oval 23,24					
	1. Maroon (gloss or flat)	(4)	**500**	2. Olive green	(4)	**550**
	3. Mojave	(4)	**500**			
158	**0-4-0** *NYC* in oval 19-23					
	1. Gray	(3)	**125**	2. Black	(4)	**175**
	3. Green	(5)	**225**			

250 E variation 2 (top), variation 1 (bottom)

203	**0-4-0 Armored Loco** (only) gray 17-21	(5)	**1200***
	1. With two 702 gray supply cars	(5)	**1800***
	2. With two 900 gray ammo cars	(5)	**1800***
248	**0-4-0** 7 1/2" 27-32		
	1. Dark green/brass RS, either strap and cast headlight. NDV U26	(4)	**225**
	2. Orange/brass RS or etched U27	(2)	**125**
	3. Dark green/maroon RS U30 (3) **225** 4. Orange/peacock RS	(2)	**125**
	5. Red/cream RS (2) **125** 6. Red/brass RS	(3)	**225**
	7. Olive green/orange RS U30 (3) **350** 8. Terra cotta/cream RS U31	(3)	**375**

Note: 248 cataloged by Ives in 1928 and 1929. Designated 3260 and made in two colors, light blue and dark blue. Late 248 cabs may be found without handrails. NDV

250	**0-4-0** (early) Dark green/brass, 8" no reversing slot on top 26	(3)	**250**
250E	**0-4-0** (late) 8" Same loco as 252E with 250 number plates. U34 Has reversing slot on top.		
	1. Orange/brass/terra cotta frame	(3)	**275**
	2. Same as 1 but *E* is RS on door	(4)	**225**
	3. Terra cotta/brass/maroon or black frame	(3)	**200**
	4. Same as 3 but *E* is RS on door	(4)	**225**
251	**0-4-0** 10" 25-32		
	1. Gray/brass or red inserts. NDV	(3)	**375**
	2. Red/brass or ivory inserts and with or without ivory stripe. NDV	(4)	**450**
251E	**0-4-0** 10" 27-32		
	1. Gray/red or brass inserts. NDV	(3)	**400**
	2. Red/ivory or brass inserts and with or without ivory stripe. NDV	(4)	**450**

Note: Gray versions of 251 and 251E exist with either red or black lettering. NDV

252	**0-4-0** 8" Same as 250 but with hand reverse 26-32		
	1. Dark green/brass	(4)	**250**
	2. Peacock/brass	(2)	**125**
	3. Olive green/brass	(2)	**125**
	4. Terra cotta/brass/maroon frame with or without cream stripe. NDV	(3)	**175**
	5. Orange/brass/terra cotta or black frame	(3)	**175**
	6. Maroon/brass/cream stripe Macy DSS	(5)	**600**
252E	**0-4-0** 8" 33-35		
	1. Terra cotta/brass/terra cotta frame (easily faked)	(3)	**200**
	2. Terra cotta/brass/maroon frame	(2)	**150**
	3. Orange/brass/terra cotta frame	(2)	**150**
253	**0-4-0** 8" 24-32		
	1. Maroon/brass (4) **400** 2. Red/brass	(4)	**450**
	3. Dark green/brass, strap headlight only	(3)	**200**
	4. Mojave/brass exists with both cast and strap headlights. NDV	(2)	**175**
	5. Peacock/orange with or without orange stripe	(2)	**175**
	6. Terra cotta/cream/maroon or black frame	(3)	**300**
	7. Pea green/orange with orange stripe U30	(5)	**750***
	8. Same as 7 but no orange stripe	(5)	**750***
	9. SG green/cream/dark green frame	(3)	**250**
	10. Gray/brass U23-26 * 11. Red/orange U31	(4)	**400**
	12. Red/cream U29 (4) **400** 13. Blue/brass U		*****

Note: Peacock and pea green versions exist with and without orange stripe. NDV

253E	**0-4-0** 9" 31-36		
	1. Peacock/orange	(3)	**150**
	2. Terra cotta/cream/maroon frame	(4)	**325**
	3. SG green/cream/dark green frame	(4)	**325**
	4. SG green/cream/black frame	(3)	**250**

Note: E is either rubber-stamped in black on door (1931 or 1932) or embossed in red on number plate. If on door, add $100.

254 **0-4-0** 9 1/2" Brass inserts 24-32

1. Dark green	(5)	**350**	2. Mojave	(3)	**325**
3. Olive green	(2)	**250**	4. Pea green	(3)	**300**
5. Pea green/dk green frame	(3)	**350**	6. Red	(5)	**500**
7. Apple green	(3)	**375**	8. Orange	(4)	**450**

Note: Variations exist having to do with red or orange celluloid inserts behind ventilators, different color hatches, and orange or red stripes. NDV.
Note: A rare export version exists with 1 headlight, no pantograph, 254 RS on ends, and underframe marked "Made in U.S. of America."

254E **0-4-0** 9 1/2" brass inserts and black frame 27-34

1. Olive green/red stripe	(4)	**350**	2. Olive green/no red stripe	(3)	**300**
3. Pea green with or without orange stripe and orange hatches. NDV				(4)	**400**
4. Orange				(5)	**500▲**

Note: On most versions, the "E" is embossed in red on number plate. On some later versions, the "E" is rubber-stamped in black on the door. The rubber-stamped versions are rarer add $25 to $50.

256 **0-4-4-0** 11 1/2" Orange only 24-30

1. Nickel trim RS *LIONEL* with border stamped HL	(5)	**1200▲**
2. Same as 1 but no border	(3)	**900**
3. Brass trim RS *LIONEL* no border diecast HL	(3)	**800**
4. *Lionel Lines* on brass plate w/border, diecast HL	(4)	**1100▲**
5. Same as 4/no border/larger letters	(3)	**800▲**

450 **0-4-0** Macy's Special 9" DSS U30

1. Red/brass	(5)	**800**
2. Apple green/brass/dark green frame	(5)	**950**

700	0-4-0 *NYC* in oval dark green 15,16				(5)	550▲
701	0-4-0 *NYC* in oval dark green 15,16					
	1. Iron wheels	(5)	550	2. Diecast wheels	(4)	450
703	4-4-4 *NYC* in oval dark green 15,16				(5)	2250▲
706	0-4-0 Dark green 15,16					
	1. *NYC* in oval	(5)	500	2. Lettered *C.P.R.*	(5)	500
728	0-4-0 *Quaker* 728 U15,16				(5)	*
732	0-4-0 *Quaker* U15,16				(5)	*
1651	0-4-0 9" Litho cab on 253-type, 33 frame, Red litho brown roof/black frame *Lionel Ives* markings, sets only				(3)	150

Steamers

Note: Gray versions in excellent or better condition of both sheet-metal and diecast locos are always harder to find than black versions.

260 Series Steamers

255E	2-4-2 Gunmetal 263W 35,36				(5)	1200▲
260E	2-4-2 30-35, with *Chugger* 33-35					
	1. Black/cream stripe 260T 8 wheels				(4)	750▲
	2. Black/green frame 260T 8 wheels				(3)	750▲
	3. Black/green frame 260T 12 wheels				(4)	800
	4. Gunmetal 263T 12 wheels (4)	850		5. Gunmetal 263W 1935	(4)	900

263E	**2-4-2** 36-39			
	1. Gunmetal 263W, 2263W		(3)	**675**
	2. Blue/dark blue 263W, 2263W, blue or red cow-catcher. NDV		(4)	**1200**

Diecast Steamers

204	**2-4-2** Same casting as 1684, U40,41					
	1. Gunmetal 1689W, 2689W (4) **125**	2. Black 1689W, 2689W			(3)	**100**
224, 224E	**2-6-2** 38-42					
	1. Gunmetal 2689W, sheet metal tender				(2)	**250**
	2. Gunmetal 2224W diecast tender				(4)	**1700**
	3. Black 2224W diecast tender				(3)	**250**
	4. Black 2224W plastic tender				(3)	**200**
	Note: Same casting used for 224, 229, 1664, 1666					
225, 225E	**2-6-2** Similar casting to Postwar 675, 38-42					
	1. Gunmetal 2225W, 2265W sheet metal tender				(3)	**325**
	2. Gunmetal 2235W, 2245W diecast tender				(4)	**1000▲**
	3. Black 2235W, 2245W diecast tender				(3)	**300**
	4. Black 2235W plastic tender				(2)	**200**
	5. Black 2225T, 2225TX, 2225W, 2225WX sheet metal tenders, uncataloged sets 39,40				(4)	**300**
226E	**2-6-4** Black with red firebox light. Great runner. 38-41					

1. 2226T, 2226W		(4)	**700**
2. 2226TX, 2226WX (lower coupler)		(4)	**650**
3. Late version with 226 plate		(5)	**800**
Note: Tender lettering both silver and white: journals came both in nickel and black. NDV			
Some 225s, 225Es, 226Es come with Lionel Lines plates rather than number plates. NDV			

229 229E	**2-4-2** 39-42					
	1. Gunmetal 2689T&W (4) **250**	2. Black 2689T&W			(3)	**150**
	3. Black 2666T&W (3) **150**					
238	**4-4-2** *Pennsylvania* Black 2225T&W U39-40				(5)	**700***
	Note: 238s are usually gunmetal in cataloged sets and black in uncataloged sets					
238E	**4-4-2** *Pennsylvania* Gunmetal 36-38					
	1. 265T&W 36,37 (3) **400**	2. 2265W 2225W 38			(4)	**450**

Normal production 250E *Prototype 250E*

250E	**4-4-2** *Hiawatha* 250W, 250WX, 250T, 2250T, 2250W 35-42	(5)	**2000**▲
264E	**2-4-2** *Commodore Vanderbilt* same as 265E but no eccentric rod 35,36,U40		
	1. Red Comet 1935 261T (5) **550** 2. Red Comet 1936 265T (4)		**475**
	3. Black 1936 265T (3) **350** 4. Black U1940 265T (3)		**375**
265E	**2-4-2** *Commodore Vanderbilt* 35-40		
	1. Black 261TX 35 (5) **350** 2. Black 265T&W (3)		**350**

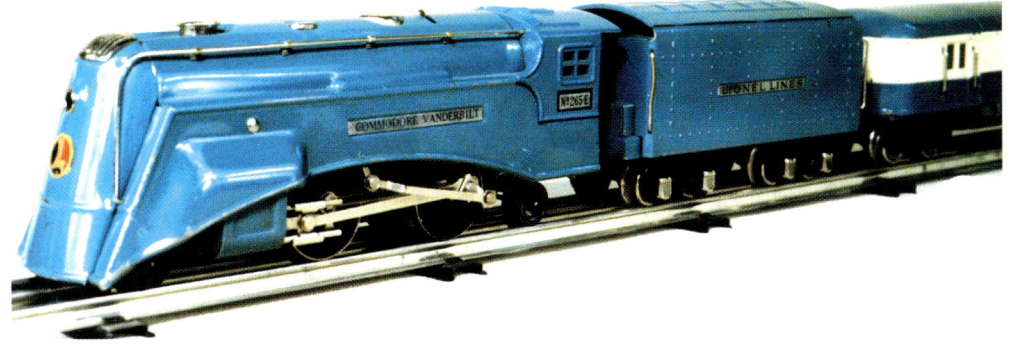

	3. Blue 265TW *Blue Streak* 36-38	(4)	**700**▲
	4. Gunmetal 265T&W 2225T&W 36-38	(3)	**400**
	5. Chrome plated 265T U35, 36		**5P**
	6. Black 2225T&W 38-40	(3)	**350**
289E	**2-4-2** *Lionel Lines* same casting as 1689		
	1. Gunmetal 1689T&W U36 (4) **500** 2. Black 1588W 1688T&W U37 (3)		**400**
1664	**2-4-2** same casting as 1666, 1938-42		
1664E	1. Gunmetal 1689W 38,39 (3) **150** 2. Black 1689T&W 39-41 (2)		**85**
	3. Black 2666T&W plastic 42 only (4) **75**		
1666	**2-6-2** same casting as 1664, 1938-42		
1666E	1. Gunmetal 2689W 2689T&W 38,39	(3)	**135**
	2. Black 2689T&W 39-41 (2) **125** 3. Black 2666T&W plastic 42 (3)		**100**

1688E Gunmetal

1668	**2-6-2** *Lionel Lines* 37-41			
1668E	1. Gunmetal 1689T&W 37,38 (3)**125**▲	2. Black 1689T&W 39-41	(2)	**100**
1684	**2-4-2** Same casting as 204 U41,42			
	1. Black (3) **100**	2. Gray	(5)	**500**
1688	**2-4-2** same casting as 1666 36-38 U37-42			
1688E	1. Gunmetal 36-38 1689T&W U37-42		(3)	**125**
	2. Black 1689T&W U40		(2)	**100**
1689E	**2-4-2** *Lionel Lines* same casting as 289E			
	1. Gunmetal 1689T&W 36 (2) **125**	2. Black 1689T&W 37	(2)	**100**

Hudsons

700E	**4-6-4** *New York Central* 700W 37-42		(5)	**5000**
700E	**Walnut Display Board**		(4)	**400**
700K	**4-6-4** *NYC,* 700KW 38-42			
	1. Original box/unassembled (5)**10000***	2. Assembled, primer gray	(4)	**3500**
700EWX	**4-6-4** Same as 700E but with tinplate flanges and blind drivers U37-38		(5)	**5000***
763E	**4-6-4** *New York Central* 37-42			

1. Gunmetal 263W, 2263W oil 37-40 (4) **2500**▲

2. Gunmetal 2226W, 2226WX coal 40 (5) **7000**▲

3. Black 2226W coal 41,42 (4) **2750**

Sheet-Metal Steamers

249	**2-4-2** 36-37 U38,39				
249E	1. Gunmetal 2225T&W 265T&W 36			(5)	**275**
	2. Black 265T&W 37	(3)	**225**	3. Dull black 265T&W 37 (5)	**275**▲
	Rare set: Gray 249 with 3 Ives 10-inch lithographed freight cars, U38			(5)	**550**▲
257	**2-4-0** Black only 30,U31,32				
	1. Orange stripe 257T	(4)	**250**▲	2. No orange stripe 257T, 259T (4)	**225**
	3. Ives plates 1931 only	(5)	**500**	4. No orange stripe 257T crackle (5)	**550**
258	**2-4-0** Black only. Same as 257 but with reverse lever in cab 30				

258 variation 1 (top), 261 (bottom)

	1. Orange stripe	(3)	**325**	2. No orange stripe, 258T (4)	**350**
	3. Cream stripe			(4)	**100**
	4. Ives plates 31,32			(4)	**700**
	Came in 2 rare sets				
	a. U32 Passenger Set - Ives 258 with Ives 1695, 1696, and 1697 12-inch passenger cars			(5)	**1500**▲
	b. 1615X U32 Freight Set - Ives 258 with Ives 1707, 1708, 1709 and 1712 9 1/2 inch lithograph freight cars			(5)	**2000**
258	**2-4-2** U41				
	1. Gunmetal 1689T&W			(4)	**125**
	2. Black 1689T			(2)	**90**
	Note: Most 258s have number board on front. A few have the number rubber-stamped under the cab window. NDV				
259	**2-4-2** Black only 259T 32			(3)	**125**
259E	**2-4-2** 33,34 36-38, U36-40				
	1. Black 259T 262T 33,34	(3)	**150**	2. Gunmetal 1689T 2689T 36-38 (3)	**150**
	3. Black 1588TX UDSS 36-40	(5)	**175**	4. Black 1689T 2689T U36-40 (3)	**150**
261	**2-4-2** Black 257T 31 only			(3)	**350**

PREWAR

261E	2-4-2 Black 261T 35 only						
	1. Red stripe	(4)	**400**	2. No red stripe	(4)	**325**

262	2-4-2 Black 262T diecast 31,32		
	1. Orange stripe	(5)	**375**
	2. No orange stripe, shiny	(3)	**275**
	3. No orange stripe, crackle finish	(5)	**350**
	4. No orange stripe, dull finish	(3)	**275**

Note: Crackle tender shell will fit frames of 257T, 258T, 261T, and 262T.

262E	2-4-2 Black 262T 33,34					
	1. No stripe	(3)	**325**	2. Orange stripe	(4)	**375**
	3. Red stripe	(4)	**400**	4. **1663** with Ives plates, 31	(5)	**600**
	5. Black satin 265T&W U35,36				(4)	**375**

Rare: Headed 2 sets of Ives 1685 series passenger cars:
| | a. Blue and silver | (5)**1200▲** | b. Vermilion | (5) | **1200▲** |

Switchers

PREWAR

201	**0-6-0** *Lionel Lines* 40-42					
	Large and small number versions, add $50 for small numbers.					
	1. 2201T	(4)	**650**	2. 2201B	(4)	**700**

203	**0-6-0** *Lionel Lines* 40,41					
	Large and small number versions, add $50 for large numbers.					
	1. 2203T	(4)	**550**	2. 2203B	(4)	**600**

227	**0-6-0** *Pennsylvania* **8976** 39-42					
	1. 2227T, 227 on boiler	(4)	**900**	2. 2227B, 227 on boiler	(4)	**900**
	3. 2227B, no 227 on boiler	(5)	**1150**			

228	**0-6-0** *Pennsylvania* **8976** same as 227 but for use with 2800 series 39-42					
	1. 2228T	(4)	**1000**	2. 2228B	(4)	**1050**

230	**0-6-0** *Pennsylvania* **8976** 39					
	1. 2230T	(5)	**1450**	2. 2230B	(5)	**1650**

231	**0-6-0** *Pennsylvania* **8976** 39					
	1. 2231T	(5)	**1150**	2. 2231B	(5)	**1650**

232	**0-6-0** *Pennsylvania* **8976** 2232B *Magic Electrol* 40-42	(4)	**1750**
233	**0-6-0** *Pennsylvania* **8976** 2232B *Magic Electrol* 40-42	(4)	**1900▲**

700E (top), 231 (bottom)

701	**0-6-0** *Pennsylvania* **8976** 701T Built to NMRA scale standards 39-42	(5)	**2300**
1662	**0-4-0** *Lionel Lines* 2203T 40-42	(3)	**350**
1663	**0-4-0** *Lionel Lines* 2201T same as 1662 but with *Magic Electrol* 40-42	(4)	**400**

Passenger Cars

Note: Price listed is for each car. The locomotives that cars came with in sets are listed on the second line.

Olive 252 with 529 cars (top), Terra Cotta 252 with 529 cars (bottom)

529 Pullman 530 Observation (152, 153, 252, 248, 259, 261) 26-32
    1. Olive green/maroon   (2)   **40**   2. Olive green/red   (2)   **40**
    3. Olive green/orange   (4)   **60**
    4. Terra cotta/cream/maroon frame   (4)   **75**

600 Pullman 601 Observation 602 Baggage (262E, 259E, 265E, 238) 33-42
    1. Gray/red/ivory   (3)   **125**   2. Blue/alum/alum   (4)   **200**
    3. Red/red/ivory   (4)   **200**

600   **Pullman** 4 wheels 5 1/2" 15-25
    1. Dark green   (5)   **125**   2. Brown   (3)   **60**

    3. Maroon   (3)   **40**   4. Orange   (3)   **45**

601 Pullman 602 Baggage 7" 8 wheels 15-23
    1. Dark green   (3)   **40**   2. Orange   (4)   **75**

603   **Pullman** Orange matches orange versions of 601 and 602, U22   (4)   **65**

603 Pullman 604 Observation 6 1/2" 8 wheels 20-25
    1. Orange with wood-grained doors   (2)   **50**
    2. Orange with maroon doors   (2)   **50**

603 Pullman 604 Observation (252, 259, 259E 264E *Red Comet*) 31-36
    Note: Same as 607, 608 but no lights.
    1. Red/black/cream   (1)   **60**   2. Orange/terra cotta/cream   (2)   **75**
    3. SG green/dark green/cream DSS   (3)   **85**
    4. Red/white air tanks   (4)   **135**   5. Red/white with underbellies   (4)   **135**

605 Pullman 606 Observation (251, 4U, 254E) 25-32
    1. Gray/maroon/*NYC*   (3)   **200**   2. Gray/maroon/*Lionel Lines*   (2)   **200**
    3. Gray/maroon/green stripe   (5)   **325**   4. Gray/red U   (3)   **200**
    5. Red/ivory   (4)   **350**   6. Orange/cream/cream doors   (4)   **325**
    7. Same with pea green doors U DSS   (5)   **400**
    8. Olive green/maroon U   (5)   **550**

606 Pullman with green door   *606 Pullman with cream door*

607 Pullman 608 Observation illuminated (252, 253, 253E, 249E, 259E) 26-37

  1. Peacock/orange/*Lionel Lines*   (3)   **50**
  2. Peacock/orange/*Illinois Central*   (5)   **125**
  3. SG green/dark green/cream   (3)   **125**
  4. Red/cream/DSS *Macy's*   (5)   **225**
  5. Maroon/cream/DSS *Macy's*   (5)   **225**
  6. Maroon/black/cream/DSS *Macy's* (no *Macy* markings)   (5)   **225**
  7. Rare DSS Set: Dark red 253 numbered 450 with red/cream 607,608 cars   (5)   **1000**

609 Pullman 611 Observation *Lionel Lines* (259E, 204) DSS U35-37,40,41   (4)   **125**
  Blue/aluminum/aluminum, Same as 603

610 Pullman 612 Observation 8 1/2" 8 wheels 15-24

  1. Dark green/maroon   (3)   **65**   2. Dark green/wood grained   (3)   **65**
  3. Maroon   (4)   **100**   4. Mojave/maroon   (4)   **100**
  5. Mojave/wood grain   (4)   **100**

610 Pullman 612 Observation (body used for 442 diner) 26-30

  1. Mojave/maroon/*NYC*   (2)   **75**   2. Same as 1 w/*Illinois Central*   (4)   **150**
  3. Mojave/red inserts *NYC*   (2)   **100**   4. Olive green/maroon   (2)   **75**
  5. Olive green/red   (3)   **75**   6. Olive green/orange   (3)   **100**
  7. Pea green/orange   (3)   **100**   8. Red/aluminum/aluminum   (4)   **200**
  9. Terra cotta/maroon/cream U33   (4)   **250**
  10. Light blue/alum/alum U36,37 DSS   (5)   **300**

613 Pullman 614 Observation 615 Baggage (262, 255 gray, 263E blue) 31-42

  1. Terra cotta/maroon/cream   (4)   **300**   2. Red/alum/aluminum 35 only   (5)   **425**
  3. Blue/dark blue/ivory *Blue Comet*   (4)   **350**

629 Pullman 630 Observation 6 1/2" 24-32

  1. Dk green/maroon 4 wheels   (3)   **40**   2. Orange/peacock 4 wheels   (3)   **40**
  3. Red/cream 4 wheels   (4)   **45**   4. Red/cream 8 wheels   (5)   **100**

629 Pullman 630 Observation (152, 248, 257, 258DSS, 259DSS) 24-32, U34, U35

  1. Dark green/maroon   (2)   **50**   2. Orange/peacock   (2)   **40**
  3. Red/cream   (3)   **60**   4. Red/cream U34 DSS   (3)   **60**
  5. Light red/cream U35 DSS   (3)   **60**

710 Pullman 712 Observation (256, 260E, U251 red) 24-34

  1. Orange/RS *Illinois Central* 4W   (5)   **450**
  2. Orange/RS *New York Central* 4W   (3)   **300**
  3. Orange/RS *Lionel Lines* 4W   (3)   **300**
  4. Red/ivory/green doors 4W or 6W   (3)   **350**
  5. Red/ivory/ivory doors U30 4W or 6W   (3)   **350**
  6. Blue/cream 6W   (4)   **400**
  Note: Add $100 for red with 6W trucks

1630 Pullman 1631 Observation Manual couplers no illumination 38-42

  1. Light blue/aluminum   (2)   **45**   2. Light blue/gray   (4)   **60**

1685 Pullman 1686 Baggage 1687 Observation Lionel-Ives U33-37
(262E, 259E, 261E, 249E, 265E, 264E, 263E)
    1. Gray/maroon/cream 6W   (5)   **500**   2. Red/maroon/cream 4W   (4)   **300**
    3. Dk red/maroon/cream 4W (4)   **300**   4. Light blue/alum/alum 4W   (4)   **300**
    5. Vermilion/maroon/cream 4W   (4)   **300**

2600 Pullman 2601 Observation 2602 Baggage Red/dark red/ivory (238, 225)38-42   (4)   **225**▲

2613 Blue

2613 Green

2613 Pullman 2614 Observation 2615 Baggage (263E, 763E (4 car sets), 226E) 38-42
    1. Blue/dark blue/cream, early trucks 38-40   (3)   **400**
    2. Green/dk green/cream, late trucks 40-42   (4)   **550**
    Note: Prototypes or color samples exist but blue version with late trucks or green version with early trucks never went into normal production

2623, 2624 Pullman If steps broken deduct 50% (763E, 226E) 41, 42
    1. Irvington Tuscan   (5)   **500**   2. Manhattan Tuscan U   (4)   **500**

2624 Pullman Manhattan Tuscan (763E, 226E) U41,42   (5)   **1500**▲

2641 variation 2(top), 2643 (bottom)

PREWAR

47

2623 Manhattan

2630 Pullman 2631 Observation automatic couplers no illumination (1666) 38-42
    1. Blue/aluminum/aluminum (2) **100** 2. Blue/gray/gray (4) **125**

2640 Pullman 2641 Observation Automatic couplers illuminated (1666) 38-42
    1. Lt blue/aluminum/alum (3) **100**▲ 2. Green/dark green/cream (3) **125**

2642 Pullman 2643 Observation Tuscan/Tuscan/gray 41,42 (4) **150**▲

Passenger Sets

Note: Complete set in set box commands a higher price than total of components sold separately. Price listed is without box. Add 100% for box.

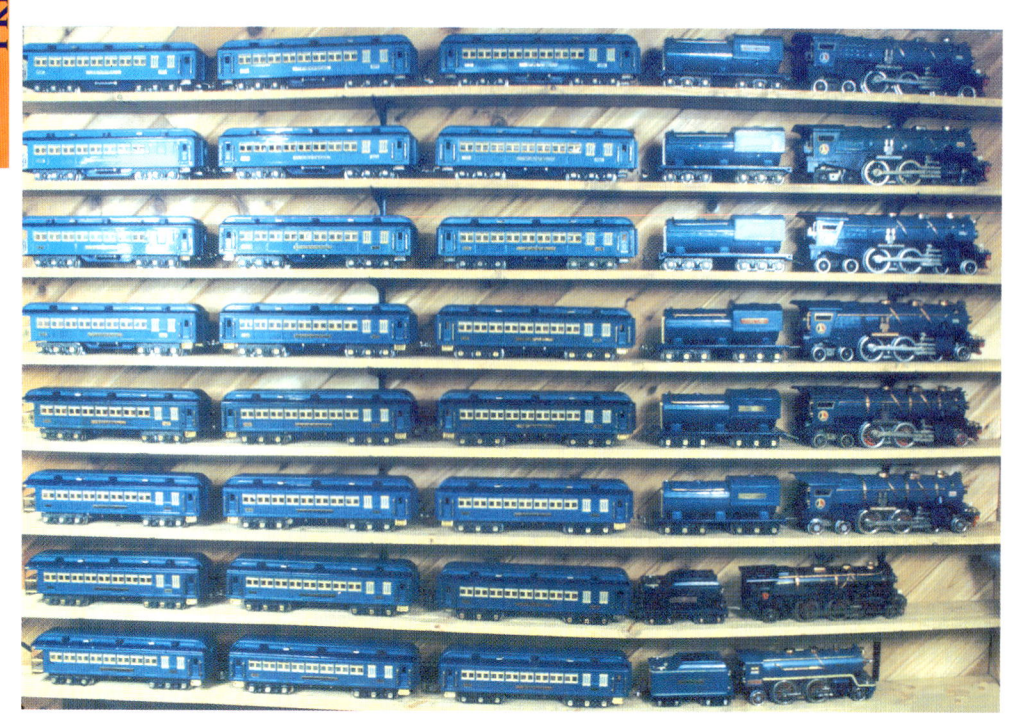

Eight different Blue Comet Sets

Set No.

97	**251,** two 605s, 606, 25-30		
	1. Gray (4) **1500** 2. Red 28,29	(5)	**2200**▲
144	**262, 262T,** two 613s, 614 Terra cotta 31,32	(4)	**800**▲
144E	**262E, 262T** 615, 613, 614 Terra cotta 33,34	(4)	**950**▲
146W	**225, 2245W,** 2602, 2600, 2604 Red 39-40	(4)	**750**▲
182E	**225E, 2265T,** 2600, 2601, 2602 Red 38 only	(4)	**900**
186W	**238E, 2265W,** 2602, 2600, 2601 Red 38 only	(4)	**850**
190W	**226E, 2226W,** 2615, 2613, 2614, 38-40		
	1. Blue 38,39 (4) **2800** 2. Green, 40	(5)	**3700**
194W	*Blue Comet* **263E, 2263W,** 2615, 2613, 2614, 38,39	(4)	**2000**
234E	**259E, 262T,** 602, 600, 601 Gray 34 only	(4)	**500**
241E	**260E, 260T,** two 710s, 712, 30-34		
	1. Red 6-wheel trucks (5)**2100**▲ 2. Blue	(4)	**1750**▲
	3. Red 4-wheel trucks (4)**1400**▲		

48

144E set (top), 246E set (bottom)

246E	**262E, 262T,** 602, 600, 601 Gray 33 only	(4)	700
267	**4U**, two 605s, 606, 1930 only	(5)	2200
268	**256,** two 710s, 712, 25-28		
	1. *Lionel* RS border/cars *IC* markings	(5)	2700
	2. *Lionel* RS no border/cars *NYC* markings	(4)	2200
	3. Brass plate/cars *NYC* markings	(3)	2000
276W	**255E, 263TW,** 615, 613, 614 Red 35	(5)	3250

PREWAR

752E set (top), 283W set (bottom)

283W	**Blue Comet 263E, 263W,** 615, 613, 614, 36,37	(4)	2250
298W	**238E, 265W,** 600, 602, 601 Red 36,37	(4)	850

Hiawatha set (top), 709W Rail Chief set (bottom)

709W	***Rail Chief*** 700EW, 700W, 792 combination 37-41 two 793 coaches, 794 observation	(5)	7500
748W	**763E, 2226WX,** Four 2623 *Irvington* or *Manhattan* pullmans 41,42, Also known to come with both.	(4)	5000

49

Union Pacific **M10000**

752E Power Car, 753 Coach, 754 Observation
    1. Yellow/brown 34-36
        a. M-10000 *Lionel Lines* RS black   (5)   *
        b. 752E *City of San Francisco* RS black   (5)   *
        c. 752E *Lionel Lines* RS in black   (4)   **950**
    2. Aluminum 34-36   (4)   **950**

752W Power Car, 753 Coach, 754 Observation
    1. Yellow/brown 35   (4) **1100**   2. Aluminum 35   (4)   **900**

752W Power Car, two 753 Coaches, 754 Observation
    1. Yellow/brown 36-41   (4) **1600**   2. Aluminum 36   (4)   **1250**

755W Hiawatha set (top), 752W set (bottom)

755W	***Hiawatha*** 250E, 250TW, 782, 783, 784, 35-41		
	1. Thick casting/diecast trucks (4) **4000▲** 2. Thin casting/stamped trucks	(4)	**4000▲**
766W	**763, 263W** Gray, 615, two 613s, 614 Blue cars 37 only	(5)	**4000**
768W	**763, 2263W** Gray 2615, two 2613s, 2614, 38-40		
	1. Blue cars 38,39 (4) **4000** 2. Green cars 1940 only	(5)	**4250**
890W	**226E, 2226WX**, three 2623 Pullmans	(4)	**2000**
1048	**Passenger Car Set** two 2630, 2631, 1019 track 38-40	(4)	**250***
1048X	**Passenger Car Set** two 2630, 2631, 41-42	(5)	**1000***
1060	**Passenger Car Set** two 1690, 1691, 36-37	(4)	**300***
1576	**Passenger Car Set** 1811, 1812, 34-37	(4)	**100***
	Note: May have come with 2 1811, 1812, 1813 in 1935-add 1 to rarity.		

Passenger Streamline Sets

Red Comet (top), 279E Silver Streak (center), Blue Streak (bottom)

Blue Streak 265E, 265TX, 619, 617, 618, 36, 37
    1. Blue/white stripe cars   (4)   **1600▲**
    2. Solid blue cars (came with black 265E only)   (5)   **2200***

Commodore Vanderbilt 265E, 265TW, 600, 601, 602, 35   (4)   **800**

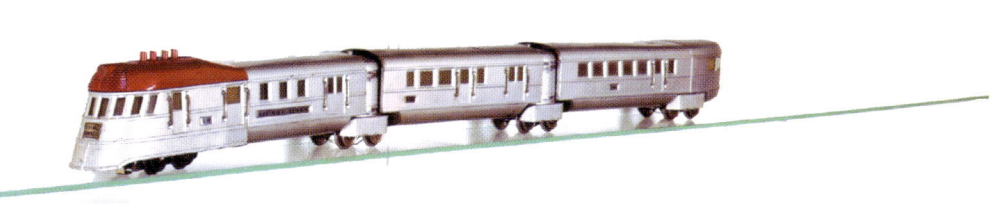

Flying Yankee 35-41
    1. 616W, two 617s, 618 All-chrome power car, black roof 35   (4)   **1800**
    2. Same consist but power car with dark gray nose 36-41   (3)   **600▲**
    3. U, DSS, painted silver, red top, one 617 with 2 doors, smooth sides   (4)   **1500**
    4. Same as 3 but 617 has one door and ribbed sides   (4)   **650**
    5. U35, 3 cars painted silver, black roof, sliding shoe pick-ups,   (5)   **900**
        smooth sides, coach car has 2 doors

Red Comet 264E, two 603s, 604, 35, 36
    1. With 261T, 1935   (4)   **1500**   2. With 265T, 1936   (4)   **1400**

UP's City of Denver 36-39
    636W, 2 637 coaches, 638 obvs
    1. Medium brown/yellow/yellow vestibules   (3)   **1000▲**
    2. Dark brown/yellow/yellow-brown vestibules   (4)   **1200▲**
    3. Dark brown/yellow/yellow vestibules   (4)   **750▲**
    4. Green/dark green (only one 637 coach) U DSS   (5)   **4500***

279E   265E, 261TX, 619, 618 (Called **Silver Streak** by collectors) 35   (4)   **1400**

PREWAR

Rolling Stock
600 Series

553 Hopper, 554 Tank, 556 Cattle and 557 Caboose

620	**Floodlight** 37-42						
	1. Red/aluminum light	(2)	65	2. Red/gray cast light	(3)	85
651	**Flatcar** 4 stakes 35-42						
	1. Green/nickel journals	(2)	40	2. Green/black journals	(3)	45
652	**Gondola** 35-42						
	1. Yellow/nickel or blk journals	(2)	50	2. Orange/latch or box couplers	(3)	60
653	**Hopper** 34-40 U41,42 SG green				(3)	55
654	**Tank Car** 34-42						
	1. Aluminum/*Sunoco* decal	(2)	40	2. Orange/*Shell* decal	(3)	65▲
	3. Light gray/*Sunoco* decal	(3)	60			
655	**Boxcar** 34-42 U39,40						
	1. Cream/maroon/brass				(3)	65
	2. Yellow/brown/black journals U39,40				(3)	80
656	**Cattle Car** 35-40						
	1. Light gray/red	(2)	100	2. Lt gray/red/vermilion doors	(3)	175
	3. Orange/maroon RS	(4)	200	4. Lt. gray/Tuscan/gray doors	(3)	100▲
657	**Caboose** 34-42						
	1. Dark red/cream	(1)	30	2. Red/cream	(1)	30
	3. Red/white	(1)	20	4. Red/Tuscan/white	(3)	35
659	**Dump** Dark green 35-42				(3)	60

800 Series

Note: First versions of the 800 Series came with no journals (no holes punched in frame). These cars are rarer than later versions with journals (holes punched in frame). Became 2800 series in 1938 when couplers were changed from manual to automatic

800 **Boxcar** *PRR* and *Wabash* 5 1/2", hook couplers no journals RS 15-26
  1. Yellow orange/maroon (5) **100**   2. Yellow orange (3) **40**
  3. Green (5) **150**   4. Orange (2) **30**

801 **Caboose** 5 1/2", hook couplers, no journals, RS15-26
  1. Brown/black *Wabash RR 4390* (4) **50**
  2. Brown/black *NYNH&H* (5) **150**
  3. Brown/black *Wabash RR 4890* (3) **40**

802 **Cattle** *Union Stock Lines* 5 1/2", hook couplers no journals RS 15-28
  1. Dark green (3) **50**   2. Green (3) **50**

803 **Hopper** 23-34
  1. Dark green RS no journals 23-28 (3) **45**
  2. Peacock/brass 29-34 (2) **35**

804 **Tank** 23-34 U35-40
  1. Gray RS no journals 23-28 (3) **40**   2. Dark gray RS 23-28 (3) **40**
  3. Terra cotta RS 23-28 (2) **30**   4. Aluminum/no decal 29-34 (2) **30**
  5. Alum/*Sunoco* decal U34 (3) **30**   6. Orange/*Shell* decal/nickel U39 (4) **60**
  7. Orange/*Shell* decal U40 (4) **70**

805 **Boxcar** 27-34
  1. Cream/orange (3) **50**   2. Terra cotta/orange (3) **50**
  3. Orange/maroon (4) **70**   4. Pea green/orange (3) **45**
  5. Pea grn/maroon no journals (4) **60**   6. Pea green/orange U31 (3) **50**

806 **Cattle Car** 27-34
  1. Pea green/terra cotta no journals U27 (4) **125**
  2. Orange/maroon no journals (3) **85**
  3. Orange/pea green (2) **75**   4. Orange/orange U31 (2) **75**

807 **Caboose** 27-34,U35-39
  1. Peacock/dark green/red nj U27,28 (4) **50**
  2. Dark red/peacock (2) **25**   3. Red/cream (3) **30**
  4. Red RS/blk journals U40,41 (4) **50**   5. Dull red/brown RS 42 (4) **50**
  Note: Variations exist having to do with nickel trim, rubber stamping, brass and nickel journals, and different color shades. NDV

809 **Dump** 31-34,U35-40
  1. Orange (5) **125**   2. Green (3) **65**
  3. Dark green U35-40 (4) **75**

810 **Derrick** 30-42
  1. Terra cotta/maroon/peacock boom (4) **300**
  2. Same/brass knobs instead of nickel (3) **300**
  3. Yellow/red/green boom (3) **350▲**

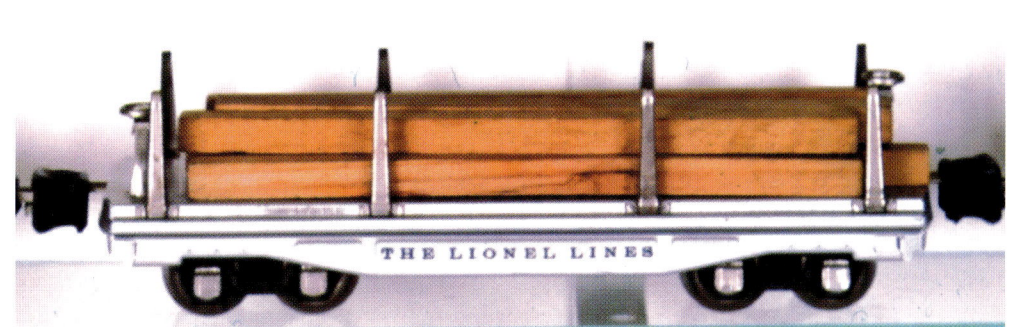

811 **Flatcar** 26-40
  1. Maroon/gold RS (2) **75**   2. Aluminum/black RS (3) **125**

PREWAR

812 Gondola variation 3, 810 Derrick variation 1, 812 Gondola variation 4

812	Gondola 26-42						
	1. Mojave	(3)	**75**	2. Dark green	(2)	**50**
	3. Apple green	(4)	**100**	4. Green 36-40	(2)	**60**

PREWAR

813 Cattle Car variation 3 (top), 814R Refrigerator Car variation 4 (bottom)

813	Cattle Car 26-42						
	1. Orange/pea green	(3)	**150**	2. Cream/maroon	(4)	**350▲**
	3. Tuscan	(5)	**2700▲**			

Note: 813 and 814 come with both large and small door handles. NDV

814	Boxcar 26-42						
	1. Yellow/brown/brass trim	(3)	**225**	2. Yellow/brown/nickel trim	(3)	**225**
	3. Cream/maroon	(4)	**250**	4. Cream/orange	(3)	**125**

Note: Door guides usually match roof color but on cream/orange cars guides can be found in peacock add $25 or pea green add $75.

814R	Refrigerator 29-42		
	1. Ivory/peacock/black frame	(3)	**200**
	2. White/blue/black frame nickel	(4)	**400**
	3. Ivory/blue/alum frame nickel	(4)	**600▲**
	4. Flat white/Tuscan/black frame HS	(5)	**2500▲**
	5. Same as 4 but w/nickel plates	(5)	*****
	6. White/blue/aluminum frame brass	(4)	**600▲**

54

815   **Tank** 26-42
- 1. Pea green/maroon frame/no decal   (5)   **400**
- 2. Pea green/black frame/no decal   (2)   **100**
- 3. Aluminum/*Sunoco* decal   (2)   **125**   4. Aluminum/no decal   (4)   **150**
- 5. Shell orange/*Shell* decal   (5)   **400**

816   **Hopper** 27-42
- 1. Olive green/brass   (3)   **175**   2. Bright red/brass   (3)   **150**
- 3. Dark red/brass   (4)   **200**   4. Dark red/nickel   (4)   **225**
- 5. Black/nickel   (5+) **1000**   6. Black/white RS   (5)   **550**
- 7. Orange, one known to exist (5+)   *   8. Dk green, one known to exist (5+)   *

817   **Caboose** 26-42
- 1. Peacock/dk green/orange   (2)   **95**   2. Peacock/dark green/brass   (3)   **95**
- 3. Red/peacock/brass   (4)   **150**   4. Red/brown/nickel plates   (4)   **300**
- 5. Red/nickel/alum railing   (2)   **125**

820   **Boxcar** *Illinois Central* and *Union Pacific* 15-26
5 1/2", hook couplers no journals RS
- 1. Yellow orange/brown   (5)   **100**   2. Yellow/orange   (4)   **75**
- 3. Orange   (3)   **60**   4. Orange/maroon   (3)   **50**
- 5. Dark olive green *AT&SF*   (5)   **250**

820   **Floodlight** RS *Lionel Lines* 31-42
- 1. Terra cotta/brass lights   (2)   **150**   2. Terra cotta/nickel lights   (4)   **200**
- 3. Green/nickel lights   (3)   **175**   4. Green/gray diecast lights   (4)   **450**

821   **Cattle** *Union Stock Lines* Green 15,16,25,26   (4)   **85**
5 1/2", hook couplers no journals RS

822   **Caboose** *NYC Lines* 5 1/2", hook couplers no journals RS 15-26
- 1. Brown/black   (3)   **60**
- 2. Maroon/black vertical ribs embossed outward, black or gold lettering   (2)   **50**
- 3. Maroon/black vertical ribs embossed inward, black lettering   (2)   **50**

831   **Flatcar** 27-34, U35-40
- 1. Black/8 stakes/no journals (4)   **100**   2. Dark green/8 stakes   (4)   **75**
- 3. Dark green/4 stakes   (2)   **25**   4. Green/4 stakes U35-40   (3)   **30**

900   **Ammunition Car** Gray, matches 203 armored loco 17-21   (4)   **275**

901   **Gondola** 19-27 *Lake Shore* and *Pennsylvania*
- 1. Maroon   (3)   **60**   2. Gray   (3)   **60**
- 3. Light gray   (3)   **60**   4. Dark green   (3)   **60**
- 5. Olive   (5)   **100**   6. Brown   (5)   **100**
- 7. Dark olive green   (3)   **60**   8. Dark gray   (3)   **60**

902   **Gondola** 27-34
- 1. Dark green   (4)   **40**   2. Peacock/no journals   (5)   **35**
- 3. Stephen Girard green   (3)   **40**

2600 Series

2620   **Floodlight** 38-42
- 1. Red/aluminum light   (2)   **100**   2. Red/gray light   (3)   **125**
- 3. Black/nickel light 43   (5)   **325**

2651   **Flatcar** 38-42
- 1. Green   (2)   **60**   2. Black 42   (4)   **175**

PREWAR

2652	**Gondola** 38-42					
	1. Yellow	(2)	**60**	2. Burnt orange	(3)	**80**
2653	**Hopper** 38-42					
	1. Stephen Girard green	(3)	**85**	2. Black RS	(4)	**300**▲
2654	**Tank Car** 38-42					
	1. Aluminum/*Sunoco* decal	(2)	**50**	2. Orange/*Shell* decal	(3)	**75**
	3. Gray/*Sunoco* decal	(3)	**85**			
2655	**Boxcar** 38-42					
	1. Cream/maroon/nickel	(2)	**100**	2. Cream/Tuscan RS	(3)	**150**
2656	**Cattle Car** 38-42					
	1. Gray/red	(3)	**150**▲	2. Burnt orange/Tuscan RS	(4)	**325**▲
2657	**Caboose** 38-42					
	1. Red/cream	(2)	**35**	2. Red/red/white RS	(3)	**40**
	3. Red/Tuscan/white 1 coupler	(3)	**50**	4. Same as 3 with 2 couplers	(3)	**60**
2659	**Dump** 38-42 Green RS				(3)	**150**▲
2660	**Derrick** Cream/red 38-42					
	1. Green boom	(3)	**175**▲	2. Unpainted black boom	(3)	**175**▲

2800 Series

2810	**Derrick** Yellow/red 38-42					
	1. Early couplers and trucks	(4)	**350**▲	2. Late couplers and trucks	(5)	**700**▲
2811	**Flatcar** Aluminum/black RS 38-42				(4)	**150**
2812	**Gondola** Green/nickel 38-42				(2)	**75**

2812X variation 2

2812X	**Gondola** Burnt orange					
	1. Nickel trim RS	(3)	**125**	2. Nickel plates	(5)	**175**
2813	**Cattle Car** 38-42 Cream/maroon				(4)	**325**
2814	**Boxcar** 38-42					
	1. Yellow/brown	(4)	**250**	2. Cream/maroon	(3)	**225**
	3. Burnt orange/Tuscan	(5)	**2000***			

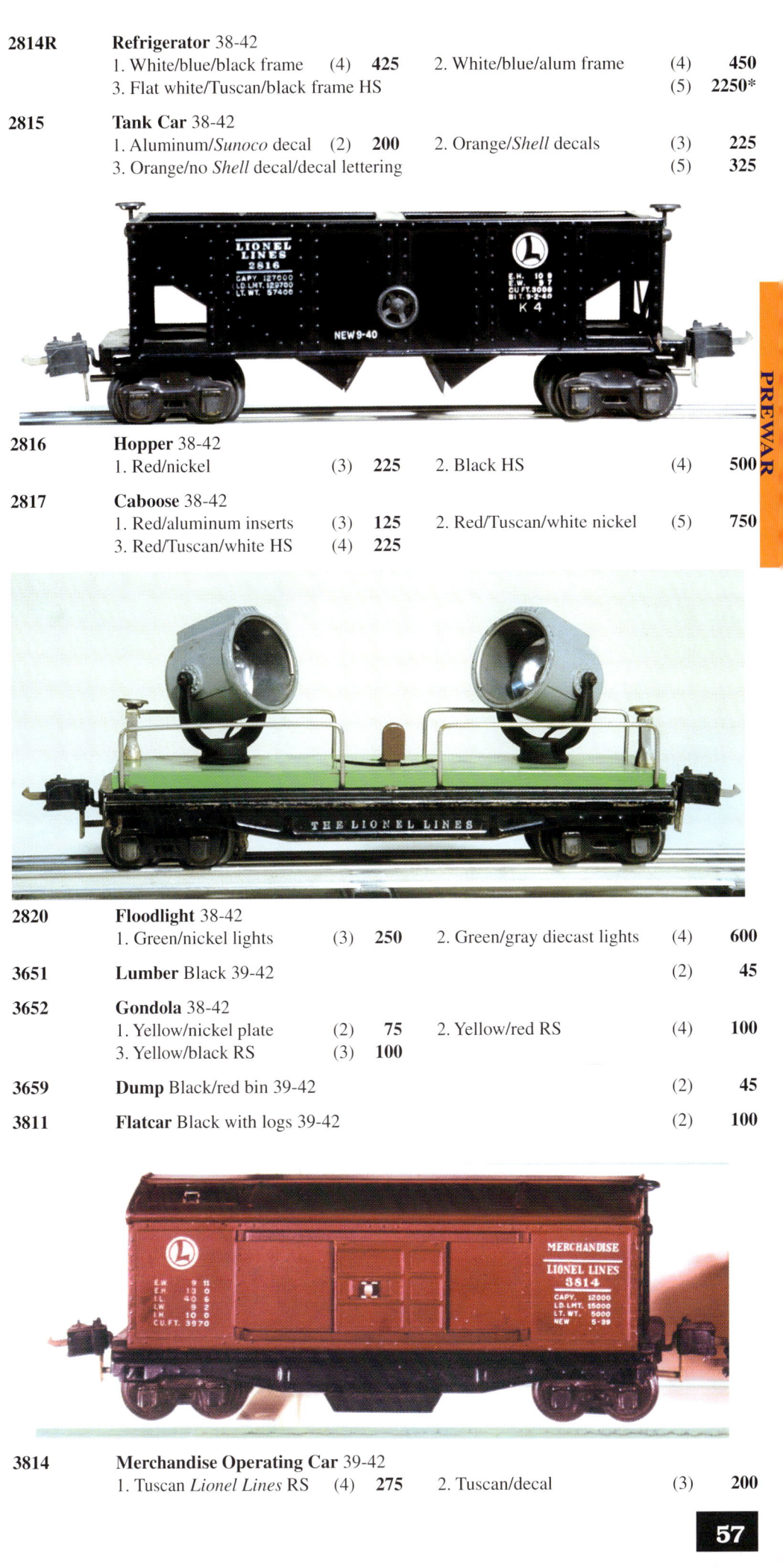

2814R	**Refrigerator** 38-42					
	1. White/blue/black frame	(4)	**425**	2. White/blue/alum frame	(4)	**450**
	3. Flat white/Tuscan/black frame HS				(5)	**2250***
2815	**Tank Car** 38-42					
	1. Aluminum/*Sunoco* decal	(2)	**200**	2. Orange/*Shell* decals	(3)	**225**
	3. Orange/no *Shell* decal/decal lettering				(5)	**325**

2816	**Hopper** 38-42					
	1. Red/nickel	(3)	**225**	2. Black HS	(4)	**500**
2817	**Caboose** 38-42					
	1. Red/aluminum inserts	(3)	**125**	2. Red/Tuscan/white nickel	(5)	**750**
	3. Red/Tuscan/white HS	(4)	**225**			

2820	**Floodlight** 38-42					
	1. Green/nickel lights	(3)	**250**	2. Green/gray diecast lights	(4)	**600**
3651	**Lumber** Black 39-42				(2)	**45**
3652	**Gondola** 38-42					
	1. Yellow/nickel plate	(2)	**75**	2. Yellow/red RS	(4)	**100**
	3. Yellow/black RS	(3)	**100**			
3659	**Dump** Black/red bin 39-42				(2)	**45**
3811	**Flatcar** Black with logs 39-42				(2)	**100**

3814	**Merchandise Operating Car** 39-42					
	1. Tuscan *Lionel Lines* RS	(4)	**275**	2. Tuscan/decal	(3)	**200**

3859	**Dump** Black/red 38-42					
	1. Early trucks and couplers	(3)	**150**	2. Late trucks and couplers	(4)	**150**

Scale and Semi-Scale Freights

Note: Kit prices based on unassembled condition in original box.

714	**Boxcar** Scale Tuscan RS *Pennsylvania* 40-42				(4)	**600**
714K	**Boxcar Kit** Scale 40-42				(5)	**1000**

715	**Tank Car** Scale 40-42					
	1. Black *Shell* decal 40	(4)	**750**	2. Black *Sunoco* decal 41, 42	(5)	**800**
715K	**Tank Car Kit** Scale 40-42					
	1. *Shell* decal	(4)	**800**	2. *Sunoco* decal	(5)	**1000**

716	**Hopper** Scale RS *B&O* Black 40-42				(5)	**800**
716K	**Hopper Kit** Scale 40-42				(5)	**1500**
717	**Caboose** Scale RS *NYC* Tuscan 40-42				(4)	**650**
717K	**Caboose Kit** Scale 40-42				(5)	**1000**
2672	**Caboose** *PRR* Tuscan 42				(3)	**75**
2755	**Tank Car** *Sunoco* 41,42					
	1. Aluminum 41	(3)	**140**	2. Gray 42	(4)	**175**
2757	**Caboose** *PRR* Tuscan Automatic coupler one end 41,42				(2)	**40**

2757X	Caboose *PRR* Tuscan Automatic couplers both ends 41,42		(3)	**40**
2758	**Boxcar** 41,42		(3)	**75**
2954	**Boxcar** Semi-scale Tuscan RS *Pennsylvania* 40-42		(4)	**400**
2955	**Tank Car** Semi-scale 40-42			
	1. Lettered *Shell* (4) **450** 2. Decal *Sunoco*		(5)	**750**
2956	**Hopper** Semi-scale Black 40-42		(5)	**700**
2957	**Caboose** Semi-scale Tuscan 40-42		(4)	**400**

Rolling Stock Outfits

Note: Must have original boxes (all interior and exterior packaging)

186	**Log Loader Outfit** 164, 3651, UCS, 40-41		(5)	**1050***
188	**Coal Loader Outfit** 97, 3659, UCS, 38-41		(4)	**1000***
801	**Freight Car Set** 2654, 2655, RCS, 38-40		(4)	**525***
801X	**Freight Car Set** 2654, 2655, 41-42		(5)	**500***
802	**Freight Car Set** 2814, 2815, RCS, 38-40		(4)	**700***
802X	**Freight Car Set** 2814, 2815, 41-42		(5)	*****
808	**Freight Car Set** One each: 803, 804, 805, 806, 807, 831, 27-34		(4)	**1400***
818	**Freight Car Set** 653, 654, 655, 657, 35-37		(4)	**1700***
1049	**Freight Car Set** 2679, 2680, 1019, 38-40		(4)	**475***
1049X	**Freight Car Set** 2679, 2680, 41-42		(5)	**475***
1061	**Freight Car Set** 1679, 1680, 1682, 36-37		(4)	**500***
1577	**Freight Car Set** 1514, 1515, 1517, 34-37		(4)	**475***

PREWAR

OO Gauge

Locomotives

OO1 Hudson (top), OO3 Hudson (bottom)

001	**Hudson** 4-6-4 **5342** Scale fully detailed 3-rail RS 38-42			
	1. 001T no whistle (3) **600** 2. 001W with whistle		(3)	**650**
002	**Hudson** 4-6-4 **5342** Modified semi-detailed 3-rail RS 39-42			
	1. 002T no whistle (4) **550** 2. 002W with whistle		(4)	**575**
003	**Hudson** 4-6-4 **5342** Scale fully detailed 2-rail RS 39-42			
	1. 003T no whistle (4) **600** 2. 003W with whistle		(4)	**675**
004	**Hudson** 4-6-4 **5342** Modified semi-detailed 2-rail RS 39-42			
	1. 004T no whistle (5) **450** 2. 004W with whistle		(5)	**475**
0081K	**Kit** containing 001 and 001T Information Requested			
0081KW	**Kit** containing 001 and 001W Information Requested			

Rolling Stock

0014	**Boxcar** Detailed 3-rail 38-42			
	1. Yellow/maroon roofwalk decal *Lionel Lines* 38		(4)	175
	2. Tuscan decal *Pennsylvania* 39-42		(3)	125
0015	**Tank** Detailed 3-rail 38-42			
	1. *Sunoco* Silver U38 (4) **125**	2. *Shell* Black 39,40,42	(3)	125
	3. *Shell* Gray 39,40,42 (3) **125**	4. *Sunoco* Black 41	(5)	175
0016	**Hopper** Detailed 3-rail 38-42			
	1. *SP* Gray U38 (4) **200**	2. *SP* Black 39-42	(4)	200
0017	**Caboose** Red, Detailed 3-rail 38-42			
	1. *NYC* 39-42 (3) **100**	2. *PRR* maroon roofwalk 38	(4)	125

PREWAR

0024	**Boxcar** Tuscan *Pennsylvania* Semi-detailed 3-rail 39-42		(3)	100
0025	**Tank** Semi-detailed 3-rail 39-42			
	1. *Shell* Black 39-42 (3) **100**	2. *Sunoco* Black 41	(4)	125

OO25 Shell Tank car   *OO27 NYC Caboose*

0027	**Caboose** Red NYC Detailed 3-rail 39-42		(3)	100
0044	**Boxcar** Tuscan *Pennsylvania* Detailed 2-rail 39-42		(3)	100
0044K	**Boxcar Kit** Tuscan *Pennsylvania* Detailed 2 or 3 rail 39-42		(4)	150
0045	**Tank** Black Detailed 2-rail 39-42			
	1. *Shell* 39,40-42 (3) **125**	2. *Sunoco* 41	(4)	135
0045K	**Tank Car Kit** Black Detailed 2 or 3 rail 39-42			
	1. *Shell* 39,40,42 (4) **150**	2. *Sunoco* 41	(4)	150
0046	**Hopper** *SP* Black Detailed 2-rail 39-42		(3)	125
0046K	**Hopper Kit** *SP* Black Detailed 2-rail 39-42		(3)	150
0047	**Caboose** Red NYC Detailed 2-rail 39-42		(3)	100
0047K	**Caboose Kit** Red NYC Detailed 2-rail 39-42		(3)	125
0074	**Boxcar** Tuscan *Pennsylvania* Semi-detailed 2-rail 39-42		(3)	100
0075	**Tank** Semi-detailed 2-rail 39-42			
	1. *Sunoco* Silver U39 (4) **150**	2. *Shell* Black 39,40,42		*
	3. *Sunoco* Black 41 *			
0077	**Caboose** Red NYC Semi-detailed 2-rail 39-42		(3)	125

Standard Gauge

From top left: 9E SG two-tone green, 10E Peacock/orange stripe, 9E Orange, 380E Dark green, 380 Mojave, 380E Maroon, 318E Pea green, 8E Red/cream stripe, 8 Olive green, 318 Gray

Electric Locomotives

8	**0-4-0** 25-32					
8E	1. Maroon/brass				(2)	**225**
	2. Olive green/brass				(3)	**250**
	3. Mojave/brass				(2)	**225**
	4. Red/cream stripe/cream trim				(3)	**275**
	5. Red/no stripe/brass				(3)	**250**
	6. Dark olive green/brass U				(5)	**500**
	7. Maroon/cream stripe/cream trim U				(4)	**350**
	8. Pea green/yellow U				(4)	**350**
	9. Peacock/orange/orange stripe U				(5)	**500**
	10. Peacock/cream stripe/cream trim U				(5)	**500**
	11. Dark green/brass U				(4)	**500**
9	**0-4-0** *NYC* Dark green, manual reverse 29				(5)	**2800**
9E	**0-4-0** *NYC* 28-30					
	1. Orange	(4)	**2000**	2. SG two-tone green	(4)	**1750**
	3. Dark gray	(3)	**1200**			
9U	**0-4-0** *U-Build It* **Kit** Orange, same as 9E but hand reverse 28,29					
	1. Unassembled in box complete				(5)	**7000***
	2. Assembled no box				(4)	**1800**
10	**0-4-0** *CM&St.P* 25-30					
10E	1. Mojave	(1)	**225**	2. Gray	(2)	**225**
	3. Peacock	(1)	**225**	4. Peacock/orange stripe	(3)	**350**
	5. Peacock/dark green frame cream stripe U				(4)	**450**
	6. Red/cream stripe U	(4)	**500**	7. Red/no cream stripe U	(4)	**400**
	8. Tan U	(3)	**500**	9. Olive U	(3)	**600**
	10. State brown/dk green frame/cream U				(4)	**600**
	11. Mojave/cream stripe				(3)	**250**
33	**0-6-0 Round Cab** (first versions) 1913 only					
	1. Dk olive green/*NYC* oval	(2)	**600**	2. Dk olive green/block *PRR*	(5)	**900**
	3. Dk olive green/red stripe	(4)	**700**	4. Black	(4)	**700**

PREWAR

61

33	**0-4-0 Round Cab** (second versions) 13-24					
	NYC markings: common. *C&O* markings: rare.					
	1. Dark olive green	(2)	**125**	2. Midnight blue DSS	(5)	**2000**
	3. Black	(2)	**125**	4. Gray	(2)	**125**
	5. Maroon	(4)	**500**	6. Red	(4)	**500**
	7. Peacock	(4)	**600**	8. Dark green	(3)	**200**
	9. Red with cream striping	(4)	**600**	10. Brown	(4)	**500**
	11. Mojave	(3)	**300**	12. Pea green	(4)	**400**
	13. Black FAOS DSS 1915	(5)	**2000**			
34	**0-6-0 Round Cab** Dark olive green RS block *NYC* or *NYC* oval 12, U13				(4)	**900**
38	**0-4-0 Round Cab** RS *NYC* oval or block lettering 13-24					
	1. Dark olive green	(3)	**275**	2. Black	(2)	**200**
	3. Maroon	(3)	**350**	4. Dark green	(3)	**400**
	5. Mojave	(4)	**500**	6. Peacock	(5)	**800**
	7. Gray	(3)	**350**	8. Brown	(3)	**300**
	9. Red/cream stripe	(4)	**600**	10. Red	(4)	**700**
	11. Dk olive green/RS *PRR*	(4)	**600**	12. Black *FAOS* 62 DSS	(5)	**1000**
42	**0-4-4-0 Square Cab** Dark green *NYC* oval or block lettering 1912					
	1. Thin rims	(5)	**1600**	2. Thick rims	(4)	**1500**

42	**0-4-4 Round Cab** *NYC* oval or block lettering 13-23					
	1. Black	(2)	**500**	2. Maroon	(5)	**2000**
	3. Dark gray	(3)	**700**	4. Dark green	(3)	**700**
	5. Mojave	(4)	**800**	6. Peacock	(5)	**1800**
	7. Gray	(2)	**500**	8. Olive green	(4)	**1200**
	9. Pea green	(4)	**1200**	10. "61 FAOS" DSS 1915	(5)	**2500**
	Note: Odd colors turn up as a result of Lionel's policy of repainting trains which were sent in for repair.					
50	**0-4-0 Round Cab** same as 38 but with Super motor 1924 only					
	1. Dark gray	(2)	**175**	2. Dark green	(3)	**225**
	3. Maroon	(4)	**400**			
53	**0-4-4-0 Square Cab** Script *NYNH&H,* oval or block *NYC* 12-14					
	1. Maroon	(4)	**1500**	2. Brown	(4)	**1500**

53 Maroon 0-4-4-0, 53 Maroon 0-4-0 square cab, 53 Maroon round cab

53	**0-4-0 Square Cab** *NYC* oval 15-19					
	1. Maroon	(2)	**800**	2. Dark olive green	(4)	**1200**
	3. Mojave	(4)	**1000**			
53	**0-4-0 Round Cab** *NYC* oval Maroon 20,21				(4)	**1000**
54	**0-4-4-0 Square Cab** Pedestal type headlight/thick rim drivers 1912 only				(5)	**3500**
54	**0-4-4-0 Round Cab** same as 42 but brass body, 13-24 red spokes, and ventilators, red cab door window frames.					
	1. Single motor	(4)	**2500**	2. Double motor	(5)	**2800**
318	**0-4-0** *NYC* 1924-35					
318E	1. Dark gray	(2)	**400**	2. Mojave	(2)	**350**
	3. Gray	(1)	**250**	4. Pea green	(2)	**350**
	5. State brown/cream stripe	(4)	**600**	6. State brown/no cream stripe	(4)	**600**
	7. Black (headed Coal Train)	(5)	**2000**			

PREWAR

From top left: 408E Mojave, 381 E reproduction, 408E Apple green, 402E Mojave (cast), 9U orange, 402 Mojave (strap)

380	**0-4-0** *CM&St.P* 23-29					
380E	1. Mojave	(4)	**700**	2. Maroon	(2)	**400**
	3. Dk grn w/weighted frame	(4)	**550**	4. Same w/o weighted frame	(3)	**450**
381	**4-4-4** *CM&St.P* 28-36					

381E	1. State green/apple green	(4)	**2500**	2. State green/red	(5)	**3000**
381U	**4-4-4** *U-Build-It Kit* (in box) 28,29					
	1. Kit in box	(5)	**6500**	2. Dark State green/381U plate	(5)	*
	3. Dark State green/381 plate	(5)	**3500**			

63

402	**0-4-4-0** *NYC* 2 motors 23-29			
402E	1. Mojave/strap headlight (4) **600**	2. Mojave/cast headlight	(3)	**575**

Note: Early 402s came with the E rubber-stamped on the door. These are rarer than those with the E on the brass plate. Add $50

408E	**0-4-4-0** *NYC* 2 motors 27-36					
	1. Mojave	(3) **1250**	2. Apple green		(3)	**1500**
	3. Dark green (State Set)	(5) **3500**	4. Tan (State Set)		(4)	**3500**
	5. Tan/dark brown roof (State Set)				(5)	**4000**
1910	**0-6-0 Square Cab** *NYNH&H* Dark olive green 10,11				(4)	**1500**
1910	**0-6-0 Round Cab** *NYC* oval Dark olive green 12				(3)	**1000**
1911	**0-4-0 Square Cab** *NYC* oval or block *NYNH&H* 10,11					
	1. Maroon	(5) **2000**	2. Dark olive green		(4)	**1800**
	Note: Add $200 for thick-rim version					
1911	**0-4-0 Round Cab** *NYNH&H* or block NYC dark olive green 1912 only				(3)	**1200**
1911	**0-4-4-0 Special Square Cab** Dark olive green/block *NYC* 11,12				(5)	**2000**
1912	**0-4-4-0 Square Cab** Dark olive green 10-12					
	1. Thin rim/script *NYNH&H* (5) **3500**	2. Thick rim/block *NYC*		(4)	**3300**

1912	**0-4-4-0 Special Square Cab** same as 1912 but made of brass 1911 only		(4)	**5000***

Note: In general square cabs and thin rims are more desirable than round bodies and thick rims. The only exception is the 1911 with thick rims.

Steam Locomotives

5	**0-4-0** Black no tender 06-26					
	1. Thin rims	(4)	**700**	2. Thick rims	(3)	**500**

Number 51

Number 5 Special variation 3

5	**Special 0-4-0** Thin rims 06-11		
	1. 4w tender/10 series solid 3-rivet truck	(5)	**1000**
	2. 4w tender/10 series open 3-rivet truck	(4)	**900**
	3. 8w tender 2 100 series trucks	(4)	**700**

Number 6, Thin rim variation

6	**4-4-0** Black/nickel trim 8w tender 06-23					
	1. Thin rims	(4)	**1500**	2. Thick rims	(3)	**1200**
6	**Special 4-4-0** Thin rims Brass/nickel 8w tender 08,09				(5)	**2000**
7	**4-4-0** Brass/nickel 8w tender 10-23					
	1. Thin rims/open 3-rivet trucks				(5)	**3000**

	2. Thick rims/single rivet trucks	(4)	**2500**

Note: In general, thin rims and split frames are more desirable than thick rims and solid frames.

51	**0-4-0** Thick rims 6w tender/two 100 series trucks 12-23	(3)	**700**
	Note: 5, 5 Special and the 51 are the same loco		
384	**2-4-0** 384T Black came with or without green stripe 30-32	(2)	**600**
384E	and either brass or green window trim. NDV		
385E	**2-4-2** 384T 385T 33-39		
	1. Gunmetal/copper and brass 384T 33	(4)	**850**
	2. Gunmetal/nickel 384T, 34	(4)	**950**
	3. Gunmetal/nickel Ives 385T 35-39	(5)	**1000**

PREWAR

390 (top), 390E variation 5 (bottom)

390	**2-4-2** 390T Black with or without orange stripe, hand rev 1929 only	(4)	**900**
390E	**2-4-2** 390T 390X 29-31,33		
	1. Black/orange stripe	(3)	**800**
	2. Blue/cream stripe *Blue Comet*	(4)	**1500**
	3. Dark green/orange stripe-dark green stripe	(4)	**1700**
	4. Same as 3 with light green stripe	(5)	**2000**
	5. Black/red stripe	(3)	**1500**
392E	**4-4-2** 384T 392T 392W 32-39		
	1. Black/brass and copper/384T with or without green stripe. NDV	(3)	**1300**
	2. Black/384T black crackle finish	(5)	**1800**
	3. Black/brass and copper/12w 392T	(5)	**2000**
	4. Black/nickel/12w 392T	(4)	**1450**
	5. Gunmetal/nickel/12w 392T	(4)	**2100**

400E variation 9   *400E variation 1*

400E	**4-4-4** 400T 400W 31-39		
	1. Black/brass and copper, brass boiler bands	(3)	**2200**
	2. Black/brass and copper, painted bands	(4)	**2700**

400E variation 3 (top), 400E variation 4 (bottom)

	3. Gunmetal/brass and copper, brass bands	(3)	**2500**
	4. Gunmetal/brass and copper painted bands	(4)	**2500**
	5. Gunmetal/nickel, painted boiler bands	(4)	**3200**
	6. Black crackle/brass (5) **5000** 7. Black crackle/nickel	(4)	**3500**
	8. Blue/brass and copper (4) **3500** 9. Light blue/nickel	(4)	**3800**
	10. Black/nickel (5) **2750**		
1835E	**2-4-2** same as 385E 34-39		
	1. Black/nickel/384T 34 (3) **800** 2. Black/nickel/1835TW 35-39	(4)	**900**

Passenger Cars
Early Passenger Cars

Note: Price listed is per car

18,19,190 Series 06-27
    1. Dark olive green/red window trim
High knobs	(5)	**1500**	Low knobs	(5)	**1500**
No knobs	(3)	**200**			

    2. Yellow orange   (4)   **750**   3. Dark orange   (3)   **200**
    4. Mojave   (4)   **700**

29   **Day Coach** 08-21
    Early same body as No. 3 trolley 08,09   (5)   **800***
    NYC & HRRR or *Pennsylvania RR*. Closed or open ends. Solid steps
    Middle 10,11
    High knobs or low knobs. *NYC&HRRR* perforated or 3-hole steps
    1. Maroon/black trim   (5)   **800***   2. Dark green   (5)   **800***
    Late Open clerestory 3-hole steps removable roof 12-21
    1. Dark olive green/maroon stripe   (4)   **650***
    2. Dark olive green/no maroon stripe   (4)   **650***

31 Combine 32 Baggage 21-25   (3)   **125**
35 Pullman 36 Observation 12-26
    RS *NYC* common RS *C&O* or *NYNH&H* rare
    1. Green   (2)   **75**   2. Dark blue DSS   (5)   **400**
    3. Orange   (4)   **125**   4. Maroon   (3)   **75**
    5. Brown   (3)   **75**   6. Dark olive green   (2)   **65**

180,181,182 Series 11-21
    1. Maroon early   (5)   **225**   2. Maroon late   (3)   **150**
    3. Brown   (4)   **175**

1910   RS 1910 and Pullman green open 3-rivet trucks 3 high knobs 09,10   (5)   **1700**

412 variation 3 (top), variation 4 (bottom)

PREWAR

67

Large Classic Era Passenger Cars

From top: Stephen Girard Set, Blue Comet Set, Brown State Set, Green State Set

State Car Series 29-35

412	**Pullman CALIFORNIA**			
	1. State green/dark green/apple green		(4)	**1600**
	2. State green/dark green/cream		(5)	**2200**
	3. State brown/dk brn-tan vents/cream		(5)	**1700**
	4. State brown/solid dark brown/cream		(5)	**2000**
413	**Pullman COLORADO**			
	1. State green/dark green/apple green		(4)	**1600**
	2. State green/dark green/cream		(5)	**2200**
	3. State brown/dk brn-tan vents/cream		(5)	**1700**
	4. State brown/solid dark brown/cream		(5)	**2000**
414	**Pullman ILLINOIS**			
	1. State green/dark green/apple green		(5)	**2000**
	2. State green/dark green/cream		(5)	**3000**
	3. State brown/dk brn-tan vents/cream		(5)	**1800**
	4. State brown/solid dark brown/cream		(5)	**2200**
416	**Observation NEW YORK**			
	1. State green/dark green/apple green		(4)	**1700**
	2. State green/dark green/cream		(4)	**2200**
	3. State brown/dk brn-tan vents/cream		(5)	**1800**
	4. State brown/solid dark brown/cream		(5)	**2000**

418, 419, 431, 490 Series 23-32
Note: Most stamped New York Central or Lionel Lines. Illinois Central markings are rare.

418	**Pullman** 23-33			
	1. Mojave/10 series 4w trucks 23-24		(2)	**300**
	2. Mojave/6w trucks 25-33		(3)	**325**
	3. Apple green/apple green/red 29-33		(4)	**425**
419	**Combine** 23-33			
	1. Mojave/10 series 4w trucks 23-24		(2)	**300**
	2. Mojave/6w trucks 25-33		(3)	**325**
	3. Apple green/apple green/red 29-33		(4)	**425**
431	**Diner** 27-33			
	1. Mojave/6w trucks 27-33		(4)	**700**
	2. Mojave/6w trucks with hinged roof		(5)	**1100**
	3. Apple green/apple green/red 29-33		(4)	**600**
	4. Apple green/apple green/red with hinged roof		(5)	**900**
490	**Observation** 23-33			
	1. Mojave/10 series 4w trucks 23-24		(2)	**275**
	2. Mojave/6w trucks 25-33		(3)	**300**
	3. Apple green/apple green/red 29-33		(4)	**400**

Blue Comet Series 30-40

420	**Pullman FAYE**			
	1. Medium blue/dark blue/brass		(4)	**1000**
	2. Light blue/dark blue/nickel and brass		(4)	**1200**
	3. Light blue/dark blue/all nickel		(5)	**1400**
421	**Pullman WESTPHAL**			
	1. Medium blue/dark blue/brass		(4)	**1000**
	2. Light blue/dark blue/nickel and brass		(4)	**1200**
	3. Light blue/dark blue/all nickel		(5)	**1400**
422	**Observation TEMPEL**			
	1. Medium blue/dark blue/brass		(4)	**1000**
	2. Light/blue/dark blue/nickel and brass		(4)	**1200**
	3. Light blue/dark blue/all nickel		(5)	**1400**

PREWAR

Stephen Girard Series Green/dark green/cream 31-40

424	**Pullman LIBERTY BELL**					
	1. Brass trim	(4) **600▼**	2. Nickel trim		(4)	**700▼**
425	**Pullman STEPHEN GIRARD**					
	1. Brass trim	(4) **600▼**	2. Nickel trim		(4)	**700▼**
426	**Observation CORAL ISLE**					
	1. Brass trim	(4) **600▼**	2. Nickel trim		(4)	**700▼**

428, 429, 430 Series *Lionel Lines* markings 26-30

427	**Diner** (made as 431)		**Never made**
428	**Pullman**		
	1. Dark green/dark green/maroon	(2)	**375**
	2. Dark green/dark green/orange	(3)	**375**
	3. Orange/orange/SG green	(5)	**650**
429	**Combine**		
	1. Dark green/dark green/maroon	(2)	**375**
	2. Dark green/dark green/orange	(3)	**375**
	3. Orange/orange/SG green	(5)	**650**
430	**Observation**		
	1. Dark green/dark green/maroon	(2)	**375**
	2. Dark green/dark green/orange	(3)	**375**
	3. Orange/orange/SG green	(5)	**650**

69

Medium Classic Era Passenger Cars

309 variation 4 (top), 339 variation 4 (bottom)

309, 310, 312 Series New York Central or Lionel Lines markings 26-40

309	**Pullman**			
	1. Mojave/mojave/maroon		(2)	**200**
	2. Pea green/pea green/orange		(1)	**150**
	3. Maroon/terra cotta/cream		(5)	**250**
	4. State brown/dark brown/cream		(4)	**250**
	5. Medium blue/dark blue/cream		(4)	**250**
	6. Stephen Girard green/dk green/cream		(5)	**300**
	7. Light blue/silver/silver		(2)	**225**
	8. Red-orange/aluminum/aluminum U			**5P**
310	**Baggage**			
	1. Mojave/mojave/maroon		(2)	**200**
	2. Pea green/pea green/orange		(1)	**150**
	3. State brown/dark brown/cream		(4)	**250**
	4. Medium blue/dark blue/cream		(4)	**250**
	5. Stephen Girard green/dk green/cream		(5)	**300**
	6. Light blue/silver/silver		(2)	**225**
	7. Red-orange/aluminum/aluminum U			**5P**
312	**Observation**			
	1. Mojave/mojave/maroon		(2)	**200**
	2. Pea green/pea green/orange		(1)	**150**
	3. Maroon/terra cotta/cream		(5)	**250**
	4. State brown/dark brown/cream		(4)	**250**
	5. Medium blue/dark blue/cream		(4)	**250**
	6. Stephen Girard green/dk green/cream		(5)	**300**
	7. Light blue/silver/silver		(2)	**225**
	8. Red-orange/aluminum/aluminum U			**5P**

319, 320, 322 Series Maroon/maroon/mojave only 24-27

319	**Pullman**						
	1. *New York Central*	(2)	**125**	2. *Illinois Central*	(4)	**400**
	3. *Lionel Lines*	(2)	**125**			

320	**Baggage** 25-27					
	1. *New York Central*	(2)	**125**	2. *Illinois Central*	(4)	**400**
	3. *Lionel Lines*	(3)	**175**	4. *Lionel Electric Railroad*	(3)	**200**
322	**Observation**					
	1. *New York Central*	(2)	**125**	2. *Illinois Central*	(4)	**400**
	3. *Lionel Lines*	(2)	**125**			

1766, 1767, 1768 Series Lionel Lines 34-40

1766	**Pullman**		

	1. Terra cotta/maroon/cream/brass	(4)	**600**▼
	2. Vermilion/maroon/nickel	(5)	**700**▼
1767	**Baggage**		
	1. Terra cotta/maroon/cream/brass	(4)	**600**▼
	2. Vermilion/maroon/nickel	(5)	**700**▼
1768	**Observation**		
	1. Terra cotta/maroon/cream/brass	(4)	**600**▼
	2. Vermilion/maroon/nickel	(5)	**700**▼

Small Classic Era Passenger Cars

332	**Baggage** came in sets with 337,338 series and 339,341 series 26-33					
	1. Gray/maroon	(2)	**100**	2. Peacock/orange/orange door	(2)	**100**
	3. Peacock/orange/red doors	(3)	**125**	4. Olive green/red	(3)	**150**
	5. Red/cream	(3)	**150**	6. Peacock/dark green/orange	(4)	**150**
	7. State brown/dark brown/cream U				(5)	**300**
	8. Peacock/orange/red doors w/divider				(3)	**150**
	9. Olive/maroon doors				(5)	*

337, 338 Series 25-32
Note: Both 337,338 and 339,341 series came with Lionel Lines, New York Central, and Illinois Central markings. NDV

337	**Pullman**					
	1. Mojave/maroon	(3)	**100**	2. Olive green/maroon	(1)	**100**
	3. Olive green/red	(2)	**100**	4. Pea green/cream Macy's U	(4)	**300**
	5. Red/cream (also came in Macy's U set)				(3)	**150**
338	**Observation**					
	1. Mojave/maroon	(3)	**100**	2. Olive green/maroon	(1)	**100**
	3. Olive green/red	(2)	**100**	4. Pea green/cream Macy's U	(4)	**300**
	5. Red/cream				(3)	**150**
	6. Red/cream with Macy's sticker on drumhead				(4)	**300**

339, 341 Series 25-33

339	**Pullman**		
	1. Gray/maroon	(2)	**100**
	2. Peacock/orange	(1)	**100**
	3. Peacock/dark green/orange	(2)	**100**
	4. State brown/dark brown/cream U	(5)	**300**
	5. Ives 1694 gray/maroon/cream U	(4)	**150**
341	**Observation**		
	1. Gray/maroon	(2)	**100**
	2. Peacock/orange	(1)	**100**
	3. Peacock/dark green/orange	(2)	**100**
	4. State brown/dark brown/cream U	(5)	**300**
	5. Ives 1694 gray/maroon/cream U	(4)	**150**
341	**Observation** RS *THE IVES RAILWAY LINES* Peacock/dark green/orange	(4)	**150**

Rolling Stock

Note: Most desirable items in the Early Period are extremely rare. In some cases, less than 10 are known to exist. Therefore, rarity ratings indicate relative rarity and desirability to other items within the Early Period.

10 Series Freights

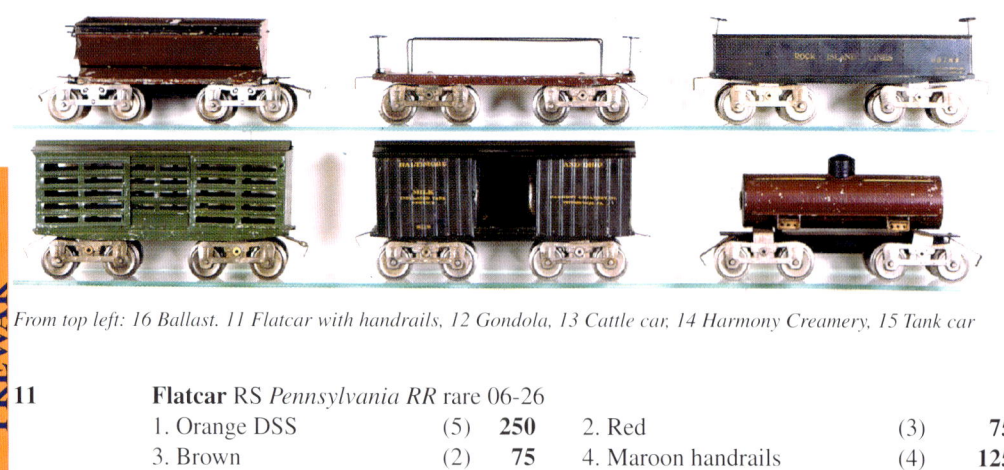

From top left: 16 Ballast, 11 Flatcar with handrails, 12 Gondola, 13 Cattle car, 14 Harmony Creamery, 15 Tank car

11   **Flatcar** RS *Pennsylvania RR* rare 06-26
- 1. Orange DSS   (5)   **250**   2. Red   (3)   **75**
- 3. Brown   (2)   **75**   4. Maroon handrails   (4)   **125**
- 5. Maroon no handrails   (2)   **75**   6. Gray DSS   (4)   **150**
- 7. Dark olive green   (3)   **75**

12   **Gondola** RS *Lake Shore* or *Rock Island* 06-26
- 1. Red   (4)   **75**   2. Brown   (4)   **75**
- 3. Gray   (4)   **75**   4. Maroon   (4)   **75**

Note: Early versions have brakewheel outside and flat edges. Later versions have brakewheel inside and rolled edges. Add $100 for early versions.

13   **Cattle Car** various shades of green 06-26
- **Early** Five slats/smooth surface, two-piece roof, *Lionel Mfg.*   (5)   **300**
- **Middle** 6 slats/embossed surface, one-piece roof, *Lionel Corp*   (3)   **75**
- **Late** 6 slats, embossed surface, no brakewheel, *Lionel Corp*   (3)   **75**

14   **Boxcar** 06-26
- 1. Red/smooth sides   (5)   **350**   2. Red/embossed sides   (4)   **300**
- 3. Yellow-orange/embossed sides   (3)   **100**
- 4. Orange/embossed sides   (2)   **75**
- 5. Dk olive grn/embossed sides DSS   (4)   **250**

14   **Harmony Creamery** Dark green 1921 only   (5+)   *****

15   **Oil Tank** 06-26
- 1. Red/wood domes, ends/U-shaped wire step/RS *416 Pennsylvania*   (5)   **350**
- 2. Wine/three-piece step/metal ends   (4)   **200**
- 3. Wine or brown/single step with three holes/metal ends   (2)   **75**

16   **Ballast** 06-26
- 1. Gray   (5)   **400**   2. Brown   (3)   **200**
- 3. Red   (3)   **200**   4. Dark green   (3)   **200**
- 5. Wine   (2)   **150**

17   **Caboose** 06-26
Early Smooth sides/awnings over main windows, no cupola awnings, vertical striping, steps formed from platform
Middle Embossed sides, no awnings over main windows, awnings over cupola windows, steps formed from platform
Late Embossed sides, no awnings over cupola or main windows, soldered on 3-hole steps, rounded windows rather than square
- 1. Red/black roof   (5)   **350**   2. Brown/black roof   (3)   **150**
- 3. Wine/black roof   (2)   **75**

100 Series Freights

Top row: 112 short olive green Gondola, 112 red Gondola. Second row: 113 green Cattle car, 114 red Boxcar. Third row: 116 maroon Hopper, 116 dark green Hopper. Fourth row: 117 brown Caboose, 117 maroon Caboose

112	**Gondola** 10-26						
	Early 10-12 (7-inches long)						
	1. Dark olive green/red RS *Lake Shore* or *NYNH&H*				(5)		300
	Middle 13-26 (9 1/2-inches long)						
	2. Red/dark olive green trim	(4)	150	3. Maroon	(3)		75
	4. Brown	(3)	75	5. Dark gray	(2)		50
	6. Gray	(3)	50	7. Orange	(5)		200
113	**Cattle Car** Green/embossed sides/no lettering 12-26				(3)		50
	Note: Early cars are darker green than later cars.						
114	**Boxcar** 12-26						
	1. Red	(4)	150	2. Yellow-orange	(3)		75
	3. Orange	(2)	50	4. Dark olive green DSS	(5)		150
116	**Ballast** 10-26						
	1. Dark olive green	(5)	75	2. Maroon	(4)		65
	3. Brown	(2)	50	4. Dark gray	(2)		50
	5. Gray	(2)	50	6. Dark green	(3)		50
117	**Caboose** RS *NYC&HRRR* 4351, 12-26						
	1. Red/black roof	(5)	75	2. Brown/black roof	(4)		65
	3. Maroon/black roof	(3)	50				

200 Series Freights

211	**Flatcar** Black/RS *Lionel Lines* 26-40				(2)	**100**
212	**Gondola** 26-40					
	1. Gray	(4)	**175**	2. Maroon	(2)	**175**
	3. Green	(3)	**175**	4. Medium green	(4)	**200**
	5. Mojave	(4)	**200**	6. Dark green	(5)	**275**

213	**Cattle Car** roofs from 213 and 214 are interchangeable 26-40					
	1. Mojave/maroon	(3)	**375**	2. Terra-cotta/pea green	(2)	**325**
	3. Cream/maroon	(5)	**700**			
214	**Boxcar** roofs from 213 and 214 are interchangeable 26-40					
	1. Terra-cotta/dark green	(4)	**400**	2. Cream/orange	(2)	**300**
	3. Yellow/brown	(3)	**650**			

214R	**Refrigerator** 29-40					
	1. Ivory/peacock	(4)	**800**	2. White/light blue/brass	(5)	**900**
	3. White/light blue/nickel	(5)	**975**			
215	**Tank Car** 26-40					
	1. Pea green	(2)	**400**	2. Pea green/Sunoco decal	(5)	**750**
	3. Ivory/Sunoco decal	(3)	**300**	4. Ivory/no Sunoco decal	(3)	**325**
	5. Alum/Sunoco decal/brass	(4)	**400**	6. Alum/Sunoco decal/nickel	(5)	**550**

216 Hopper variation 2   *218 Dump variation 3*

216	**Hopper** Dark green 26-38					
	1. Brass	(3)	**400**	2. Nickel	(5)	**1500**▲
217	**Caboose** 26-40					
	1. Orange/maroon	(5)	**450**	2. Light red/nickel	(4)	**250**
	3. Red/peacock/red cupola	(3)	**200**	4. Red/peacock/peacock cupola	(4)	**500**
	5. Pea green/red/brass		**5P**			
218	**Dump** 26-38					
	1. Mojave/2 brass knobs/brass ends				(3)	**325**
	2. Mojave/1 brass knob/brass ends				(2)	**275**
	3. Mojave/1 brass knob/mojave ends				(2)	**275**
	4. Green/red/brass ends 1926					**5P**
	5. Gray/brass ends					**5P**
	6. Pea green/maroon ends					**5P**

PREWAR

219	**Derrick** 26-40		
	1. Peacock/red boom	(2)	**275**
	2. Yellow/red/green or red boom NDV	(4)	**450**
	3. Ivory/red/green boom	(5)	**550**

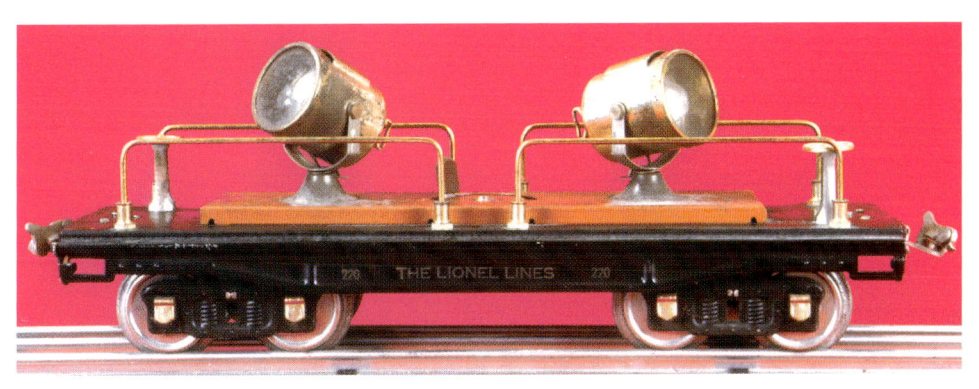

220	**Floodlight Car** 31-40					
	1. Terra-cotta/brass lights	(2)	**375**	2. Green/nickel-plated lights	(3)	**400**

75

500 Series Freights

511	**Flatcar** 27-39						
	1. Dark green/gold RS lettering					(2)	75
	2. Medium green/silver RS lettering					(3)	80
	3. Medium green/gold RS lettering					(2)	80
	Note: Brakewheel placed differently through the years. NDV						
512	**Gondola** 27-39						
	1. Peacock	(2)	**50**	2. Green		(2)	**50**
513	**Cattle Car** 27-38						
	1. Olive green/orange	(3)	**250**	2. Orange/pea green		(2)	**175**
	3. Cream/maroon	(5)	**500**				
514	**Boxcar** 29-40						
	1. Cream/orange	(2)	**200**	2. Yellow/brown		(3)	**275**
514	**Refrigerator** Ivory/peacock 27,28					(3)	**300**

PREWAR

514R **Refrigerator** 29-40
1. Ivory/peacock   (3) **300**   2. White/light blue   (5) **500**

515	**Tank Car** 27-40						
	1. Terra cotta/no decal	(2)	**175**	2. Ivory/no Sunoco decal		(2)	**200**
	3. Ivory/Sunoco decal	(3)	**200**	4. Alum/Sunoco decal		(3)	**250**
	5. Tan w&w/o Sunoco decal	(4)	**250**	6. Shell orange/Shell decal		(5)	**1600***
	Note: Brakewheel on left side on early versions; right side on later versions. NDV						
516	**Hopper** Red 28-40						
	1. No coal load/brass	(2)	**225**	2. Coal load/brass		(3)	**275**
	3. Coal load/RS lettering	(4)	**375**	4. Coal load/nickel		(5)	**425**
517	**Caboose** 27-40						
	1. Pea green/red/brass	(2)	**100**	2. Pea green/red/orange		(2)	**100**
	3. Red/black/orange	(5)	**850**	4. Red/aluminum		(4)	**250**
	5. Red/alum/no number plates, number rubber-stamped on bottom					(4)	**500**
520	**Floodlight Car** 31-40						
	1. Terra-cotta/brass lights	(2)	**225**	2. Green/nickel plated lights		(3)	**250**
	Early: brakewheel left. Late: right. NDV						

Trolleys

Note: All 1, 2, 3, and 4 series trolleys and trailers had number plus Electric Rapid Transit on side, except as indicated.

1	**Trolley** 4-wheels 5 window, no reverse, no headlight/smooth sides 06 *New Departure Motor* Orange/cream	(5)	**3000**
1	**Trailer** 5 window Blue/cream 07	(5)	**2500**

Number 1 variation 1   *Number 100 variation 3*

1	**Trolley** 6 window Embossed sides/standard motor 08					
	1. Blue/cream	(4)	**2500**	2. Dark green/cream	(5)	**3000**
1	**Trailer** 6 windows blue/cream 08				(3)	**2000**
1	**Trolley** 6 window, used 1908/09 version of 2 trolley body 10-14					
	1. Blue/cream	(4)	**2500**	2. Blue/cream *Curtis Bay*	(5)	**3000**
2	**Trolley** 4-wheels headlight and reverse 06-14					
	1. Cream/red/open ends 06				(5)	**2000**
	2. Blue/cream windows/open ends 08				(4)	**2000**
	3. Red/cream windows closed offset ends 10-12				(4)	**2000**
	4. Dark olive green/orange windows closed flush ends 13-16				(5)	**2200**
	5. Cream/red/closed flush ends				(4)	**1800**
2	**Trailer**					
200	1. Cream/red/matches no. 1 above				(5)	**1800**
	2. Red/cream/matches no. 3 above				(4)	**1500**
3	**Trolley** 8-wheels 06-13					
	1. Cream/dark olive green/flat windows open ends 1906				(5)	**3000**
	2. Cream/dark olive green/inset windows open ends 1908				(5)	**3000**
	3. Cream/orange/open ends inset windows 1908				(5)	**3000**
	4. Orange/cream/open ends inset windows 1908				(5)	**3000**
	5. Dark olive green/cream/closed offset ends 1910				(5)	**3000**
	6. Dark olive green/cream/closed flush ends 1913				(5)	**3000**
	7. Same but lettered *Bay Shore*				(5)	**3000**
3	**Trailer** 08				(5)	**2800**
300	Matches nos. 2,3, and 4					
4	**Trolley** 8 wheels Same body as 3 but with 2 motors - early 06-13					
	1. Dark olive green/cream, open ends - late				(5)	**5000**
	2. Dark olive green/cream/flush ends				(5)	**5000**

PREWAR

77

8	**Trolley** *PAY AS YOU ENTER* 8-wheels single motor 09-15		
	1. Cream/orange/9 windows	(5)	**6000**
	2. Dark olive green/cream 11 windows	(5)	**6000**
9	**Trolley** *PAY AS YOU ENTER* 8-wheels double motor 09-12		
	1. Cream/orange/9 windows	(5)	**6000**
	2. Dark olive green/cream/11 windows	(5)	**6000**
10	**Interurban** 10-16	(5)	**4000**
1010	**Trailer** (powered and trailer units stamped 1010)		
	1. Maroon/gold/high knobs (5) **4000** 2. Dk olive green/low knobs	(4)	**3000**
	3. Dk olive green/no knobs (4) **1500** 4. Same but RS *WB&A*, both		∗
100	**Trolley** 5 windows Blue/cream 1910	(4)	**2000**
1000	**Trailer** Blue/cream 1910	(4)	**1500**
100	**Trolley** 5 windows 13-14		
	1. Red/cream (4) **2000** 2. Blue/cream	(4)	**2000**
	3. Blue/cream/*Linden Ave* (5) **4000**		
1000	**Trailer** matches nos. 1 and 2 NDV 13-14	(4)	**1500**
1000	**Trailer** *Linden Ave* 13-14	(5)	**3500**
100	**Trolley** 6 windows 14-16		
	1. Red/cream (4) **2000** 2. Blue/cream	(4)	**2000**
1000	**Trailer** matches nos. 1 and 2 NDV 14-16	(4)	**1500**
101	**Open Summer Trolley** four wheels 10-13		
	1. Blue roof and ends (4) **2000** 2. Same as 1 w/*101 Wilkins Ave*	(5)	**2500**
	3. Red roof and ends (4) **2000**		
1100	**Trailer** matches 101		
202	**Open Summer Trolley** 4-wheels Red/cream/black 10-13	(5)	**3000**
2200	**Trailer** matches 202	(5)	**2500**
303	**Open Summer Trolley** 8-wheels Green/cream/maroon 10-13	(5)	**3000**
3300	**Trailer** matches 303	(5)	**2500**

Number 300 Converse Trolley 2 7/8 gauge

2 7/8-Inch Gauge

Note: These were the first trains Joshua Lionel Cowen made. They are extremely rare. About 30 collectible variations exist. The largest known 2 7/8-inch gauge collection has nine pieces. Few items in this category are ever sold so the prices listed are estimates. All metal and iron cars have black frames, 4 wheels, and Lionel Manufacturing Company stamped on floor. Reproductions exist.

100 Electric Locomotive varaition 1    *600 Derrick*

100	**Electric Locomotive** 01-05				
	1. Maroon/black roof	(5) **5000**	2. Apple green	(5)	**5000**
200	**Electric Express** 01-05				
	1. Electric Express/wooden car body no corner braces			(5)	6000
	2. Same with corner braces			(5)	5000
	3. Sheet-metal body/maroon			(5)	5000
	4. Sheet-metal body/apple green			(5)	5000
300	**Electric Trolley** Maroon/light green/6 reversible seats, 01-05 lettered *City Hall Park* on one end and *Union Depot* on the other			(5)	5000
309	**Trolley Trailer** matches 300, 01-05				
400	**Express Trailer** matches 200, RS lettering				
	1. Gold *Lake Shore*	(5) **3000**	2. Green/gold *B&O*	(5)	3000
500	**Electric Derrick** Maroon/black 03,04			(5)	3000
	Derrick made of cast iron, brass chain with tackle attached				
600	**Derrick Trailer** Same as 500 but without motor 03,04			(5)	3000
800	**Electric Box** Maroon/maroon roof/gold RS lettering 04,05 *Metropolitan Express*			(5)	3000
900	**Electric Box Trailer** Matches 800 04,05			(5)	3000
1000	**Electric Passenger** 05				
	1. Maroon/black roof/gold RS lettering *Metropolitan St. R.R. CO.*			(5)	5000
	2. Same as 1 but lettered *Maryland St. RY Co.*			(5)	5000
1050	**Passenger Trailer** Matches 1000, 04,05				
	1. Maroon/black roof/gold RS lettering *Metropolitan St. R.R. Co.*			(5)	5000
	2. Lettered *Maryland St. RY Co.*			(5)	5000
	3. Lettered *Philadelphia R.T. Co.*			(5)	5000

PREWAR

Postwar 1945-1969
Diesels
Alcos

Note: Later Alcos (1957 and beyond) often turn up with cracked pilots. Be sure to check pilots before buying.

208 Santa Fe (top), 209 New Haven (center), 210 Texas Special Alcos (bottom)

202	**Union Pacific A** Orange/black 57		(3)	**100**
204	**Santa Fe AA** Blue/yellow 57		(4)	**200**
205	**Missouri Pacific AA** Blue/white 57,58			
	1. Blue/white (2) **175** 2. Dark blue/white		(4)	**250**
208	**Santa Fe AA** Blue/yellow 58,59		(3)	**200**
209	**New Haven AA** Black/orange/white 58		(4)	**900**
210	**Texas Special AA** Red/white 58		(3)	**175**
211	**Texas Special AA** Red/white 62,63,65,66			
	1. Glossy Red (3) **150** 2. Flat Red		(4)	**150**
212	**US Marine Corps A** Blue/white, fixed rear coupler only 58,59 No coupler opening in front, came w/Blue unpainted shell, Red shell painted blue, Black shell painted blue NDV			
	1. Magnetraction/E unit		(3)	**175▼**
	2. No Magnetraction/E unit (no E Unit slot to be legitimate)		(4)	**275**
212T	**US Marine Corps** Blue/white 58,59 Dummy unit made to match 212. Fixed couplers front and rear		(4)	**650▲**
212	**Santa Fe AA** Silver/red 64-66			
	1. Gray shell (3) **200** 2. Black shell		(4)	**350**
213	**Minneapolis & St. Louis** Red/white **AA** 64		(3)	**250▲**
215	**Santa Fe AA** Silver/red/black-yellow stripes U64,65 Power A **215**, Dummy A **212**		(3)	**250**
216	**Burlington A** Silver/red 58		(4)	**400**
216	**Minneapolis & St. Louis A** Red/white U		(3)	**175**
217	**Boston & Maine AB** Black/blue/white 59		(3)	**225**
218	**Santa Fe AA** Silver/red 59-63			
	1. Front decal red, yellow and black		(3)	**200**
	2. Front decal yellow and black		(5)	**250***
218	**Santa Fe AB** Silver/red 61		(3)	**250**

80

219	**Missouri Pacific AA** Blue/white U59	(3)	**225**
220	**Santa Fe A** Silver/red 61	(2)	**185**
221	**Rio Grande A** Yellow/black 63,64	(2)	**90**

221	**USMC A** Olive drab/white U64	(4)	**375**
221	**Santa Fe A** Olive drab/white U64	(4)	**475**
222	**Rio Grande A** Yellow/black stripes 62	(2)	**85**
223,212	**Santa Fe AA** Silver/red U64		*****
223,218C	**Santa Fe AB** Silver/red 63	(5)	**350**
224	**US Navy AB** Blue/white 60	(3+)	**275**
225	**Chesapeake & Ohio A** Dark blue/yellow 60	(3)	**200**
226	**Boston & Maine AB** Black/blue/white U59 1. Unpainted blue shell (3) **275** 2. A unit w/painted gray shell (5)		**550**
227	**Canadian National A** Green/yellow U59,60	(3)	**175**
228	**Canadian National A** Green/yellow U60,61	(4)	**200**
229	**Minneapolis & St. Louis A** Red/white 61	(3)	**150**
229	**Minneapolis & St. Louis AB** 62,63A 1. Red/white (3) **250** 2. Olive drab uncataloged (5)		**750***
230	**Chesapeake & Ohio A** Blue/yellow 61	(2)	**150**
231	**Rock Island A** Black 61-63 1. Red stripe and white stripe (3) **175** 2. Red stripe/no white stripe (3) 3. White stripe/no red stripe (4+)**600▲***		**200**
232	**New Haven A** 62 Orange/black	(3)	**200**
1055	**Texas Special A** Red/white U59,60	(2)	**90**
1065	**Union Pacific A** Yellow/red U61	(2)	**115**
1066	**Union Pacific A** Yellow/red U64	(2)	**115**
2023	**Union Pacific AA** 50,51 1. Yellow/gray nose, roof & trucks 50	(5)	**4000▲**

	2. Yellow/gray roof & black trucks 50	(2)	**375**
	3. Silver/gray roof & black trucks 51	(4)	**425**
2024	**Chesapeake & Ohio A** Blue/yellow 69	(2)	**125**
2031	**Rock Island AA** Black/white 52-54	(4)	**550**

| 2032 | **Erie AA** Black/yellow 52-54 | (4) | **350** |

2023 Union Pacific (top), 2033 Union Pacific Alcos (bottom)

2033	**Union Pacific AA** Silver/black 52-54		(3)	**375**
2041	**Rock Island AA** Black 69			
	1. White lettering/red stripe (3) **200**	2. No lettering, no red stripe	(3)	**175**

Budd Cars

| 400 | **Baltimore & Ohio** Silver/blue 56-58 | (3) | **400** |

| 404 | **Baltimore & Ohio** Silver/blue 57, 58 | (3+) | **400** |
| 2550 | **Baltimore & Ohio** dummy 57, 58 | (4) | **600** |

| 2559 | **Baltimore & Ohio** dummy 57, 58 | (4) | **425** |

F-3 Units

Note: Most reproductions have silk-screen lettering; however, some 2345 reproductions exist with heat-stamped lettering

2245 Texas Special AB (top), 2344 A and 2344C B (center), 2343A and 2343C B (bottom)

2240	**Wabash AB** Gray/blue/white 56	(3)	900
2242	**New Haven AB** Silver/black/orange 58,59	(4)	1200
2243	**Santa Fe AB** Silver/red 55-57	(3)	450
2243C	**Santa Fe B Unit** Silver/red 55-57	(3)	225
2245	**Texas Special AB** 54,55		
	1. Silver trucks/red pilot/portholes	(3)	850
	2. Black trucks/silver pilot/A w/portholes/B w/solid portholes late 55 only	(5)	1400
	3. Same as 2 but A and B have solid portholes	(5)	1600*
	Note: possible dealer replacement shells		
2333	**Santa Fe AA** Silver/red 48,49		
	1. RS larger lettering (3+) 650 2. HS smaller lettering	(3)	600
2333	**Santa Fe** Clear bodies (Vol. 5, pg 65)		5X
2333	**New York Central AA** Dark gray/gray/white 48,49		
	1. RS larger lettering (4) 900 2. HS smaller lettering	(3)	800
	Note: Original NYC's had black or red decals and original Santa Fe's had red decals. Replacement decals are available and can be applied to either.		
2343	**Santa Fe AA** Silver/red 50-52	(2)	550
2343C	**Santa Fe B Unit** Silver/red 50-55		
	1. Screen roof vents matches 2343 50-52	(4)	300
	2. Louver vents matches 2353 53-55	(3)	250
2344	**New York Central AA** 50-52	(3)	650
2344C	**New York Central B Unit** 50-55		
	1. Screen roof vents matches 2344 50-52	(4)	300
	2. Louver vents matches 2354 53-55	(3)	275
2345	**Western Pacific AA** Silver/orange/black 52	(4)	1500
2353	**Santa Fe AA** Silver/red 53-55	(3)	550
2354	**New York Central AA** Dark gray/gray/white 53-55	(3+)	650
2355	**Western Pacific AA** Silver/orange/black 53	(4)	1300
	Also reported no lettering on one side, NDV		
2356	**Southern AA** Green/gray/yellow 54-56	(4)	1000
2356C	**Southern B Unit** Green/gray/yellow 54-56	(4)	400
2363	**Illinois Central AB** Brown/orange/yellow 55,56		
	1. Black lettering (4) 900 2. Brown lettering	(5)	1000
2367	**Wabash AB** Gray/blue/white 55,56	(4)	850

POSTWAR

83

| 2368 | **Baltimore & Ohio AB** Blue/white/black 56 | (4) | **1700** |

| 2373 | **Canadian Pacific AA** Gray/maroon/yellow 57 | (4) | **2500** |

2378 **Milwaukee Road AB** 56
1. No yellow stripe along roof (4) **1500** 
2. Yellow stripe along roof (4) **1900**
3. A unit no stripe, B unit with stripe (4) **1900**

| 2379 | **Rio Grande AB** Yellow/silver/black 57,58 | (4) | **1000** |
| 2383 | **Santa Fe AA** Silver/red 58-66 | (3) | **575** |

FM Units

Note: Watch for Jersey Central reproductions being sold as originals. The best way to tell an original is by checking the spacing between Jersey and Central. On the original, there is more space between the words on one side than there is on the other. On reproductions, the space between the words is the same on both sides.

2321 **Lackawanna** Gray body 54-56
    1. Maroon roof 54 (3+) **700** 2. Gray roof 55,56 (3) **550**

2322 **Virginian** Blue/yellow 65,66
    1. Unpainted blue shell (3+) **800** 2. Painted blue shell (4) **950**

2331 **Virginian** 55-58
    Note: The yellow on the second version is much lighter than the yellow on the third version, which is almost gold.
    1. Yellow/black both colors painted on gray mold (4) **1000**
    2. Blue/light yellow/both colors painted on/gray mold (4+) **1100**
    3. Blue/yellow - yellow only painted on blue plastic mold (3+) **800**

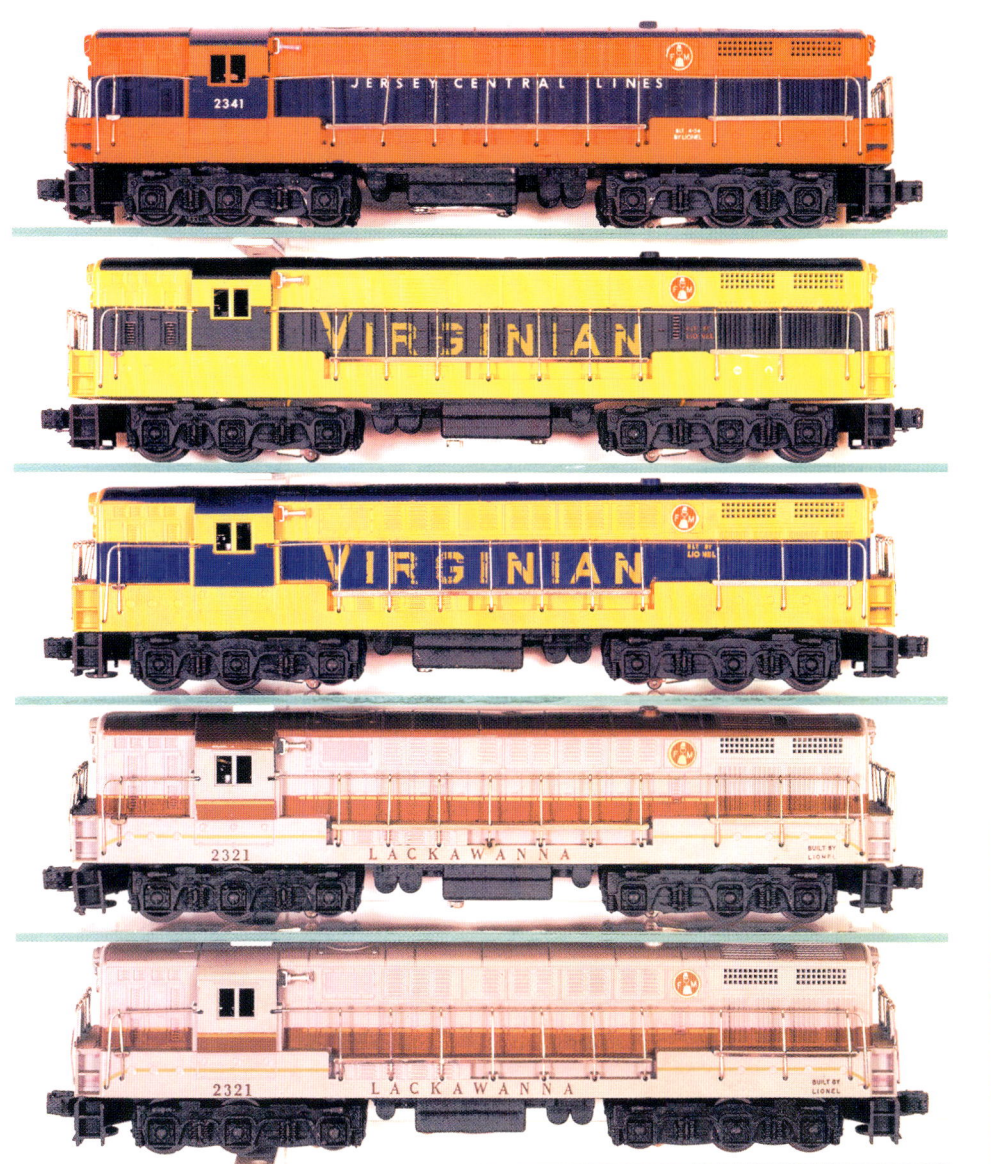

From top: 2341 Jersey Central, 2331 Virginian variation 2, 2331 Virginian variation 3, 2321 Lackawanna variation 1, 2321 Lackawanna variation 2

2341	**Jersey Central** Orange/blue/blue stripe 56					
	Note: Originals are heat-stamped; reproductions are silk-screened					
	1. Glossy finish	(5)	**2200**	2. Dull finish	(4)	**1800**

GE 44-Ton Switchers

Note: Difficult to find in Like New condition. All have a tendency to flake and are usually found with broken screw holes.

625	**Lehigh Valley** Red/black/white 57, 58	(3)	**150**

626	**Baltimore & Ohio** Blue/yellow 57	(4)	**475**
627	**Lehigh Valley** Red/white 56, 57	(2)	**175**
628	**Northern Pacific** Black/yellow 56, 57	(3)	**175**
629	**Burlington** Silver/red 56	(4)	**700**

GM Switchers

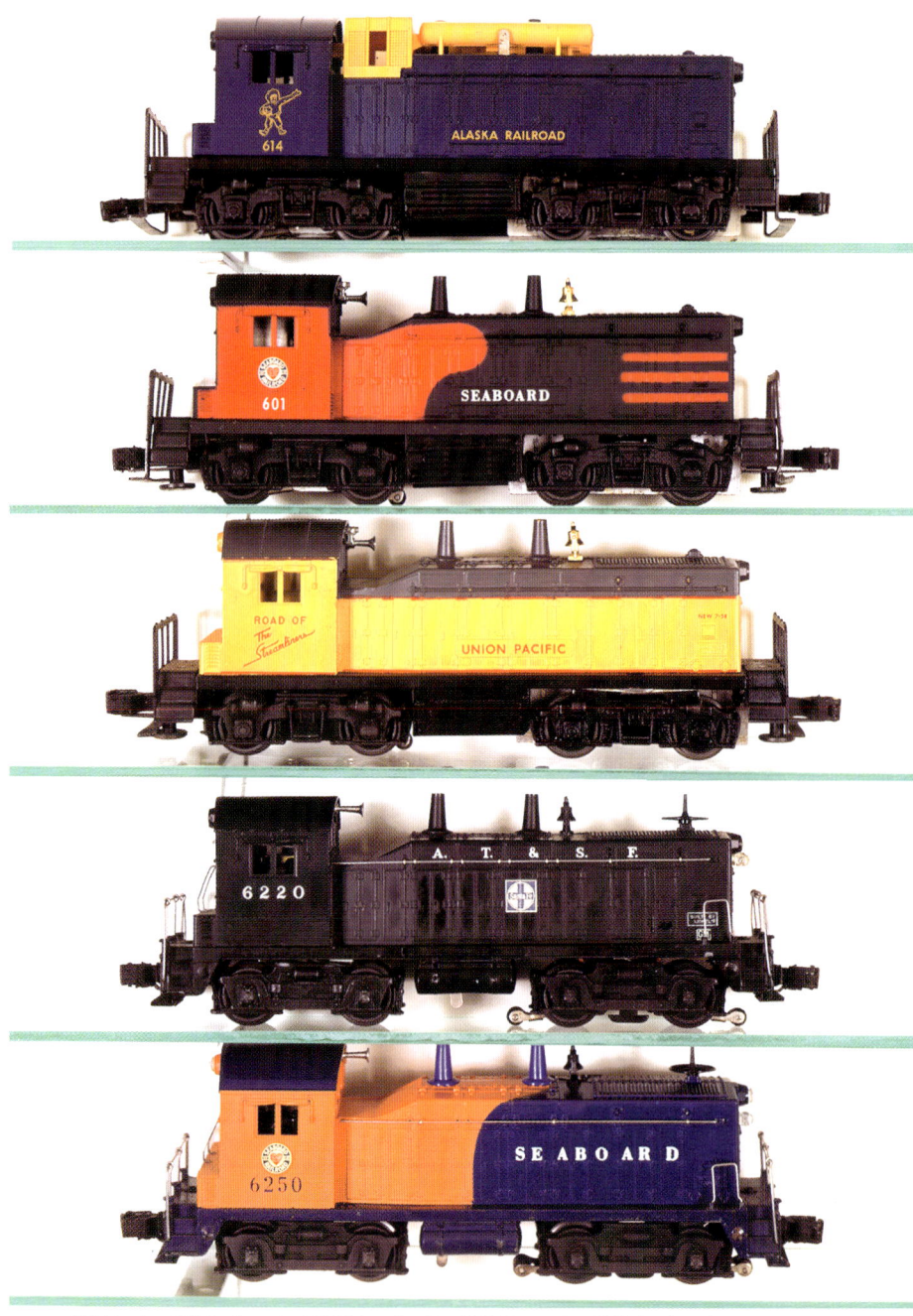

From top: 614 Alaska, 601 Seaboard, 613 Union Pacific, 6220 Santa Fe, 6250 Seaboard

600	**MKT** Red/white 55						
	1. Black frame/black rails	(3)	**175**	2. Gray frame/yellow rails	(3+)	**225**
	3. Gray frame/black rails	(4)	**250**			
601	**Seaboard** Black/red/white 56					
	1. Red stripes/rounded ends	(3)	**275**	2. Red stripes/squared ends	(4)	**300**
602	**Seaboard** Black/red/red 57,58				(3)	**225**
610	**Erie** 55 Black/yellow					
	1. Black frame	(3)	**225**	2. Yellow frame	(4)	**400▲**
	3. Lionel dealer replacement shell with raised nameplate				(4)	**300▲**
611	**Jersey Central** Orange/blue 57,58				(3)	**225**
613	**Union Pacific** Yellow/gray/red 58				(4)	**400**
614	**Alaska** Blue/yellow with dynamic brake unit 59,60					
	1. *Built by Lionel* in blue raised letters				(3)	**300**
	2. *Built by Lionel* in yellow raised letters				(4)	**500▲**

POSTWAR

86

616	**Santa Fe** Black/white/safety stripes 61,62				
	1. No dummy horn, bell, or E unit slot			(5)	**375**▲
	2. Has dummy horn, bell, & E unit slot			(4)	**275**▲
617	**Santa Fe** Black/white/safety stripes 63			(4)	**400**
621	**Jersey Central** Blue/orange 56,57			(3)	**250**
622	**Santa Fe** Black/white, operating bell 49,50				
	1. Large *GM* decal	(4+) **500**	2. Small *GM* decal	(3)	**200**
	3. Large *GM* decal and *Built by Lionel* in white			(4)	**425**
	4. Same as 3 plus small decal			(4+)	**450**
623	**Santa Fe** Black/white 52-54				
	1. 10 Handrail stanchions	(4) **250**	2. 3 Handrail stanchions	(3)	**225**
624	**Chesapeake & Ohio** Blue/yellow 52-54				
	1. 10 Handrail stanchions	(4) **325**	2. 3 Handrail stanchions	(3)	**250**
633	**Santa Fe** Blue/yellow 62				
	1. No safety stripes	(3) **150**	2. Safety stripes	(3+)	**185**
634	**Santa Fe** Blue/yellow 63,65,66				
	1. Safety Stripes	(2) **150**	2. No Safety Stripes	(3)	**175**
635	**Union Pacific** Yellow/red U65			(4)	**200**
645	**Union Pacific** Yellow/red 69			(3)	**175**
6220	**Santa Fe** Black/white, operating bell 49,50				
	1. Large *GM* decal, 1949	(4+) **375**	2. Small *GM* decal, 1950	(3)	**325**
6250	**Seaboard** Blue/orange/white-blue 54,55				
	Note: Fewer rubber-stamped versions produced but decal version with decal in excellent condition is more desirable.				
	1. Decal	(4) **400**	2. Rubber-stamped	(4)	**375**

GP-7s and GP-9s

Note: Originals have HS lettering. Reproductions have RS lettering or are silk-screened. Known reproductions include 2337, 2339, 2349, 2347, 2365.

2028	**Pennsylvania GP-7** Tuscan 55			
	1. Yellow RS lettering/gold frame		(4)	**500**
	2. Gold RS lettering/gold frame		(4+)	**500**

	3. Gold RS lettering/tan frame		(5)	**1000**
2328	**Burlington GP-7** Silver/black/red 55,56		(3)	**600**
2337	**Wabash GP-7** Blue/gray/white 58		(4)	**450**
2338	**Milwaukee Road GP-7** 55,56			
	1. Orange stripe through cab (5) **1800**	2. All-black cab	(3)	**300**▼
2339	**Wabash GP-7** Blue/gray/white 57		(3+)	**375**▼
2346	**Boston & Maine GP-9** 65,66		(3)	**400**
2347	**Chesapeake & Ohio GP-7** Blue/yellow *Sears*U65		(5)	**3000**
2348	**Minneapolis & St. Louis GP-9** 58,59			
	1. Red/white (4) **450**	2. Red/yellow		**FAKE**
2349	**Northern Pacific GP-9** Black/gold/red 59,60		(4)	**700**

From top: 2337 Wabash GP-7, 2338 Milwaukee Road variation 1, 2338 Milwaukee Road GP-7 variation 2

2359	**Boston & Maine GP-9** Blue/black/white 61,62	(3)	**350**▲
2365	**Chesapeake & Ohio GP-7** Dummy couplers 62,63		
	1. Blue/yellow (3) **300** 2. Blue/white		**FAKE**

Electrics

520	**Box Cab** Red/white 56,57		
	1. Black plastic pantograph (3) **125** 2. Copper plastic pantograph	(4)	**175**
2329	**Virginian EL-C** Rectifier Blue/yellow 58,59	(4)	**650**

EP-5s

Note: Difficult to find EP-5s in Like New condition due to flaking and fading. Beware of repaints, particularly Milwaukee Road because of no decal. 2352 price not commensurate with its rarity because of its drab color scheme.

2350	**New Haven EP-5** Black/white/orange 56-58		
	Note: The major variation of the New Haven has to do with the color of the N and H. The common version has a white N and orange H. The rare version has an orange N and black H. Both versions come with either the nose trim painted or a decal. The versions with the painted nose trim are far more sought after than the decal versions.		
	1. White *N* orange *H*/nose trim decal	(3)	**400**▼
	2. White *N* orange *H*/painted nose trim	(4)	**600**▼
	3. Orange *N* black *H*/nose trim decal	(4)	**1500**
	4. Orange *N* black *H*/painted nose trim	(5)	**1750**
2351	**Milwaukee Road EP-5** Yellow/black/red 57,58	(3)	**700**
2352	**Pennsylvania EP-5** Tuscan/gold 58,59	(3)	**750**
2358	**GN EP-5** Orange/green/yellow 59,60	(4)	**1200**

EP-5s from top: 2358 Great Northern, 2352 Pennsylvania, 2351 Milwaukee Road, 2350 New Haven

GG1s

2332 (left), 2340 (center), 2360 (right)

2330	**GG-1** Dark green/5 gold stripes 50	(4)	**1500**
2330	**GG-1** Nickel-plate		**5P**

2332 **GG-1** single motor 47-49
Note: Only came with electric horn that soundslike the buzz of a doorbell. All other GG1's came with same horn as the Alcos.

1. Black/5 silver stripes	(5)	**3000**	2. Black/5 gold stripes		(5)	**2500**
3. Dark green/5 gold stripes decaled keystones					(3)	**900**
4. Dark green/5 gold stripes RS keystones					(4)	**1400**
5. Dark green/5 silver stripes RS keystones					(4)	**1500**

2340-1 **GG-1** Tuscan 5 gold stripes *Congressional Set* 55	(4)	**1800**
2340-25 **GG-1** Brunswick Green 5 gold stripes 55	(4)	**1800**

2332 Pennsylvania GG-1

2360-1	**GG-1** Tuscan 56-58, 61-63		
	Note: Variations exist having to do with louvres, shape of headlights, and steps. NDV.		
	1. 1956/5 gold stripes/RS/small *PRR* keystone	(4)	**2000**
	2. Same as 1 but large *PRR* keystone usually found on solid-stripe versions	(5)	**2200**
	3. 1957,58 Solid stripe/RS/OB marked 2360-10/large *PRR* keystone	(3)	**1600**
	4. 1961-63 Solid stripe/painted/HS markings	(3)	**1200**
	5. Late 1963 Solid stripe/painted/decaled markings	(3)	**1200**
	6. Very glossy finish/5 gold stripes		**5P**
2360-25	**GG-1** Brunswick green 5 RS gold stripes 56-58	(4)	**1600**

Powered Units

Note: High prices, restorations and reissues have lessened the demand. Beware of repaired window struts. Like New, 54, 55, and 3360 must be complete with track actuator.

41	**US Army** 55-57		
	1. Unpainted black plastic w/white lettering	(3)	**180**
	2. Yellow lettering		**FAKE**

42 Picatinny Arsenal   *51 Navy*

42	**Picatinny Arsenal** Olive drab/white 57	(4)	**450▲**
44	**US Army** Blue/white/gray 59-62	(3)	**325▲**
45	**US Marines** Olive drab/white/gray 60-62	(3+)	**375▲**
50	**Gang Car** Orange/blue 54-64		
	1. Gray bumpers (54 only). Men in reversed colors	(5)	**1500**
	2. Same, blue bumpers	(3)	**90**
	3. Horn changed to solid type attached off-center. Blue bumpers	(1)	**75**
51	**Navy Yard** Blue/white 56,57	(2)	**275▲**
52	**Fire Car** Red/white 58-61	(3)	**275**

52 Fire Car   *53 Rio Grande Snowolow*

53	**Rio Grande Snowplow** Black/yellow 57-60				
	1. *a* printed backwards	(4) **350**▲	2. *a* printed correctly	(5)	**800**▲
54	**Ballast Tamper** Black/yellow 58-62,66,68,69			(3)	**250**
55	**Tie-Jector** Red/white 57-61			(4)	**225**
	Some came with a horizontal opening behind man, some didn't. NDV				

56 Minneapolis & St. Louis   *57 AEC Switcher*

56	**Minneapolis & St. Louis** Red/white 58	(4+)	**700**
57	**AEC Switcher** White/red/white 59,60	(4)	**875**▲

58 Great Northern Rotary Snowplow   *59 Minuteman*

58	**GN Rotary Snowplow** Green/white 59-61	(4)	**850**▲
59	**Minuteman** White/blue 62,63	(4)	**825**▲
60	**Lionelville Trolley** Yellow/red/blue 55-58		

Note: Some cars with red lettering may actually be faded black cars since black pigment has red in it.

1. Yellow/black lettering 55	(3+)	**200**	2. Yellow/blue lettering	(3)	**175**▲
3. Roof vents	(4)	**250**	4. Yellow/red lettering	(5)	**2200**
5. The first versions off the production line had black silhouettes of				(5)	**350**▲

motormen at each end of the trolley. They would appear and disappear according to which direction the car was traveling. However, the motormen silhouettes were rather indistinct and Lionel soon discontinued putting them on. The motormen remained available for separate sale and today trolleys exist with motormen, but most were put on by collectors.

65	**Handcar** 62-66	(4)	**450**

1. First versions were made of light yellow plastic which had a tendency to melt and are almost impossible to find in Like New condition. This version came with two sizes of rectifiers: thick (extends through slot in chassis wall) and thin (clipped to chassis wall). The thick

version (two rubber-tire wheels) is harder to find than the thin version (one rubber-tire wheel). NDV
2. Dark yellow (4+) **500▲**

68 Executive Inspection Car variation 3   *68 Executive Inspection Car variation 1*

68	**Executive Inspection Car** 58-61			
	1. Red/cream (3+)**400▲**	2. Red throughout		**5P**
	3. Blue/cream stripe **5P**			
69	**Maintenance Car** Dark gray/black 60-62		(3)	**350**

3360 Burro Crane   *3927 Track Cleaning Car*

3360	**Burro Crane** 56,57					
	1. Yellow	(3)	**275**	2. Brown		**5P**
3927	**Track Cleaning Car** Complete with 2 bottles, brush, and wiper 56-60					
	1. Orange/blue	(3)	**150**	2. Orange/black	(4)	**175**

Steamers
Berkshires

726	2-8-4 2426W Turned stanchions, *Atomic Motor* double worm drive, 46 horizontal motor, Baldwin drivers	(4)	**800**
726	2-8-4 2426W Cotter pin stanchions, single worm drive and 47-49 slanted motor, Baldwin drivers	(3)	**550▼**

726	2-8-4 2046W Korean War issue Spoked drivers, no Magnetraction 52					
	1. 726RR stamped on cab	(3)	**325**	2. No RR	(4)	**325**
736	2-8-4 2671WX 12-wheels, diecast trailing trucks, Magnetraction, 50,51 smoke, rubber-stamped cab number				(3)	**350**
736	2-8-4 2046W 8-wheels, diecast trailing trucks, Magnetraction, 53-55 smoke, heat-stamped cab number				(2)	**325**
736	2-8-4 2046W,736 sheet-metal trucks with plastic side frames, 55-66 Magnetraction, smoke, HS cab number				(2)	**300**

746   4-8-4 *Norfolk & Western* 746W 57-60
         1. Short stripe tender   (4)   **900**   2. Long stripe tender   (4)   **1100**

The General

1862   4-4-0 1862T Gray/red, no smoke, no MT, headlight 59-62   (3)   **225**▼
Note: Red or black headlight housings are interchangeable. NDV

1872   4-4-0 1872T Gray/red, smoke, MT, headlight, oper. couplers 59-62   (3+)   **400**

1882   4-4-0 1882T Black/orange MT but no smoke, sold by *Sears* U60   (4)   **600**▼
Note: See Set Section as Generals usually are sold in sets.

Hudsons

646	4-6-4 2046W, S, MT 54-58		
	1. Plastic side frames on stamped trailing trucks, larger *646* RS in silver	(3)	**225**▼
	2. Same as 2 but *646* HS in white	(3)	**200**▼

665	4-6-4, S, MT Same as 685 but with feedwater heater and lower 54-59,66 marker lights. Both HS and RS cab number. NDV. Plastic side frames on TT.		
	1. 6026W *Lionel Lines* (3+) **225** 2. 2046W *Lionel Lines*	(3+)	**225**
	3. 736W *Pennsylvania* 66 (3) **200**		
685	4-6-4 6026W Smoke, Magnetraction 53		
	1. *685* RS in silver below cab window	(4)	**300**
	2. *685* HS in white below cab window	(3)	**250**▼

773	4-6-4 50, S, MT 64-66		
	1. 1950/2426W tender, has slide valve guide, silver RS *773* on cab/white, HS *Lionel Line*s lettering on tender	(4)	**1800**
	2. 1964/736W tender, no slide valve guide/larger, thicker *773* RS in white on cab/HS *Pennsylvania* on tender	(4)	**1000**
	3. 1965,66, same as 65 version but with *New York Central* on 773W tender	(4)	**1200**
2046	4-6-4 2046W 50,53		
	1. Early 1950, *2046* RS in silver/metal TT	(3+)	**275**
	2. Later 1950, *2046* HS in white/metal TT	(3+)	**275**
	3. 1953/2046 HS in white/plastic TT	(3)	**250**
2055	4-6-4 2046W, 6026W, S, MT 53-56		
	1. 1953, *2055* RS in silver/6026W	(3)	**250**
	2. 1954-56, *2055* HS in white/2046W	(2)	**225**
2055	4-6-4 6026W Blue Boy's Train (Locomotive only)		*****
2056	4-6-4 2046W S (*Lionel Lines* in larger lettering than 50-51 2046W) 52	(3)	**350**
2065	4-6-4 2046W,6026W, S, MT 54-56		
	1. 1954, *2065* RS in silver, 2046W	(3+)	**275**▲
	2. 1955,56, *2065* HS in white, 6026W	(2)	**250**▼

K-4 Pacific Type

675	2-6-2 *Lionel Lines* 47-49		
	1. Early 47, *675* HS on boiler front, Baldwin disc drivers, 2466WX, 2466T	(4)	**250**
	2. Late 47, red decal *5690* on boiler front RS on cab, 2466WX, 2466T	(3)	**200**
	3. 48, 2466WX/2466T	(3)	**200**
	4. 49, 6466WX	(3)	**200**

675	2-6-4 2046W Sintered iron spoked drivers, 5690 decal 52	(3+)	**200**
2025	2-6-2 2466WX,6466WX Die-cast trailing truck, Baldwin disc drivers 47-49		
	1. Early 47, 2025 HS on boiler front, 2466WX	(3)	**250**
	2. Later 47, red *5690* decal, 2466WX 2025 RS on cab	(2)	**150**
	3. 48,49 6466WX	(2)	**150**
2025	2-6-4 6466WX No MT, Spoked drivers, 5690 or 6200 on red decal 52	(2)	**125**
2026X	2-6-2 6466T Same as 2025 but no smoke U49	(5)	**400**
2035	2-6-4 6466W MT, Spoked drivers, stamped four-wheel trailing truck 50,51	(3)	**175**

Streamlined 2-6-4

221	2-6-4 221W,221T *New York Central* 46,47		
	1. Gray/aluminum-colored wheels/46	(5)	**400**▲
	2. Gray/black wheels/46	(3)	**200**
	3. Black/black drivers with nickel rims	(3)	**200**

Prairie Type

224	2-6-2 2466W,2466T 45,46		
	1. Black handrails, 1945 (4) **250** 2. Stainless handrails, 1946	(3)	**175**
637	2-6-42046W Magnetraction, 2037 boiler casting 59-63	(3+)	**175**
1666	2-6-2 2466WX,2466T Number plates, Nickel-rimmed drivers 46	(2+)	**130**
1666	2-6-2 2466WX, RS number U47	(3+)	**150**
2016	2-6-4 6026W Same as 2037, no Magnetraction or smoke 55,56	(3)	**200**
2018	2-6-4 6026W,6026T,1130T Smoke, no Magnetraction 56-59	(2)	**150**▲
2018	2-6-4 6026W Blue Boy's Train		*
2026	2-6-2 6466WX Wire handrails, smoke 48,49		
	1. Visible smoke-unit wire, 1948	(3)	**150**
	2. Hidden smoke-unit wire, 1949	(3)	**150**

95

2018 Boys Train

2026	2-6-4 6466W,6466T,6066T Cast handrails, smoke, no MT 51-53	(2)	**150**
2029	2-6-4 1060T,243W 64-66	(2)	**225**
2029	2-6-4 243W *PRR* markings 68,69	(4)	**350▲**
2036	2-6-4 6466W Magnetraction, no smoke 50	(2)	**225▲**
2037	2-6-4 6066T,6026T 53-64 6026W,243W 57-63	(2)	**150**

2037-500	2-6-4 1130T-500 Pink Girl's Loco, Either RS or HS numbers. NDV 57,58	(4+)	**1000**

Scout and Scout Type

233	243W, 233W, S, HL, MT 61,62	(3)	**250**
234	Not known to exist but 234W does exist		
235	1130T, S, HL, MT U61	(4)	**150**
236	1130T, 1050T, S, HL, MT 61,62	(3)	**100▲**

237	1130T, S, HL 63-66				
	1. Narrow white stripe	(3) **115▲**	2. Thick white stripe	(4)	**115▲**

238	243W, 63,64		(3)	100▲
239	243W, 242T HS and RS numbers. RS rarer but NDV 65,66		(2)	100▲
240	242T, 2P, S,HL, RT *Sears* 9820 U64		(4)	325▼
241	1130T Diecast, S, 1 RT *JC Penney* U65			
	1. Thick white stripe (4) **165**	2. Narrow white stripe	(2)	120
242	1130T, 1062T, 1060T 62-66			
	1. Thin-sided walkway (2) **75**	2. Thick-sided walkway	(2)	75
243	243W, HL, RT 60		(3)	100
244	244T, 1130T, S, HL 60,61		(2)	75
245	1130T Timken trucks, 2P U59		(4)	225▲
246	1130T, 244T, HL, MT 59-61,A62		(1)	60

247	247T, S, No MT Blue stripe *B&O* A60,A61 Also came with uncataloged whistle tender	(3)	125
248	1130T U58	(4)	175▲
249	250T Red stripe/*Pennsylvania* liquid smoke unit 58	(4)	100
250	250T Red stripe/*Pennsylvania* 57	(3)	100

POSTWAR

251	1130T, 244T slope back, U66	(4+)	400

1001	1001T Only plastic Scout locomotive 48 Some diecast 1101s show up rubber-stamped *1001*				
	1. White HS *1001* on cab (3) **60**	2. Silver RS *1001* on cab	(4)	125
	3. Diecast 1101 RS *1001* (4) **150▲**			
1050	0-4-0 1050T U59		(4+)	225▲

97

1060	1060T A60,A61	(3)	40▼
1061	1061T, 1062T A63,A64,69		
	1. 0-4-0/no tire on drive wheel/1061T	(2)	40▼
	2. 0-4-0/1062-50/1061T, tire on drive wheel	(2)	40▼
	3. 2-4-2/tire on drive wheel/1062T	(4)	40▼
	4. 2-4-2/tire on drive wheel/ number printed on paper and glued to cab, one geared drive wheel instead of two	(4)	90
1062	1061T, 1062T 63,64		
	1. No tire on drive wheel/1061T	(2)	40
	2. Tire on drive wheel (1062-50)/1062T	(3)	50
1101	1001T Scout, diecast, 3P U48		
	1. Heat-stamped 1101 (2) **75** 2. RS 1001	(4+)	150▲
1110	1001T Scout, diecast 49,51,52		
	1. Wire handrails (3) **60** 2. No wire handrails	(2)	50
	3. Same with hole in boiler front over light, silver reverse lever	(3)	75
1120	1001T Scout 50	(2)	65
1130	1130T, 6066T 53,54		
	1. Plastic boiler/3P/1130T or 6066T	(2)	60
	2. Die-cast boiler/3P/6066T	(4)	250
1654	1654T, 1654W, Diecast, 3P 46,47	(3)	60
1655	6654W, Diecast, 3P 48,49	(3)	60
2034	6066T,3P 52	(3)	80▲
6110	6001T, Diecast, 2P, MT, Smoke, no light 50	(3)	60

Switchers

1615	0-4-0 1615T No bell, back-up light, or handrails 55-57		
	1. Silver RS numbers, early 1955	(3+)	275
	2. White HS numbers, later 1955-57	(2)	200▼

1625	0-4-0 1625T No bell, back-up light, or handrails, dummy front coupler 58	(4)	450▲
1656	0-4-0 6403B Tender has handrails, back-up light, and bell. 48,49 Some come misnumbered 6043B.		
	1. Sans-serif numerals on cab & *Lionel Lines* lettering on tender condensed	(4)	550
	2. Serif numerals on cab and lettering on tender elongated	(4)	550
1665	0-4-0 2403B Similar to prewar 1662. Usually found with red and green marker lights broken. Tender has handrails, back-up light, and bell. Number rubber-stamped in silver on cab/elongated heat-stamped lettering on tender	(5)	750

1656 0-4-0 variation 2 (top), 1656 0-4-0 variation 1 (bottom)

Turbines

671	6-8-6 671W 46-49		
	1. Dbl worm drive, horz motor, 671W 46	(3)	**250**
	2. Sgl worm drive, slanted motor 671W 47	(3)	**300**
	3. 2671W with back-up lights early 48	(5)	**500**▲
	4. 2671W no back-up lights later 48 and 49	(2)	**300**
671(671RR)	6-8-6 2046W-50 No Magnetraction S 52	(4)	**400**
	This version came with or without RR (re-run) printed below 671. NDV		
671R	6-8-6 4671W Engine and tender only. White on black 46-48 electronic control decals. 671R on box only. *Electronic Control Set*	(4)	**350**▼
681	6-8-6 50,51,53		
	1. 2671W, 12-wheel tender 50, 51	(3)	**400**
	2. 2046-50, 8-wheel tender 53	(3)	**250**
 **682**	6-8-6 2046W-50 White stripe and oiler linkage 54,55	(4)	**500**
2020	6-8-6 2020W, 2466WX 027 gauge version of 671 Double worm drive/horizontal motor 46	(3)	**300**
2020	6-8-6 2020W,6020W Single worm drive & slanted motor 47-49	(3)	**225**
4681	6-8-6 4681W 50	**Not known to exist**	

POSTWAR

99

Passenger Cars
The General Cars

1865	**Western & Atlantic** Yellow/brown 59-62	(2)	75
1866	**Western & Atlantic** Yellow/brown 59-62	(2)	75
1875	**Western & Atlantic** Yellow/Tuscan 59,60	(4+)	500
1875W	**Western & Atlantic** Yellow/Tuscan, whistle 59-62	(4)	275
1876	**Western & Atlantic** Yellow/brown 59-62	(2)	150
1885	**Western & Atlantic** *Sears,* Blue/black/white U60	(4)	500

Sheet-Metal Cars

Note: Sets consist of 2 Pullmans and 1 Observation. Cars came with both silver and white lettering. Silver is rarer. Prices are for white lettering. Add 20% if silver lettering.

2430	Pullman Blue/silver 46,47	(3)	100
2431	Observation Blue/silver 46,47	(3)	100
2440	Pullman Green/cream 46,47	(3)	65
2441	Observation Green/cream 46,47	(3)	65
2442	Pullman Brown/gray 46-48	(3)	80
2443	Observation Brown/gray 46-48	(3)	80
6440	Pullman Green/cream 48,49	(3+)	75
6441	Observation Green/cream 48,49	(3+)	75
6442	Pullman Brown/gray 49	(3+)	80
6443	Observation Brown/gray 49	(3+)	80

Streamline Passenger Cars (Small)

Green/yellow 48,49 ▲

2400	**Maplewood** Pullman		(4)	175
2401	**Hillside** Observation		(4)	175
2402	**Chatham** Pullman		(4)	175

Aluminum/blue (no lights) 64,65 ▲
2404	**Santa Fe** Vista Dome		(3)	90

2405	**Santa Fe** Pullman		(3)	90
2406	**Santa Fe** Observation		(3)	75

Aluminum/blue 66 ▲
2408	**Santa Fe** Vista Dome		(3)	90
2409	**Santa Fe** Pullman		(3)	90
2410	**Santa Fe** Observation		(3)	90

Aluminum/blue/blue stripe 59-63 ▲
2412	**Santa Fe** Vista Dome		(3)	110
2414	**Santa Fe** Pullman		(3)	110
2416	**Santa Fe** Observation		(3)	90

Aluminum/black 52,53 ▲
2421	**Maplewood** Pullman		(3)	110
2422	**Chatham** Pullman		(3)	110
2423	**Hillside** Observation		(3)	110
2429	**Livingston** Pullman 52,53 only		(4)	125

Aluminum/black/black stripe gray roof 50,51 ▲
2421	**Maplewood** Pullman		(4)	110
2422	**Chatham** Pullman		(4)	110
2423	**Hillside** Observation		(4)	110

Aluminum/red 54-58 ▲
2432	**Clifton** Vista Dome		(3)	100
2434	**Newark** Pullman		(3)	100
2435	**Elizabeth** Pullman		(4)	160
2436	**Summit** Observation		(3)	100
2436	**Mooseheart** Observation 57,58 only		(4)	90

POSTWAR

101

Aluminum/red/red stripe 56 ▲

2442	**Clifton** Vista Dome	(4)	150
2444	**Newark** Pullman	(4)	150
2445	**Elizabeth** Pullman (sold separately) 56	(5)	450
2446	**Summit** Observation	(4)	150

Yellow/red 50 ▼

2481	**Plainfield** Pullman	(5)	325
2482	**Westfield** Pullman	(5)	325
2483	**Livingston** Observation	(5)	325

Streamline Passenger Cars (Large)

Presidential 62-66

2521	**McKinley** Observation	(4)	150
2522	**Harrison** Vista Dome	(4)	150
2523	**Garfield** Pullman	(4)	150
2530	**Railway Express Agency** Baggage Car 54-60		
	1. Small doors (3) 250 2. Large doors	(5)	**700**▲

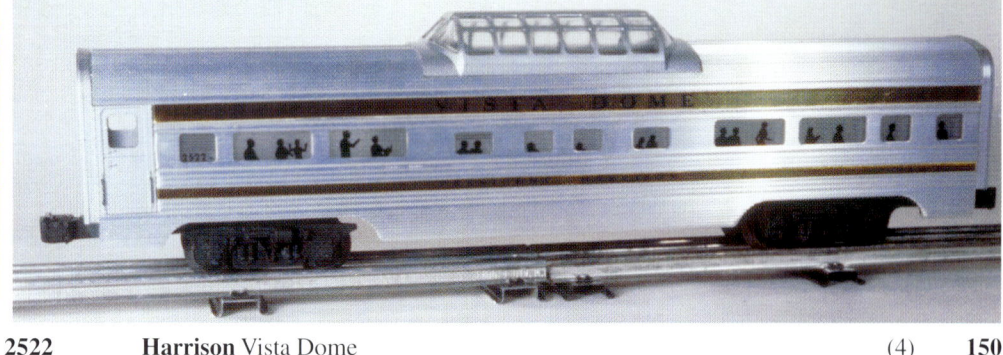

Super Speedliner 52-60 ▲

Note: Some plates have dots, others don't. Different wiring methods are used to connect the lights to the pick-up assemblies. These minor variations don't affect the price. Some plates are glued on, some are secured by rivets; others by hex nuts. If hex nuts add $50. per car. The other important variation has to do with the channel along the side of the car. Most are ribbed. A few are smooth. If smooth, add 20% to the prices listed.

2531	**Silver Dawn** Observation	(3)	175
2532	**Silver Range** Vista Dome	(3)	175
2533	**Silver Cloud** Pullman	(3)	175
2534	**Silver Bluff** Pullman	(3)	175

Presidential Set (top), Congressional Set (bottom)

Congressional 55,56 ▲
2541	**Alexander Hamilton** Observation	(4)	400
2542	**Betsy Ross** Vista Dome	(4)	400
2543	**William Penn** Pullman	(4)	400
2544	**Molly Pitcher** Pullman	(4)	400

Canadian Pacific 57
2551	**Banff Park** Observation	(4)	375
2552	**Skyline 500** Vista Dome	(4)	375
2553	**Blair Manor** (separate sale only)	(5)	700 ▲

2554	**Craig Manor** (separate sale only)	(5)	700 ▲

Super Chief 59-61 ▲

2561	**Vista Valley** Observation	(4)	350
2562	**Regal Pass** Vista Dome	(4)	350
2563	**Indian Falls** Pullman	(4)	350

Irvington Cars 46-50 ▲

Note: Prices for cars with plain window inserts. Add $75 -$125 for Like New with all boxes and components, including inserts with people in silhouette but beware of reproductions. The original Irvington cars had heat-stamped lettering, and it has dulled with age. Reproductions have silk-screened lettering, which is bright, and the rivets around the area of the lettering have been removed to accommodate the silk screen.

2625	**Irvington**	(4)	350
2625	**Manhattan** 47 only	(4+)	400
2625	**Madison** 47 only	(4+)	425

2627	**Madison**	(4)	325
2628	**Manhattan**	(4)	325

POSTWAR

103

Rolling Stock
Action and Animated Cars

Note: See also Military and Space. Operating cars are in there normal sections.

3357   **Cop and Hobo Car** Also known as Hydraulic Platform Maintenance 62-64
Car. Comes with cop, hobo, and platform. First reissued in 1982 as 7901
1. Blue/white	(3)	**100**	2. Aqua/white	(4)	**150**
3. Prototype (Vol. 5)		**5P**			

3370   **Sheriff and Outlaw** 61-64
1. Green/yellow   (3)   **90**
2. Decal version (Vol. 5)   **5P**
3. Arch-bar trucks/blue car/no lettering   **5P**
4. Same but green car/no lettering   **5P**

3376   **Operating Giraffe Car** 60-64, 69
1. Blue car/white lettering   (2)   **75**   2. Green car/yellow lettering   (3)   **150**

3. Blue car/yellow lettering   (4) **300▲**   4. Blue car/no lettering   (3)   **175**
5. Mock-up (Vol. 5)   **5+**   6. Decal version mock-up   **5+**
Note: Giraffe comes two ways: yellow with brown spots and solid yellow. NDV.

3386   **Operating Giraffe Car** U66
1. Blue, white lettering   (3)   **125**   2. Bongo and Bobo (Vol. 4)   **5P**

3424   **Wabash** Two tell-tale poles 56-58
1. Blue/white/blue man   (3)   **100**   2. Same but white man   (4)   **125**

3434   **Operating Chicken Car** (Poultry Dispatch) Brown/white 59,60 64-68
1. Blue sweeper man   (4)   **250**   2. Gray sweeper man   (3)   **175**

3435   **Aquarium Car** Green (reissued in 1981 as 9308) 59-62
1. Yellow lettering/no circle around L/no tank designation   (3)   **275**

2. Same as 1 but gold lettering   (3+)   **300**

POSTWAR

104

3. Gold lettering/circle around L/*Tank No. 1* and *Tank No. 2* (5) **1200**
4. Same as 3 but no circle around L (5) **800▲**
5. White lettering **FAKE**

3444	**Erie Animated Gondola** Red/white (reissued in 1980 as 9307) 57-59	(2)	**100**
6473	**Horse Transport Rodeo Car** with red & brown lettering 62-66, 69		
	1. Light yellow (3) **35** 2. Dark yellow	(3)	**35**

Boxcars

638-2361	**Van Camps Pork & Beans** Scout-Type, Bank slot U62,63		
	1. Light red/white-yellow (4) **60** 2. Dark red/white-yellow	(3+)	**50**
1004	**Baby Ruth** Scout-Type Orange/blue 48,49,51,52		
	1. Blue outlined *Baby Ruth* (1) **15** 2. Solid blue *Baby Ruth*	(1)	**15**
X2454	**Pennsylvania** 9 1/4", Orange/black, Early-Style 46		

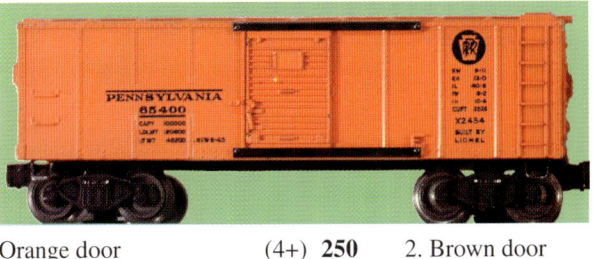

	1. Orange door (4+) **250** 2. Brown door	(3+)	**225**
X2454	**Baby Ruth** Orange/black lettering/brown door, Early-Style 46,47	(2+)	**65**
X2458	**Pennsylvania** Auto box Dark brown/white 45-48	(3+)	**100**
2758	**Pennsylvania** Auto box U45,46	(3)	**100**
	Note: Cataloged as 2458. Lionel had left-over 2758 bodies so they were fitted with a postwar frame and trucks and sold as a 2458.		
3428	**United States Mail** Type 3, Operating, Red/white/blue 59,60,65,66 w/gray man or blue man. NDV	(3)	**175▲**
3454	**PRR Merchandise Car** 46,47		
	Note: Baby Ruth on original cartons but not on reproductions.		
	1. Silver/blue (3) **175** 2. Silver/red	(5)	**1000**

3464	**AT&SF** Early-Style Operating 49-52			
	1. Orange/black, brown painted door 1949 Information requested			*
	2. Orange/black, blackened metal door 1949		(3)	50
	3. Unpainted orange plastic/black plastic doors		(4)	80
	4. *NYC* Tan/White		(5)	1000 ▲
X3464	**New York Central** Early-Style Operating 50-52		(3)	60

3474	**Western Pacific** Silver/black Early-Style Operating 52,53		(4)	100
3484	**Pennsylvania** Type 1 Tuscan/white Operating 53,U54			
	1. Non-painted man 53 (2) **90**	2. Flesh tones painted on		(3) 90
3484-25	**AT&SF** Orange Operating 54,56			
	1. HS black/Type 1 2A 2B (5) **1500**	2. RS white/Type 1		(3) 150
	3. HS white/Type 1 2A 2B (4) **175**			

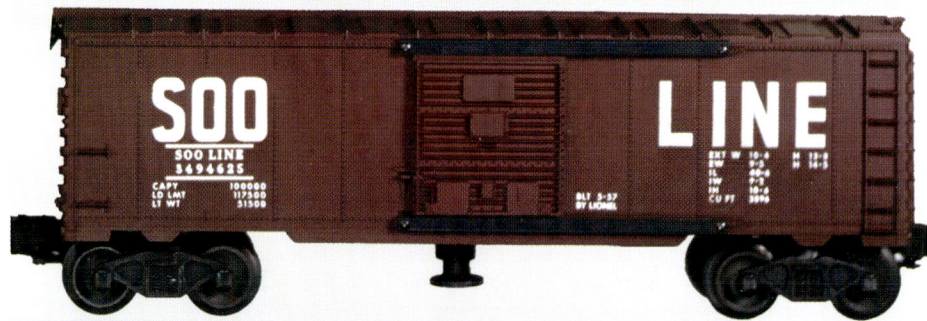

3484 Santa Fe (top), 3494-625 Soo Line (center), 3494-550 Monon (bottom)

3494-1	**NYC Pacemaker** Type 2A Gray/red/white Operating 55			(4)	**175**
3494-150	**Missouri Pacific** Type 2B Blue/gray/yellow door Operating 56			(4)	**175**
3494-275	**State of Maine** Type 2B Operating 56-58				
	1. Line above and below B.A.R. and 3494275			(3)	**150**
	2. No line above or below B.A.R. and 3494275 omitted, 56 only			(4)	**250**
3494-550	**Monon** Type 2B Maroon/white Operating 57,58				
	1. Built Date (4) **400**	2. No built date		(4+)	**425**
3494-625	**Soo** Type 2B Tuscan/white Operating 57,58			(4)	**450▲**
3854	**Pennsylvania Merchandise Car** Dark brown/white, 11" long 46,47				
	1. Brown door 46 only (4+) **600**	2. Black door 46,47		(4)	**500**
4454	**Baby Ruth** Orange/black lettering, Early-Style 46-48			(4)	**250**
	brown-painted doors, *Electronic Set*				
	Note: Black doors questionable				

From top left: 6014 Airex, 6014 Wix, 6044 Airex, 6014 Chun King, 638-2361 Van Camps, 6024 Whirlpool

6004	**Baby Ruth** Orange/blue Scout-Type Blue outlined only 50			(3)	**15**
6014	**Airex** Red/yellow-white Scout-Type SM59, A60				
	1. Regular style lettering (3) **50**	2. Bold style lettering		(4)	**75**
X6014	**Baby Ruth** *PRR* Scout-Type 51,52,54-56				
	1. White/black 51,52 (2) **15**	2. Red/white 54-56		(2)	**15**
6014	**Bosco** Scout-Type 58				
	1. White/black (4) **75**	2. Red/white		(2)	**15**
	3. Orange/black (3) **15**				
6014	**Campbell Soup** Red/white Scout-Type U69				*****
6014	**Chun King** Red/white Scout-Type U56			(4)	**125**
6014	**Frisco** White/black 57,58				
	1. White/black (1) **15**	2. Red/white		(2)	**15**
	3. Orange/black (4) **30**				
6014	**Wix** White/red Scout-Type U59			(4)	**150**
6014-85	**Frisco** Scout-Type 69				
	1. Orange/bright blue (2) **20**	2. Orange/dark blue		(2)	**20**
	3. In Hagerstown box (4) **50**				
6014-335	**Frisco** White/black Scout-Type 63-66,68				
	1. With coin slot (4) **125**	2. Without coin slot		(1)	**15**

6024	**Nabisco Shredded Wheat** Orange/black, Scout-Type 57				
	1. No bank slot	(2)	**25**	2. Bank slot	**5P**
	3. Orange/brn, no bank slot	(4)	**75**		
6024-60	**RCA Whirlpool** Red/wht Scout-Type U57,58			(4)	**85**
6034	**Baby Ruth** *PRR* Scout-Type 53,54				
	1. Orange/dark blue	(2)	**15**	2. Orange/blue (1)	**15**
6044	**Airex** Scout-Type U A59,A60				
	1. Blue/yellow-white	(1)	**25**	2. Dark blue/yellow-white (5)	**350**
	3. Teal blue	(4)	**150**		
6044-1X	Scout-Type Blue Plastic/No lettering, *McCall/Nestle's* decal			(5)	**800**
	Note: Reproduction decals available				
6050	**Libby's Tomato Juice** Scout-Type 63,63				
	1. With green stems	(2)	**40**	2. Without green stems (4)	**250**
	3. Without white lines between tomatoes			(3)	**100**
6050	**Lionel Savings Bank** White/green Scout-Type 61				
	1. *Built by Lionel* spelled out	(4)	**100**	2. *Blt by Lionel* (3)	**35**
6050	**Swift** Red/white Scout-Type 62,63				
	1. Bank slot	(2)	**25**	2. No bank slot	**5X**
	3. Minus two rows of rivets left of door			(3)	**35**
6352-1	**Pacific Fruit Express** Type 2B Operating 55-57				
	1. Lettering with *CU. FT.*	(3)	**100**	2. No *CU. FT.* (4)	**150**
	3. As replacement accessory (must have box), came with 352 Ice Depot			(5)	**2000***
	and 5 cubes of ice. Original cubes have bubbles, reproductions don't.				
6428	**US Mail** Red/white/blue w/HS Black/white lettering 60, 61, 65, 66				
	1. Lettering on both sides	(3)	**60**	2. Lettering on one side (4)	**75**
6454	**Baby Ruth** Dark orange/black lettering/brown doors Early-Style 48			(4+)	**300**

6454 NYC variation 2 (top), variation 1 (center), variation 3 (bottom)

6454	**New York Central** Early-Style 48,49		
	1. Brown/white/brown door	(2)	75
	2. Bright orange/black/brown door	(4)	200
	3. Burnt orange/white/brown door	(2)	75
6454	**Santa Fe** Orange/black lettering brown doors Early-Style U48,49	(2)	75
6454	**Southern Pacific** Early-Style Made in 49,52 and 53 but not cataloged 50,51		
	1. Brown/white/large circular herald with 1/16" break in outside circle between *R* and *N* 1949	(4)	85
	2. Same with small herald no break in outside circle 1950	(3)	75
	3. Reddish brown/white/small herald/no break/51-52	(3)	75
X6454	**Erie** Brown/white/brown doors Early-Style U49, 50-53	(3)	65
X6454	**Pennsylvania** Tuscan/white Early-Style U49-53		
	1. Tuscan doors (4) **100** 2. Black plastic doors	(4+)	200

6464 Boxcars

The 6464 boxcars are the most popular category of Lionel's postwar rolling stock. Their splashy graphics make them some of the best-looking cars Lionel ever made in the postwar era. There are so many variations – both major and minor – that they present an endless challenge to collectors. The category also contains some of the rarest and most valuable items of the postwar era.

To understand the variations, the collector must be familiar with the different body and door types that were used. The identification and labeling of the different body types, which has become the accepted standard of the hobby, was first published by Charles Weber of Norristown, Pennsylvania.

Doors used in 1953, 1954, and early 1955 had a single, large block in the middle. Those used in 1955 through 1969 had three additional blocks. The first door is called the 1953 single block (SB) door and the second is called the 1955 multiple block (MB) door.

Body Type 1, SB Door

In 1953, the first body type had four rows of rivets to the left of the door (rows 1 through 4) and four rows of rivets to the right of the door (rows 5 through 8). The rows to the right of the door were not interrupted but three of the rows to the left of the door were interrupted by smooth areas. The rivets were removed because they interfered with the heat-stamping process used in applying graphics. Row 4 was the only row on the left side that was not interrupted.

The Type 1 body type comes with the SB door only.

Body Type 2A, SB Door

In 1954, the increase in the size of graphics necessitated more changes in the rivet detail. The middle portion of row 2 and all of row 7 were removed.

Most Type 2As come with the SB door but some 2As were still being used in 1955 after the MB door was introduced so Type 2A exists with both SB and MB doors. The most common examples of Type 2A with MB doors are the 6464-125 NYC, 6464-150 Missouri Pacific and the 6464-275 State of Maine.

Body Type 2B, MB Door

In 1955, the only change on the body had to do with the roof. The Pacific Fruit Express car was introduced and it used the same mold as the 6464 boxcars. To make the PFE, Lionel altered the die to make an opening for the ice hatch. When the die was used again to make 6464 boxcars, a plug was inserted in the die to cover the opening but a thin plastic ridge was discernible on the roof. This third body type is called 2B.

It was a transition year for doors. Lionel started using the multiple-block doors about mid-way through the year. So Type 2B exists with both MB and SB doors.

Body Type 3, MB Door

A new mold was introduced in 1958. The result was a boxcar made of lighter weight plastic with ribs on the underside of the roof. The thin line from the ice hatch was gone and the rivet detail changed slightly, for no apparent reason. The change had to do with row 7. Two rivets were added to the top and two rivets were added to the bottom.

Body Type

In 1960, the number of rivets changed in row 3. They were almost all removed.
As with other categories, we recommend the collector concern himself with only major variations, i.e. those that can be readily seen on the exterior of the car and those generally accepted by the majority of experienced collectors.

6464-1	**Western Pacific** Type 1 53,54					
	1. Silver/blue	(3)	**125**	2. Silver/blue inside roof ribs	(4+)	**450**
	3. Silver/red	(5)	**1800**	4. Silver/black		**5P**
	5. Orange/white		**5P**	6. Orange/silver		**5P**
	7. Powder blue/black		**5P**	8. Dark blue/white		**5P**
	9. Orange/black		**5P**			
	10. Silver/light blue feather RS both sides					*
6464-25	**Great Northern** Type 1 53,54					
	1. Orange/white	(2)	**100**	2. Tuscan/white		**5P**
	3. Same, red/green decals				(5)	**600***
	To be legitimate, decal must be applied over smooth surface. If traces of heat-stamping can be detected under decal, it was applied outside the Lionel factory.					

From top left: 6464-4 WP, 6464-25 GN, 6464-50, 6464-75, 6464-125, 6464-175, 225 SP, 6464-250 WP

6464-50	**Minneapolis & St. Louis** Type 1 53-56				
	1. Tuscan/white	(2)	**85**	2. Dark green/gold	**5P**
	3. Tuscan/yellow		**5P**	4. Light bluish green/black	**5P**
	5. Copper primer/Tuscan and white			(5)	**500***

6464-75	**Rock Island** Dark green/gold 53,54,69				
	1. Type 1 53,54	(3)	**100**	2. Type 4 69	(2)	**100**

6464-100	**Western Pacific** 54,55		
	1. Orange/white/blue feather *1954* Type 1	(5+)	**6000**
	2. Same but no *1954* Type 1	(5)	**2000***
	3. Silver/black/yellow feather Type 1 54	(4)	**225**
	4. Silver/black/yellow feather Type 2A 54,55	(3)	**150**
	Long feather or short feather NDV		
	5. Orange/white or gray/blue feather Type 2A 54,55	(4)	**650**

6464-125	**New York Central** 54-56				
	1. Gray-red/HS white, gray top row of rivets, SB no cedilia Type 2A 54	(4)	**150**		
	2. Gray-red/RS white red top row of rivets, SB, cedilia, Type 2A 55,56	(3)	**125**		
	3. Same as 2 but no cedilia	(4)	**200**	4. Same as 2 but MB	(3)	**125**
	5. Lilac/red Type 2B		**5X**	6. Pink/red Type 2B		**5X**

6464-150	**Missouri Pacific** 54,55,57

Note: The 6464-150 has more variations than any other boxcar. The seven listed below represent a reasonable number to collect. The number is limited to keep the collector (and the authors) from going crazy. The variations listed are in chronological order. Many more variations – all worth about $150 – were made by Lionel by interchanging the various kinds of doors, using grooves, not using grooves, changing the sizes of the Eagle and using different shades of blue paint and plastic.

	1. Blue-gray/RS black, gray stripe on SB door, no *XME*, 3/4-inch *Eagle* and *New 3-54* to right, 6464-150 to left, no grooves, no *Built by Lionel*, blue plastic/painted gray stripe, Type 2A, early 54 first run	(3)	**150**
	2. *New 3/54* moves to the left, *BLT by Lionel* and *XME* are added to the right, late 54 second run	(3)	**150**
	3. White shell painted blue-gray, grooves, 5/8-inch *Eagle*, *BLT by Lionel* and *XME* to right, *BLT 3/54* and *6464-150* to left, gray stripe on SB door, early 55	(4)	**350**
	4. Same as 3 but blue plastic shell early 55	(3)	**125**
	5. Blue-gray, RS black solid yellow SB door, *XME*, 5/8 inch *Eagle* to right, *New 3-54* and *6464-150* to left, grooves, *Built by Lionel,* MP seal in first panel to left of door, blue plastic, painted gray stripe, Type 2A, 55	(5)	**1250**

110

      6. Same as 4 but white plastic SB door painted yellow, last run 1955   (4) **200**
      7. Blue-gray, RS black/solid yellow MB door, *XME*, 1/2 inch *Eagle* and   (2) **125**
        New 3-54 to left, *6464-150* to right, no grooves, *Built by Lionel*,
        gray plastic painted blue, Type 2B, 57

6464-175   **Rock Island** 54,55
      1. Silver/blue   (3) **150**   2. Silver/black   (5) **1200**

6464-200   **Pennsylvania** Tuscan/white 54,55,69
      1. Type 1   (4) **175**   2. Type 2A   (4) **175**
      3. Type 4   (3) **125**

6464-225   **Southern Pacific** Black/white 54-56
      1. Red/yell herald Type 2A   (3+) **150**   2. Red/yellow herald Type 1   (5) **1500***
      3. White herald Type 2A   (5) **2000***

6464-250   **Western Pacific** Orange/white 66
      1. Type 4   (4) **250**   2. Type 3   (5) **1000**

6464-275   **State of Maine** 55,57-59
      Note: 2A is HS, 2B both HS and RS. NDV
      1. Red-white-blue/white-black Type 2A, 2B   (3) **100**
      2. White body, painted red and blue stripes, solid red door Type 2A   (4) **250**
      3. Red-white-blue, no 6464-275, same shell used on 3494-275 Type 2B   (4+) **250**
      4. Red-white-blue Type 3   (3) **100**

6464-300   **Rutland** 55,56
      Note: Fakes have devalued #5 and #6
      1. Green-yellow/RS green-yellow, yellow plastic door Type 2A   (3) **175**
      2. Same, white plastic door painted yellow   (3) **175**
      3. Irregular spacing HS MB Type 2B 56   (4) **175**
      4. Gray body painted green/yellow   (4) *****
      5. Yellow body and door models, RS yellow-green, yellow and green   (5) **600**
        SB door, Type 2A
      6. Yellow body painted glossy green solid yellow plastic SB door,   (5) **1500***
        solid shield herald, Type 2A

From top left: 6464-100 WP variation 3, 6464-100 WP variation 4, 6464-150 variation 1, 6464-150 variation 6, 6464-275 variation 2, 6464-275 variation 1, 6464-300 variation 1, 6464-300 variation 2

6464-325   **Sentinel** Type 2B 56
      1. Normal production   (4) **800**   2. Decaled one side only   **5P**

Top row: 6464-325 Sentinel, 6464-350 MKT, 6464-375 Central of Georgia. Row 2: 6464-400 B&O, 6464-425 New Haven, 6464-425 New Haven. Row 3: 6464-450 Great Northern, 6464-475 B&M, 6464-500 Timken. Row 4: 6464-510 NYC, 6464-515 MKT, 6464-525 M&St. L. Row 5: 6464-650 D&RG, 6464-700 Santa Fe, 6464-725 New Haven, Row 6: 6464-725 New Haven, 6464-825 Alaska, 6464-900 NYC

6464-350	**Katy** Type 2B 56			
	1. Maroon/white	(4) **350**	2. Pink/black	**5X**
6464-375	**Central of Georgia** 56,57,66			
	Note: Types 2B and 4 come with both maroon and red lettering. NDV			
	1. Maroon plastic, painted silver oval & roof, red-white lettering 3-56 built date Type 2B 56,57	(3)		**125**
	2. No built date Type 4 66	(2)		**125**
	3. Gray plastic painted red, painted silver oval and roof, red/white lettering, 3-56 built date Type 4 66	(5)		**2000**
	4. Red decal lettering, silver oval Type 2B			**5P**
6464-400	**B&O Time-Saver** 56,57,69			
	1. Blue-silver-orange/blue-white, Built 5-54 Type 2B	(3+)		**150**
	2. Same, built 2-56 Type 2B	(4)		**200**
	3. Two different built dates: 5-54 on one side and 2-56 on the other Type 2B	(5)		**1500***
	4. Blue-silver-orange/blue-white Type 4	(3)		**125**
	5. *B&O* markings Timken colors Type 4	(5)		**1200***
	6. Solid green/white Type 4	(5)		**1200***
6464-425	**New Haven** Black/white 56-58			
	1. Half-serif N Type 2B 56,57 (3) **150**	2. Full-serif N Type 2B 57,58	(3)	**75**
	3. Type 3, 58 (2) **50**			
6464-450	**Great Northern** Olive-orange/yellow stripe 56,57,66			
	1. Type 2B (3+) **150**	2. Type 3	(5)	**1500***
	3. Type 4 (3) **125**			
	4. White lettering, white stripe Type 4			**FAKE**
	5. White lettering, yellow stripe Type 4			**FAKE**
6464-475	**Boston & Maine** 57-60,65,66,68			
	Note: This car comes in many different shades of blue w/ and w/o built dates (harder to find). NDV			
	1. Blue/black-white Type 2B	(2)		**75**
	2. Same but Type 3,4	(3)		**150**
	3. Purplish/black-white, gray mold, 66	(4)		**250**▲
	4. Same as 3 but blue mold	(4)		**400**

112

6468-1 Baltimore & Ohio (top), 6468x Baltimore & Ohio (bottom)

6464-500	**Timken** 57,58,69					
	1. Yellow/blue-gray Type 2B	(3+)	**150**	2. Decal markings Type 2B		**5P**
	3. Yellow/black Type 4	(3+)	**150**	4. Same as 3 but Type 3	(4)	**200**
	5. Yellow/red Type 4		**5X**	6. Green/white Type 4		**5X**
	7. Green/red Type 4		**5X**	8. Green/gold Type 4		**5X**
	9. Beige/black Type 3	(4+)	**400**▼			
6464-510	**NYC Pacemaker** Girl's Train, Type 2B 57,58					
	1. Bluish green/black	(4)	**800**	2. Sky blue/black	(5)	**900***
	3. Yellow/black		**5X**			
6464-515	**Katy** Girl's Train, Type 2B 57,58					
	1. Yellow/black	(4)	**800**	2. White/black	(5+)	*****
	3. Beige/black		**5P**	4. Blue/black		**5X**
6464-525	**Minneapolis & St. Louis** 57,58,54-66					
	1. Red/white Type 2B Gray mold				(2)	**75**
	2. Red/white Type 2B Black mold				(2)	**150**
	3. Red/white Type 3				(3)	**125**
	4. Red/white Type 4				(2)	**75**
	5. Red/yellow Type 2B					**5X**
	6. Red/yellow Type 4					**5X**
	7. Bright-pink purple/white Type 4					**5X**
	8. Raspberry-gray/white Type 4					**5X**
6464-650	**Rio Grande** Yellow-silver 57,58,66					
	Note: The rare painted yellow-roof version is on a gray Type 4 body mold. Type 2s with a yellow roof (unpainted) are created by removing the silver paint.					
	1. Black/roof painted silver/built date/Type 2B				(3)	**175**
	2. No built date Type 4				(3)	**175**
	3. Yellow-painted roof, built date Type 4				(5)	**1200**▼
6464-700	**Santa Fe** Red/white 61,66					
	1. Type 4	(3)	**150**	2. Type 3	(5)	**1500***
6464-725	**New Haven** 62-66,68,69					
	1. Orange/black Type 4 62-66, 68				(2)	**150**
	2. Black/white Type 4 69				(4)	**275**

POSTWAR

113

6464-825	**Alaska** 59, 60		
	Note: Types 3 and 4 came in both blue and gray body molds. NDV		
	1. Blue/yellow, yellow stripe, Type 3,4	(4)	**400**
	2. Blue/yellow, yellow stripe, yellow door Type 4	(5)	**350***
	3. Blue/white, white stripe, Type 3,4		**FAKE**
	4. Blue/white, yellow stripe, Type 3,4		**FAKE**
	5. Blue/white, white stripe, white door		**FAKE**
6464-900	**New York Central** 60-63, 65, 66		
	1. Jade green/black-red-white Type 4	(3)	**150**
	2. Same as #1 but w/black doors	(3)	**200**
	3. Same as #1 but Type 3	(5)	**1200***
	4. No red lettering or black trim, *NYC* Type 4		**5X**
	5. No red lettering or white date Type 4		**5X**
	6. Yellow/black-red-white Type 4		**5X**
6468-1	**Baltimore & Ohio** Auto box Blue/white 53-55	(3)	**85**
6468X	**Baltimore & Ohio** Auto box Tuscan/white, 027 *Santa Fe* Freight Set 55	(4+)	**475**

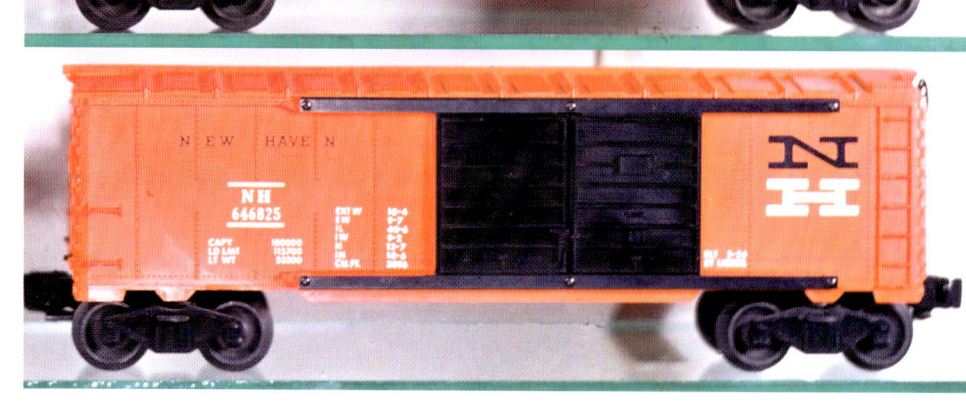

6468-25 New Haven variation 4 (top), variation 3 (center), variation 1 (bottom)

6468-25	**New Haven** Auto box 56-58		
	1. Black N with full serif, H in white, black doors	(2)	**100▼**
	2. Same, darker orange and Tuscan doors	(3)	**100▼**
	3. Black N with half serif, H in white	(2)	**100**
	4. White N with half serif, H in black	(4)	**350***
6530	**Fire Safety Training Car** 60, 61		
	1. Red/white (3) **125** 2. Black/white	(5)	**3000***

Cabooses
Bay Window

6517 Lionel Lines(top), 6517-75 Erie(bottom)

6517	**Lionel Lines** Red/white 55-59		
	1. *Lionel* underscored	(4)	**135**
	2. *Lionel* not underscored	(3)	**100**
6517-75	**Erie** Red/white 66	(5)	**500**
6517-1966	**Train Collectors Association** Orange/white U66	(4)	**475**▼

Early Cupola Type

2457	**Pennsylvania** Red/white 45-47		
	1. Tool box, generator, steps and 2 couplers, *Eastern Div.* lettering	(3)	**50**
	2. Same, no steps	(2)	**45**
	3. Brown/white left-over inventory from the prewar 2757 caboose.	(4)	**85**
2472	**Pennsylvania** Red/white, sintered iron wheels, one coupler, 45-47		
	1. Late 1945 trucks *Eastern Div.* lettering	(2)	**40**
	2. Late 1945 trucks without *Eastern Div.* lettering	(3)	**40**
	3. 1947 trucks without *Eastern Div.* lettering	(1)	**40**
4457	**Pennsylvania** Red/white, *Electronic Set* 46,47	(4)	**175**

POSTWAR

115

N5c Pennsy Type

6417	**Pennsylvania** Tuscan/white 53-57				
	1. *New York Zone*	(2)	**50**	2. No *New York Zone* (4)	**250**
6417-25	**Lionel Lines** Tuscan/white 54			(2)	**40**

6417-50	**Lehigh Valley** 54				
	1. Gray/red	(3)	**175**▲	2. Tuscan/white (5)	**1200**

6427 Lionel Lines   *6427-60 Virginian*

6427	**Lionel Lines** Tuscan/white 54-60		(2+)	**85**
6427-60	**Virginian** 58			
	Note: Reproduction Virginian cabooses exist. Originals are heat-stamped with rivet detail. Reproductions are silk-screened with rivet detail removed.			
	1. Blue/yellow (4) **350**▲ 2. Dark blue/white			**FAKE**
6427-500	**Pennsylvania** Sky blue/white, *Girl's Train* 57,58		(4)	**350**
6437	**Pennsylvania** Tuscan/white 61-68		(3)	**45**
6447	**Pennsylvania** Tuscan/white 63		(5)	**500**

Southern-Pacific Type

1007	**Lionel Lines** Red/white 48-52		(1)	**10**
2257	**SP** No light, 1 coupler, brake wheels U47,48			
	1. Bright red/white (2) **40** 2. Brown/white		(5)	**500**
2357	**SP** U47,48			
	Note: Though not in the 47 catalog, both the 2257 and 2357 were available in 1947.			
	1. Red with red stack (5) **600** 2. Brown with brown stack		(2)	**75**
4357	**SP** Brown/white Electronic Set 48		(4)	**125**
6007	**Lionel Lines** Red/white 50		(2)	**10**
	Note: 6007 and 6017 were the cheapest cabooses Lionel made other than Scout cabooses. Similar to the 6257 but without brakewheels. Usually unpainted plastic and no trim.			
6017	**Lionel Lines** Common, inexpensive caboose made in many colors 51-61 and shades. Major colors:			
	1. Red/white metal trucks (1) **10** 2. Tuscan/white metal trucks (2)			**10**
	3. Tuscan/wht Timken trucks (1) **10** 4. Lt Tuscan/wht Timken trucks (1)			**10**
	5. Brown/wht Timken trucks (1) **10** 6. Olive drab/U (5)			**375**
6017-50	**US Marine Corps** Blue/white Box marked 6017-60, 58		(3)	**75**
6017-85	**Lionel Lines** Gray/black		(3)	**60**

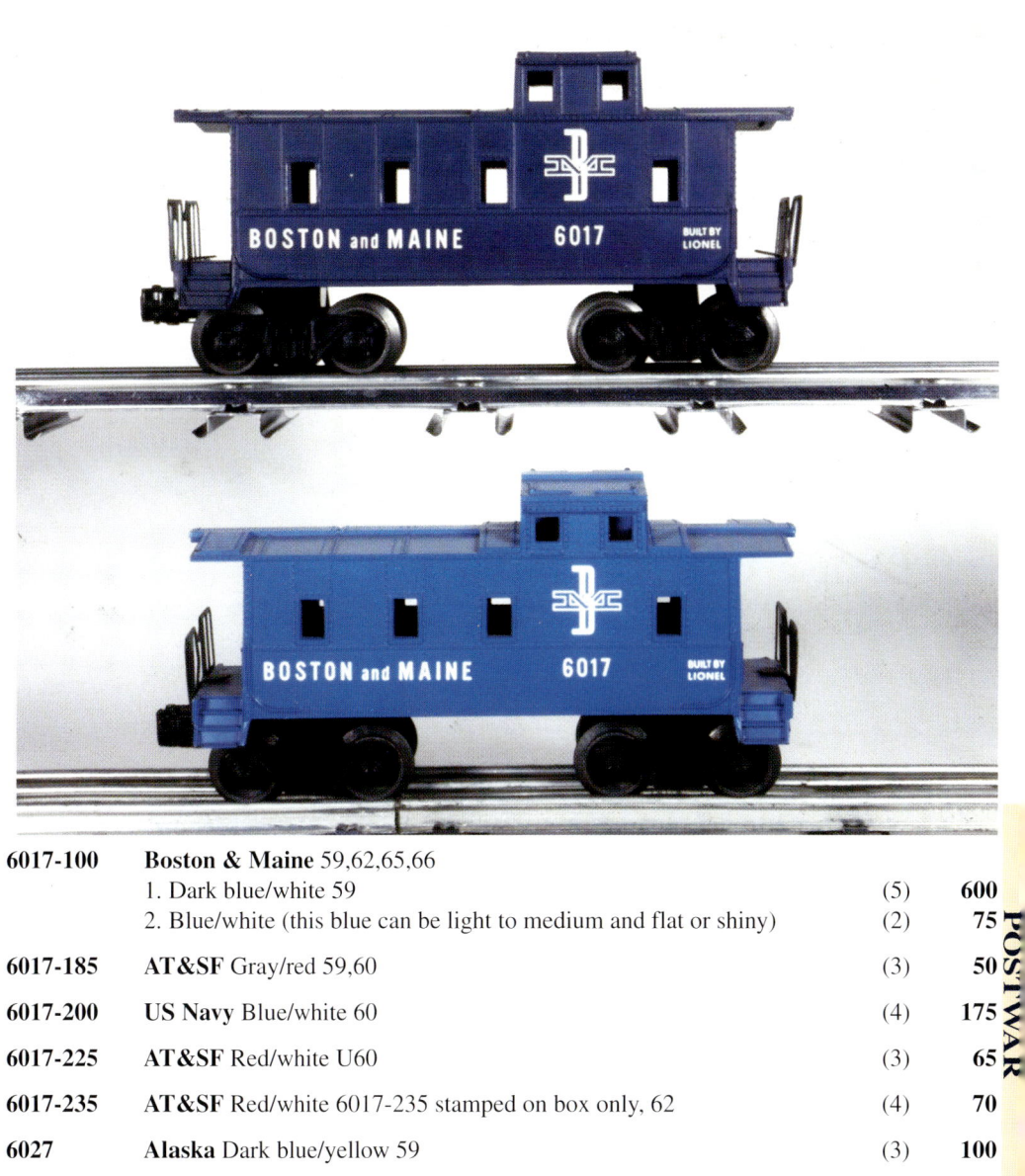

6017-100	**Boston & Maine** 59,62,65,66					
	1. Dark blue/white 59				(5)	**600**
	2. Blue/white (this blue can be light to medium and flat or shiny)				(2)	**75**
6017-185	**AT&SF** Gray/red 59,60				(3)	**50**
6017-200	**US Navy** Blue/white 60				(4)	**175**
6017-225	**AT&SF** Red/white U60				(3)	**65**
6017-235	**AT&SF** Red/white 6017-235 stamped on box only, 62				(4)	**70**
6027	**Alaska** Dark blue/yellow 59				(3)	**100**
6037	**Lionel Lines** 52-54					
	1. Brown/white	(1)	**10**	2. Light brown/white	(1)	**10**
	3. Tuscan/white	(2)	**25**	4. Red/white	(2)	**25**
6047	**Lionel Lines** 62					
	1. Various shades of red/wht	(1)	**10**	2. Unpainted Tuscan plastic	(4)	**40**
6057	**Lionel Lines** 59-62					
	1. Red/white	(1)	**10**	2. Brown/white	(3)	**100**
	3. Orange-red/white	(1)	**10**			
6057-50	**Lionel Lines** Orange/black 62,69					
	1. Regular production	(3)	**35**	2. TTOS 1969 convention 69	(3)	*****
6058	**Chesapeake & Ohio** Yellow/black many shades of yellow NDV 61					
	1. Painted black frame, rails	(3)	**75**	2. Unpainted frame, no rails	(3)	**75**
6059	**Minneapolis & St. Louis** 61,62,65-67,69					
	1. Painted dark red plastic/white				(1)	**20**
	2. Unpainted red plastic/white				(1)	**20**
	3. Unpainted brown plastic/white				(1)	**10**
6059-50	**Minneapolis & St. Louis** 63,64					
	1. Painted dark red/white	(3)	**85**	2. Unpainted red plastic/white	(2)	**30**
6067	Not known to exist. Parts list shows this car but number for body is 6257					
6157-125	No Lettering					
	1. Red	(1)	**10**	2. Light red	(1)	**10**
	3. Brown	(1)	**10**			

117

6057-50 Lionel Lines redecorated for 1969 TTOS Convention

6167	**Lionel Lines** 63			
	1. Red/white		(1)	10
	2. Red/no lettering in Hagerstown box		(3)	50
6167-25	No Lettering Red 64		(1)	10
6167-50	No Lettering Yellow 63		(2)	10
6167-85	**Union Pacific** Yellow/black 64-69		(3)	25
6167-100	No Lettering Red 64		(1)	10
6167-125	No Lettering 64			
	1. Brown (1) **10**	2. Red	(1)	10
6167-150	No Lettering Yellow		(1)	20

6058 C&O variation 1 (top), variation 2 (bottom)

6257 Lionel Tan/black color sample

6257	**Southern Pacific** or **Lionel** markings 48-56	(1)	**10**
	Note: Previously 2257. Very common. Made in many colors & variations		
6257X	Same as 6257 but with 2 couplers 48,49		
	1. Bright red/white	(4)	**35**
	2. Dull red/white, came in 1425B set with 1656 switcher	(4)	**35**
6257-100	**Lionel Lines** 56-63	(1)	**10**
6357	**SP** or **Lionel** markings 1 coupler, light, inserts, 2 brakewheels 48-61		
	1. SP Dull red/white, 2357 on side, 6357, RS on base	(5)	**35**
	2. Same, 6357 on side	(2)	**25**
	3. SP Bright red/white	(2)	**25**
	4. *Lionel* Maroon/white	(2)	**25**
6357-50	**AT&SF** Red/white Came in rare 2555W set, called both the 60	(5)	**1000**
	Over and Under and the *Father and Son* set.		
6457	**Lionel** (previously 2357) 2 couplers, 49-52		
	light, inserts, ladders, tool boxes, smokestack		
	1. Brown/white 49 (3) **40** 2. Semi-gloss brown/white 50 (3)		**40**
	3. Reddish brown/white 52 (4) **50**		
6557	**Lionel** Tuscan/white smoking caboose 58,59	(4)	**225**

6657   **Rio Grande** Yellow/silver/black (not made w/smoke unit by Lionel) 57,58 (4)   **250**

POSTWAR

Work Cabooses

Note: Cabs, tool boxes easily switched

From top left: 6419-100 N&W, 6119 DL&W, 6219 C&O, 6130 SF

2419	**DL&W** Light gray/black 46,47	(2)	**75**
2420	**DL&W** 46-48		
	1. Dark gray/black HS serif *Lionel Lines*	(4)	**125**
	Note: Variations exist having to do with style of lettering, couplers, color of frame, and shade of gray. NDV		
	2. Black/RS sans-serif *Lionel Lines* factory repaint		
6119	**DL&W** 55,56		
	1. Red cab and tray, white HS serif *Lionel*, black painted frame	(2)	**25**
	2. Same as 1 but gray tray	(1)	**40**
	3. Same as 1 but sans-serif *Lionel*	(1)	**40**
6119-25	**DL&W** Orange cab and tray, painted frame, black HS *Lionel* 57		
	1. Glossy orange frame (4) **65**▲ 2. Flat orange frame	(2)	**60**
6119-50	**DL&W** Brown cab and tray, white HS *Lionel* brown painted frame 56	(3)	**75**
6119-75	**DL&W** Gray cab and tray, black HS sans-serif *Lionel* 57 on glossy or flat gray painted frame	(3)	**50**
6119-100	**DL&W** White or gray lettering, serif and sans-serif. NDV 63-66		
	1. Red cab, gray tray, white RS serif *Lionel* black painted frame	(1)	**30**
	2. Same but no *Lionel* on blue metal frame, *Built by Lionel* HS on cab	(4)	**40**
6119-125	No Lettering Information requested 60		
6120	No Lettering U61,62		
	1. Yellow cab and tray, black painted frame, no stack but hole for one	(1)	**20**
	2. Same but without hole for stack	(2)	**25**
6130	**AT&SF** 65-68		
	1. Painted red cab and tray, white RS serif, *Lionel* black painted frame	(1)	**30**
	2. Same but unpainted gray tray, blue frame	(5)	**60**
	3. Unpainted red cab and tray, gold metal frame	(3)	**250**
6219	**Chesapeake & Ohio** Blue/yellow 60	(4)	**85**
6419	**DL&W** 48-50 52-57		
	Note: Numerous minor variations. NDV		
	1. Painted gray cab, tool boxes and frame, black HS serif *Lionel*	(2)	**50**
	2. Same but black RS sans-serif *Lionel Lines* (factory repaint)	(5)	**60**
	3. Same as 1 but unpainted gray cab, tool boxes and frame	(2)	**50**
6419-25	**DL&W** Gray/black 55	(3)	**50**
6419-50	**DL&W** Gray/black 56,57	(3)	**60**
6419-75	**DL&W** Gray/black 56,57	(3)	**50**
6419-100	**Norfolk & Western 576419** on cab, Unpainted gray plastic cab, 57,58 molded tool boxes and frame, black HS serif *Lionel Lines*	(4)	**175**
6420	**DL&W** Dark gray/black, searchlight 49,50	(4)	**150**

6429	DL&W Gray/black 63	(4)	400
6814	**First Aid Medical Car** White/red, man, 2 stretchers, oxygen tank unit 59-61		
	1. Black RS serif *Lionel,*/gray frame	(3)	150
6824-50	2. White HS serif *Lionel,*/black frame/no tray insert/no man, stretchers or oxygen unit/*Sears* U64	(4)	300
6824	**USMC First Aid Medical Car** 60		
	1. Olive drab and gray tray, white RS *USMC*, olive drab painted frame, tray insert, white HS 6824 on tray. Came in *Land, Sea, and Air Gift Pack 1805*	(4)	200
6119-125	2. Same except white RS serif *Lionel* on black painted frame, no tray insert, no "6824" on tray. Came in *19334 JC Penney* set	(4)	250

Coal Dump Cars

3359-55	**Lionel Lines Twin Dump** Black/red frame/two gray bins 55-58	(3+)	75
3459	**Lionel Lines** 46-48		
	1. Black/white	(2)	75
	2. Unpainted aluminum bin, blue lettering	(3)	300
	3. Same but blank on one side/FM	(4)	350
	4. Painted green bin, white lettering	(3)	100
	5. Painted yellow, black lettering	(5)	8000*
	6. Red/white	(5)	*
3469	**Lionel Lines** Black/white 49-55	(2)	60
3559	**Coal Dump** Black/red 46-48	(2)	100
5459	**Electronic Set** Black/white/decal 46-48	(4)	200

Crane Cars

2460	**Bucyrus Erie** 6-wheel trucks 46-50		
	1. Glossy gray cab/black lettering 46	(4)	350▼
	2. Black cab/white lettering 46-50	(3)	125▼
2560	**Lionel Lines** 46,47		
	1. Green, brown or black Bakelite boom 46	(2)	100▼
	2. Black plastic boom 47	(2)	100▼
4460	**Bucyrus Erie** 6-wheel trucks 50		NM
6460	**Bucyrus Erie** 52-54		
	1. Black cab/white lettering 52-54	(2)	80
	2. Red cab/white lettering (6460-25 on box) 54	(4)	175▼

From top: 2560 Prewar style, 2460 variation 1, 2460 variation 2

6560 **Bucyrus Erie** 55-64,66,68,69
  1. Gray cab/black lettering Lionel used a screw to attach the trucks (2) **75▼**
     (not a horseshoe clip) on the first run. A number of different frames and
     cabs were used on these early versions. They were molded plastic in
     either an orange/red (4) **125** or black (5) **225**. A few had no printing
     at all on the frames or printing without the 6560 number
  2. Red cab/white lettering (1) **40▼**

6560-25 **Bucyrus Erie** Red/white 56 (3) **60▼**

Depressed Center Flatcars

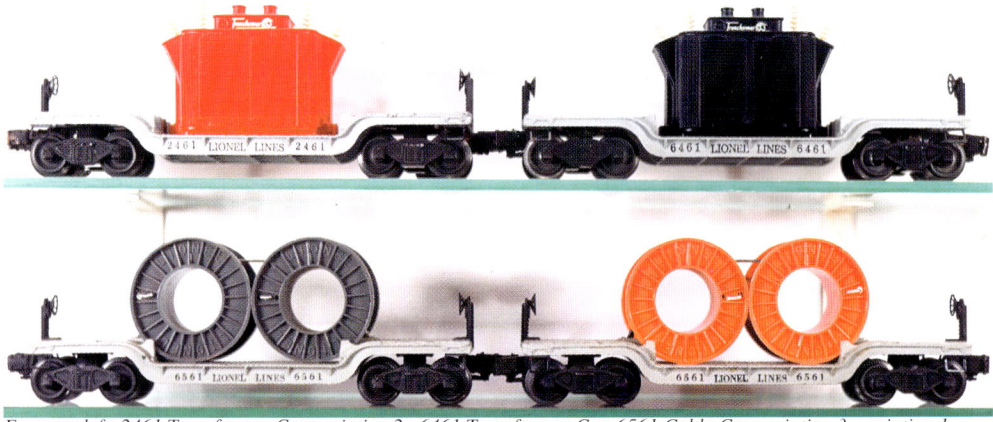

From top left: 2461 Transformer Car variation 2, 6461 Transformer Car, 6561 Cable Car variation 3, variation 1

2461 **Transformer Car** 47-48
  1. Light gray/black/red transformer/2462 RS on frame (3+) **150**
  2. Same but no lettering *2461* RS on bottom (4) **175**
  3. Same as 1 but black transformer (3) **90**

POSTWAR

122

6418	**Girder Bridge Car** Gray Four 4-wheel trucks. O gauge only 55-57 Will not negotiate 027 switches		
	1. Orange girders/*Lionel* in raised letters	(3)	125
	2. Pinkish-orange girders/black *US Steel*	(2)	125
	3. Black girders/raised lettering *US Steel*	(3)	125
6461	**Transformer Car** Gray/black Insulators usually broken 49 Originals are brittle and yellowed with age, Repros are flexible. Applies to 2461 also	(3)	85
6518	**Transformer Car** Gray/black transformer/white lettering.56-58 Four 4-wheel trucks. O gauge only. Will not negotiate 027 switches	(3+)	125
6561	**Cable Car** Gray/black lettering w/two plastic reels of aluminum wire 53-56		
	1. Orange reels (2) 75 2. Gray reels	(2)	75
	3. Dark gray reels (3) 85		

Flatcars

1877	**Fence and Horses** 59-62		
	1. Brown/yellow, 2 each white, black and brown horses, plastic arch-bar trucks, 2 operating couplers	(3)	90
	2. Same, Timken trucks	(3)	90
1887	**Fence and Horses** *Sears* Brown/yellow, same as 1877, U60 plastic arch-bar trucks, 2 operating couplers	(4)	175
2411	**Big Inch Flatcar** Lt gray/black, same frame as 2419 Work Caboose 46-48		
	1. 46 only came with metal pipes. Original pipes have ridge inside. Reproductions are smooth inside	(4)	125
	2. In 47 and 48 came with 3 wood logs, stained or unstained	(2)	50
3361-55	**Log Dump** Gray/black 55-59 Variations: different shades of gray, different types of lettering. NDV This car is a 6362 rail car w/dumping mechanism added.	(2)	60
3362	**Helium Tank Unloading** Dk green/white/3 silver-painted wood tanks 61-63		
	1. White lettering	(3)	50
	2. No lettering in Hagerstown box (3362/3364 Unloader Car) came as Helium Tank car only w/2 tanks *Note: RS lettering is easy to remove and leave no trace*	(3)	70
3364	**Operating Log Dump** Dark green/white with 3 dark stained logs 65-69 *Note: Same car as 3362 but with logs. Catalog showed picture of 3362 but listed 3364.* *In 1969, box stamped 3362/3364; no number on car. NDV*	(2)	60
3451	**Log Dump** Black/white 5 unstained logs 46-48		
	1. Rubber-stamped (3) 60 2. Heat-stamped	(2)	50

POSTWAR

123

From top left: 2411 Big Inch Flat car, 3361 Log car op., 3451 Log car op., 6361 Log car, 3461 Log car op., 3362 Helium Tanks op.

3460	**Flatcar w/Trailers** Unpainted red/white, 2 dark green *Lionel Trains* 55-57 (2) vans. Original vans have *Fruehauf* labels in back on a silver background		**70**
3461	**Log Dump** 49-55 *Note: Logs stained dark for the first time in 54*		
	1. Black/wht RS & HS 49-54 (2) **50** 2. Green/white/dark logs 54,55 (3)		**80**
3512	**Operating Fireman and Ladder Car** Unpainted red/white. 59-61 Repro ladders available, same ladders used on 494 Beacon Tower		
	1. Black ladder (2) **175** 2. Silver ladder (4)		**225**
3545	**TV Car** Black/white Two men/yellow TV camera/blue base 61,62 (3)		**200**
3545	Mock-up		**5X**
6111/6121	**Flatcar with Logs or Pipes** Steel-stamped car made in a number of 55-58 colors. HS lettering is either serif or non-serif, the latter being harder to find. Add $5. Some boxes stamped with different suffixes. NDV		
	1. Red/white (1) **25** 2. Yellow/black (1)		**25**
	3. Lt and medium gray/white (3) **40** 4. Dark gray/white (3)		**125**
6151	**Range Patrol Truck** White/black plastic *Range Patrol* truck 58		
	1. Orange/black (2) **125** 2. Light lemon yellow/black (2)		**150**
	3. Dark yellow/black (2) **125** 4. Cream/black (4)		**100**

POSTWAR

6262	**Wheel Car** (8 pairs of wheels with axles) 56,57		
	1. Black/white, metal trucks (2) **75** 2. Red/white, metal trucks (5)		**500**
6264	**Fork-Lift Car** Red/white, came with 264 Operating Fork Lift. 57-60 Hard to find in original box.		
	1. Plastic trucks (2) **100** 2. Metal trucks (2)		**100**
	3. As replacement accessory (must have box) (4)		**200***

124

6416 Boat Loader

6311	**Pipe Car** Reddish brown/white 55	(3)	65
6343	**Barrel Ramp Car** Red/white 6 stained barrels. Came in set 11222, 61,62	(2)	45
6361	**Timber Transport Car** Gold or black chains NDV 60,61, 64-69		
	1. Green/white	(3)	75
	2. Green/no lettering in Hagerstown box	(4)	150
	Note: Gold chain version believed to come from Madison Hardware		
6362-55	**Railway Truck Car** Orange/black, w/3 trucks only, 55, 56 no couplers, small & large lettering NDV	(2)	60
6401-1	**Flatcar** Gray no lettering 64		
	1. No box (1) **10** 2. With separate sale box	(4)	125*
	Note: 6401-1 through 6406 are General-type flat cars which came with a number of different loads. All were unnumbered except 6404 and 6405.		
6402	**Flatcar with Reels or Boat** Gray plastic, *Timken* trucks, 64,65,69 1 operating and 1 non-operating coupler. Came with the following loads		
	1. Blue and white boat (3) **45** 2. 2 Dark orange cable reels	(3)	35
	3. 2 Light orange cable reels, 2 operating couplers	(3)	35
6402-25	**Flatcar** Gray no lettering 64	(2)	10
6404	**Auto** Black/white/one auto, general-type flat car A60		
	1. Red auto/gray bumpers (2) **70** 2. Yellow auto	(3)	150
	3. Green auto (4) **400*** 4. Brown auto/gray bumpers	(4)	400*
6405	**Flatcar with Trailer** Maroon/yellow 61		
	1. Yellow van/no markings (3) **75** 2. Gray van/no markings	(4)	75
6406	**Auto** Tuscan or Gray Flat/no markings		
	1. Dark yellow auto/gray bumpers A61	(5)	*
	2. Medium yellow auto/gray bumpers A61	(4)	125
	3. Brown auto/gray bumpers U61-63	(4+)	300
	4. Green auto/gray bumpers U61-63	(4+)	300
6407	See Military and Space Chapter		
6408	**Flatcar with Pipes** 63	(3)	50
6409-25	**Flatcar with Pipes** no number, Red/white 63	(2)	50
6411	**Flatcar** Logs 48-50		
	1. Flat light gray/black (2) **45** 2. Glossy medium gray/black	(4)	100
6414	**Autoloader** Flatcar (6511-2 mold) Red/white, with black superstructure added. 55-66 Came with premium cars and cheapened cars. The premium cars had bumpers, windshields, axles and rubber tires. The cheapened versions had no bumpers, windshields, axles or tires.		
	1. Metal trucks, 6414 to right of *Lionel*. Red, white, blue and yellow premium cars.	(2)	125
	2. Timken trucks, 6414 to left of *Lionel*	(2)	125
	3. Same with 4 red premium cars, gray plastic bumpers	(4)	200
	4. Same with 4 yellow premium cars, gray plastic bumpers	(4)	400
	5. Same with 4 green premium cars, gray plastic bumpers	(5)	900
	6. Same with 4 brown premium cars, gray plastic bumpers	(5)	1000

POSTWAR

125

	7. 6414-85, 4 cheapened cars, 2 red and 2 yellow, 6414 on left	(4)	650
	8. Decal on superstructure. 6414 on decal, not on flatcar. 4 red premium cars, gray plastic bumpers. Reproduction decals available.	(4)	600▲
	9. Black/white		**FAKE**
6416	**Boatloader** Red/white/black 61-63	(4)	350▲

Note: Timken or Arch-bar trucks. NDV. Car originally came with 4 boats. The boats were made by Athearn and had a white hull, blue top, and brown interior. Athearn made the boat in a number of different colors but only the blue/white boat came with this car originally. In 1958, the same boat (in red/white) was cataloged on the HO gauge 0801 flatcar.

6424	**2 Autos** Two premium autos in many of the common colors. NDV 56-59		
	1. Black/white, plastic trucks	(2)	60
	2. Black/white, metal trucks	(2)	60
	3. Same as 2 on 6805 mold w/1 cream auto w/chrome bumpers and 1 red auto w/chrome bumpers	(5)	250*
	4. Red/white	(5)	500*
6430	**Piggy-Back Car** Red/white 56-58		
	1. Metal trucks, 2 green 4-wheel vans, *Lionel Trains* plates	(3)	75
	2. Same, 2 gray vans, *Cooper Jarrett* plates (aluminum background)	(2)	75
	3. Same except white vans, black background on plates	(2)	75
	4. Same except Timken trucks, 2 gray, *Cooper Jarrett* plates (Aluminum background) and *Fruehauf* labels	(5)	85
6431	**Piggy-Back Car** Red/white w/*Midge* Toy Tractor and two white 66 unmarked vans. Some of the vans had holes on the sides for a sign. Most didn't have holes.		
	1. White vans with holes for name plates	(4+)	300▲
	2. Yellow vans without holes	(5)	500▲
	Note: Midge Toy Tractor has been re-issued by the Midge Toy Company		
6440	**Piggy-Back Van Car** Red/white 60-63		
	1. 2 gray 2-wheel vans, no plates 2 operating couplers	(2)	85
	2. Same except 1 operating coupler 1 non-operating coupler	(4)	100
	3. Sears vans (Vol. 5)		5P
6467	**Miscellaneous Car** Red/white black bulkheads stakes, metal trucks 56	(2)	60
6469	**Liquified Gas Car** Red/white 63	(4)	250
6477	**Miscellaneous Car** Red/white, black bulkheads/5 plastic pipes 57,58 w/plastic or metal trucks	(2)	75
6500	**Bonanza Airplane Car** Black/white 62,63		
	1. Airplane w/red top/white bottom/red wings	(4)	450▲
	2. White top/red bottom/white wings	(4)	550▲
	Note: Airplane reproductions exist. Originals have Lionel Corp. *in raised lettering.*		
6501	**Jet Boat Car** Red/white w/white/brown boat 62,63	(3)	150
6502	**Girder Car** Black/white, no number/light orange *Lionel* girder 62	(3)	50▼
6502-50	**Girder Car** Blue/white, no lettering/dark orange *Lionel* girder A62	(2)	40▼
6502-75	**Girder Car** Aqua/white, no lettering/dark orange *Lionel* girder 64	(2)	40▼

6500 Bonanza Airplane Car

6511	**Pipe Car** 5 aluminum-colored plastic pipes 53-56		
	1. Painted Red/white lettering	(2)	35
	2. Unpainted Brown/white lettering	(3)	60
	3. Same as 1 w/die-cast plates securing trucks	(5)	250*
6512	See Military and Space		

6519 Allis Chalmers Condenser Car prototype

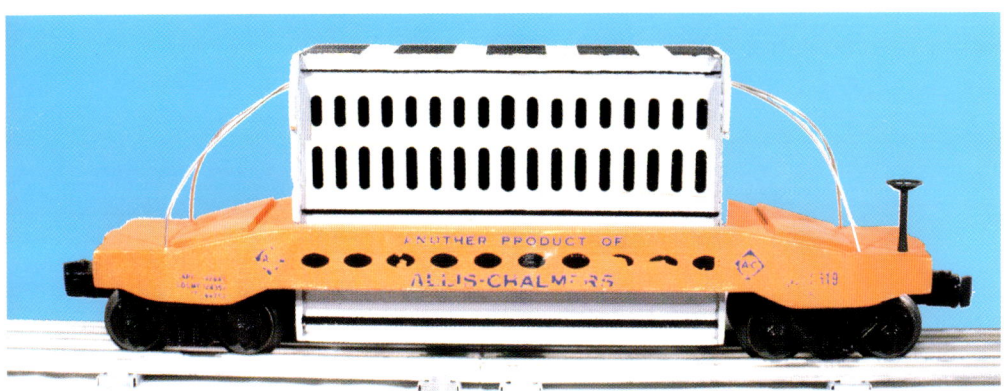

6519	**Allis Chalmers Condenser Car** 58-61		
	1. Light orange/blue/gray condenser	(2)	75▲
	2. Dark orange/blue/gray condenser	(3)	100▲
	3. Medium orange/blue/gray condenser	(3)	75▲
6660	**Boom Car** Red/white, yellow boom on black metal base 58	(3)	85
6670	**Derrick Car** 59,60		
	1. 6670 to left of *Lionel* (3) **80** 2. 6670 to right of *Lionel*	(4)	200
6800	**Airplane Car** Red/white 57-60		
	1. Airplane/black top/yellow bottom, plastic trucks	(4)	175
	2. Airplane/yellow top/black bottom, metal trucks	(4+)	200
	Came in light and dark yellow. Reproduction planes available		
6801	**Boat Car** Red/white 57-60		
	Note: Reproduction boats available		
	1. Boat – white hull/brown deck/6801	(3)	75
	2. Boat – yellow hull/wht deck/6801-50	(4)	100
	3. Boat – blue hull/white deck/6801-75 (early box)	(2)	65
	4. Boat – aqua hull/cream deck 6801-75 (late box)	(3)	75
6802	**US Steel Girder** Red/white, black *US Steel* girders come with 58,59 and without 6418. NDV	(2)	65
6810	**Piggy-Back Car** Red/white, one white van, 58	(3)	75▲
	Cooper Jarrett plates (black background)		
6812	**Track Maintenance Car** Red/white bases and tops are interchangeable 59-61		
	Note: Repro men available.		
	1. Dark yellow base and top (3) **100** 2. Black base, gray top	(2)	100
	3. Gray base, black top (2) **100** 4. Cream base and top	(4)	200
	5. Light yellow base and top (2) **100**		

POSTWAR

127

6816	**Allis Chalmers Bulldozer Car** 59,60			
	1. Red/white, light orange bulldozer, *Allis Chalmers* in black		(4)	**550**
	2. Red/white, dark-orange bulldozer, *AllisChalmers* in white		(4)	**400**
	3. Black/white, light orange bulldozer		(5)	**800**
6817	**Allis Chalmers Scraper Car** 59,60			
	1. Red/white, light orange scraper		(4)	**500**
	2. Red/white, dark orange scraper, wire windshield, white *Allis Chalmers*		(4)	**800▲**
	3. Black/white		(5)	**800▲**
6818	**Transformer Car** Red/white, black transformer **58**		(2)	**75**
6821	**Crate Car** Red/white, tan crates 59,60		(2)	**65**
6825	**Trestle Bridge Car** Red/white, black trestle 59-62		(2)	**60**
	Note: the same trestle also came in gray			
6826	**Christmas Tree Car** Red/white with original (pitiful looking) trees 59,60		(4)	**125**
6827	**P&H Steam Shovel** (kit) Black/white 60-63			
	1. Dark yellow steam shovel (4) **250▲** 2. Light yellow steam shovel		(4)	**175**
6828	**P&H Crane** (kit) 60-63, 66			
	1. Black/white flatcar, lt yellow crane		(4)	**250**
	2. Black/white flatcar, dk yellow crane		(4)	**350**
	3. Red/white flatcar		(5)	**800▲**
	Note: 6827 and 6828 came with booklet depicting the history of P&H. Among the many fascinating tidbits is the derivation of P&H. The P is for Alonzo Pawling and the H is for Henry Harnischfeger.			

Gondolas

1002	**Lionel Scout** 48-52			
	1. Blue/white, Scout couplers		(2)	**20**
	2. Black/white, Scout couplers		(1)	**10**
	3. Yellow/black, knuckle couplers		(4)	**400***
	4. Silver/black, knuckle couplers		(4)	**400***
	5. Red/white, knuckle couplers		(4)	**400***
	6. Black/white, knuckle couplers			*****
2452	**Pennsylvania** Black/white brakewheels, some came with barrels 45-47			
	1. Regular wheels (1) **15** 2. Whirly wheels		(4)	**40**
	3. Dished-out wheels (4) **40** 4. Stamped 6462 not 2452		(4)	**300***
2452X	**Pennsylvania** Black/white, 2452X stamped on frame 46,47		(1)	**20**
3562	**AT&SF** Barrel Car Operating 54-58			
	1. 3562-1 Black/white/black trough 54		(3)	**250**
	2. 3562-1 Black/white/yellow trough 54		(3)	**185**
	3. 3562-25 Gray/red 54		(4)	**400**
	4. 3562-1 Gray/red 54		(5)	**1000**
	5. 3562-25 Gray/blue 55		(2)	**75**
	6. 3562-50 Painted yellow/black		(4)	**150**
	7. 3562-50 Unpainted yellow plastic/black 55,56		(2)	**75**
	8. 3562-75 Unpainted orange plastic/black 57,58		(3)	**110**
	9. White/black		**Not Known To Exist**	
4452	**Pennsylvania** *Electronic Set* 46-48		(4)	**100**
6002	**Gondola** Black/white 50		(3)	**15**

3562 Operating Barrel Cars From top: variation 1, variation 3, variation 5, variation 7, variation 8

6012	**Lionel** Black/white 51-56		(1)	**10**
6032	**Lionel** 52,53		(1)	**10**
6042	**Lionel** U59-61			
	1. Black unpainted/white (3) **10**	2. Blue painted/white	(1)	**10**
6062	**New York Central** Black/white 59-64			
	1. Unpainted black plastic (3) **25**	2. Painted	(4)	**60**
6062-50	**New York Central** Black/white 69		(3)	**25**
6112	**Lionel** Black/white 4 red canisters 56-58			
	1. Black/white (1) **10**	2. Blue unpainted/white	(1)	**10**
	3. White/black (4) **30**			
6142	**Lionel** Black/white 61-66		(1)	**10**
6162	**NYC** Blue/white 61-63		(2)	**15**
6162-60	**Alaska** 59			
	1. Yellow/blue (3) **65**	2. Tan/blue		**FAKE**
6162-110	**NYC** w/2 red canisters 64-69			
	1. Blue/white (2) **15**	2. Aqua blue/white	(3)	**50**
	3. Red /white (4) **200**			

POSTWAR

From top left: 6462 NYC variation 2, 1002 Lionel variation 1, 6462 NYC variation 3, 1002 Lionel variation 4, 6562 NYC variation 4, 1002 Lionel variation 3

129

6342	**New York Central** Red/white 56-58, 64-69					
	1. Metal trucks			(3)		45
	2. Plastic trucks			(4)		100
	3. In separate sale box (overstamped). One example asking $2000.			(5)		*
6452	**Pennsylvania** Black/white (cataloged in 1949 but not available) 48 only					
	1. 6462 on side, 6452 stamped on base			(3)		50
	2. 6452 on side and base			(2)		40
6462	**New York Central** 49-56					
	Note: Also came in - Painted orange, Painted gold, Gray/black Gray/white,					
	Gray/red, Glossy green/white and Blue/black. All are 5X, NDV.					
	1. Black/white	(1)	**15**	2. Red/white	(1)	**15**
	3. Green/white	(2)	**40**			
6462-500	**New York Central** Pink/blue Girl's Train			(4)		**250▲**
6562	**New York Central** 56-58					
	1. Gray/maroon **6562-1**	(2)	**50**	2. Gray/red **6562-1**	(3)	**60**
	3. Red/white **6562-25**	(2)	**50**	4. Black/white **6562-50**	(2)	**50**

Hoppers

From top left: 6456 Lehigh Valley variation 1, 6456 Lehigh Valley variation 2, 6456 Lehigh Valley variation 3, 6456 Lehigh Valley variation 4, 3456 N&W, 2856-2956 B&O

2456	**Lehigh Valley** 48					
	1. Matte black/white	(3)	**50**	2. Glossy black/white Information Requested		
2856/2956	**B&O** Black/white 46, 47			(4)		**300**
	Note: This was the prewar 2956 which was cataloged in 46 and 47 in gray with postwar trucks and the number 2856. 2856 was never made but some black 2956 hoppers turn up with postwar trucks. Whether Lionel or a service station or a customer put the trucks on, no one knows. But it's a nice car anyway.					
3456	**Norfolk & Western** Black/white Operating bottom hatches 50-55					
	1. Corner braces	(2)	**70**	2. No corner braces	(3)	**85**
6076	**Lehigh Valley** U63					
	1. Gray/black	(1)	**15**	2. Black/white	(1)	**15**
	3. Red/white	(1)	**15**	4. Yellow/black	(3)	**20**
6076	**AT&SF** Gray/black U63					
	1. Regular production			(1)		**10**
	2. **TTOS Convention Car** (overstamped)			(4)		**50**
6176	**Lehigh Valley** 64-66, 69					
	1. Different shades of yellow with black or blue lettering			(1)		**10**
	2. Lemon yellow	(3)	**50**	3. Gray/black	(1)	**10**
	4. Black/white	(1)	**10**	5. Black/gray	(2)	**10**
6176-100	Unpainted Olive drab/no lettering			(4)		**100**

130

6176-1967	**TTOS Convention Car** 67				(4)	**65**
6346-56	**Alcoa** Silver/blue Quad/hatch covers/no center brace hole 56					
	1. Silver/blue HS	(2)	**85**	2. Silver/red HS		**FAKE**
	3. Silver/blue decal		**5P**			
6436-1	**Lehigh Valley** Black/white 55					
	1. No spreader bar holes	(3)	**75**	2. Spreader bar and holes	(2)	**50**
6436-25	**Lehigh Valley** Maroon/white, no covers/spreader bar 55-57				(3)	**65**
6436-110	**Lehigh Valley** Red/white 63-66,68					
	1. *Built Date 3/5*/63	(4)	**100**	2. No built date 63,64-66,68	(2)	**40**
6436-500	**Lehigh Valley** Girl's Set Lilac/maroon/w or w/o spreader bar holes 57,58				(4)	**400**
6436-1969	**TCA Convention Car** Red/white, spreader bar/no cover U 69				(4)	**160**
6446-1	**N&W Hopper** Gray/black covered 54,55,57,63					
	1. 546446 on car, 1954	(2)	**75**	2. 6446-25 on car, 1955,57	(3)	**75**
	3. 6446-25 on car/spreader bar/plastic AAR trucks, 1963				(4)	**150**
6446-25	**N&W** Black/white covered					
	1. 54-6446 on car	(2)	**75**	2. 6446-25 on car	(2)	**75**
6446-25	**Norfolk & Western** specials made for *N&W RR* 55-57					
	1. Gold/white		**5P**	2. Pink/black		**5P**
	3. Light blue/white		**5P**	4. Silver/white		**5P**
6446-60	**Lehigh Valley** Red/white, covered 63				(4)	**350**
6456	**Lehigh Valley** 48-55					
	1. Black/white 49-51	(1)	**20**	2. Maroon/white 51	(2)	**25**
	3. Gray/maroon 54	(3)	**75**	4. Glossy red/yellow 55	(4)	**200**
	5. Glossy red/white 55	(5)	**750**	6. Gray/white		*****

POSTWAR

From top left: 6446-25 N&W variation 1, 6536 M&St. L variation 1, 6436-25 Lehigh Valley, 6636 Alaska, 6346 Alcoa Aluminum variation 1, 6736Detroit & Mackinac variation 1

6476	**Lehigh Valley** Unpainted 57-69				
	Note: Made through 1969 in many different colors, some with road names and some without, cataloged and uncataloged. None are worth more than $20.				
	1. Red plastic/white 57	(1)	**10**	2. Black plastic/white 57 (2)	**10**
	3. Gray plastic/black 57	(3)	**15**		
6476-1	**TTOS 69 Convention Car**			(4)	**60**
6476-125	**Lehigh Valley** Yellow/black (6176 on car) 64			(2)	**15**
6476-135	**Lehigh Valley** Unpainted mustard yellow plastic/red 68,69			(2)	**10**
6536	**Minneapolis & St. Louis** 58,59,63				
	1. Red/white 58,59	(3)	**85**	2. Shinier Red/white 63 (4)	**95**
6636	**Alaska** Black/yellow 59,60			(4)	**125**
6736	**Detroit & Mackinac** 60-62				
	1. Red/white			(3)	**60**
	2. Red/white, *Mackinac Mac's* face filled in due to flaw in die			(4)	**150**

Military and Space

943	**Exploding Ammo Dump** 59,60			(3)	**60**
3309	**Turbo Missile Launching Car** one missile, arch-bar trucks, 63,64 two fixed couplers, no missile holder			(2)	**50**
	1. Light red/white	(2)	**40**	2. Cherry red/white (2)	**40**

3330	**Flat Car with Operating Submarine Kit** 60,61				
	1. Submarine assembled	(3)	**90**	2. Submarine unassembled (5)	**175**
3330-100	**Operating Submarine Kit (must have box)**			(5)	**400**

3349	**Turbo Missile Launching Car** 62-65		
	Missile holder/Timken trucks/no number or lettering on car		
	1. Lt red/white/2 operating couplers	(2)	65
	2. Dk red/white/2 operating couplers	(2)	75
	3. Olive drab/one operating coupler and one fixed coupler	(4)	600▲
3409	**Helicopter Launching Car** Blue/white 61,62	(3)	125
	Note: Manually cocked and released. Gray Navy helicopter with one propeller, yellow tail assembly. Flatcars are available and so are reproduction helicopters.		
3410	**Helicopter Launching Car** 61,62		
	1. Blue/white w/yellow unmarked helicopter/one propeller	(3)	175
	2. Blue/white w/Navy helecopter	(2)	125
	3. Aqua/white w/yellow unmarked helicopter/one propeller	(5)	350
3413	**Mercury Capsule Car** Red/white, Gray base/red launcher, 62-64 parachute inside of white/red rocket with gray nose		
	1. Light gray base (4) 275 2. Dark gray base	(4)	275

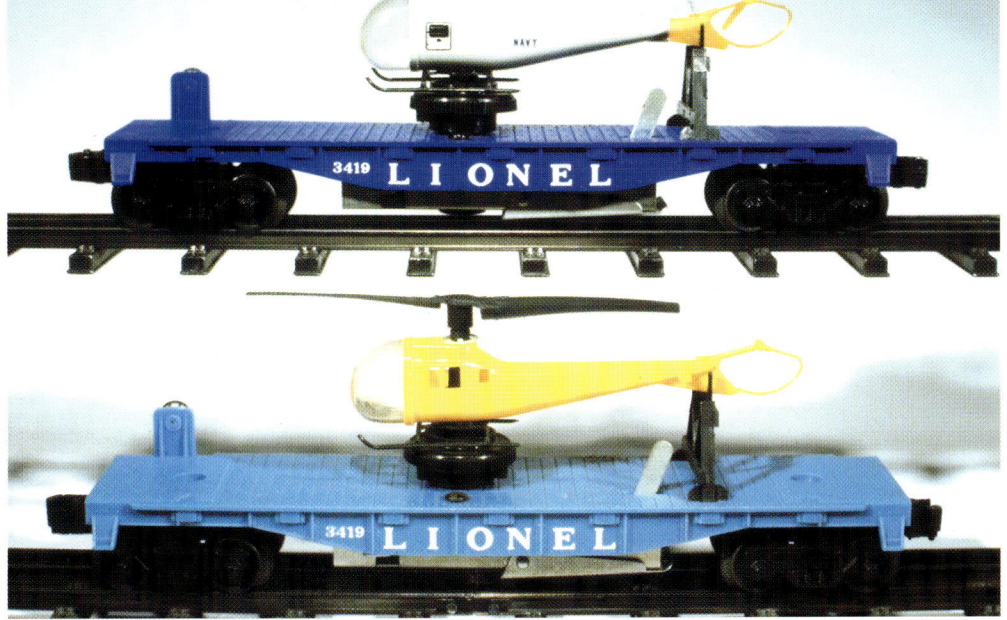

3419 Helicopter Launching Car variation 3 (top), bottom variation 5 (bottom)

3419	**Helicopter Launching Car** 59-65		
	Note: Helicopters with 2 props are more desirable than helicopters with one propeller.		
	1. Light blue/gray *US Navy* copter with 2 props/large winding mechanism	(3)	200
	2. Same as 1 but dark blue	(2)	150
	3. Same as 2 but small winding mechanism	(2)	125
	4. Light blue/small winding mechanism	(3)	125
	5. Light blue/small winding mechanism/yellow copter/one propeller	(3)	225
	6. Same as 4 but dark blue	(3)	125

POSTWAR

| 3429 | **USMC Helicopter Launching Car,** Olive drab/same mechanism as 60 3419/gray, one prop gray helicopter with *USMC* markings. Included in *1805 Land, Sea, and Air Gift Pack*. | (4) | 500▲ |

3470	**Target Launcher** 62-64		
	Note: Blower nozzle may be switched.		
	1. Dark blue flat w/clear nozzle	(2)	100
	2. Dark blue flat w/red nozzle	(2)	150
	3. Dark blue flat w/gray nozzle	(2)	125
	4. Light blue flat w/clear nozzle	(4)	150
	5. Light blue flat w/yellow nozzle	(5+)	2000*
3509	**Satellite Car** Green/white/black/silver satellite, 61,62 gray superstructure/yellow microwave disc	(3)	110▲
3510	**Satellite Car** Red/white/*Lionel* only on side/no number A62 plastic Timken trucks, fixed couplers, black & silver satellite, gray superstructure/yellow microwave dish.	(3)	100▼
3519	**Satellite Car** Green/white, gray superstructure, yellow dish 61-64 operated by remote control	(2)	75
3535	**AEC Security** Red/white, gray plastic roof gun usually missing, 60,61 gray rotating searchlight, similar cab to 520 electric	(3)	125
3540	**Operating Radar Car** Red/white, gray base, yellow dish, 59,60 black & silver radar	(3)	150
3619	**Helicopter Recon Car** 62-64		
	1. Operating Yellow/black roof/red and black lettering/same body & roof as 3665 and 3666/red copter	(3)	150
	2. Same w/darker yellow body	(4)	200
3665	**Minuteman** White/blue with rocket 61-64		
	1. Dark blue roof	(3)	100
	2. Light blue roof, (3619 mold)1964	(4)	275
3666	**Cannon Boxcar** Sears Set 3-9820, White/lt blue roof/blue lettering U64 Operating cannon fires silver painted wooden shells. *Note: Reproduction roofs available*	(5)	500▲
3820	**Operating Submarine** Olive/white *USMC* markings on car/*US Navy* 60 markings on gray sub/part of 1805 *Land, Sea, and Air Gift Pack*	(4)	175
3830	**Operating Submarine** Blue/white, gray sub/*US Navy* markings 60-63	(3+)	125
6175	**Flatcar with Rocket** (same gray cradle used with 6801 Boat Car) 58-61 *US Navy* rocket/red/white/blue lettering, same rocket as 175 launcher		
	1. Red/white 58 (3) **90** 2. Black/white 59-61	(2)	100
6402-Type	**Flat Car** (mold 1877-3) w/green tank *Sears* U64	(4)	175
6407	**Flatcar with Large Missile** Red/white (gray cradle is same used on 63 6501) holds large white-red rocket with removable blue nose with and without pencil sharpener. Reproduction sharpeners available	(5)	700

6413	**Mercury Capsule Carrying Car** Blue/white, 2 gray unlettered 62,63 Mercury capsules secured by bands, same chassis as 6519 *Note: Brakewheels may be added, reproduction capsules available*			
	1. Blue/white (4) **150** 2. Aqua/white		(4+)	**275**
6448	**Target Car** 61-64 *Note: Solid white can be made by combining 1 and 2*			
	1. Red sides/white lettering (2) **75** 2. White sides/red lettering		(3)	**75**
6463	**Rocket Fuel** White/red 62,63		(3)	**85**
6470	**Exploding Boxcar** Red/white, spring-loaded 59-63		(2)	**50**
6480	**Exploding Boxcar** Red/white 61		(4)	**100**
6512	**Cherry Picker** Black/white, gray base holds black metal ladder, 62,63 Original vestibule orange, repros exist in both orange & black		(3)	**125**

6544	**Missile Launching Car** Blue/white, gray launching mechanism 60-64 usually found with brakewheels broken, used 6519 chassis and 44 launching base, same firing mechanism as 448 range set			
	1. White lettered console (2) **150**▲ 2. Black lettered console		(4)	**375**
6630	**Missile Launcher** Black/white/blue base, *Sears* U60-64 Black missile firing ramp		(3)	**90**
6640	**USMC Missile Launcher** 60			
	1. Olive/white (6511-3 mold) (3) **250** 2. No lettering (6424-11 mold)		(3+)	**300**
6650	**Lionel Missile Launcher** Red/white, Blue launcher (same as 6630) 59-63 Black launching pad, white/red missile with blue nose			
	1. 6511-3 mold (3) **65** 2. 6424-11 mold		(3)	**75**
6651	**USMC Cannon** Olive/white U65 Came in *JC Penney* set headed by 221 *USMC* Alco		(4)	**150**
6803	**USMC Tank & Microwave Truck** Gray microwave truck and tank 58,59		(4)	**200**
6804	**USMC Trucks** Red/white gray microwave truck and truck w/2 guns 58,59		(4)	**250**
6805	**Radioactive Waste** Red/white/black plastic containers painted gray 58,59 *Note: Reissued 9234 in 1980. Reissued containers are gray plastic. Sometimes found with 4 different shades of painted tan containers made for the 462 derrick platform. NDV*		(2)	**175**
6806	**USMC Radar & Navy Hospital Trucks** Red/white/1 gray USMC 58,59 radar dish truck and 1 *US Navy* hospital truck		(4)	**250**
6807	**Flatcar with USMC Boat** Red/white, large gray amphibious boat 58,59		(4)	**125**
6808	**Flatcar with USMC Truck & Tank** Red/white 58,59 Gray searchlight truck & two-gun tank		(4)	**275**
6809	**Flatcar with 2 USMC Trucks** Red/white 58,59 Gray cannon truck & *Navy* hospital truck		(4)	**200**
6814	**First Aid Medical Car** White/red, man, 2 stretchers, oxygen tank unit 59-61, U64			
	1. Black RS serif *Lionel*/gray frame		(3)	**125**
	2. White HS serif *Lionel*/black frame, no tray insert, no man or stretchers or oxygen unit, *Sears* U64		(4)	**150**

Top row; 6175 Flatcar with rocket, 6844 Missle Carring car, 6823 ICBM Missle car. Row 2: 3413 Mercury Capsule car, 6544 Missle Launching car, 3349 Turbo Missle Launching car. Row 3: 3666 Canon Boxcar, 3419 Helicopter Launching car, 3619 Helicopter Recon car. Row 4: 6470 Exploding Boxcar, 6448 Target car, 6463Rocket Fuel. Row 5: 6413 Mercury Capsule Carring car, 6805 Radioactive Waste, 3540 Operating Radar car. Row 6: 6814 First Aid Medical car, 3330 Submarine car, 3535 AEC Security

POSTWAR

6819	**Helicopter** Red/white Gray *Navy* one-prop helicopter, 59,60 with prop end weights, reproduction helicopters available			(3)	120
6820	**Navy Helicopter** Gray *Navy* one-prop copter with 2 missiles 60,61 Reproduction helicopters available				
	1. Light blue/white	(4) 175	2. Dark blue/white	(3)	150
6823	**ICBM Missiles** Red/white, 2 red/white ICBM-type missiles 59,60 Same missiles as on 6650			(3)	85
	Note: Missile and rocket parts interchangeable; therefore all color combinations are possible.				
6830	**US Navy Submarine** Gray non-operating sub with black lettering 60,61			(3+)	140
	1. Painted flat blue	(3) 140	2. Painted gloss blue	(5)	350*
6844	**Missile Carrying Car** 6 white missiles, gray missile holder base 59,60 Reproductions of gray base available in gray and black				
	1. Black/white	(2) 85	2. Red/white	(4+)	700

Mint Car

6445	**Fort Knox Gold Reserve** Silver/black 61-63		(3)	225

136

Refrigerator Cars

3462	**Milk Car** Unpainted alum doors operating 47,48			
	1. Glossy white/brass-base mechanism		(4)	75
	2. Dull white/later mechanism		(2)	45
3472	**Milk Car** operating 49-53			
	1. Metal doors 49 only (3) **75**	2. Plastic doors	(2)	50
3482	**Milk Car** operating 54,55			
	1. 3472 lower right/early production		(3)	75
	2. 3482 lower right		(2)	50
3662-1	**Milk Car** White/brown operating 55-60, 64-66			
	1. Built date/55-60 (3) **90**	2. No built date/64-66	(3+)	125
3672	**Bosco** Yellow/Tuscan operating 59,60			
	1. Painted yellow (4) **500▲**	2. Yellow plastic	(3)	300
6472	**Milk Car** Dull white 50-53		(2)	35
6482	**Milk Car** White 57		(4)	85
6572	**Railway Express** 58,59,U64			
	1. Dark green/metal Timken trucks 58.59		(4)	175
	2. Light green *Madison Hardware* 4WPT U64		(2)	90

POSTWAR

6672	**Santa Fe** White/brown non-operating 54-56		
	1. Black lettering/L in circle	(3+)	**100**
	2. Same but no L in circle	(3+)	**100**
	3. Blue lettering/L in circle	(3)	**75**
	4. Blue/3 lines of data right of door	(5)	**500**

Note: Roof is either reddish brown or chocolate brown. NDV

Searchlight Cars

3520	**Lionel Lines** Gray/black, orange generator/gray searchlight 52,53 on-off switch, serif and non-serif lettering. NDV	(2)	**65**

3530	**Operating Generator Car** 56-58		
	1. Orange generator, short stripe	(3+)	**200**
	2. Orange generator, long stripe	(4)	**300**
	3. Gray generator	(5)	*

Note: The base of pole came in black (common), blue (hard to find) and yellow (rare). Some fuel tanks are black and some are blue. On some cars the white stripe goes through the ladder (long stripe) and on others it does not (short stripe).

3620	**Lionel Lines** Gray/black 54-56		
	1. Searchlight gray plastic	(2)	**50**
	2. Searchlight orange plastic painted gray	(4)	**100**
	3. Searchlight orange plastic		**FAKE**

Note: Shown in 54 catalog, p. 20. Beware of painted gray version with the paint removed.

3650	**Lionel Lines** Extension Searchlight 56-59					
	1. Gray frame/black	(3)	**85**	2. Dark gray frame/black	(4)	**175**
	3. Olive gray frame/black	(4)	**250**			

6520	**Lionel Lines** Gray/black/gray housing 49-51					
	Same die-cast depressed-center frame as 2461					
	1. Green generator 49	(4)	**350▲**	2. Orange generator	(2)	**65**
	3. Unpainted gray generator		*	4. Unpainted maroon generator	(3)	**75**
	5. Tan generator	(5)	**1000**			

Note: Some cars have faded orange generators and black housings. NDV

6822	**Lionel** Red/white 61-69					
	1. Gray searchlight housing	(2)	**60**	2. Black searchlight housing	(3)	**75**

6520 Searchlight Car variation 5

Stock Cars

3356	**Operating Horse Car & Corral** Green/yellow, 56-60, 64-66	(3)	**150**
	plastic & metal trucks		
	Car only, no box	(2)	**75**
	Separate sale car w/box	(5)	**500**
3366	**Circus and 3356-150 Corral** White/red, 59-62	(4)	**400▲**
	Car only	(3)	**150**
3656	**Armour Stock Car** Orange w/cattle and corral 49-55		
	1. Black lettering/*Armour* sticker 49	(4)	**350**
	2. White lettering/*Armour* 49,50	(3)	**100**
	3. White lettering/no *Armour* 50-55	(2)	**85**
6356-1	**NYC** Yellow/black 54,55	(2)	**60**
6376	**Lionel Lines Circus Car** White/red 56,57	(2+)	**85**
6434	**Poultry** Red/white/gray doors 58,59	(3)	**75**
6473	See Action Cars		
6556	**Katy** Red/white *Set 2513W* headed by 2329 Virginian 58	(4)	**275**
6646	**Lionel Lines** Orange/black 57	(3)	**50**
6656	**Lionel Lines** Yellow/black 50-55		
	1. *Armour* sticker 50 (4) **100** 2. No *Armour* sticker 50-55	(2+)	**30**

POSTWAR

139

Tank Cars

1005	**Sunoco** Gray tank Scout Type 48-50 1d		(1)	10
2465	**Sunoco** Silver 46-48 2d			
	1. Black lettering/decal in center 46		(4)	400
	2. Same but decal off to one side 46		(1)	15
	3. Blue lettering 47		(2)	25
	4. Silk screening 48		(2)	25
2555	**Sunoco** Aluminum, same as 2755, 46-48 1d		(3)	100

2755	**Sunoco** Aluminum Prewar tank car with postwar trucks 45 1d		(4)	200

2855	**Sunoco** Black 46,47 1d					
	1. Gas-Oil in decal 46	(4)	250▲	2. No Gas-Oil 47	(4)	300▲

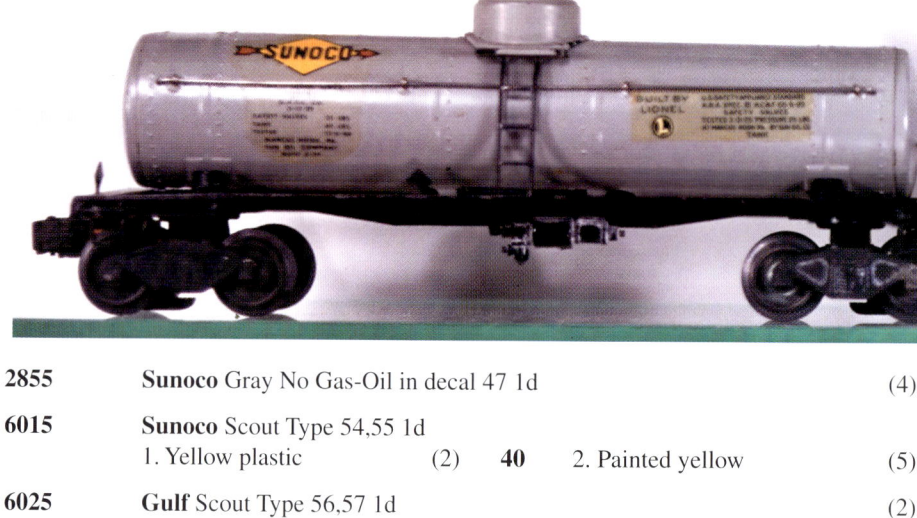

2855	**Sunoco** Gray No Gas-Oil in decal 47 1d					(4)	300▲
6015	**Sunoco** Scout Type 54,55 1d						
	1. Yellow plastic	(2)	40	2. Painted yellow		(5)	70*
6025	**Gulf** Scout Type 56,57 1d					(2)	45
6035	**Sunoco** Scout Type 52,53 1d					(1)	12
6045	**Lionel Lines** 58-63 2d					(1)	50

140

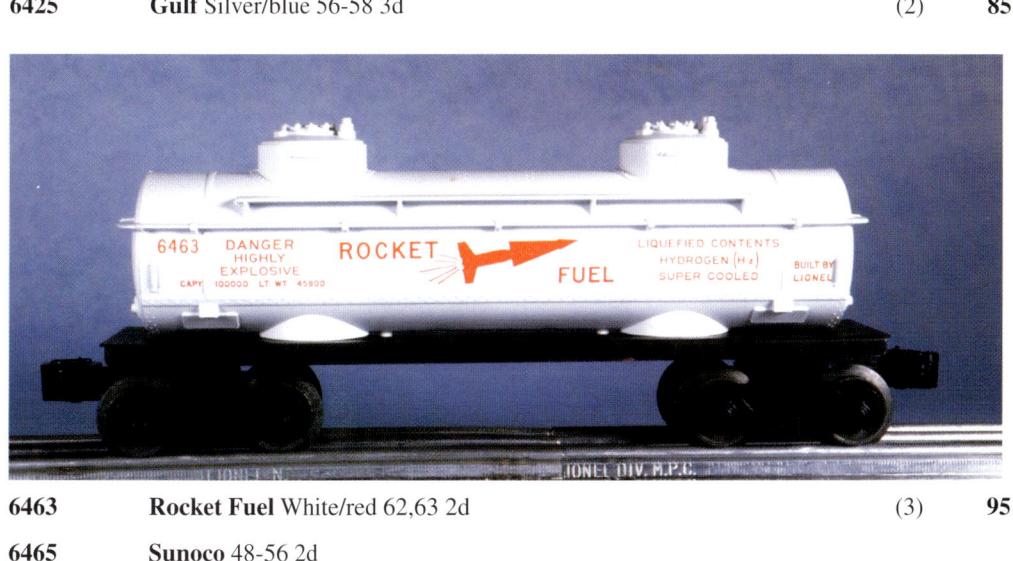

| 6045 | **Cities Service** Green/white, non-operating couplers U60 2d | (2) | **175** |

6315	**Gulf** 56-59,66-69 1d		
	1. Glossy orange/black tank	(3)	**100**
	2. Flat orange/black tank	(3)	**75**
	3. Solid orange tank	(2)	**100**
	4. Solid orange tank with *6315 Chemical Tank Car* on ends	(2)	**100**
6315	**Lionel Lines** Orange/black, plastic trucks 63-65 1d	(2)	**40**
6315-60	**Lionel Lines** 63,64 1d		
	1. Unpainted orange plastic no built date	(3)	**40**
	2. Same as 1 with built date	(4)	**50**
	3. Painted orange	(4)	**125**
6415	**Sunoco** Silver/black 53-55 3d	(1)	**40**

| 6425 | **Gulf** Silver/blue 56-58 3d | (2) | **85** |

6463	**Rocket Fuel** White/red 62,63 2d	(3)	**95**
6465	**Sunoco** 48-56 2d		
	Note: Common car with lots of variations, only one of which (so far) is worth more than $20		
	1. Silver/Sunoco decal normal production	(1)	**20**
	2. Painted black/Sunoco decal (Rare version owned by Nick Vernola)	(5)	*****
6465	**Gulf** 58 2d		
	1. Unpainted blk plastic tank (3) **75** 2. Painted black plastic tank	(3)	**75**
	3. Painted gray plastic tank (3) **75**		

141

6465	Lionel Lines Gray, orange or black. NDV 58,59 2d	(1)	25
6465	Cities Service Green/white, operating couplers 60-62 2d	(3)	50
6465-60	Gulf Gray/blue/black 58 2d	(2)	60
6555	Sunoco Silver/black 49,50 1d	(3)	100

TCA Convention Cars 1965-1967

Note: Special 6464 cars with brass and aluminum doors made for the Train Collecters Association. Fakes have turned up. Check the doors. The inside of the doors on originals is aluminum, outside is brass. On fakes, the doors are all brass. No reported sales for boxed/mint condition.

6464-250	Western Pacific (159 made) 67	(5)	350
6464-375	Central of Georgia (100 made) 67	(5)	350
6464-475	Boston & Maine Decal version 67		5P
6464-475	Boston & Maine (3 made) 67		5X
6464-525	Minneapolis & St. Louis (7 made) 67		5X
6464-650	Denver & Rio Grande Western (137 made) 67	(5)	350
6464-700	A.T. & S.F. (92 made) 67	(5)	350
6464-735	New Haven (3 made) 67		5X
6464-900	New York Central (2 made) 67		5X

6464-1965	TCA Pittsburgh 65	(5)	300
6464-1965X	Pittsburgh 65	(5)	350
6517-1966	TCA Bay Window Caboose 66	(4)	500

Vat Cars

| 6475 | Libby's Crushed Pineapple 4 vats w/silver labels/red & blue lettering U63 | | |
| | 1. Blue/white (2) 100 2. Aqua blue/white | (4) | 225 |

Prototype made for Libbys

6475	Pickle Car Tan/brown/green 60-62		
	1. Slats on pickle vats (2) 75 2. No slats on pickle vats	(4)	250
	3. Blank vats (3) 175		
6475	Heinz 57 Pickle Car Tan/brown/green		*

Accessories

30	**Water Tower** 47-50			
	1. Brown roof, black superstructure/doubled-walled tank, fill hole in roof, 30 RS in black on base		(4)	**250**
	2. Red roof, brown superstructure/singled-walled tank, fill hole in roof, 30 RS in black on base		(4)	**225**
	3. Same as 2, gray roof brown superstructure		(3)	**150**
	4. Gray roof, brown superstructure, single-walled tank, no fill hole, no RS number		(3)	**150**
35	**Boulevard Lamp** 45-49			
	1. Aluminum (2) **50** 2. Gray		(3)	**60**
38	**Water Tower** Clear, plastic funnel w/packet of water coloring tablets 46,47			
	1. Red roof/tan base (4) **425** 2. Brown roof/tan base		(4+)	**450**
45	**Gateman** White/red/green base 46-49		(2)	**50**
45N	**Gateman** White/red/green base 45		(2)	**75**
56	**Lamp Post** two shades of green NDV 46-49		(3)	**75**
58	**Goose Neck Lamp Post** Ivory, diecast 46-50		(3)	**50**
64	**Highway Lamp Post** L452W bulb, Green, diecast 45-49		(3)	**75**▲
70	**Yard Lamp** Black, swivel light, round, Bakelite base 49,50 Came with early 397 coal loader		(4)	**75**▲
71	**Lamp Post** Gray, diecast, bayonet bulb 49-59		(2)	**20**
75	**Goose Neck Lamps** Black, (2 per box) Price is for two. 61-73		(2)	**65**
76	**Boulevard Street Lamps** 2-pin bulb, Dark green, 55-66,68,69 unpainted plastic, (3/box). Price for 3.		(2)	**30**
89	**Flagpole** White pole/tan base w/Lionel, pennant and American flag 56-58			
	1. Dark blue pennant (5) **150** 2. Purple pennant		(4)	**85**
93	**Water Tower** "Lionel Lines" Aluminum/red base/black spout 46-49		(3)	**85**

POSTWAR

97	**Coal Elevator** Yellow bunker with red roof/black Bakelite base, 46-50 97C controller.		(3)	**225**
110	**Trestle Set** Package of 22 or 24 trestles 55-69			
	1. Gray trestles (2) **30** 2. Black trestles		(4)	**35**
111	**Trestle Set** Pkg of 10 Trestles 56-69		(2)	**30**
114	**Newsstand with Horn** Yellow building/silver roof/brn base control 57-59		(3)	**125**
115	**Lionel City Station** Prewar carry over 46-49 Cream/red/red base w/auto train stop		(4)	**500**

143

118	Newsstand with Whistle Yellow/silver/brown base 58		(3)	125
125	Whistle Shack White sides/red roof 50-55 Similar to 145 Automatic Gateman with whistle			
	1. Light gray base (2) **50**	2. Dark gray base	(3)	90
	3. Apple green base (4) **100**			
128	Animated Newsstand came with newspaper inserted in boy's hand 57-60 reissued by *Fundimensions* in 1982 as 2308.			
	1. Dark green stand (3) **250**	2. Apple green stand	(4)	300
132	Passenger Station illuminated White/green roof/maroon base/auto 49-55 train stop, maroon chimney, green chimney, NDV.		(3)	80
133	Passenger Station White/green roof and chimney, 57,61,62,66 maroon base, no automatic train stop, illuminated		(2)	80

246 Forklift Platform, 138 Watertower

138	Water Tower Brown tank and frame/gray base/black operating spout 53-57			
	1. Gray roof, 53 only (4) **150**▲	2. Orange roof, 54-57	(3)	**125**▲
140	Automatic Banjo Signal Black with operating arm 54-66		(2)	35
145	Automatic Gateman White shack/green base, plastic crossbuck, 50-66 red-gold *Lionelville* sticker above door, blue plastic man or painted with flesh-colored hands & face NDV			
	1. Maroon roof (2) **40**	2. Red roof	(4)	75
148	Dwarf Trackside Light Tan/black 57-60 Requires 148C switch for operation. Can also use 153C.		(4)	50

152 and 162 Crossing Gates

150	**Telegraph Pole Set** Brown, set of 6 w/track clips 47-50	(3)	**75**
151	**Semaphore** Operating plastic blade/painted yellow tip w/red/green 47-69 translucent plastic inserts.		
	1. Black base/painted aluminum pole	(1)	**40**
	2. Black base/unpainted aluminum pole	(3)	**75**
	3. Green base/painted aluminum pole	(4)	**80**
	4. Same as 1 but packaged in blister pack	(5)	*****
152	**Automatic Crossing Gate** Red, diecast base with pedestrian gate 45-49 Deduct $10-$20 if missing pedestrian gate	(3)	**50**
153	**Automatic Block Control** Green base 45-69		
	1. Painted aluminum pole (2) **50** 2. Unpainted aluminum pole	(3)	**60**

154 Automatic Highway Signals, orange base is a prewar version

455 Oil Derrick variation 1

154	**Automatic Highway Signal** Black base, silver post 45-59		
	1. Diecast sign, screw-type bulbs	(3)	**65**
	2. Plastic sign, bayonet-type bulbs	(3)	**40**
155	**Ringing Highway Signal** Black/white plastic base w/bell, 55-57 same lights as 154	(3)	**85**

156	**Station Platform** illuminated Green base/red roof/diecast posts, 46-49 picket fence with signs, also prewar 39-42	(3)	**160**
157	**Station Platform** illuminated Green roof, black metal posts/signs 58,59		
	1. Maroon base (3) **70** 2. Molded, red base	(4)	**125**
161	**Mail Pick-Up Set** Tan base/red bag holder arm/gray painted 61-63 bag with magnet plus second magnet to be glued to car. Price assumes second magnet	(4)	**75**

145

163	**Single Target Block Signal** 61-69		
	1. Painted tan base	(2)	**50**
	2. Molded darker tan plastic unpainted base	(4)	*

164 Log Loader and 97 Coal Elevator with 2023 UP gray nose FA

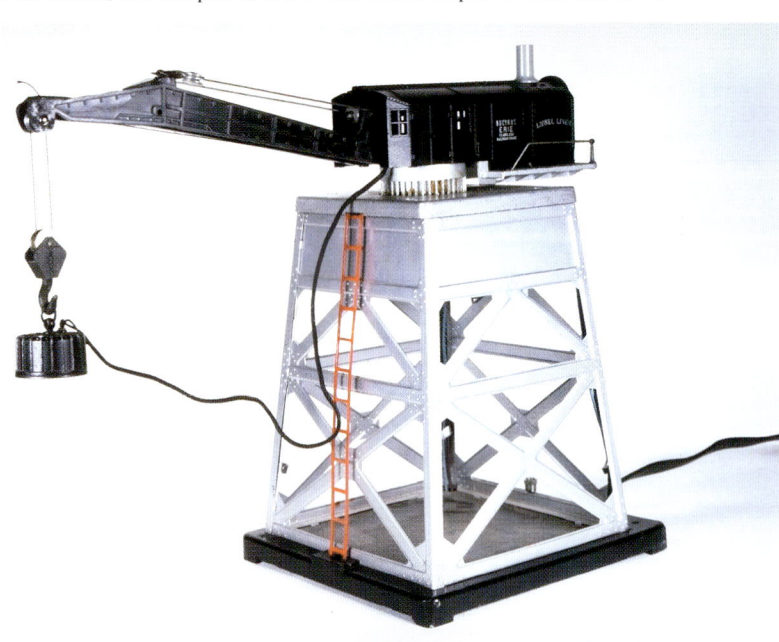

164	**Log Loader** Green/yellow/red, two-button controller 46-50	(3)	**300**
175	**Rocket Launcher** Price assumes complete with original 58-60 175-50 rocket, control panel, tower and crane. Repro rockets available	(4)	**300**
182	**Magnet Crane** With 165C controller/black base 46-49 aluminum painted frame, same cab as 2460 crane car w/added stack	(4)	**295▲**
192	**Operating Control Tower** Yellow tower/green frame/gray base, 59,60 beware of heat damage to roof, usually found with top piece missing	(4)	**250**
193	**Industrial Water Tower** Green shed/gray base/silver top with 53-55 red flashing light		
	1. Red superstructure (2) **175** 2. Black superstructure	(5)	**350**

| 195 | **Floodlight Tower** Tan base/gray tower, eight two-pin bulbs 57-66,69 Eight-light extension designed to be clipped to other side | (2) | 85 |

193 Industrial Watertowers *197 Radar Towers*

197	**Rotating Radar Antenna** Black plastic gridwork/*Lionel* 58,59 in orange letters				
	1. Gray platform	(4)	**100**	2. Orange platform (4)	**125**
199	**Microwave Relay Tower** Gray tower/white antenna/gray or tan base 58,59 (4) (interchangeable with 195 Floodlight Tower)				**125**
213	**Lift Bridge**				5P
214	**Girder Plate Bridge** 53-69				
	1. *LIONEL* on sides	(2)	**35**	2. *US Steel* girders (from 6418) (2)	**60**
252	**Automatic Crossing Gate** Black base, black/white gate, 50-62,63 two red lanterns	(2)			**35**

POSTWAR

282 Gantry Crane

147

253	**Block Control Signal** Tan base, white pole 56-59					
	1. Black control box	(3)	**60**	2. Tan control box	(2)	5(
256	**Freight Station** Maroon/white/green, picket fence w/billboards 50-53				(2)	9(
257	**Freight Station** Diesel horn, same as 256 w/battery-powered horn 56,57 and control button					
	1. Maroon base	(2)	**150**	2. Brown base	(4)	25(
262	**Highway Crossing Gate** 62-66,69					
	1. Black/white gate	(3)	**40**	2. Red/white gate	(4)	4!
264	**Operating Fork Lift Platform** Black base/brown deck area, 57-60 orange lift truck with blue man, white crane, red 6264 with lumber				(4)	35(
282	**Gantry Crane** Gray frame, black superstructure, white lettering, 54,55 3 lever controller 282C, comes with both gray glued-on smokestack and black smokestack molded in plastic. NDV					
	1. Black magnet 54	(3)	**250▲**	2. Nickel plated magnet, 55	(4)	250▲
282R	**Gantry Crane** 282 w/modified motor and platform 56,57 "R" means redesigned. Cab is one piece molded plastic including stack. 282 secured with screws to base. 282R snapped on base				(3)	275▲
299	**Code Transmitter Beacon Set** 61-63				(3)	225
308	**Railroad Sign Set** Five die-cast signs 45-49				(3)	75
309	**Yard Sign Set** 12 plastic signs with diecast bases 50-59				(2)	35
310	**Billboard Set** with 3 different billboards 50-68					
	1. Dark green frame	(3)	**45**	2. Light green frame	(4)	*
	3. Yellow frame	(5)	*	4. Red frame	(5)	*
313	**Bascule Bridge** Green base, yellow/red shack, black alignment 46-49 frame, aluminum bridge. Reissued in 97				(4)	550
314	**Plate Girder Bridge** Gray sheet metal base/diecast sides 45-48,50				(3)	4!
315	**Trestle Bridge** Aluminum, Illuminated 46,47				(3)	125
316	**Trestle Bridge** same as 315 but painted gray, and no light 49				(2)	35
317	**Trestle Bridge** Gray, same as 316, 50-56				(2)	35
321	**Trestle Bridge** Aluminum Sheet metal base/gray plastic sides 58-64				(2)	75

| 332 | **Arch Under Bridge** Black metal span/gray plastic sides 59-66 | (3) | 50 |
| 334 | **Operating Dispatching Board** Green board/tan base/blue man 57-60 | (4) | 325 |

342	**Culvert Loader** Black metal base, red/gray building 56-58 operates with 345 and 6342 culvert car	(4)	350▲
345	**Culvert Unloading Station** Black metal base, gray ramp, 57-59 red-gray tower, operates with 342 and 6342	(4)	400
346	**Culvert Unloader** *Sears* Manual identical to 348/9836 set with U64,65 2347 C&O GP-7, hand operated with crank	(4+)	275
347	**Cannon Firing Range Set** Olive drab, 4 cannons, 4 silver shells U64 *9820 Sears Military Set*	(4+)	600
348	**Culvert Unloader** Manual 348s are 346s with a piece of tape, 66-69 348 rubber-stamped on it placed over the 346 number on the box	(4)	275

POSTWAR

350	**Engine Transfer Table** Black metal base, yellow building, red light 57-60 on top with 350-89 rail brackets	(4)	400
350-50	**Transfer Table Extension** Black metal base, w/350-89 rail brackets 57-60	(4)	225▲
352	**Ice Depot** White shed, red roof, blue man w/orange arms 55-57 and paddle, with 6352-1 car		
	1. Brown base (4+) **350** 2. Red base	(4)	225
353	**Trackside Control Signal** Tan base, white pole/2 target lamp cover 60,61	(2)	40

149

356	**Operating Freight Station** Maroon/white, picket fence with signs 52-57 two blue baggage men with carts, green, orange, or red carts known to exist, some baggage loads lithographed		
	1. Dark green roof (2) **125▲** 2. Light green roof	(5)	**325**
362	**Barrel Loader** Gray base/yellow ramp 52-57 brown plastic fence, cream or blue man. NDV		
	1. Gray molded plastic base (3) **150** 2. Painted gray base	(3+)	**175**
364	**Conveyor Lumber Loader** 48-54		
	1. Painted gray, smooth finish	(3)	**125**
	2. Painted darker gray, crackle finish	(4)	**125**
365	**Dispatch Station** gray base, red control room, gray roof, 59 yellow microwave tower, 2 yellow speakers	(3)	**200▲**
375	**Turntable** Battery operated 62-64	(4)	**275**
394	**Rotary Beacon** Beware of repro beacons. 49-53		
	1. Tower, base, top painted red	(2)	**50**
	2. Tower, base, top painted green	(4)	**115**
	3. Tower, base, top unpainted aluminum	(3)	**75**
	4. Tower, base, top painted aluminum	(3)	**60**
	5. Tower, top unpainted aluminum painted red base	(4)	**125**
	6. Tower unpainted aluminum/red base and top	(5)	*****
395	**Floodlight Tower** 49,50,52-56		
	1. Tower, base, top painted yellow	(5)	**175**
	2. Tower, base, top painted silver	(3)	**50**
	3. Tower, base, top painted red	(4)	**85**
	4. Tower, base, top unpainted aluminum	(3)	**50**
	5. Tower, base, top painted green	(3)	**80**
397	**Diesel Operating Coal Loader** Gray metal base/red tray 48-57		
	1. Yellow motor cover, yard light	(5)	**450▲**
	2. Blue motor cover, no yard light	(3)	**175▲**
410	**Billboard Blinker** Black, goes w/310 billboard 56-58	(4)	**60**
415	**Diesel Fueling Station** White/red/gray base/blue tank/white 55-67	(4)	**150**
419	**Heliport Control Tower** Red tower/gray roof, spring mechanism, 62 yellow dish/yellow-black copter, one-piece prop	(5)	**500**
443	**Missile Launching Platform** Blue launcher on tan base, 60-62 with exploding ammo dump	(3)	**95**
445	**Switch Tower** Two blue men white tower/green roof/maroon base 52-57	(2)	**85**

448	**Missile Firing Range Set** Gray launcher/tan base/6448 Target car 61-63	(4)	**175**
450	**Signal Bridge** Spans 2 tracks Gray base/black metal gridwork, 52-58 Two lights	(3)	**75**
452	**Gantry Signal** Gray base/black metal gridwork, one signal light 61-63	(4)	**125**
455	**Oil Derrick** Red base/green tower/metal Sunoco sign. 50-54		
	1. Green tower, red top (4) **350** 2. Green tower, green top	(3)	**200**
	3. Light green tower, red top (5) **400** 4. Light green tower, green top	(5)	*****

456	**Coal Ramp** w/3456 *N&W* Operating Hopper designed to operate 50-55 with 397 Coal Loader, red light, 456C controller, red tray		
	1. Dark gray ramp (3) **350** 2. Light gray ramp	(2)	**225**
460	**Piggyback Transportation** Came with 2 versions of lift trucks 55-57 *Note: Must have lift truck driver*		
	1. White heat-stamped lettering	(3)	**150**
	2. Black stick-on label, white lettering	(3)	**150**
460P	**Piggyback Platform** 460P on box (must have box) 55-57	(5)	**100**
461	**Platform with Truck & Midge** Gray base/white *Midge Toy* trailer U66	(4)	**250**
462	**Derrick Platform Set** 61,62 Tan base/yellow crane, 3 black cranks	(5)	**500▲**
464	**Lumber Mill** Gray base/red roof 56-60 Reissued as 2301 in 1980, original has 464 in window	(3)	**225▲**
465	**Sound Dispatching Station** Tan base/red room/gray roof 56,57 yellow dish with gray microphone and internal speaker	(3)	**150▲**
470	**Missile Launching Platform** Tan base/blue launcher, 59-62 with 6470 Target car	(4)	**125**
494	**Rotary Beacon** 54-66		
	1. Tower, base, platform painted red	(3)	**50**
	2. Tower, base, platform unpainted alum	(3)	**50**
	3. Tower, base, platform painted alum	(3)	**50**
497	**Coaling Station** 53-58		
	1. Dk green roof/metal brace (4) **350** 2. Dark green roof/no brace	(3)	**225**
	3. Light green roof/no brace (3) **225**		
902	**Lionel Elevated Trestle Set** Packaged in paper bag. Parts punched U59 out of heavy cardboard sheets.	(5)	**350**
908	**Cardboard Railroad Station** U59-62 Came with uncataloged sets X810NA, 19394, 19395.	(5)	**1200**
910	**Cardboard Submarine Base** U61 Included in uncataloged set X-625 w/228 CN Alco X-714 w USMC.	(5)	**2500***
920	**Scenic Display Set** 57,58	(3)	**150**
920-2	**Tunnel Portals** "Hillside" 57	(3)	**50**

POSTWAR

151

Two variations of the 497 Coaling Station

943	**Exploding Ammo Dump** Gray base, olive drab body, 59,60 mousetrap mechanism	(4)	**60**
970	**Ticket Booth** Cardboard, 46"h x 23w x 11deep 58-60	(3)	**175**
1045	**Operating Watchman** Requires 1045C, Red base/blue man 46-50 w/flesh-colored hands & face, aluminum pole, nickel or brass RR warning sign. NDV	(3)	**85**
1047	**Operating Switchman** Green metal base/blue switchman with 59-61 red flag/blue or black fuel tank on base. NDV	(4)	**200▼**

Replacement Accessories

Note: These were the smaller items, such as the cans for the operating milk car, that were often lost or broken. Lionel sold replacements, usually in a group, which came in their own boxes or other packages. Each box had its own catalog number. Most items are extremely hard to find. Values and rarity ratings are based on the items being in their original packaging. **Prices are for Excellent with the box with any additional packaging.**

B909	Same as 909 but in blister pack 66		*
L363	**Miniature Lamps**	(3)	**15**
L461	**Miniature Lamps**	(3)	**15**
SP	**Smoke Pellets** (box of 12) 48-69	(4)	**500**
28	**Lamp "r"**		*
35-30	**Telephone Pole** for Generator Car	(3)	**250***
39-3	**12-Volt Lamp**		*
40	**Dealer display box** wire on eight plastic cables	(5)	**300**
40-25	**4-conductor Wire** on cable (envelope)	(4)	**50**
40-40	Same as 40-25 but 3-conductor wire	(4)	**75**
44-80	**Four Missiles** (envelope) 59-60	(2)	**15**
47-73	**12-Volt Red Lamps** (box of 12)	(4)	**25**
55-150	**24 Ties for Tie-Jector** (envelope) 59,60	(3)	**15**
64-15	**12-Volt Opal Lamps** (box of 12)	(4)	**25**
111-50	**Trestle Set** (Father-Son Set)	(5)	**250**

From top left: 0209 Six Small Barrels, 362-78 Six Barrels, 3424-100 Low Bridge Signal Set, 195-75 Eight Bulb Floodlight Head, 394-37 Rotating Beacon Lantern, 450L Signal Light Head, 3462 Seven Magnetic Milk Cans

111-100	**Two Trestle Tiers** (envelope) 60	(3)	20
122	**Lamp Assortment Kit**	(4)	85
123	**Lamp Assortment**	(4)	300
123-60	**Lamp Assortment Kit**	(5)	125
152-33	**12-Volt Red Lamps** (box of 12)	(4)	75
153-23	**6-8-Volt Red Lamps** (box of 12)	(4)	75
160	**Unloading bin** w/separate sale box		
	1. Multicolored (4+) 60 2. Black	(4)	50
	3. Tuscan (4+) 60 4. Sheet-metal (no box)	(5)	200*
164-64	**Five Logs** 52-58	(3)	35
165-53	**18-Volt Red Lamps** (box of 12)	(4)	25
175-50	**Rocket** (zip-lock plastic bag) 58-60	(4)	100
182-22	**Metal punch-outs** in cloth bag w/drawstring, for use with magnetic cranes	(5)	150*
195-75	**Eight Bulb Floodlight Head**		
	1. In early box (4) 250 2. In late box	(5)	350
196	**Smoke Pellets,** in clear plastic "lunchbox" containers (12 pack) 46,47 only	(5)	100*
197-75	**Radar Screen** for 197		
	1. Silver screen (5) 500* 2. Chrome screen	(5)	500*
206	**Bag of Artificial Coal**, 46-59	(3)	35
207	**Bag of Artificial Coal** smaller than 206, usually included with operating coal cars and accessories	(5)	75*
0209	**Six Small Barrels**	(3)	25
216	**Miniature Lamps**	(3)	25
264-150	**12 Boards for Forklift Platform** (envelope) 57-59	(4)	50
352-55	**7 Ice Cubes for Icing Station** (envelope) 55-57	(4)	55
356-35	**Two Baggage Trucks** 52-56		
	1. No load (3) 65 2. With load	(4)	150
362-78	**Six Barrels** 52-58	(2)	35
394-37	**Rotating Beacon Latern**, 54-60	(3)	25
450L	**Signal Light Head** 52-58	(4)	150

POSTWAR

153

6800-60 Airplane, 460-150 Vans green, 460-150 Vans and 6801-60 Boat

460-150	**Two Piggyback Vans** w/either 2 white or 2 green vans 55-57	(5)	**450***
464-150	**6 Boards for Lumber Mill** (envelope) 56-58	(3)	**45**
479 and 479-1 Trucks for 6362 Railway Truck Car (envelope)		(2)	**35***
480-25	**Conversion Coupler** 50-60	(2)	**20***
480-32	**Conversion Coupler** 61-69	(2)	**20***
671S	**Conversion Kit** 47-49	(3)	**250***
671-75	**Smoke Lamps**	(4)	**50**
703-10	**Smoke Lamp**	(4)	**50**
726S	**Conversion Kit** 47-49	(5)	**300***
909	**Smoke Fluid** (box of 4) 58-69	(4)	**100**
919	**Artificial Grass** 46-64	(2)	**25**

3330-100 Submarine

920-3	**Green Grass** (Scenic Display Set) 57,58	(3)	**35**
920-4	**Yellow Grass** (Scenic Display Set) 57,58	(3)	**35**
920-5	**Artificial Rock** (Scenic Display Set) 57,58	(4)	**50**
920-8	**Lichen** (Scenic Display Set) 57,58	(4)	**50**
925	**Lubricant** 2-oz 46-69 (with box)	(2)	**35**
926	**Lubricant** 1/2-oz (same as above)		

927	**Lubricant and Maintenance Kit** 1-track cleaner, 1-lubricant, 1-oil, 1-wooden tamper, 1-brush, 2-pointed sticks, 6-emery boards	(4)	65
928	**Lubricant & Maintenance Kit** 60-63 oiler, eraser rail cleaner, grease, track cleaner	(5)	150*
1640-100	**1960 Presidential Special Kit** 60	(5)	500*
3330-100	**Operating Submarine Kit** 60	(5)	750*
3356-2	**Operating Horse Car** in separate sale box	(4)	750*
3356-100	**Nine Horses** 56-59	(4)	75
3356-150	**Horse Corral** 56,57	(4)	500
3357-27	**Components for Cop & Hobo Car**	(4)	150*
3366-100	**Nine White Horses** 59,60	(3)	200
3424-50	**One Tell-Tale Pole**	(5)	500*
3424-100	**Two Tell-Tale Poles** 56-58	(4)	75*
3454-51	**Baby Ruth Packing Cases**	(5)	150*
3462P	**Milk Car Platform** 52-55	(3)	1500*
3462-70	**Seven Magnetic Milk Cans** 52-59	(3)	40
3530-50	**Telephone Pole** searchlight 56,57	(4)	125
3656-34	**Nine Cattle** 52-58	(3)	75
3656-150	**Cattle Corral** 52-55	(4)	1000*
3662-79	**Seven Milk Cans** (envelope) 55-57,59	(5)	40*
3672P	**Bosco Platform**	(5)	4000*
3672-79	**Seven Bosco Milk Cans** 59,60	(5)	125*
3927-50	**Cotton Track Cleaning Patches** (qty 25) 57-60	(2)	35
3927-75	**Track Cleaner** 56-69	(4)	35
5159	**Lubricant & Maintenance Kit** for slotcars, 65,65	(3)	75
6112-25	**Four Canisters** either 1 red & 1-white, or 2 of either color 56-58 1. White lettering (3) **50** 2. Black lettering	(3)	600*
6352-25	**Box for Ice Car**	(5)	2000*
6414-25	**Four Automobiles** 55-57	(4)	500
6454	**Replacement Car Bodies**	(4)	50
6511-24	**Five Pipes** 55-58	(3)	65

POSTWAR

Two 6827-100 Power Shovels and two 6828-100 Truck Cranes

6650-80	Missile 59,60	(3)	75
6800-60	Airplane 57,58	(4)	400*
6801-60	Boat 57,58	(4)	200
6816-100	Bulldozer 59,60	(4)	1000*
6817-100	Earth Scraper 59,60	(4)	1500*
6827-100	Power Shovel 60	(4)	200*▲
6828-100	Truck Crane 60	(4)	200*▲

Track

OC	Curved Track O gauge, 45-61	(1)	10
OCS	Insulated Curved Track O gauge, 50		*
OS	Straight Track O gauge, 45-61	(1)	10
OSS	Insulated Straight Track O gauge 46,50		*
OTC	Lockon 55-59	(1)	3
RCS	Remote Control Track O gauge w/RCS-20 two-button controller 46-48	(3)	20
UCS	Remote Control Track O gauge 49-66, 68,69	(3)	25
TOC	Same as OC		
TOS	Same as OS		
TO20	90 Degree Crossing O gauge 62-66,69	(3)	20
UCS	Remote Control Track O gauge		
1/2 OC	1/2 Curve Track O gauge		25*
1/2OS	1/2 Straight Track O gauge		*
5/F	Test Set	(4)	5000▲
O20X	45 Degree Crossover 46-59	(1)	20
O20	90 Degree Crossover 45-61	(1)	20
O22	Remote Control Switches (price per pair) 45-61	(1)	125
O22A	Remote Control Switch 47U	(4)	100
O22LH	Remote Control Switch 45-61	(2)	75
O22RH	Remote Control Switch 45-61	(2)	75
O25	Bumper Black, O gauge 46,47	(3)	30
O26	Bumper 48-50		
	1. Gray, 48 only (4) 125 2. Red	(1)	40
O42	Manual Switches (pair) 47-59	(3)	75
31	Curved Track Super O 57-66	(3)	3
32	Straight Track Super O 57-66	(3)	3
33	1/2 Curved Track Super O 57-66	(3)	2
34	1/2 Straight Track Super O 57-66	(3)	2
36	Remote Control Set Super O includes 90 controller and wires 57-66	(3)	20
37	Uncoupling Track Set Super O includes 90 controller and wires 57-66	(3)	20
38	Adapter Track Super O Adapts other track to Super O 57-51 (pair of straight sections)	(3)	20
43	Power Track Super O 59-66	(3)	12
48	Straight Track Super O insulated 57-66	(3)	12

49	**Curved Track** Super O insulated, 57-66	(3)	12
112	**Super O Switches** (pair)	(4)	150
112-125 & 112LH **Super O Switch** Left Hand 57-60		(4)	75
112-150 & 112RH **Super O Switch** Right Hand 57-60		(4)	75
120	**Super O 90 Degree Crossing** 57-66	(3)	15
130	**Super O 60 Degree Crossing** 57-66	(4)	50
142	**Super O Manual Switches** (price per pair) 57-66	(3)	60
142-125	**Super O LH Manual Switch** 57-60	(3)	40
142-150	**Super O RH Manual Switch** 57-60	(3)	40
260	**Bumper** 51-69		
	1. Red diecast for regular O (2) **30** 2. Black plastic for Super O	(5)	150
760	**O72 Track Package 16 Sections** (72" circle) 50, 54-57	(4)	60
1008	**O27 Uncoupling Clip** 57-62	(3)	10
1008-50	**O27 Track** w/uncoupling clip	(3)	10
1009	**Manumatic Track Section** Used with Scout Sets 48-52	(3)	10
1013	**O27 Curved Track** 45-66, 68,69	(1)	1
1018	**O27 Straight Track** 45-66, 68,69	(1)	1
1019	**Remote Control 0-27 Track** w/RCS 20, 46-48	(2)	15
1020	**O27 90 Degree Crossing** 55-66, 68,69	(2)	10
1022	**O27 Manual Switches** (price per pair) 53-66, 69,69	(2)	30
1023	**O27 45 Degree Crossing** 56-66, 68,69	(2)	5
1024	**0-27 Manual Switches** (price per pair) 46-52	(2)	30
1025	**O27 Bumper** Black w/lamp, 46,47	(2)	15
1121	**O27 Remote Control Switches** (price per pair) 46-51	(3)	75
1122	**O27 Remote Control Switches** (price per pair) 52	(2)	75
1122E	**O27 Remote Control Switches** (price per pair) 53-66, 68,69	(3)	75
1122LH	**O27 LH Remote Control Switch** 55-66,68,69	(3)	50
1122RH	**O27 RH Remote Control Switch** 55-66,68,69	(3)	50
6009	**O27 Uncoupling track** 53-55	(2)	20
6019	**O27 Remote Control Track** 48-66	(2)	20
6029	**O27 Remote Control Track** 55-63	(2)	25
6149	**O27 Remote Control Track** 64-66, 68,69	(2)	10

Transformers and Controllers

ECU-1	**Train Control Unit** Electronic set	(4)	100
KW	190 Watts 50-65	(4)	150
LW	125 Watts 55-66	(3)	125
Q	75 Watts 46	(2)	60
R	100 Watt or 110 Watt 46, 47	(3)	80
RW	110 Watt 48-54	(3)	75
S	80 Watts 47	(2)	40
SW	130 Watts 61-66	(4)	100
TW	175 Watts 53-60	(3)	150

POSTWAR

V	150 Watts 46,47	(3)	150
VW	150 Watts 48,49	(3)	200
Z	250 Watts 45-47	(4)	250
ZW	250 Watts 48,49	(3)	300
ZW	275 Watts 50-66	(4)	325
88	**Controller** 46-50	(1)	10
90	**Controller** 55-66	(2)	15
91	**Circuit Breaker**	(3)	25
92	**Circuit Breaker**	(2)	20
96C	**Controller** 45-54	(2)	20
145C	**Contactor** 50-60	(1)	7
147	**Whistle Controller**	(2)	13
148-100	**Double Pole Switch** 57,58	(2)	25
153C	**Contactor** 46-66, 68,69	(1)	5
167	**Whistle Controller**	(2)	15
364C	**Switch** 59-64	(2)	15
390C	**Switch** 60-64	(3)	30
413	**Countdown Control Panel** Gray (can be used with any operating car) 62	(3)	75
1010	35 Watt	(2)	25
1011	25 Watt	(2)	25
1012	35 Watt	(2)	25
1014	40 Watt	(2)	25
1015	45 Watt	(3)	25
1016	35 Watt	(3)	25
1025	45 Watt	(3)	25
1026	25 Watt	(2)	25
1032	75 Watt	(3)	75
1033	90 Watt	(3)	75
1034	75 Watt	(3)	75
1037	40 Watt	(2)	40
1041	60 Watt	(2)	40
1042	75 Watt	(3)	50
1043	50 Watt Black Case	(2)	25
1043-500	**Girls Train Transformer** 60 Watt (Ivory case)	(4)	200
1044	90 Watt	(3)	75
1053	60 Watt	(2)	25
1063	75 Watt	(3)	50
1073	60 Watt	(3)	50

Lionel Cataloged Sets 1945-1969

Note: Prices listed are for Like New Boxed w/all inserts and packaging, also Like New

From top: Girls Train, Electronic Set, Alaska, Sears General, Five Star General

463W	O Gauge 4-Car Freight Set (224, 2466W, 2458, 2452, 2555, 2457) 45	(5)	**650**
1000W	027 3-Car Set (2016, 6026W, 6014 red, 6012, 6017) 55	(4)	**225**
1001	027 3-Car Set (610, 6012, 6014 red, 6017) 55	(3)	**325**
1111	Lionel Scout Set (1001, 1001T, 1002 blue, 1005, 1007) 48	(2)	**150**
1112	Lionel Scout Set (1101, 1001T, 1002 blue, 1004, 1005, 1007) 48	(4)	**200**
1113	Lionel Scout Train (1120, 1001T, 1002 black, 1005, 1007) 50	(3)	**150**
1115	Lionel Scout (1110, 1001T, 1002 black, 1005, 1007) 49	(4)	**150**
1117	Lionel Scout (1110, 1001T, 1002 black, 1005, 1004, 1007) 49	(3)	**150**
1119	Scout 3-Car Freight (1110, 1001T, 1002 black, 1004, 1007) 51, 52	(2)	**150**
1400	Lionel 027 Passenger Set (221, 221T, two blue 2430s, blue 2431) 46	(4)	**675**
1400W	Lionel 027 Passenger Set (221, 221W, two blue 2430s, blue 2431) 46	(5)	**800**
1401	Lionel 027 Freight Outfit (1654, 1654T, 2452X, 2465, 2472) 46	(3)	**150**
1401W	Lionel 027 Freight Outfit (1654, 1654W, 2452X, 2465, 2472) 46	(5)	**250**
1402	Lionel 027 Passenger Set (1666, 2466T, two green 2440s, green 2441) 46	(4)	**500**
1402W	Lionel 027 Passenger Set (1666, 2466W, two green 2440s, green 2441) 46	(5)	**600**
1403	Lionel 027 Freight Train (221, 221T, 2411, 2465, 2472) 46	(4)	**425**
1403W	Lionel 027 Freight Train (221, 221W, 2411, 2465, 2472) 46	(5)	**525**
1405	Lionel 027 Freight Train (1666, 2466T, 2452X, 2465, 2472) 46	(3)	**175**
1405W	Lionel 027 Freight Train (1666, 2466W, 2452X, 2465, 2472) 46	(5)	**250**

POSTWAR

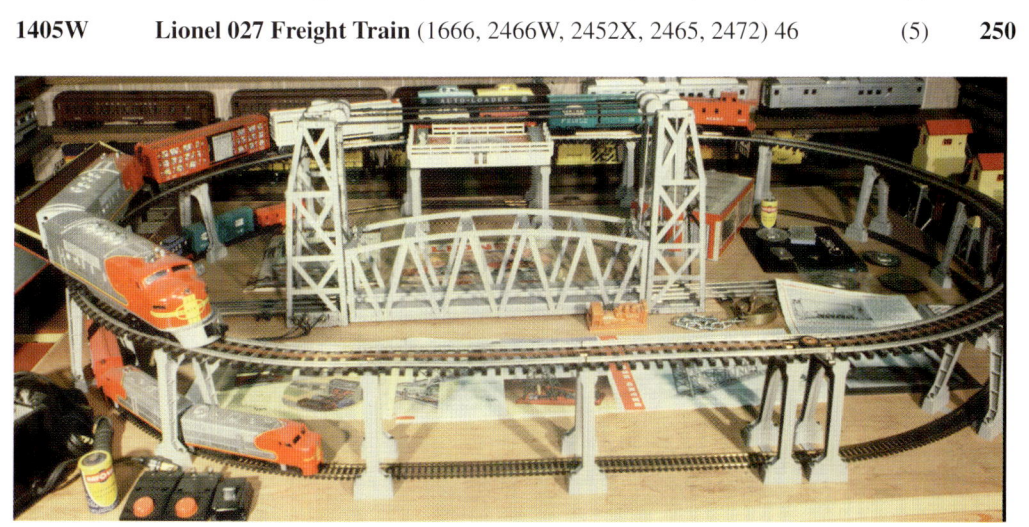

2555W Father and Son Set

159

From Top: Santa Fe Set 1962, New Haven Set 1958, Burlington GP-7 Set with extra pullman 1957, 2056 Set 1952, Alco Set 1951, Anniversary Set 1950, 671 Set 1948, 675 Set 1947, 2026 Set 1948, Empire State Set 1947

1407B	Lionel 027 Switcher Bell Outfit (1665, 2403B, 2452X, 2560, 2419) 46	(5)	900
1409	Lionel 027 Freight Train (1666, 2466T, 3559, 2465, 3454, 2472) 46	(4)	400
1409W	Lionel 027 Freight Train (1666, 2466W, 3559, 2465, 3454, 2472) 46	(5)	500
1411W	Freight Outfit (1666, 2466WX, 2452X, 2465, 2454, 2472) 46	(4)	225
1413WS	Lionel 027 Freight Train (2020, 2020W, 2452X, 2465, 2454, 2472) 46	(3)	350
1415WS	Lionel 027 Freight Set (2020, 2020W, 3459, 3454, 2465, 2472) 46	(4)	550
1417WS	Lionel 027 Freight Outfit (2020, 2020W, 2465, 3451, 2560, 2419) 46	(4)	750
1419WS	Lionel 027 Freight Train (2020, 2020W, 3459, 97, 2452X, 2560, 2419) 46	(5)	900
1421WS	Lionel 027 Freight Train (2020, 2020W, 3451, 164, 2465, 3454, 2472) 46	(5)	1000
1423W	Lionel 3-Car Freight Outfit 48, 49		
	(1655, 6654W, 6452, 6465, 6257) 48	(3)	150
	(1655, 6654W, 6462, 6465, 6257) 49	(3)	150
1425B	Switcher Freight 48, 49		
	(1656, 6403B, 6456 black, 6465, 6257X) 48	(4)	850
	(1656, 6403B, 6456 black, 6465, 6257) 49	(4)	850
1426WS	Lionel Passenger Set (2026, 6466WX, two green 2440s, grn 2441) 48, 49	(4)	600
1427WS	Lionel Three-Car Freight Set (2026, 6466WX, 6465, 6454, 6257) 48	(3)	250
1429WS	Four-Car Freight Set (2026, 6466WX, 3451, 6465, 6454, 6357) 48	(3)	225
1430WS	Passenger Train (2025, 6466WX, 2400, 2402, 2401) 48, 49	(4)	800
1431	Lionel Freight Train (1654, 1654T, 2452X, 2465, 2472) 47	(4)	150
1431W	Lionel Freight Train (1654, 1654W, 2452X, 2465, 2472) 47	(4)	150
1432	Lionel Passenger Set (221, 221T, two blue 2430s, blue 2431) 47	(4)	900
1432W	Lionel Passenger Set (221, 221W, two blue 2430s, blue 2431) 47	(4)	900
1433	Lionel Freight Train (221, 221T, 2411, 2465, 2472) 47	(4)	400
1433W	Lionel Freight Train (221, 221W, 2411, 2465, 2472) 47	(4)	400
1434WS	Passenger Train (2025, 2466WX, two green 2440s, green 2441) 47	(4)	400
1435WS	Lionel Freight Train (2025, 2466WX, 2452X, 2454, 2472) 47	(3)	250
1437WS	Lionel Freight Set (2025, 2466WX, 2452X, 2465, 2454, 2472) 47	(3)	275
1439WS	Lionel Freight Outfit (2025, 2466WX, 3559, 2465, 3454, 2472) 47	(4)	425

Number	Description	Cond	Price
1441WS	De Luxe Work Outfit (2020, 2020W, 2461, 3451, 2560, 2419) 47	(4)	550
1443WS	4-Car Freight (2020, 2020W, 3459, 3462, 2465, 2472) 47	(4)	425
1445WS	4-Car Freight (2025, 6466WX, 3559, 6465, 6454, 6357) 48	(4)	325
1447WS	De Luxe Work Train 48, 49 (2020, 6020W, 3451, 2461, 2460, 6419) 48 (2020, 6020W, 3461, 6461, 2460, 6419) 49	(4)	525
1449WS	5-Car Freight Outfit (2020, 6020W, 3462, 6465, 3459, 6411, 6357) 48	(4)	450
1451WS	3-Car Freight (2026, 6466WX, 6462, 3464, 6257) 49	(3)	275
1453WS	4-Car Freight (2026, 6466WX, 3464, 6465, 3461, 6357) 49	(3)	325
1455WS	4-Car 027 Freight (2025, 6466WX, 6462, 6465, 3472, 6357) 49	(3)	400
1457B	4-Car Diesel Freight (6220, 6462, 3464, 6520, 6419) 49, 50	(4)	625
1459WS	027 5-Car Freight Outfit 49 (2020, 6020W, 6411, 3656, 6465, 3469, 6357)	(4)	550
1461S	3-Car Freight With Smoke (6110, 6001T, 6002, 6004, 6007) 50	(2)	150
1463W	027 3-Car Freight (2036, 6466W, 6462, 6465, 6257) 50	(2)	150
1463WS	027 3-Car Freight (2026, 6466W, 6462, 6465, 6257) 51	(3)	200
1464W	027 Diesel 3-Car Pullman (2023 AA yellow, 2481, 2482, 2483) 50	(4)	2000
1464W	027 Diesel 3-Car Pullman 51 (2023 AA silver, 2421, 2422, 2423 cars w/gray roof)	(4)	900
1464W	3-Car Pullman 52, 53 (2033 AA silver, 2421, 2422, 2423 cars w/silver roof)	(4)	1000
1465	3-Car Freight (2034, 6066T, 6032, 6035, 6037) 52	(2)	150
1467W	027 Diesel 4-Car Freight 50, 51 (2023 AA yellow, 6656, 6465, 6456, 6357) 50 (2023 AA silver, 6656, 6465, 6456, 6357) 51	(3)	650
1467W	4-Car Freight (Twin 2032, 6656, 6456, 6465, 6357) 52, 53	(4)	525
1469WS	027 4-Car Freight 50, 51 (2035, 6466W, 6462, 6465, 6456 black, 6257) 50 (2035, 6466W, 6462, 6465, 6456 maroon, 6257) 51	(2)	225
1471WS	5-Car Freight 50, 51 (2035, 6466W, 3469X, 6465, 6454, 3461X, 6357)	(3)	350
1473WS	4-Car Freight (2046, 2046W, 3464, 6465, 6520, 6357) 50	(3)	425
1475WS	5-Car Freight 50 (2046, 2046W, 3656, 3461X, 6472, 3469X, 6419)	(3)	525
1477S	027 3-Car Freight (2026, 6466T, 6012, 6014 white, 6017) 51, 52	(3)	200
1479WS	027 4-Car Freight (2056, 2046W, 6462, 6465, 6456, 6257) 52	(3)	425
1481WS	5-Car Freight (2035, 6466W, 3464, 6465, 3472, 6462, 6357) 51	(3)	325
1483WS	5-Car Freight (2056, 2046W, 3472, 6462, 3474, 6465, 6357) 52	(4)	625
1484WS	4-Car Pullman 52 (2056, 2046W, 2421, 2422, 2429, 2423 cars w/silver roof)	(4)	1000
1485WS	027 3-Car Freight (2025, 6466W, 6462, 6465, 6257) 52	(3)	225
1500	027 3-Car Freight (1130, 6066T, 6032, 6034, 6037) 53, 54	(1)	150
1501S	027 3-Car Freight (2026, 6066T, 6032, 6035, 6037) 53	(2)	150
1502WS	027 3-Car Pullman (2055, 2046W, 2421, 2422, 2423) 53	(4)	750
1503WS	027 4-Car Freight 53, 54 (2055, 6026W, 6462 black, 6456 black, 6465, 6257) 53 (2055, 6026W, 6462 black, 6456 green, 6465, 6257) 54	(2)	325

POSTWAR

Set	Description	Rarity	Price
1505WS	**027 4-Car Freight** (2046, 2046W, 6464-1, 6462, 6415, 6357) 53	(3)	**450**
1507WS	**027 5-Car Freight** (2046, 2046W, 3472, 6415, 6462, 6468, 6357) 53	(3)	**425**
1509WS	**027 5-Car Freight** (2046, 2046W, 3520, 6456, 3469, 6460, 6419) 53	(2)	**500**
1511S	**027 4-Car Freight** (2037, 6066T, 6032, 3474, 6035, 6037) 53	(4)	**300**
1513S	**027 4-Car Freight** (2037, 6026T, 6012, 6014 red, 6015, 6017) 54, 55	(1)	**175**
1515WS	**027 5-Car Freight** (2065, 2046W, 6415, 6462, 6464-25, 6456, 6357) 54	(4)	**500**
1516WS	**027 3-Car Passenger** (2065, 2046W, 2434, 2432, 2436) 54	(4)	**750**
1517W	**027 4-Car Freight** (2245P/C AB, 6464-225, 6561, 6462 green, 6427) 54	(4)	**1000**
1519WS	**027 5-Car Freight** (2065, 6026W, 3461, 6462 red, 6356, 3482, 6427) 54	(4)	**550**
1520W	**027 Texas Special 3-Car Passenger** (2245P/C AB, 2432, 2435, 2436) 54	(5)	**2000**
1521WS	**027 5-Car Freight** 54 (2065, 2046W, 3620, 3562 black, 6561, 6460 black cab, 6419)	(4)	**750**
1523	**027 4-Car Work Train** (6250, 6511, 6456 gray, 6460 red cab, 6419) 54	(4)	**750**
1527	**027 3-Car Work Train** (1615, 1615T, 6462, 6560 gray cab, 6119) 55	(4)	**500**
1529	**027 3-Car Freight** (2028, 6311, 6436, 6257) 55	(5)	**750**
1531W	**027 4-Car Freight** (2328, 6462 red, 6456, 6465, 6257) 55	(4)	**650**
1533WS	**027 Freight Hauler** (2055, 6026W, 3562 yellow, 6436, 6465, 6357) 55	(4)	**450**
1534W	**027 3-Car Passenger** (2328, 2434, 2432, 2436) 55	(4)	**1000**
1536W	**027 3-Car Passenger** (2245P/C AB, 2432, 2432, 2436) 55	(4)	**2000**
1537WS	**027 4-Car Freight** 55 (2065, 2046W, 3562 yellow, 3469, 6464-275, 6357)	(4)	**575**
1538WS	**027 4-Car Passenger** (2065, 2046W, 2435, 2434, 2432, 2436) 55	(4)	**900**
1539W	**027 5-Car Freight** (2243P/C AB, 3620, 6446, 6561, 6560, 6419) 55	(4)	**900**
1541WS	**027 5-Car Freight** (2065, 2046W, 3482, 3461, 6415, 3494, 6427) 55	(4)	**600**
1542	**027 3-Car Freight** (520, 6014 red, 6012, 6017) 56	(3)	**225**
1543	**027 3-Car Freight** (627, 6121, 6112, 6017) 56	(4)	**250**
1545	**027 4-Car Freight** (628, 6424, 6014 red, 6257) 56	(4)	**325**
1547S	**027 Freight Hauler** (2018, 6026T, 6121, 6112, 6014 red, 6257) 56	(4)	**175**
1549S	**027 3-Car Work Train** (1615, 1615T, 6262, 6560, 6119 orange) 56	(4)	**900**
1551S	**027 4-Car Freight** (621, 6362, 6425, 6562, 6257) 56	(4)	**400**
1552	**027 Passenger** (629, 2434, 2432, 2436) 56	(5)	**1200**
1553W	**027 5-Car Freight** (2338, 6430, 6462 red, 6464-425, 6346, 6257) 56	(4)	**700**
1555WS	**027 Freight Hauler** (2018, 6026W, 3361, 6464-400, 6462 red, 6257) 56	(3)	**400**
1557W	**027 5-Car Work Train** (621, 6436, 6511, 3620, 6560, 6119) 56	(4)	**525**
1559W	**027 5-Car Freight** 56 (2338, 6414, 3562 yellow, 6362, 3494-275, 6357)	(4)	**750**
1561WS	**027 5-Car Freight** 56 (2065, 6026W, 6430, 3424, 6262, 6562, 6257)	(4)	**600**
1562W	**027 4-Car Passenger** (2328, 2442, 2442, 2444, 2446) 56	(4)	**2000**
1563W	**027 5-Car Freight** (2240P/C AB, 6467, 3562 yellow, 3620, 6414, 6357) 56	(4)	**1750**
1565W	**027 5-Car Freight** (2065, 6026W, 3662, 3650, 6414, 6346, 6357) 56	(4)	**600**
1567W	**027 5-Car Freight** 56 (2243P/C AB, 3356, 3424, 6672, 6430, 6357)	(4)	**1000**
1569	**027 4-Car Freight** (202, 6014 white, 6111, 6112, 6017) 57	(3)	**300**

1571	**027 5-Car Freight** (625, 6424, 6476, 6121, 6112, 6017) 57	(4)	**450**
1573	**027 5-Car Freight** (250LT, 250T , 6025, 6112, 6464-425, 6476, 6017) 57	(4)	**250**
1575	**027 5-Car Freight** (205P/T AA, 6111, 6121, 6112, 6560, 6119) 57	(4)	**400**
1577S	**027 6-Car Freight** 57 (2018, 1130T, 6121, 6464-475, 6111, 6014 red, 6112, 6017)	(4)	**250**
1578S	**027 3-Car Passenger** (2018, 1130T, 2434, 2432, 2436) 57	(5)	**550**
1579S	**027 7-Car Freight** 57 (2037, 1130T, 6111, 6025, 6476, 6468, 6112, 6121, 6017)	(4)	**300**
1581	**027 7-Car Freight** 57 (611, 6476, 6024, 6424, 6464-650, 6025, 6560, 6119)	(4)	**600**
1583WS	**027 6-Car Freight** 57 (2037, 6026W, 6482, 6112, 6646, 6121, 6476 black, 6017)	(3)	**250**
1585W	**027 9-Car Freight Train** 57 (602, 6014 white,6121, 6025, 6464-525, 6112, 6024, 6476 gray, 6111, 6017)	(4)	**425**
1586	**027 3-Car Passenger** (204P/T AA, 2432, 2432, 2436) 57	(4)	**700**
1587S	**Lady Lionel Pastel Train Set** 57, 58 (2037-500, 1130T-500, 6462-500, 6464-515, 6436-500, 6464-510, 6427-500)	(4)	**4000**
1589WS	**027 7-Car Freight** 57 (2037, 6026W, 6464-450, 6111, 6025 orange, 6024, 6424, 6112, 6017)	(4)	**500**
1590	**027 4-Car Steam Freight** 58 (249, 250T, 6014 red Bosco, 6151, 6112, 6017)	(3)	**300**
1591	**U.S. Marine Land & Sea Limited** (212, 6809, 6807, 6803, 6017-50) 58	(4)	**1100**
1593	**5-Car UP Diesel Work Train** (613, 6476, 6818, 6660, 6112, 6119) 58	(4)	**650**
1595	**027 Marine Battlefront Special** 58 (1625, 1625T, 6804, 6808, 6806, 6017 gray)	(5)	**1675**
1597S	**027 6-Car Coal King Smoking Freighter** 58 (2018, 1130T, 6014 orange, 6818, 6476 red, 6025 black, 6112 blue, 6017)	(4)	**325**
1599	**027 6-Car Texas Special Freight** 58 (210 AA, 6801-50 w/yellow hull boat, 6112-1 black, 6014 orange Bosco or red Frico, 6424-60, 6465-60 gray, 6017)	(3)	**450**
1600	**027 3-Car Burlington Passenger** (216, 6572, 2432, 2436) 58	(4)	**900**
1601W	**027 5-Car Diesel Freight** (2337, 6800, 6464-425, 6801, 6810, 6017) 58	(4)	**925**
1603WS	**027 5-Car Whistling Mountain Climber Steam Freight** 58 (2037, 6026W, 6424, 6014-60 white Bosco, 6818, 6112, 6017)	(4)	**375**
1605W	**027 6-Car Santa Fe Diesel Freight** 58 (208 AA, 6800, 6464-425, 6801, 6477, 6802, 6017)	(4)	**1000**
1607W	**027 6-Car Trouble Shooter Work Set** 58 (2037, 6026W, 6465, 6818, 6464-425, 6112, 6660, 6119)	(4)	**475**
1608W	**027 4-Car Merchants Limited Diesel Passenger** 58 (209P/T AA, 2434, 2432, 2432, 2436)	(5)	**1650**
1609	**027 3-Car Steam Freight** 59, 60 (246, 1130T, 6162-25 blue, 6476 red, 6057)	(2)	**125**
1611	**027 4-Car Alaskan Freight** (614, 6825, 6162-50, 6465 black, 6027) 59	(3)	**650**
1612	**The General Old-Timer Outfit** (1862, 1862T, 1866, 1865) 59, 60	(1)	**375**
1613S	**4-Car B&O Steam Freight** (247, 247T, 6826, 6819, 6821, 6017) 59	(4)	**300**
1615	**5-Car Boston & Maine Diesel Freight** 59 (217P/C AB, 6800, 6464-475, 6812, 6825, 6017-100)	(4)	**625**
1617S	**5-Car Busy Beaver Steam Work Train** 59 (2018, 1130T, 6816, 6536, 6812, 6670, 6119)	(4)	**825**

1619W	5-Car Santa Fe Diesel Freight 59 (218P/T AA, 6819, 6802, 6801, 6519, 6017-185 gray)	(3)	425
1621WS	5-Car Construction Special Steam Freight 59 (2037, 6026W, 6825, 6519, 6062, 6464-475, 6017)	(3)	325
1623W	5-Car NP Diesel Freight (2349, 3512, 3435, 6424, 6062, 6017) 59	(5)	1250
1625WS	5-Car Action King Steam Freight 59 (2037, 6026W, 6636, 3512, 6470, 6650, 6017)	(4)	400
1626W	4-Car Santa Fe Diesel Passenger 59 (208P/T AA, 3428, 2412 blue stripe, 2412 blue stripe, 2416 blue stripe)	(4)	750
1627S	027 3-Car Steam Freight (244, 244T, 6062, 6825, 6017) 60	(1)	125
1629	4-Car C & O Diesel Freight (225, 6650, 6470, 6819, 6219) 60	(1)	325
1631WS	4-Car Industrial Steam Freight (243, 243W, 6519, 6812, 6465, 6017) 60	(2)	325
1633	Land-Sea-Air 2-Unit Diesel Freight 60 (224P/C AB, 6544, 6830, 6820, 6017-200)	(3)	1000
1635WS	5-Car Heavy-Duty Special Steam Freight 60 (2037, 243W, 6361, 6826, 6636, 6821, 6017)	(4)	450
1637W	5-Car Twin Unit Diesel Freight 60 (218P/T AA, 6475, 6175, 6464-475, 6801, 6017-185)	(4)	550
1639WS	6-Car Power House Special Steam Freight 60 (2037, 243W, 6816, 6817, 6812, 6530, 6560, 6119)	(5)	1750
1640W	5-Car Presidential Campaign Special 60 (218P/T AA, 3428, two 2412s blue stripe, 2416 blue stripe, 1640-100)	(3)	650
1641	3-Car Headliner Steam Freight (246, 244T, 3362, 6162, 6057) 61	(1)	125
1642	3-Car Circus Special Steam Freight (244, 1130T, 3376, 6405, 6119) 61	(2)	175
1643	4-Car Sky-Scout Diesel Freight (230, 3509, 6050, 6175, 6058) 61	(2)	275
1644	Frontier Special General Passenger (1862, 1862T, 3370, 1866, 1865) 61	(2)	475
1645	027 4-Car Diesel Freight (229, 3410, 6465, 6825, 6059) 61	(3)	240
1646	4-Car Utility Steam Freight (233, 233W, 6162, 6343, 6476 red, 6017) 61	(2)	350
1647	Freedom Fighter Missile Launcher Outfit 61 (45, 3665, 3519, 6830, 6448, 6814)	(4)	950
1648	5-Car Supply Line Steam Freight 61 (2037, 233W, 6062, 6465, 6519, 6476 red, 6017)	(2)	275
1649	027 5-Car Two Unit Diesel Freight 61 (218P/C AB, 6343, 6445, 6475, 6405, 6017)	(5)	525
1650	5-Car Guardian Steam Freight 61 (2037, 233W, 6544, 6470, 3330, 3419, 6017)	(4)	450
1651	4-Car All Passenger Diesel 61 (218P/T AA, 2414 blue stripe, two 2412s blue stripe, 2416 blue stripe)	(3)	750
1800	The General Frontier Pack 59, 60 (1862, 1862T, 1877, 1866, 1865, General Story Book)	(2)	400
1805	Land-Sea-And Air Gift Pack (45, 3429, 3820, 6640, 6824) 60	(4)	1750
1809	The Western Gift Pack (244, 1130 T, 3370, 3376, 1877, 6017) 61	(2)	300
1810	The Space Age Gift Pack (231, 3665, 3519, 3820, 6017) 61	(2)	550
2100	O Gauge 3-Car Passenger (224, 2466T, two brown 2442s, brn 2443) 46	(5)	550
2100W	O Gauge 3-Car Passenger (224, 2466W, two brown 2442s, brn 2443) 46	(4)	500
2101	O Gauge 3-Car Freight (224, 2466T, 2555, 2452, 2457) 46	(5)	400
2101W	O Gauge 3-Car Freight (224, 2466W, 2555, 2452, 2457) 46	(4)	325

POSTWAR

Number	Description	Rarity	Price
2103W	**O Gauge 4-Car Freight** (224, 2466W, 2458, 3559, 2555, 2457) 46	(4)	425
2105WS	**3-Car Freight Outfit** (671, 671W, 2555, 2454, 2457) 46	(4)	450
2110WS	**3-Car Passenger** (671, 671W, three 2625s) 46	(5)	1750
2111WS	**4-Car Freight** (671, 671W, 3459, 2411, 2460, 2420) 46	(5)	825
2113WS	**O Gauge 3-Car Freight Outfit** (726, 2426W, 2855, 3854, 2457) 46	(5)	2000
2114WS	**O Gauge 3-Car Passenger Outfit** (726, 2426W, three 2625 Irvingtons) 46	(5)	2500
2115WS	**O Gauge 4-Car Work Train** with Smoke 46 (726, 2426W, 2458, 3451, 2460, 2420)	(5)	1400
2120S	**3-Car De Luxe Passenger** (675, 2466T, two brown 2442s, brn 2443) 47	(5)	500
2120WS	**3-Car De Luxe Passenger** (675, 2466WX, two brown 2442s, brn 2443) 47	(4)	525
2121S	**3-Car Freight** (675, 2466T, 2452, 2555, 2457) 47	(5)	375
2121WS	**3-Car Freight** (675, 2466WX, 2452, 2555, 2457) 47	(4)	375
2123WS	**4-Car Freight** (675, 2466WX, 2458, 3559, 2555, 2457) 47	(4)	450
2124W	**3-Car Passenger** (2625 Irvington, 2625 Madison, 2625 Manhattan) 47 1. With 2332 GG-1 Dark green 2. With 2332 GG-1 Black	(4) (5)	3300 7500*
2125WS	**4-Car Freight** (671, 671W, 2411, 2454, 2452, 2457) 47	(4)	575
2126WS	**3-Car Passenger** 47 (671, 671W, 2625 Irvington, 2625 Madison, 2625 Manhattan)	(4)	1750
2127WS	**Lionel Work Train** (671, 671W, 3459, 2461, 2460, 2420) 47	(4)	750
2129WS	**4-Car Freight** (726, 2426W, 3854, 2411, 2855, 2457) 47	(4)	2000
2131WS	**4-Car De Luxe Work Train** (726, 2426W, 3462, 3451, 2460, 2420) 47	(4)	1500
2133W	**Twin Diesel O Gauge Freight** (2333P/T AA, 2458, 3459, 2555, 2357) 48	(4)	1250
2135WS	**3-Car Freight** 48, 49 (675, 2466WX, 2456, 2411, 2357) 48 (675, 6466WX, 6456, 6411, 6457) 49	(3)	350
2136WS	**3-Car Passenger** 48, 49 (675, 2466WX, two brown 2442s, brown 2443) 48 (675, 6466WX, two brown 6442s, brown 6443) 49	(4)	600
2137WS	**4-Car De Luxe Freight** (675, 2466WX, 2458, 3459, 2456, 2357) 48	(3)	400
2139W	**4-Car Freight** (2332, 3451, 2458, 2456, 2357) 48	(3)	1500
2139W	**O Gauge 4-Car Freight Outfit** (2332, 6456, 3464, 3461, 6457) 49	(3)	1400
2140WS	**3-Car De Luxe Passenger** (671, 2671W, 2400, 2402, 2401) 48, 49	(4)	900
2141WS	**4-Car Freight** 48, 49 (671, 2671W, 3451, 3462, 2456, 2357) 48 (671, 2671W, 3461, 3472, 6456, 6457) 49	(3)	500
2143WS	**4-Car De Luxe Work Train** (671, 2671W, 3459, 2461, 2460, 2420) 48	(4)	700
2144W	**3-Car De Luxe Passenger Outfit** (2332, 2625, 2627, 2628) 48, 49	(4)	2500
2145WS	**4-Car Freight** (726, 2426W, 3462, 2411, 2460, 2357) 48	(4)	850
2146WS	**3-Car Pullman** (726, 2426W, 2625, 2627, 2628) 48, 49	(5)	2300
2147WS	**4-Car Freight Set** (675, 6466WX, 3472, 6465, 3469, 6457) 49	(3)	400
2148WS	**O Gauge 3-Car Deluxe Pullman** (773, 2426W, 2625, 2627, 2628) 50	(5)	5000
2149B	**O Gauge 4-Car Diesel Work Train** (622, 6520, 3469, 2460, 6419) 49	(4)	750
2150WS	**O Gauge Deluxe Passenger** (681, 2671W, 2421, 2422, 2423) 50	(4)	850
2151W	**O Gauge 5-Car Diesel** (2333P/T AA, 3464, 6555, 3469, 6520, 6457) 49	(3)	1100
2153WS	**4-Car De Luxe Work Train** (671, 2671W, 3469, 6520, 2460, 6419) 49	(4)	600

2155WS	**4-Car Freight** (726, 2426W, 6411, 3656, 2460, 6457) 49	(4)	850
2159W	**5-Car Freight** (2330, 3464, 6462, 3461X, 6456, 6457) 50	(5)	2000
2161W	**SF Twin Diesel Freight** (2343 AA, 3469X, 3464, 3461X, 6520, 6457) 50	(3)	1500
2163WS	**4-Car Freight** 50, 51 (736, 2671WX, 6472, 6462, 6555, 6457) 50 (736, 2671WX, 6472, 6462, 6465, 6457) 51	(3)	575
2165WS	**O Gauge 4-Car Freight** (736, 2671WX, 3472, 6456, 3461X, 6457) 50	(3)	650
2167WS	**3-Car Freight** (681, 2671W, 6462, 3464, 6457) 50, 51	(3)	425
2169WS	**5-Car Freight** w/smoke and whistle 50 (773, 2426W, 3656, 6456, 3469X, 6411, 6457)	(5)	2750
2171W	**NYC Twin Diesel Freight** (2344 AA, 3469X, 3464, 3461X, 6520, 6457) 50	(3)	1250
2173WS	**4-Car Freight** 50, 51 (681, 2671W, 3472, 6555, 3469X, 6457) 50 (681, 2671W, 3472, 6465, 3469X, 6457) 51	(3)	550
2175W	**5-Car Santa Fe Twin Diesel Freight** 50, 51 (2343 AA, 6456 black, 3464, 6555, 6462, 6457) 50 (2343 AA, 6456 maroon, 3464, 6465, 6462, 6457) 51	(3)	1200
2177WS	**3-Car Freight** (675, 2046W, 6462, 6465, 6457) 52	(4)	325
2179WS	**4-Car Freight** (671, 2046WX, 3464, 6465, 6462, 6457) 52	(3)	425
2183WS	**4-Car Freight** (726, 2046W, 3464, 6462, 6465, 6457) 52	(2)	550
2185W	**5-Car New York Central Twin Diesel Freight** 50, 51 (2344 AA, 6456 black, 3464, 6555, 6462, 6457) 50 (2344 AA, 6456 maroon, 3464, 6465, 6462, 6457) 51	(3)	1200
2187WS	**5-Car Freight** (671, 2046WX, 6462, 3472, 6456 maroon, 3469, 6457) 52	(4)	500
2189WS	**5-Car Transcontinental Fast Freight** 52 (726, 2046W, 3520, 3656, 6462, 3461, 6457)	(4)	650
2190W	**4-Car Super Speedliner Passenger** 52, 53 (2343 AA, 2533, 2532, 2534, 2531) 52 (2353 AA, 2533, 2532, 2534, 2531) 53	(3)	2000
2191W	**4-Car Diesel Freight** (2343 AA, 2343C B Unit, 6462, 6656, 6456, 6457) 52	(3)	1500
2193W	**4-Car Diesel Freight** (2344 AA, 2344C B-Unit, 6462, 6656, 6456, 6457) 52	(3)	1500
2201WS	**4-Car Freight** 53, 54 (685, 6026W, 6462, 6464-50, 6465, 6357) 53 (665, 6026W, 6462, 6464-50, 6465, 6357) 54	(3)	700
2203WS	**4-Car Freight** (681, 2046WX, 3520, 6415, 6464-25, 6417) 53	(4)	750
2205WS	**5-Car Freight** (736, 2046W, 3484, 6415, 6468 blue, 6456, 6417) 53	(3)	700
2207W	**Triple Diesel Freight** (2353 AA, 2343C B Unit, 3484, 6415, 6462, 6417) 53	(3)	1500
2209W	**Triple Diesel Freight** (2354 AA, 2344C B Unit, 3484, 6415, 6462, 6417) 53	(3)	1500
2211WS	**4-Car Freight** (681, 2046WX, 3656, 3461, 6464-75, 6417) 53	(4)	700
2213WS	**5-Car Freight** (736, 2046W, 3461, 3520, 3469, 6460, 6419) 53	(3)	600
2217WS	**O Gauge 4-Car Freight** 54 (682, 2046WX, 3562 gray, 6464-175, 6356, 6417)	(4)	1000
2219W	**5-Car Fairbanks-Morse Power Giant Freight** 54 (2321, 6415, 6462 green, 6464-50, 6456 gray, 6417)	(4)	1250
2221WS	**O Gauge 5-Car Freight** 54 (646, 2046W, 3620, 3469, 6468 blue, 6456 gray, 6417)	(3)	600
2222WS	**O Gauge 3-Car Pullman** (646, 2046W, 2530, 2532, 2531) 54	(4)	1800
2223W	**O Gauge 5-Car Freight** (2321, 3482, 3461, 6464-100, 6462 red, 6417) 54	(5)	2500

2225WS	5-Car Work Freight 54 (736, 2046W, 3461, 3620, 3562 gray, 6460 black cab, 6419)	(4)	750
2227W	O Gauge 5-Car Freight 54 (2353, AA3562 gray, 6356, 6456 red, 6468 blue, 6417)	(3)	1500
2229W	O Gauge 5-Car Freight 54 (2354 AA3562 gray, 6356, 6456 red, 6468 blue, 6417)	(4)	1500
2231W	O Gauge 5-Car Freight 54 (2356 AA, 2356C B Unit, 6561, 6511, 3482, 6415, 6417)	(4)	2500
2234W	4-Car Super-Streamliner (2353 AA, 2530, 2532, 2533, 2531) 54	(3)	3000
2235W	O Gauge 4-Car Freight (2338, 6436, 6362, 6560 red, 6419) 55	(3)	550
2237WS	O Gauge 3-Car Freight (665, 6026W, 3562 yellow, 6415, 6417) 55	(3)	400
2239W	O Gauge Streak-Liner (2363P/C AB, 6672, 6464-125, 6414, 6517) 55	(4)	2000
2241WS	O Gauge Freight Snorter (646, 2046W, 3359, 6446, 3620, 6417) 55	(4)	550
2243W	O Gauge 5-Car Freight (2321, 3662, 6511, 6462 red, 6464-300, 6417) 55	(4)	1500
2244W	3-Car Passenger (2367P/C AB, 2530, 2533, 2531) 55	(4)	4000
2245WS	O Gauge 5-Car Freight (682, 2046W, 3562, 6436, 6561, 6560, 6419) 55	(4)	850
2247W	O Gauge 5-Car Freight 55 (2367P/C AB, 6462 red, 3662, 6464-150, 3361, 6517)	(4)	2500
2249WS	O Gauge 5-Car Freight 55 (736, 2046W, 3359, 3562 yellow, 6414, 6464-275, 6517)	(4)	900
2251W	O Gauge 5-Car Freight 55 (2331, 3359, 3562 yellow, 6414, 6464-275, 6517)	(4)	2500
2253W	O Gauge 5-Car Freight 55 (2340-25 green, 3620, 6414, 3361, 6464-300, 6417)	(4)	2500
2254W	The Congressional (2340-1 Tuscan, 2544, 2543, 2542, 2541) 55	(4)	6000
2255W	O Gauge 4-Car Work Train (601, 3424, 6362, 6560, 6119 orange) 56	(4)	600
2257WS	O Gauge 5-Car Freight (665, 2046W, 3361, 6346, 6467, 6462 red, 6427) 56	(3)	500
2259W	O Gauge 5-Car Freight (2350, 6464-425, 6430, 3650, 6511, 6427) 56	(3)	850
2261WS	O Gauge Freight Hauler, 56 (646, 2046W, 3562 yellow, 6414, 6436, 6376, 6417)	(4)	650
2263W	O Gauge 5-Car Freight (2350, 3359, 6468, 6414, 3662, 6517) 56	(4)	1000
2265WS	O Gauge 5-Car Freight (736, 2046W, 3620, 6430, 3424, 6467, 6517) 56	(4)	750
2267W	5-Car Freight (2331, 3562 yellow, 3359, 3361, 6560, 6419) 56	(4)	1650
2269W	O Gauge 5-Car Freight 56 (2368P/C AB, 3356, 6518, 6315, 3361, 6517)	(5)	3900
2270W	3-Car Jersey Central Passenger (2341, 2533, 2532, 2531) 56	(5)	5500
2271W	O Gauge 5-Car Freight 56 (2360-25 green, 3424, 3662, 6414, 6418, 6417)	(4)	3000
2273W	6-Car Milwaukee Road Diesel Freight 56 (2378P/C AB, 342, 6342, 3562 yellow, 3662, 3359, 6517)	(5)	4000
2274W	The Great Congressional (2360-1 Tuscan, 2544, 2543, 2542, 2541) 56	(5)	5000
2275W	O Gauge 4-Car Freight (2339, 3444, 6464-475, 6425, 6427) 57	(3)	750
2276W	Budd RDC Commuter Set (404, 2559, 2559) 57	(4)	3000
2277WS	O Gauge 4-Car Work Train (665, 2046W, 3650, 6446, 6560, 6119) 57	(4)	550
2279W	O Gauge 5-Car Freight (2350, 6464-425, 6424, 3424, 6477, 6427) 57	(3)	825
2281W	O Gauge 5-Car Freight 57 (2243 AB, 3562 orange, 6464-150, 3361, 6560, 6119)	(3)	1200

2283WS	O Gauge 5-Car Freight 57 (646, 2046W, 3424, 3361, 6464-525, 6562 black, 6357)		(4)	625
2285W	O Gauge 5-Car Freight (2331, 6418, 6414, 3662, 6425, 6517) 57		(4)	1750
2287W	O Gauge 5-Car Freight (2351, 342, 6342, 6464-500, 3650, 6315, 6427) 57		(5)	1800
2289WS	Super O 5-Car Freight (736, 2046W, 3359, 3494-275, 3361, 6430, 6427) 57		(4)	750
2291W	Super O 5-Car Freight 57 (2379P/C AB, 3562 orange, 3530, 3444, 6464-525, 6657)		(4)	2750
2292WS	Super O Steam Luxury Liner (646, 2046W, 2530, 2533, 2532, 2531) 57		(4)	1500
2293W	5-Car Freight (2360 Tuscan, 3662, 3650, 6414, 6518, 6417) 57		(5)	2750
2295WS	6-Car Steam Freight 57 (746, 746W, 342, 6342, 3530, 3361, 6560, 6419-100 no. 576419 on car)		(5)	3000
2296W	Super O Diesel Luxury Liner (2373P/T AA, 2552, 2552, 2552, 2551) 57		(4)	6500
2297SW	The 16 Wheeler Class J 57 (746, 746W, 264, 6264, 3356, 345, 6342, 3662, 6517)		(5)	3250
2501W	Super O Work Train (2348, 6464-525, 6802, 6560, 6119) 58		(4)	825
2502W	Super O Rail-Diesel Commuter (400, 2559, 2550) 58		(5)	1900
2503WS	Timberland Special Freight 58 (665, 2046W, 3361, 6434, 6801, 6536, 6357)		(4)	600
2505W	Super O 5-Car Freight (2329, 6805, 6519, 6800, 6464-500, 6357) 58		(4)	1550
2507W	Super O 5-Car Diesel Freight 58 (2242P/C AB, 3444, 6464-425, 6424, 6468-25, 6357)		(5)	2000
2509WS	The Owl 5-Car Freight 58 (665, 2046W, 6414, 3650, 6464-475, 6805, 6357)		(4)	800
2511W	Super O 5-Car Electric Work Train 58 (2352, 3562 orange, 3424, 3361, 6560, 6119)		(4)	1150
2513W	Super O 6-Car Freight Train 58 (2329, 6556, 6425, 6414, 6434, 3359, 6427-60)		(5)	2000
2515WS	5-Car Mainliner Steam Freight 58 (646, 2046W, 3662, 6424, 3444, 6800, 6427)		(4)	825
2517W	Super O 5-Car Diesel Freight (2379 AB, 6519, 6805, 6434, 6800, 6657) 58		(5)	2500
2518W	Super O 3-Car Passenger (2352, 2533, 2534, 2531) 58		(5)	1650
2519W	Super O 6-Car Diesel Freight 58 (2331, 6434, 3530, 6801, 6414, 6464-275, 6557)		(4)	1900
2521WS	Super O 6-Car Freight 58 (746, 746W, 6805, 3361, 6430, 3356, 6557)		(5)	2350
2523W	Super O Super Chief Freight 58 (2383 AA, 264, 6264, 6434, 6800, 3662, 6517)		(5)	1900
2525WS	Super O 6-Car Work Train 58 (746, 746W, 345, 342, 6519, 6518, 6560, 6419-100)		(5)	3000
2526W	Super Chief Passenger (2383P/T AA, 2530, 2532, 2532, 2531) 58		(4)	2000
2527	Super O Missile Launcher Outfit (44, 3419, 6844, 6823, 6814, 943) 59, 60		(3)	725
2528WS	5-Star Frontier Special Outfit (1872, 1872T, 1877, 1876, 1875W) 59-61		(2)	750
2529W	5-Car Virginian Rectifier Work Train 59 (2329, 3512, 6819, 6812, 6560, 6119)		(4)	1275
2531WS	Super O 5-Car Steam Freight 59 (637, 2046W, 3435, 6817, 6636, 6825, 6119)		(5)	1250
2533W	5-Car Great Northern Electric Freight 59 (2358, 6650, 6414, 3444, 6470, 6357)		(5)	1850

2535WS	Super O 5-Car Hudson Steam Freight 59 (665, 2046W, 3434, 6823, 3672, 6812, 6357)	(4)	**1000**
2537W	5-Car New Haven Diesel Freight 59 (2242P/C AB, 3435, 3650, 6464-275, 6819, 6427)	(5)	**2500**
2539WS	5-Car Hudson Steam Freight 59 (665, 2046W, 3361, 464, 6464-825, 3512, 6812, 6357)	(5)	**1500**
2541W	5-Car Super Chief Freight 59 (2383P/T AA, 3356, 3512, 6519, 6816, 6427)	(5)	**2350**
2543WS	6-Car Berkshire Steam Freight 59 (736, 2046W, 264, 6264, 3435, 6823, 6434, 6812, 6557)	(5)	**2000**
2544W	4-Car Super Chief Streamliner 59, 60 (2383P/T AA, 2530, 2563 red stripe, 2562 red stripe, 2561 red stripe)	(4)	**4000**
2545WS	6-Car N&W Space-Freight 59 (746, 746W, 175, 6175, 6470, 3419, 6650, 3540, 6517)	(5)	**3000**
2547WS	4-Car Variety Special Steam Freight 60 (637, 2046W, 3330, 6475, 6361, 6357)	(4)	**650**
2549W	A Mighty Military Diesel Outfit (2349, 3540, 6470, 6819, 6650, 3535) 60	(2)	**1200**
2551W	6-Car Great Northern Diesel Freight 60 (2358, 6828, 3512, 6827, 6736, 6812, 6427)	(5)	**2250**
2553WS	The Majestic Berkshire 5-Car Freight 60 (736, 2046W, 3830, 3435, 3419, 3672, 6357)	(4)	**1500**
2555W	Over & Under Twin Railroad Empire 60 (2383P/T AA, 3434, 3366, 6414, 6464-900, 6357-50, 110-85) Includes matching set of Lionel HO trains	(5+)	**12000**
2570	5-Car Husky Diesel Freight (616, 6822, 6828, 6812, 6736, 6130) 61	(4)	**625**
2571	Fort Knox Special Steam Freight (637, 736W, 3419, 6445, 6361, 6119) 61	(4)	**650**
2572	5-Car Space Age Diesel Freighter (2359, 6544, 3830, 6448, 3519, 3535) 61	(3)	**850**
2573	5-Car TV Special Steam Freight 61 (736, 736W, 3545, 6416, 6475, 6440, 6357)	(4)	**1250**
2574	5-Car Defender Diesel Freight 61 (2383P/T AA, 3665, 3419, 448, 6448, 3830, 6437)	(4)	**1750**
2575	7-Car Dynamo Electric Freight 61 (2360 single stripe, 6530, 6828, 6464-900, 6827, 6560, 6437)	(5)	**3000**
2576	4-Car Super Chief Streamline (2383P/T AA, 2563, 2562, 2562, 2561) 61	(4)	**4000**
4109WS	Electronic Control Set (671R, 4671W, 4452, 4454, 5459, 4457) 46, 47	(4)	**1000**
4110WS	Lionel Electronic Railroad 48, 49 (671R, 4671W, 4452, 4454, 5459, 4357, 97, 151)	(5)	**2000**
11201	Fast Starter Steam Freight (242, 1060T, 6042-75, 6502, 6047) 62	(1)	**150**
11212	4-Unit Cyclone Diesel Freight (633, 3349, 6825, 6057) 62	(2)	**250**
11222	5-Unit Vagabond Steam Freight (236, 1050T, 3357, 6343, 6119) 62	(2)	**150**
11232	027 5-Unit Diesel Freight (232, 3410, 6062, 6413, 6057-50 orange) 62	(4)	**425**
11242	Trail Blazer Steam Freight (233, 233W, 6465, 6476 red, 6162, 6017) 62	(2)	**125**
11252	027 7-Unit Diesel Freight (211 AA, 3509, 6448, 3349, 6463, 6057) 62	(4)	**425**
11268	027 6-Unit Diesel Freight (2365, 3619, 3470, 3349, 6501, 6017) 62	(3)	**1000**
11278	7-Unit Plainsman Steam Freight 62 (2037, 233W, 6473, 6162, 6050-110, 6825, 6017)	(3)	**250**
11288	7-Unit Orbitor Diesel Freight 62 (229P/C AB, 3413, 6512, 6413, 6463, 6059)	(4)	**800**
11298	7-Unit Vigilant Steam Freight 62 (2037, 233W, 3419, 6544, 6448, 3330, 6017)	(4)	**450**

POSTWAR

11308	**027 6-Unit Diesel Passenger** 62 (218P/T AA 2414 blue stripe, two 2412s blue stripe, 2416 blue stripe)		(3)	**650**
11311	**Value Packed Steam Freight** (1062, 1061T, 6409-25, 6076-100, 6167) 63		(2)	**100**
11321	**027 5-Unit Diesel Freighter** 63 (221, 3309, 6076-75, 6042-75, 6167-50 yellow)		(2)	**250**
11331	**Outdoorsman Steam Freight** 63 (242, 1060T, 6473, 6476-25, 6142, 6059-50)		(2)	**150**
11341	**Space-Prober Diesel Freight** 63 (634, 3410, 6407, 6014-335 white, 6463, 6059-50)		(4)	**1100**
11351	**Land Rover Steam Freight** 63 (237, 1060T, 6050-100, 6465-100, 6408, 6162, 6119-100)		(2)	**225**
11361	**Shooting Star Diesel Freight** 63 (211P/T AA, 3665-100, 3413-150, 6470, 6413, 6257-100)		(4)	**750**
11375	**Cargomaster Steam Freight** 63 (238, 234W, 6822-50, 6414-150, 6465-150, 6476-75, 6162, 6257-100)		(4)	**700**
11385	**Space Conqueror Diesel Freight** 63 (223P/218C AB, 3619-100, 3470-100, 3349-100, 6407, 6257-100)		(5)	**2000**
11395	**Muscleman Steam Freight** 63 (2037, 234W, 6464-725, 6469-50, 6536, 6440-50, 6560-50, 6119-100)		(4)	**600**
11405	**027 6 Unit Diesel Passenger** 63 (218 AA, 2414 blue stripe, two 2412s blue stripe, 2416 blue stripe)		(3)	**725**
11420	**4-Unit Steam Freight** (1061, 1061T, 6042-250, 6167-25) 64		(2)	**100**
11430	**5-Unit Steam Freight** (1062, 1061T, 6176, 6142, 6167-125) 64		(2)	**125**
11440	**5-Unit Diesel Freight** 64 (221, 3309, 6176-50 black, 6142-125 blue, 6167-100 red)		(2)	**225**
11450	**6-Unit Steam Freight** 64 (242, 1060T, 6473, 6142-75 green, 6176-50 black, 6059-50)		(2)	**150**
11460	**7-Unit Steam Freight** 64 (238, 234W, 6014-335 white, 6465-150 orange, 6142-100 blue, 6176-75 yellow, 6119-100)		(3)	**150**
11470	**7-Unit Steam Freight** 64 (237, 1060T, 6014-335 white, 6465-150 orange, 6142-100 blue, 6176-50 yellow, 6119-100)		(4)	**225**
11480	**7-Unit Diesel Freight** 64 (213P/T AA, 6473, 6176-50 black, 6142-150, 6014-335 white, 6257-100)		(4)	**650**
11490	**5-Unit Diesel Passenger** (212P/T AA, 2404, 2405, 2406) 64, 65		(3)	**700**
11500	**7-Unit Steam Freight** 64-66 (2029, 234W, 6465-150 org, 6402-50, 6176-75 yell, 6014-335 wht, 6257-100) 64 (2029, 234W, 6465-150 org, 6402-50, 6176 blk, 6014-335 wht, 6059) 65 (2029, 234W, 6465-150 org, 6402-50, 6176-75 yell, 6014-335 wht, 6059) 66		(3)	**250**
11510	**7-Unit Steam Freight** 64 (2029, 1060T, 6465-150 org, 6402-50, 6176-75 yell, 6014-335 wht, 6257-100)		(4)	**275**
11520	**6-Unit Steam Freight** (242, 1062T, 6176, 3364, 6142, 6059) 65, 66		(2)	**150**
11530	**5-Unit Diesel Freight** (634, 6014-335 white, 6142, 6402, 6130) 65, 66		(2)	**250**
11540	**6-Unit Steam Freight** (239, 242T, 6473, 6465, 6176, 6119) 65, 66		(4)	**225**
11550	**6-Unit Steam Freight** (239, 234W, 6473, 6465, 6176, 6119) 65, 66		(3)	**225**
11560	**7-Unit Diesel Freight** (211P/T AA, 6473, 6176, 6142, 6465, 6059) 65, 66		(2)	**300**
11590	**5-Unit Illuminated Passenger** (212P/T AA, 2408, 2409, 2410) 66		(3)	**750**
11600	**7-Unit Steam Freight** 68 (2029, 234W, 6014-335 white, 6476 yellow, 6315, 6560, 6130)		(3)	**800**

11710	**5-Unit Steam Freight** (1061, 1062T, 6402, 6142, 6059) 69	(3)	**150**
11720	**5-Unit Diesel Freight** (2024, 6142, 6402, 6176 yellow, 6057 brown) 69	(4)	**250**
11730	**6-Unit Diesel Freight** 69 (645, 6402, 6014-85 orange, 6142, 6176 black, 6167)	(3)	**325**
11740	**7-Unit Diesel Freight** 69 (2041 AA, 6315, 6142, 6014-410 white, 6476 yellow, 6057 brown)	(4)	**350**
11750	**7-Unit Steam Freight** 69 (2029, 234T, 6014-85 orange, 6476 black, 6473, 6315, 6130)	(5)	**500**
11760	**7-Unit Steam Freight** 69 (2029, 234W, 6014-410 white, 6315, 6476 black, 3376, 6119)	(3)	**300**
12502	**Prairie-Rider Gift Pack** (1862, 1862T, 3376, 1877, 1866, 1865) 62	(4)	**600**
12512	**Enforcer Gift Pack** (45, 3413, 3619, 3470, 3349, 6017) 62	(4)	**950**
12700	**7-Unit Steam Freight** Same as 12710 without transformer 64	(4)	**1000**
12710	**7-Unit Steam Freight** 64-66 (736, 736W, 6464-725, 6162-100 blue, 6414-75, 6476-135 yellow, 6437) 64 (736, 736W, 6464-725, 6162-100 blue, 6414, 6476-135 yellow, 6437) 65, 66	(4)	**1000**
12720	**7-Unit Diesel Freight** Same as 12730 without transformer 64	(4)	**1500**
12730	**7-Unit Diesel Freight** 64-66 (2383P/T AA, 6464-725, 6162-100 blue, 6414-75, 6476-135 yell, 6437) 64 (2383P/T AA, 6464-725, 6162-100 blue, 6414, 6476-135 yellow, 6437) 65,66	(4)	**1500**
12740	**9-Unit Diesel Freight** Same as 12750 without transformer 64	(5)	**1500**
12750	**9-Unit Diesel Freight** 64 (2383P/T AA, 3662, 6822, 6361, 6464-525, 6436-110, 6315-60, 6437)	(5)	**1500**
12760	**9-Unit Steam Freight** Same as 12770 without transformer 64	(4)	**1500**
12770	**9-Unit Steam Freight** 64 (736, 736W, 3662, 6822, 6361, 6464-525, 6436-110, 6315-60, 6437)	(5)	**1500**
12780	**6-Unit Diesel Passenger** (2383P/T AA, 2523, 2522, 2523, 2521) 64-66	(4)	**3500**
12800	**6-Unit Diesel Freight** (2346, 6428, 6436-110, 6464-475, 6415, 6017) 65, 66	(2)	**650**
12820	**8-Unit Diesel Freight** 65 (2322, 3662, 6822, 6361, 6464-725, 6436-110, 6315, 6437)	(4)	**1500**
12840	**7-Unit Steam Freight** 66 (665, 736W, 6464-375, 6464-450, 6431, 6415, 6437)	(4)	**1000**
12850	**8-Unit Diesel Freight** 66 (2322, 3662, 6822, 6361, 6464-725, 6436-110, 6315, 6437)	(4)	**1500**
13008	**6-Unit Champion Steam Freight** (637, 736W, 3349, 6448, 6501, 6119) 62	(4)	**450**
13018	**6-Unit Starfire Diesel Freight** (616, 6500, 6650, 3519, 6448, 6017-235) 62	(5)	**1250**
13028	**6-Unit Defender Diesel Freight** 62 (2359, 3665, 3349, 3820, 3470, 6017-100)	(2)	**857**
13036	**6-Unit Plainsman Steam Outfit** 62 (1872, 1872T, 6445, 3370, 1876, 1875W)	(4)	**950**
13048	**7-Unit Steam Freight** 62 (736, 736W, 6822, 6414, 3362, 6440, 6437)	(3)	**850**
13058	**7-Unit Vanguard Diesel Freight** 62 (2383P/T AA, 3619, 3413, 6512, 470, 6470, 6437)	(3)	**1650**
13068	**8-Unit Goliath Electric Freight** 62 (2360 single stripe, 6464-725, 6828, 6416, 6827, 6530, 6475, 6437)	(5)	**3000**
13078	**5-Unit Presidential Passenger** 62 (2360 single stripe, 2523, 2522, 2522, 2521)	(5)	**3500**
13088	**6-Unit Presidential Passenger** (2383P/T AA, 2523, 2522, 2522, 2521) 62	(4)	**2600**
13098	**Goliath Steam Freight** (637, 736W, 6469, 6464-900, 6414, 6446, 6447) 63	(5)	**2000**

POSTWAR

13108	Super O 7-Unit Diesel Freight 63 (617, 3665, 3419, 6448, 3830, 3470, 6119-100)		(4)	1050
13118	Super O 8-Unit Steam Freight 63 (736, 736W, 6446-60, 6827, 3362, 6315-60, 6560, 6429)		(4)	1500
13128	Super O 7-Unit Diesel Freight 63 (2383P/T AA, 3619, 3413, 6512, 448, 6448, 6437)		(4)	1825
13138	Majestic Electric Freight 63 (2360 single stripe, 6464-725, 6828, 6416, 6827, 6315-60, 6436-110, 6437)		(5)	3000
13148	Super Chief Passenger (2383 AA, 2523, 2523, 2522, 2521) 63		(4)	2600
13150	Super O 9-Unit Steam Freight 64-66 (773, 736W, 3434, 6361, 3662, 6415, 3356, 6436-110, 6437) 64 (773, 773W, 3434, 6361, 3662, 6415, 3356, 6436-110, 6437) 65, 66		(5)	3000

Postwar Boxes

Prices based on LN with inserts and all flaps intact. No Rarity Rating indicates not enough information to assign one.

ECU-1	Electronic Control Unit	(4)	30
ZW	Transformer	(2)	20
30	Water Tower	(3)	35
38	Water Tower	(4+)	75
41	US Army Switcher	(2)	25
42	Picatinny Arsenal Switcher	(4)	60
44	US Army Mobile Missile Launcher	(3)	50
45	USMC Mobile Missile Launcher	(3+)	75
50	Gang Car (O&B)	(3)	20
51	Navy Yard Switcher	(2+)	60
52	Fire Fighting Car	(3)	75
53	Rio Grande Snow Plow	(3)	50
54	Ballast Tamper	(3)	40
55	Tie-Jector	(3+)	45
56	Minn. & St. Louis Min Steamer	(4)	150
57	AEC Switcher	(4+)	150
58	GN Rotary Snowplow	(4)	150
59	Minuteman Switcher	(4+)	150
60	Trolley	(2)	25
65	Motorized Handcar	(3+)	75
68	Executive Inspection Car	(3)	75
69	Motorized Maintenance Car	(3+)	100
89	Flagpole	(4)	20
97	Coal Elevator	(3)	35
110-85	Trestle Set	(5)	150
114	Newsstand with horn	(3)	35
115	Lionel City Station	(3+)	45
118	Newsstand with whistle	(3)	30
128	Animated Newsstand	(2)	40
132	Passenger Station	(3)	20
133	Passenger Station	(2)	20

138	Water Tower	(3)	30
150	Telegraph Pole Set	(2)	20
164	Log Loader	(3)	40
175	Rocket Launcher	(3)	45
182	Magnetic Crane	(3)	45
192	Operating Control Tower	(4)	75
193	Industrial Water Tower	(3)	40
197	Rotating Radar Antenna	(3+)	30
202	Union Pacific A	(3+)	40
204P	Santa Fe Alco Powered A Unit	(3)	45
204T	Santa Fe Alco Dummy A Unit	(3)	45
205P	MP Alco Powered A Unit	(4)	50
205T	MP Alco Dummy A Unit	(4)	50
208P	Santa Fe Alco Powered A Unit	(3)	50
208T	Santa Fe Alco Dummy A Unit	(3)	50
209P	New Haven Alco Powered A Unit	(4+)	85
209T	New Haven Alco Dummy A Unit	(4+)	85
210P	Texas Special Alco Powered A	(2)	40
210T	Texas Special Alco Dummy A	(2)	40
211P	Texas Special Alco Powered A	(3)	25
211T	Texas Special Alco Dummy A	(3)	25
212	USMC Alco Powered A Unit	(3)	50
212T	USMC Alco Dummy A Unit	(5)	400
212P	Santa Fe Alco Powered A Unit	(4)	40
212T	Santa Fe Alco Dummy A Unit	(4)	40
213P	Minn. & Stl. Alco Powered A	(4)	70
213T	Minn. & Stl. Alco Dummy A	(4)	70
215	Santa Fe Alco Powered A Unit		
216P	Burlington Alco Powered A	(4+)	90
216	Minn & Stl. Alco Powered A		
217P	Boston & Maine Alco Powered A Unit	(3+)	45

217C	Boston & Maine Alco Dummy B Unit	(3+)	45
218P	Santa Fe Alco Powered A Unit	(2)	30
218C	Santa Fe Alco Dummy B Unit	(3+)	40
218T	Santa Fe Alco Dummy A Unit	(3)	35
219	Missouri Pacific Alco AA		
220P	Santa Fe Alco Powered A Unit	(4)	45
221	Rio Grande Alco Powered A		NOB
221	Santa Fe Powered A Unit		NOB
221	USMC Powered A Unit		NOB
221	2-6-4 Steamer	(3+)	45
221T	Tender	(3+)	35
221W	Tender	(3+)	40
222	Rio Grande Alco Powered A		NOB
223P	Santa Fe Alco Powered A Unit	(4)	70
224P	Navy Alco Powered A Unit	(4)	75
224C	Navy Alco Dummy B Unit	(4)	60
224	2-6-2 Steamer	(3)	35
225	C&O Alco Powered A Unit		
226	Boston & Maine Alco AB		125
227	CN Alco Powered A Unit		NOB
228	CN Alco Powered A Unit	(3)	35
229P	Minn. & St. Louis Alco Powered A Unit	(3+)	45
229C	Minn. & St. Louis Alco Dummy B Unit	(3+)	45
230	C&O Alco Powered A Unit		25
231	Rock Island Powered A Unit		35
232	New Haven Alco A		25
233	2-4-2 Steamer	(3)	30
233W	Tender	(3)	65
235	2-4-2 Steamer		NOB
236	2-4-2 Steamer	(2)	25
237	2-4-2 Steamer	(3)	25
238	2-4-2 Steamer	(3)	45
239	2-4-2 Steamer	(3)	25
240	2-4-2 Steamer		NOB
241	2-4-2 Steamer		NOB
242	2-4-2 Steamer		
242T	Tender	(3)	25
243	2-4-2 Steamer	(3)	40
243W	Tender	(3)	25
244	2-4-2 Steamer	(3)	30
244T	Tender	(4)	30
245	2-4-2 Steamer	(4)	35
247	2-4-2 Steamer	(3)	35
247T	Tender	(3)	20

248	2-4-2 Steamer	(3)	40
249	2-4-2 Steamer	(3)	35
250	2-4-2 Steamer	(3)	35
250T	Tender	(3)	25
251	2-4-2 Steamer		NOB
256	Freight Station	(2)	20
257	Freight Station with horn	(4)	60
264	Operating Forklift Platform	(3)	45
282	Gantry Crane	(3)	45
282R	Gantry Crane	(3+)	55
299	Code Transmitter Beacon Set	(2)	75
350-50	Transfer Table Extension	(4+)	75
313	Bascule Bridge	(3+)	100
334	Operating Dispatching Board	(3)	70
342	Operating Culvert Loader	(2)	45
345	Operating Culvert Unloader	(3)	50
346	Manual Culvert Unloader	(4+)	95
347	Cannon Firing Range		NOB
348	Manual Culvert Unloader	(4)	100
350	Transfer Table	(4)	75
352	Ice Depot	(2)	35
362	Barrel Loader	(2)	25
364	Lumber Loader	(3)	20
365	Dispatch Station	(2)	50
375	Turntable	(2)	35
397	Diesel Operating Coal Loader	(2)	30
400	B&O Budd Car	(3)	65
404	B&O Budd Car	(3+)	75
415	Diesel Fueling Station	(3)	35
419	Heliport Control Tower	(4+)	125
443	Missile Launching Platform	(3)	25
445	Switch Tower	(2+)	20
448	Missile Firing Range Set	(3)	40
452	Gantry Signal	(3+)	35
455	Oil Derrick	(2+)	40
456	Coal Ramp	(2)	30
460	Piggyback Transportation	(2)	25
460P	Piggyback Platform	(5)	1000
461	Platform with truck and trailer	(4)	60
462	Derrick Platform Set	(4)	125
463W	O Gauge 4-Car Freight Set 45		200
464	Lumber Mill	(2)	35
465	Sound Dispatching Station	(2+)	30
470	Missile Launching Platform	(2)	25
497	Coaling Station	(3+)	45
520	Box Cab Electric		NOB

POSTWAR

POSTWAR

600	MKT GM Switcher	(3)	45	
601	Seaboard GM Switcher	(2+)	40	
602	Seaboard GM Switcher	(2+)	40	
610	Erie GM Switcher	(3)	45	
611	Jersey Central	(3)	40	
613	Union Pacific GM Switcher	(4)	85	
614	Alaska GM Switchers	(4)	75	
616	Santa Fe GM Switcher	(3+)	60	
617	Santa Fe GM Switcher	(4)	95	
621	Jersey Central GM Switcher	(3)	40	
646-25	Great Northern Boxcar	(2)	25	
622	Santa Fe GM Switcher	(3)	50	
623	Santa Fe GM Switcher	(2+)	45	
624	C & O GM Switcher	(3)	40	
625	Lehigh Valley GE 44-Ton	(3+)	40	
626	Baltimore & Ohio GE 44-Ton	(4)	65	
627	Lehigh Valley GE 44-Ton	(3)	40	
628	Northern Pacific GE 44-Ton	(3)	40	
629	Burlington GE 44-Ton	(4)	75	
633	Santa Fe GM Switcher	(4)	40	
634	Santa Fe GM Switcher	(4)	40	
635	Union Pacific GM Switcher			
637	2-6-4 Steamer	(3+)	35	
645	Union Pacific GM Switcher		NOB	
646	4-6-4 Steamer	(3)	45	
665	4-6-4 Steamer	(2+)	45	
671	6-8-6 Steamer	(2+)	45	
671R	6-8-6 Steamer	(4)	75	
671W	Tender	(3+)	50	
675	2-6-2 Steamer	(3)	35	
681	6-8-6 Steamer	(3)	40	
682	6-8-6 Steamer	(3+)	65	
685	4-6-4 Steamer	(2+)	40	
726	2-8-4 Steamer	(3)	60	
726RR	2-8-4 Steamer	(3)	100	
736	2-8-4 Steamer	(2+)	50	
736W	Tender	(4)	75	
746	4-8-4 N&W Steamer	(4)	100	
746W	Tender (Short Stripe)	(3+)	75	
746WX	Tender (Long Stripe)	(4+)	125	
773	4-6-4 Hudson Steamer (1950)	(4)	200	
773	4-6-4 Hudson Steamer (1964)	(4)	200	
773W	Tender	(4+)	140	
920	Scenic Display Set	(2)	20	
958	Vehicle Set (white box only)	(4+)	100	

963-100	Frontier Set	(4)	100	
970	Ticket Booth	(2)	40	
986	Farm Set	(4)	100	
987	Town Set	(4+)	100	
988	Railroad Structure Set	(4+)	100	
1000W	027 3-Car Set, 55	(2)	30	
1001	027 3-Car Set, 55	(2)	50	
1047	Operating Switchman	(4)	50	
1050	0-4-0 Steamer		NOB	
1050T	Tender		NOB	
1055	Texas Special Alco Powered A		NOB	
1065	Union Pacific Alco Powered A		NOB	
1066	Union Pacific Alco Powered A		NOB	
1111	Lionel Scout Set, 48	(2)	20	
1112	Lionel Scout Set, 48		30	
1113	Lionel Scout Train, 50		20	
1115	Lionel Scout, 49		20	
1117	Lionel Scout, 49		20	
1119	Scout 3-Car Freight, 51, 52		20	
1130T	Tender	(3)	20	
1130T-500	Tender (Girls Train)	(5)	150	
1400	Lionel 027 Passenger Set, 46		200	
1400W	Lionel 027 Passenger Set, 46		250	
1401	Lionel 027 Freight Outfit, 46		30	
1401W	Lionel 027 Freight Outfit, 46		30	
1402	Lionel 027 Passenger Set 46		100	
1402W	Lionel 027 Passenger Set 46		150	
1403	Lionel 027 Freight Train 46		50	
1403W	Lionel 027 Freight Train 46		50	
1405	Lionel 027 Freight Train 46		30	
1405W	Lionel 027 Freight Train 46		40	
1407B	Lionel 027 Switcher Bell Outfit 46		150	
1409	Lionel 027 Freight Train 46		50	
1409W	Lionel 027 Freight Train 46		30	
1411W	Freight Outfit 46		30	
1413WS	Lionel 027 Freight Train 46		40	
1415WS	Lionel 027 Freight Set 46		50	
1417WS	Lionel 027 Freight Outfit 46		50	
1419WS	Lionel 027 Freight Train 46		125	
1421WS	Lionel 027 Freight Train 46		150	
1423W	Lionel 3-Car Freight Outfit 48, 49		30	
1425B	027 O Gauge Switcher Freight 48, 49		125	
1426WS	Lionel Passenger Set 48, 49		100	
1427WS	Lionel Three-Car Freight Set 48		30	
1429WS	Four-Car Freight Set 48		30	

1430WS	Passenger Train 48, 49	200
1431	Lionel Freight Train 47	30
1431W	Lionel Freight Train 47	30
1432	Lionel Passenger Set 47	200
1432W	Lionel Passenger Set, 47	200
1433	Lionel Freight Train 47	30
1433W	Lionel Freight Train 47	30
1434WS	Passenger Train 47	150
1435WS	Lionel Freight Train 47	30
1437WS	Lionel Freight Set 47	30
1439WS	Lionel Freight Outfit 47	40
1441WS	De Luxe Work Outfit 47	50
1443WS	Lionel Freight Set 47	50
1445WS	Lionel Freight Train, 48	30
1447WS	Lionel De Luxe Work Train 48, 49 Set	50
1449WS	027 Lionel 5-Car Freight Outfit 48	50
1451WS	Three-Car Freight 49	30
1453WS	Four-Car Freight Train 49	40
1455WS	Four-Car 027 Freight Set 49	40
1457B	Diesel Freight 49, 50	100
1459WS	027 Gauge 5-Car Freight Outfit 49	50
1461S	3-Car Freight With Smoke, 50	20
1463W	Lionel 027 3-Car Freight, 50	30
1463WS	027 3-Car Freight, 51	30
1464W	027 Diesel 3-Car Pullman 50	400
1464W	027 Diesel 3-Car Pullman 51	200
1464W	3-Car Pullman 52, 53	200
1465	3-Car Freight 52	20
1467W	027 Diesel 4-Car Freight 50, 51	100
1467W	4-Car Freight 52, 53	100
1469WS	Lionel 027 4-Car Freight 50, 51	30
1471WS	Lionel 5-Car Freight Set 50, 51	30
1473WS	Lionel 4-Car Freight 50	30
1475WS	Lionel 5-Car Freight Set 50	50
1477S	027 3-Car Freight 51, 52	30
1479WS	027 4-Car Freight 52	40
1481WS	5-Car Freight 51	40
1483WS	5-Car Freight 52	50
1484WS	4-Car Pullman 52	200
1485WS	027 3-Car Freight 52	30
1500	027 3-Car Freight 53, 54	20
1501S	027 3-Car Freight 53	30
1502WS	027 3-Car Pullman 53	150
1503WS	027 4-Car Freight 53	30

1505WS	027 4-Car Freight 53	50
1507WS	027 5-Car Freight 53	50
1509WS	027 5-Car Freight 53	50
1511S	027 4-Car Freight 53	30
1513S	027 4-Car Freight 54, 55	30
1515WS	027 5-Car Freight 54	50
1516WS	027 3-Car Passenger 54	100
1517W	027 4-Car Freight 54	150
1519WS	027 5-Car Freight 54	50
1520W	The Flashing Star of the 54 South West	300
1521WS	027 5-Car Freight 54	70
1523	Lionel Work Train 54	150
1527	027 3-Car Work Train 55	75
1529	027 3-Car Freight 55	100
1531W	027 4-Car Freight 55	100
1533WS	027 Freight Hauler 55	50
1534W	027 Passenger Train 55	150
1536W	Pride of the Katy and Frisco 55	300
1537WS	027 4-Car Freight 55	50
1538WS	027 Passenger Train 55	100
1539W	027 5-Car Freight 55	100
1541WS	027 5-Car Freight 55	50
1542	027 3-Car Freight 56	30
1543	027 3-Car Freight 56	40
1545	027 4-Car Freight 56	40
1547S	027 Freight Hauler 56	30
1549S	027 3-Car Work Train 56	100
1551S	027 4-Car Freight 56	50
1552	027 Passenger Train 56	150
1553W	027 5-Car Freight 56	75
1555WS	027 Freight Hauler 56	40
1557W	027 5-Car Work Train 56	50
1559W	027 5-Car Freight Train 56	75
1561WS	027 5-Car Freight Train 56	50
1562W	027 Passenger Train 56	300
1563W	027 5-Car Freight 56	250
1565W	027 5-Car Freight 56	75
1567W	The Pride of the Santa Fe 56	100
1569	027 4-Car Freight 57	30
1571	027 5-Car Freight 57	50
1573	027 5-Car Freight 57	30
1575	027 5-Car Freight 57	50
1577S	027 6-Car Freight 57	50
1578S	027 Passenger Train 57	100
1579S	027 7-Car Freight 57	30

POSTWAR

Number	Description	Price
1581	027 7-Car Freight 57	75
1583WS	027 King of the High Iron 57	50
1585W	027 9-Car Freight Train 57	50
1586	027 Passenger Train 57	100
1587S	Lady Lionel Pastel Train 57, 58 Set	400
1589WS	027 King of the High Iron 57	50
1590	027 4-Car Steam Freight 58	40
1591	U.S. Marine Land & Sea 58 Limited	125
1593	5-Car Diesel Work Train 58	75
1595	027 Marine Battlefront Special 58	150
1597S	6-Car Coal King Smoking 58 Freighter	30
1599	027 6-Car Freight 58	50
1600	027 3-Car Passenger Set 58	150
1601W	027 5-Car Diesel Freight 58	100
1603WS	Whistling Mountain Climber 58	40
1605W	027 6-Car Diesel Freight 58	100
1607W	Trouble Shooter Work Set 58	50
1608W	Merchants Limited Diesel 58 Passenger Set	200
1609	027 3-Car Steam Freight 59, 60	20
1611	027 4-Car Alaskan Freight 59	75
1612	The General Old-Timer 59, 60 Outfit	50
1613S	4-Car B&O Steam Freight 59	30
1615	0-4-0 Steamer (2+)	45
1615T	Tender (3)	50
1615	5-Car B&M Diesel Freight 59	75
1617S	5-Car Busy Beaver Steam 59 Work Train	75
1619W	5-Car Santa Fe Diesel Freight 59	50
1621WS	Construction Special Steam 59 Freight	30
1623W	5-Car Northern Pacific Diesel 59 Freight	100
1625	0-4-0 Steamer (4)	90
1625T	Tender (4)	75
1625WS	5-Car Action King Steam 59 Freight	40
1626W	4-Car Santa Fe Diesel Passenger 59	100
1627S	027 3-Car Steam Freight 60	30
1629	4-Car C & O Diesel Freight 60	40
1631WS	4-Car Industrial Steam Freight 60	30
1633	Land-Sea-Air Two Unit 60 Diesel Freight	100
1635WS	Heavy-Duty Special Steam 60 Freight	50
1637W	5-Car Twin Unit Diesel Freight 60	50
1639WS	Power House Special 60 Steam Freight	150
1640W	Presidential Campaign Special 60	100
1640-100	Presidential Kit (3)	50
1641	3-Car Headliner Steam 61 Freight	20
1642	3-Car Circus Special Steam 61 Freight	30
1643	4-Car Sky-Scout Diesel Freight 61	30
1644	Frontier Special General 61 Passenger	75
1645	027 4-Car Diesel Freight 61	30
1646	4-Car Utility Steam Freight 61	30
1647	Freedom Fighter Missile 61 Launcher Outfit	100
1648	5-Car Supply Line Steam Freight 61	30
1649	027 5-Car Two Unit Diesel Freight 61	50
1650	5-Car Guardian Steam Freight 61	40
1651	4-Car All Passenger Diesel 61	100
1656	0-4-0 Steamer (4+)	65
1665	0-4-0 Steamer (4)	75
1666	2-6-2 Steamer (3)	35
1800	The General Frontier Pack 59, 60	75
1805	Land-Sea-And Air Gift Pack 60	175
1809	The Western Gift Pack 61	50
1810	The Space Age Gift Pack 61	75
1862	4-4-0 Steamer (4)	50
1862T	Tender (4)	50
1865	W & A Passenger Car (3)	40
1866	W & A Passenger Car (3)	35
1872	4-4-0 Steamer (4)	60
1872T	Tender (4)	40
1875	W & A Passenger Car (5)	150
1875W	W & A Passenger Car (3)	75
1876	W & A Passenger Car (3)	30
1877	Flat with horses and fences (2)	30
1882	4-4-0, 1882T	NOB
1885	W & A Passenger Car	NOB
1887	Flat Car w/horses and fences	NOB
2016	2-6-4 Steamer (3)	50
2018	2-6-4 Steamer (2)	30
2020	6-8-6 Steamer (2+)	40
2020W	Tender (3)	35
2023(MC)	Union Pacific Alco AA (3)	85
2024	C&O Alco A	NOB
2025	2-6-2 Steamer (2)	30

POSTWAR

Number	Description		Value
2026	2-6-2 Steamer	(2)	30
2026X	2-6-2 Steamer		
2028	Pennsylvania GP-7	(3)	65
2029	2-6-4 Steamer	(2+)	35
2031(MC)	Rock Island Alco AA	(3)	75
2032(MC)	Erie Alco AA	(3)	75
2033(MC)	Union Pacific Alco AA	(4)	85
2034	2-4-2 Steamer	(2)	30
2035	2-6-4 Steamer	(2)	30
2036	2-6-4 Steamer	(3)	30
2037	2-6-4 Steamer	(2)	30
2037-500	2-6-4 Steamer (Girls Train)	(4+)	150
2041	Rock Island Alco AA		100
2046	4-6-4 Steamer	(2+)	45
2046W	Tender	(2)	35
2046WX	Tender	(4)	45
2046W-50	PRR Tender	(4)	45
2055	4-6-4 Steamer	(3)	40
2056	4-6-4 Steamer	(3)	45
2065	4-6-4 Steamer	(2)	45
2100	Lionel O Passenger Train 46		100
2100W	Lionel O Passenger Train 46		100
2101	Lionel O Gauge Freight Set 46		50
2101W	Lionel O Gauge Freight Set 46		50
2103W	Lionel O Gauge Freight Set 46		50
2105WS	Lionel Freight Outfit 46		50
2110WS	Lionel Passenger Train 46		200
2111WS	Lionel Freight Train 46		100
2113WS	Lionel O Gauge Freight Outfit 46		200
2114WS	O Passenger Outfit 46		300
2115WS	Lionel O Gauge Freight 46 Work Train w/smoke		150
2120S	De Luxe Passenger 47		100
2120WS	De Luxe Passenger 47		100
2121S	Lionel Freight Set 47		40
2121WS	Lionel Freight Set 47		40
2123WS	Lionel Freight Set 47		50
2124W	Lionel Passenger Set 47		350
2125WS	Lionel Freight Train 47		75
2126WS	Lionel Passenger Set 47		200
2127WS	Lionel Work Train 47		75
2129WS	Lionel Freight Set 47		200
2131WS	De Luxe Work Train 47		125
2133W	4-Car Twin Diesel O Gauge 48 Freight Train		125
2135WS	Lionel Freight Train 48, 49		40
2136WS	Passenger Train 48, 49		100
2137WS	De Luxe Freight Train 48		50
2139W	Lionel Four-Car Freight Set 48		125
2139W	O Gauge Four-Car 49 Freight Outfit		125
2140WS	De Luxe Passenger Set 48, 49		100
2141WS	Four-Car Freight Train 48, 49		50
2143WS	De Luxe Work Train 48		75
2144W	3-Car De Luxe Passenger 48, 49 Outfit		300
2145WS	Four-Car Freight Set 48		100
2146WS	Lionel Pullman Train 48, 49		250
2147WS	Four-Car Freight Set 49		50
2148WS	Lionel O Deluxe Pullman Set 50		500
2149B	O Gauge Four-Car Diesel 49 Work Train		100
2150WS	O Deluxe Passenger Set 50		100
2151W	Five-Car O Gauge Diesel Set 49		125
2153WS	Four-Car De Luxe 49 Work Train		75
2155WS	Four-Car Freight Train 49		100
2159W	Lionel 5-Car Freight 50		200
2161W	Twin Diesel Freight 50		125
2163WS	4-Car Freight 50, 51		100
2165WS	O 4-Car Freight Set 50		100
2167WS	3-Car Freight 50, 51		50
2169WS	Lionel 5-Car Freight 50 w/smoke and whistle		300
2171W	Twin Diesel Freight 50		125
2173WS	Lionel 4-Car Freight 50		50
2175W	Magnificent Lionel Twin 50, 51 Diesel Freights		150
2177WS	3-Car Freight 52		40
2179WS	4-Car Freight 52		40
2183WS	4-Car Freight 52		50
2185W	Magnificent Lionel Twin 50, 51 Diesel Freights		125
2187WS	5-Car Freight 52		50
2189WS	Transcontinental Fast Freight 52		75
2190W	Lionel Super Speedliner 52, 53		250
2191W	4-Car Diesel Freights 52		150
2193W	4-Car Diesel Freights 52		150
2201WS	Highballing Freight 53, 54		75
2203WS	Highballing Freight 53		75
2205WS	5-Car Freight 53		75
2207W	Triple Diesel Freight 53		150
2209W	Triple Diesel Freight 53		150
2211WS	4-Car Freight 53		75

POSTWAR

177

Cat. No.	Description	Price	Cat. No.	Description	Price
2213WS	5-Car Freight 53	75	2276W	Budd RDC Commuter Set 57	250
2217WS	O Gauge 4-Car Freight 54	100	2277SW	O Gauge 4-Car Work Train 57	75
2219W	Fairbanks-Morse Power Giant 54	150	2279W	O Gauge 5-Car Freight 57	100
2221WS	O Gauge 5-Car Freight, 54	75	2281W	O Gauge 5-Car Freight 57	125
2222WS	Lionel O Gauge 3-Car Pullman Set	200	2283WS	O Gauge 5-Car Freight 57	75
2223W	O Gauge 5-Car Freight 54	250	2285W	O Gauge 5-Car Freight 57	200
2225WS	Lionel O Gauge 5-Car 54 Work Freight	75	2287W	O Gauge 5-Car Freight 57	200
2227W	O Gauge 5-Car Freight 54	150	2289WS	Super O Freight Train 57	100
2229W	O Gauge 5-Car Freight 54	150	2291W	Dream-Liner of the 57 Western Roads	300
2231W	O Gauge 5-Car Freight 54	250	2292WS	Crack Super O Luxury Liner 57	250
2234W	Super-Streamliner 54	300	2293W	Pride of the Eastern Lines 57	300
2235W	O Gauge 4-Car Freight 55	75	2295WS	The Grand Daddy of 57 all Steamers	300
2237WS	O Gauge 3-Car Freight 55	50	2296W	Crack Super O Luxury Liner 57	700
2239W	O Gauge Streak-Liner 55	200	2297WS	The 16 Wheeler Class J 57	325
2240P	Wabash F3 Powered A Unit (3)	150	2340-25	GG-1/Green 5 gold stripes (4)	250
2240C	Wabash F3 Dummy B Unit (3+)	150	2321	Lackawanna FM (3)	125
2241WS	O Gauge Freight Snorter 55	50	2322	Virginian FM (3)	100
2242P	New Haven F3 Powered A Unit (4)	175	2328	Burlington GP-7 (2+)	85
2242C	New Haven F3 Dummy B Unit (4)	175	2329	Virginian Electric (4)	150
2243P	Santa Fe F3 Powered A Unit (2+)	65	2330	GGI (4+)	250
2243C	Santa Fe F3 Dummy B Unit (3)	65	2331	Virginian FM (3)	150
2243W	The High and the Mighty 55	150	2332	GGI (3)	125
2244W	The Sweetest Sight on Rails 55	250	2333P	Santa Fe F-3 Powered A Unit (2+)	65
2245P	Texas Special F3 Powered A (3)	125	2333T	Santa Fe F-3 Dummy A Unit (3)	65
2245C	Texas Special F3 Dummy B Unit (3+)	125	2333P	NYC F-3 Powered A Unit (3)	75
2245WS	Whistles While She Works 55	75	2333T	NYC F-3 Dummy A Unit (3+)	75
2247W	O Gauge 5-Car Freight 55	250	2360-25	GG-1 Brunswick green (4)	275
2249WS	O Gauge 5-Car Freight 55	100	2337	Wabash GP-7 (4)	75
2251W	The High and the Mighty 55	250	2338	Milwaukee Road GP-7 (2)	65
2253W	A Miracle of Modeling 55 Accuracy	250	2339	Wabash GP-7 (3+)	75
2254W	The Congressional 55	750	2340-1	GG-1/Tuscan 5 gold stripes (4)	250
2255W	O Gauge 4-Car Work Train 56	75	2341	Jersey Central FM (4+)	500
2257WS	O Gauge 5-Car Freight 56	50	2343P	Santa Fe F-3 Powered A Unit (2)	65
2259W	O Gauge 5-Car Freight 56	100	2343T	Santa Fe F-3 Dummy A Unit (3)	65
2261WS	O Gauge Freight Hauler 56	75	2343C	Santa Fe F3 Dummy B Unit (2+)	75
2263W	O Gauge 5-Car Freight 56	100	2344P	NYC F-3 Powered A Unit (3)	70
2265SW	O Gauge 5-Car Freight 56	75	2344T	NYC Dummy A Unit (3+)	70
2267W	Proud Giant of the Rails 56	200	2344C	NYC Dummy B Unit (3)	80
2269W	Majestic O Gauge Freight Set 56	550	2345P	Western Pacific F-3 Powered A (3+)	175
2270W	Proud Giant of the Rails, 56	700	2345T	Western Pacific F-3 Dummy A (4)	175
2271W	O Gauge 5-Car Freight Train 56	400	2346	Boston & Maine GP-7 (4)	85
2273W	From the Midwest to the East 56	600	2347	C&0 GP-7 (5)	300
2274W	The Great Congressional 56	700	2348	Minn & St. Louis GP-9 (3+)	95
2275W	O Gauge 4-Car Freight 57	150	2349	Northern Pacific GP-9 (3)	95

POSTWAR

Cat#	Description	Cond	Price
2350	New Haven EP-5	(2+)	85
2351	Milwaukee Road EP-5	(3+)	125
2352	Pennsylvania EP-5	(3+)	150
2353P	Santa Fe F-3 Powered A Unit	(2)	75
2353T	Santa Fe F-3 Dummy A Unit	(3)	75
2354P	NYC F-3 Powered A Unit	(3)	85
2354T	NYC F-3 Dummy A Unit	(3+)	85
2355P	Western Pacific F-3 Powered A	(3+)	175
2355T	Western Pacific F-3 Dummy A	(4)	175
2356P	Southern F-3 Powered A Unit	(3)	150
2356T	Southern F-3 Dummy A Unit	(3+)	150
2356C	Southern F-3 Dummy B Unit	(3+)	175
2358	Great Northern EP-5	(4+)	250
2359	Boston & Maine GP-9	(3)	85
2360-1	GG-1	(4)	250
2363P	Illinois Central F-3 Powered A	(3)	150
2363C	Illinois Central F-3 Dummy B	(3+)	150
2365	Chesapeake & Ohio GP-7	(3+)	95
2367P	Wabash F-3 Powered A Unit	(3)	135
2367C	Wabash F-3 Dummy B Unit	(3+)	135
2368P	B&O F-3 Powered A Unit	(4)	275
2368C	B&O F-3 Dummy B Unit	(4)	275
2373P	Canadian Pacific F-3 Powered A	(4)	250
2373T	Canadian Pacific F-3 Dummy A	(4)	250
2378P	Milwaukee Road F-3 Powered A	(4)	275
2378C	Milwaukee Road F-3 Dummy B	(4)	275
2379P	Rio Grande F-3 Powered A Unit	(3)	165
2379C	Rio Grande F-3 Dummy B Unit	(3+)	165
2383P	Santa Fe F-3 Powered A Unit	(3)	65
2383T	Santa Fe F-3 Dummy A Unit	(2)	65
2400	Maplewood Pullman	(4)	50
2401	Hillside Observation	(4)	50
2402	Chatham Pullman	(4)	50
2403B	Tender	(4)	75
2404	Santa Fe Vista Dome	(3+)	30
2405	Santa Pullman	(3+)	35
2406	Santa Fe Observation	(3+)	30
2408	Santa Vista Dome	(4)	30
2409	Santa Fe Pullman	(4)	35
2410	Santa Fe Observation	(4)	30
2412	Santa Fe Vista Dome	(3)	35
2414	Santa Fe Pullman	(3)	35
2416	Santa Fe Observation	(3)	30
2419	DL&W Work Caboose	(3)	25
2420	DL&W Work Caboose	(3)	25
2421	Maplewood Pullman	(2)	25
2422	Chatham Pullman	(2)	25
2423	Hillside Observation	(2)	20
2429	Livingston Pullman	(3)	35
2430	Pullman	(3+)	30
2431	Observation	(3+)	25
2432	Clifton Vista Dome	(2+)	25
2434	Newark Pullman	(2+)	25
2435	Elizabeth Pullman	(2+)	25
2436	Mooseheart Observation	(3)	35
2440	Observation	(3)	25
2441	Observation	(3)	25
2442	Pullman	(3)	25
2442	Clifton Vista Dome	(4)	45
2443	Observation	(3)	25
2444	Newark Pullman	(4)	55
2445	Elizabeth Pullman	(5-)	100
2446	Summit Observation	(4)	40
2454	Pennsylvania Boxcar	(4)	50
2460	Bucyrus Erie Crane Car	(3+)	45
2461	Transformer Car	(3)	30
2466T	Tender	(3)	30
2466W	Tender	(3)	30
2466WX	Tender	(4)	35
2481	Plainfield Pullman	(4+)	125
2482	Westfield Pullman	(4+)	125
2483	Livingston Observation	(4+)	125
2501W	Super O Work Train, 58		100
2502W	Super O Rail-Diesel 58 Commuter		250
2503WS	Timberland Special Freight 58		75
2505W	5-Car Super O Freight 58		175
2507W	5-Car Super O Diesel Freight 58		200
2509WS	The Owl 5-Car Freight 58		75
2511W	Super O Electric Work Train 58		125
2513W	6-Car Super O Freight Train 58		200
2515WS	5-Car Mainliner Steam Freight 58		100
2517W	5-Car Super O Diesel Freight 58		300
2518W	Super O Passenger Train 58		250
2519W	6-Car Super O Diesel Freight 58		200
2521	President McKinley Obsv	(3+)	85
2521WS	6-Car Super O Freight Train 58		250
2522	President Harrison Vista Dome	(3+)	85
2523	President Garfield Pullman	(3+)	95
2523W	Super O Super Chief Freight, 58		200
2525WS	6-Car Super O Work Train, 58		350

POSTWAR

No.	Description	Cond.	Price
2526W	Super Chief Passenger, 58		250
2527	Super O Missile Launcher 59, 60 Outfit		100
2528WS	5-Star Frontier Special 59-61 Outfit		100
2529W	5-Car Virginian Rectifier 59 Work Train		150
2530	Baggage Car (B & O)	(2+)	60
2530	Baggage Car (OPerf)	(5)	150
2531	Silver Dawn Observation	(2)	35
2531WS	Super O 5-Car Steam Freight 59		125
2532	Silver Range Vista Dome	(2)	40
2533	Silver Cloud Pullman	(2+)	40
2533W	5-Car GN Electric Freight 59		200
2534	Silver Bluff Pullman	(2+)	40
2535WS	Super O 5-Car Hudson 59 Steam Freight		100
2537W	5-Car New Haven 59 Diesel Freight		250
2539WS	5-Car Hudson Steam Freight 59		150
2541	Alexander Hamilton Observation	(3)	95
2541W	5-Car Super Chief Freight 59		250
2542	Betsy Ross Vista Dome	(3+)	95
2543	William Penn Pullman	(3+)	95
2543WS	6-Car Berkshire Steam Freight 59		150
2544	Molly Pitcher Pullman	(3+)	95
2544W	4-Car Super Chief 59, 60 Streamliner		400
2545WS	6-Car N&W Space-Freight 59		300
2547WS	4-Car Variety Special 60 Steam Freight		75
2549W	A Mighty Military Diesel Outfit 60		125
2550	Baltimore & Ohio Budd	(4)	100
2551	Banff Park Observation	(4)	100
2551W	6-Car GN Diesel Freight 60		225
2552	Skyline 500 Vista Dome	(4)	100
2553	Blair Manor Pullman	(4+)	175
2553WS	The Majestic Berkshire 60 5-Car Freight		150
2554	Craig Manor	(4+)	175
2555	Sunoco Tank Car	(3+)	25
2555W	Over & Under Twin 60 Railroad Empire		1000
2559	Baltimore & Ohio Budd	(3+)	85
2560	Lionel Lines Crane	(4)	35
2561	Vista Valley Observation	(4)	100
2562	Regal Pass Vista Dome	(4)	115
2563	Indian Falls Pullman	(4)	115
2570	5-Car Husky Diesel Freight, 61		75
2571	Fort Knox Special Steam Freight 61		50
2572	5-Car Space Age Diesel Freighter 61		100
2573	5-Car TV Special Steam Freight 61		125
2574	5-Car Defender Diesel Freight 61		175
2575	7-Car Dynamo Electric Freight 61		300
2576	4-Car Super Chief Streamline 61		400
6517-1966	TCA 1966 Conv Car	(4)	35
2625	Irvington (1946-1949)	(3)	85
2625	Irvington (1950)	(4+)	100
2625	Madison (1947)	(3)	85
2625	Manhattan (1947)	(3)	85
2627	Madison (1948,1949)	(3)	85
2627	Madison (1950)	(4+)	100
2628	Manhattan (1948, 1949)	(3)	85
2628	Manhattan (1950)	(4+)	100
2671W	Tender	(3)	35
2671WX	Tender	(4)	45
2755	Sunoco Tank Car aluminum	(3)	25
2758	Pennsylvania Automobile Boxcar	(2)	20
2855	Sunoco Tank Car	(4)	65
3330	Flat Car with Operating Sub Kit	(3)	50
3330-100	Operating Submarine Kit	(4)	125
3349	Turbo Launching Car	(3)	20
3356	Operating Horse Car w/corral	(2)	35
3356-2	Operating Horse Car	(4)	25
3356-150	Operating Horse Car Corral	(5)	125
3357	Cop and Hobo Car	(2)	25
3359-55	Lionel Lines Twin Dump Car	(3)	30
3360	Burro Crane	(3)	45
3366	Operating Circus Car w/corral	(3+)	75
3370	Sheriff & Outlaw Car	(3+)	35
3376	Operating Giraffe Car	(2)	25
3376-160	Operating Giraffe Car	(4)	35
3386	Operating Giraffe Car		NOB
3409	Operating Helicopter Car		NOB
3410	Operating Helicopter Car		NOB
3413	Mercury Capsule Car	(4)	35
3419	Operating Helicopter Car	(2+)	25
3424	Wabash Brakeman Car	(2)	20
3428	US Mail Car	(3+)	30
3429	USMC Helicopter Launch Car		NOB
3434	Operating Chicken Car	(3)	30
3435	Aquarium Car	(3)	60
3444	Erie Animated Gondola	(3)	40
3454	PRR Merchandise Car	(3+)	75
3460	Flatcar with trailers	(3)	25
3470	Aerial Target Launching Car	(3)	25
3474	Western Pacific Op. Boxcar	(3)	25
3484	PRR Operating Boxcar	(3)	20
3484-25	Santa Fe Operating Boxcar	(3)	30
3494-1	NYC Operating Boxcar	(3)	25
3494-150	Missouri Pacific Op. Boxcar	(3+)	35
3494-275	State Of Maine Op. Boxcar	(2+)	30
3494-550	Monon Operating Boxcar	(4)	85
3494-625	Soo Operating Boxcar	(4)	85
3509	Satellite Car	(5)	100
3510	Satellite Car		NOB
3512	Operating Fireman and Ladder Car	(3)	50

Number	Description	Condition	Price
3519	Operating Satellite Car	(3)	25
3530	Operating Generator Car	(3)	30
3535	AEC Security Car	(3)	25
3540	Operating Radar Car	(4)	40
3545	Operating TV Monitor Car	(4)	40
3562-1	Operating Barrel Car	(3)	25
3562-25	Operating Barrel Car	(2)	20
3562-50	Operating Barrel Car	(2)	20
3562-75	Operating Barrel Car	(3)	25
3619	Helicopter Reconnaissance Car	(3+)	40
3665	Minuteman Missile Launching Car	(3)	30
3666	Cannon Box Car		NOB
3672	Operating Bosco Milk Car	(3+)	75
3820	Operating Submarine Car		NOB
3830	Operating Submarine Car	(3)	30
3854	Pennsylvania Merchandise Car	(4)	85
3927	Track Cleaning Car	(2)	20
4109WS	Electronic Control Set 46, 47		125
4110WS	Lionel Electronic Railroad 48, 49		225
4357	SP Caboose	(4)	45
4452	Pennsylvania Gondola	(4)	45
4454	Baby Ruth Boxcar	(4)	45
4457	Pennsylvania Caboose	(4)	40
5459	Operating Dump Car	(4)	45
6014	Chun King Boxcar		
6014-60	Bosco Boxcar	(4)	35
6014-100	Airex Boxcar	(3)	25
6014-150	Wix Boxcar	(4+)	75
6014-410	Frisco Boxcar	(4)	25
6017-50	USMC Caboose	(3)	35
6017-85	Lionel Lines Caboose	(4)	45
6017-100	Boston & Maine Caboose	(3+)	25
6017-200	US Navy Caboose	(4+)	50
6020W	Tender	(3)	45
6024-60	RCA Whirlpool Boxcar	(4)	35
6026T	Tender	(3)	20
6026W	Tender	(3)	25
6027	Alaska Caboose	(4)	85
6044-1X	McCall/Nestle's Boxcar	(5)	200
6050	Libby's Tomato Juice Boxcar		NOB
6119	DL&W Work Caboose	(2+)	20
6119-25	DL&W Work Caboose	(3)	20
6119-50	DL&W Work Caboose	(3)	20
6119-100	DL&W Work Caboose	(3)	20
6119-125	Lionel Rescue Unit		NOB
6151	Flat Car w/Range Patrol Truck	(3)	30
6162-60	Alaska Gondola	(3)	40
6162-110	NYC Blue Gondola	(3)	20
6162-110	NYC Red Gondola (Paste-On-Label)	(4+)	35
6175	Flat Car with rocket	(3)	25
6220	Santa Fe GM Switcher	(3)	60
6250	Seaboard GM Switcher	(3)	60
6257X	SP Caboose	(4)	50
6262	Wheel Car	(3)	25
6264	Lumber Car	(4+)	125
6311	Flat Car with pipes	(4)	75
6315	Gulf Tank Car	(2)	25
6343	Barrel Ramp Car	(3)	20
6346-56	Alcoa Covered Hopper	(3)	30
6352-25	Ice Car	(5)	75
6356	NYC Stock Car	(2+)	20
6357-50	AT&SF	(4+)	125
6362	Railway Truck Car	(3+)	30
6376	Circus Car	(3)	25
6401	Flat Car	(5)	100
6403B	Tender	(3+)	60
6405	Flat with trailer	(4)	35
6406	Flat Car with single auto		NOB
6407	Flat Car with missile	(5-)	125
6408	Flat Car with pipes		NOB
6409	Flat Car with pipes		NOB
6409-25	Flat Car with pipes		NOB
6411	Flat Car with logs		
6413	Mercury Capsule Car	(3+)	35
6414	Automobile Car (B&O)	(2+)	25
6414	Automobile Transport Car (OPerf)	(4)	45
6414	Automobile Transport Car (OPix)	(3)	30
6414	RS 6414 on end flap (WB)	(4)	75
6414-25	Four Autos	(4)	100
6414-85	Automobile Transport Car	(5-)	100
6416	Boat Loader	(3+)	50
6417	NYC Porthole Caboose	(2)	20
6417-50	Lehigh Valley Caboose	(3)	35
6418	Machinery Car	(3+)	35
6419-100	DL&W Work Caboose	(3)	20
6420	DL&W Work Caboose	(3)	35
6424-110	Flat Car with two autos	(2+)	25
6427-60	Virginian	(4)	85
6427-500	Pennsylvania Caboose	(4+)	100
6429	DL&W	(4+)	150
6430	Flat Car with trailers	(3)	25
6431	Piggy-Back Car with Midge Toy Tractor	(4)	100
6434	Poultry Car	(3)	30
6436	Lehigh Valley Hopper	(2+)	20
6436-25	Lehigh Valley Hopper	(2+)	20
6436-110	Lehigh Valley Hopper	(3)	25
6436-500	Lehigh Valley Hopper	(4+)	100
6440	Pullman	(3)	30
6441	Observation	(3)	30
6442	Pullman	(3)	30
6443	Observation	(3)	30
6445	Fort Knox Gold Bullion Car	(3+)	35
6446	N&W Covered Hopper (B&O)	(2+)	20
6446	Cement Car (OPR)	(4+)	35
6446-25	N&W Covered Hopper	(2+)	20
6446-60	Lehigh Valley Covered Hopper	(5-)	85
6447	Pennsylvania Caboose	(5-)	125

POSTWAR

181

POSTWAR

6448	Exploding Boxcar	(2+)	20
6454	Baby Ruth Boxcar	(4)	75
6460	Bucyrus Erie Crane Car	(2)	25
6461	Transformer Car	(3+)	25
6462-500	NYC Gondola (Girls Train)	(4+)	100
6463	Rocket Fuel Tank Car	(3+)	35
6464-1	Western Pacific Boxcar	(2)	30
6464-50	M&STl. Boxcar	(2)	25
6464-75	Rock Island Boxcar	(3)	25
6464-100	WP Boxcar (Yellow Feather)	(3)	35
6464-125	New York Central Boxcar	(3)	35
6464-150	Missouri Pacific Boxcar	(3)	40
6464-175	Rock Island Boxcar (50, Silver, Overstamp)	(3+)	30
6464-175	Rock Island Boxcar (175 Stamped on Box)	(4+)	65
6464-175	Rock Island Boxcar (C)	(3)	20
6464-200	Pennsylvania Boxcar (B&O)	(3+)	40
6464-200	Pennsylvania Boxcar (C)	(3)	30
6464-225	Southern Pacific Boxcar	(2+)	30
6464-250	Western Pacific Boxcar (WB)	(3)	40
6464-250	Western Pacific Boxcar (B&O)	(5)	175
6464-275	State of Maine Boxcar	(3)	35
6464-300	Rutland Boxcar	(3)	40
6464-325	Sentinel Boxcar	(4)	135
6464-350	MKT Boxcar	(4)	75
6464-375	Central of Georgia Boxcar (B&O)	(3)	30
6464-375	Central of Georgia Boxcar (WB)	(2)	25
6464-400	B&O Boxcar (B&O)	(3)	30
6464-400	Baltimore & Ohio Boxcar (C)	(3)	25
6464-425	New Haven Boxcar	(2)	20
6464-450	Great Northern Boxcar (B&O)	(3)	30
6464-450	Great Northern Boxcar (WB)	(2)	25
6464-475	Boston & Maine Boxcar	(3)	20
6464-475	Boston & Maine Boxcar (OPerf)	(2+)	35
6464-500	Timken Boxcar (B&O)	(3)	30
6464-500	Timken Boxcar (C)	(3)	25
6464-510	NYC Pacmaker Boxcar (Girls Train)	(4+)	150
6464-515	Katy Boxcar Type	(4+)	150
6464-525	M&STl. Boxcar	(3)	20
6464-650	Rio Grande Boxcar (B&O)	(3)	40
6464-650	Rio Grande Boxcar (WB)	(3)	35
6464-700	Santa Fe Boxcar (OPI)	(3+)	35
6464-700	Santa Fe Boxcar (WB)	(3)	30
6464-725	New Haven Boxcar (OPix) (735 on box)	(2+)	20
6464-725	New Haven Boxcar (WB) (735 on box)	(3+)	25
6464-725	New Haven Boxcar (C) (425 on box)	(4)	40
6464-825	Alaska Boxcar	(4)	125
6464-900	NYC Boxcar	(3)	25
6464-1965	TCA Pittsburgh Boxcar	(4)	45
6466W	Tender	(3)	20
6466WX	Tender	(4)	35
6467	Miscellaneous Car	(3)	20
6468	Baltimore & Ohio Boxcar	(2)	20
6468X	Baltimore & Ohio Boxcar	(5-)	95
6469	Liquified Gas Car	(4)	75
6475	Pickle Car	(2)	20
6475	Libbys Pickle Car		NOB
6475	Heinz Pickle Car		
6477	Miscellaneous Car with pipes	(3)	30
6480	Exploding Boxcar		NOB
6500	Beechcraft Bonanza Transport Car (OPix)	(4+)	150
6500	Beechcraft Bonanza Transport Car (OPP)	(5-)	150
6501	Jet Boat Car	(3+)	50
6502	Girder Car, Black/white		NOB
6502-50	Girder Car, Blue/white		NOB
6502-75	Girder Car, Light blue/white		NOB
6511	Flatcar with pipes	(3)	20
6512	Cherry Picker Car	(3+)	35
6517	Lionel Lines Bay Window Caboose	(2)	25
6517-75	Erie Bay Window Caboose	(4)	100
6518	Transformer Car	(3+)	35
6519	Allis Chalmers Car	(3+)	25
6520	Searchlight Car	(3)	20
6530	Fire And Safety Training Car	(3+)	35
6544	Missile Launching Car	(3)	25
6556	Katy Stock Car	(4)	55
6557	Lionel Smoking Caboose	(3)	40
6560	Bucyrus Erie Crane Car	(2)	20
6560-25	Bucyrus Erie Crane Car	(3)	20
6561	Cable Car	(3)	25
6572	Railway Express Car (B&O)	(3+)	35
6572	Railway Express Car (OPix)	(3)	30
6630	Missile Launcher		NOB
6640	USMC Missile Launcher		NOB
6650	Missile Launching Flat Car	(3)	25
6651	USMC Cannon Car		NOB
6657	Rio Grande Caboose	(3+)	45
6660	Boom Car	(4)	25
6670	Derrick Car	(4)	25
6672	Refrigerator Car	(3)	25
6736	Detroit & Mackinac Hopper	(3+)	30
6800	Airplane Car (B&O)	(3)	35
6800	Airplane Car (OPix)	(4+)	50
6800-60	Airplane	(4)	150
6801	Flat Car with boat	(3)	25
6801-50	Flat Car with boat	(3+)	25
6801-75	Flat Car with boat	(3)	25
6802	Flat Car with girders	(4)	20
6803	Flat Car with Military Units	(3+)	45
6804	Flat Car with Military Units	(3+)	45
6805	Radioactive Waste	(3+)	35
6806	Flat Car with Military Units	(3+)	45
6807	Flat Car with Military Unit	(3)	35
6808	Flat Car with Military Units	(3+)	45

6809	Flat Car with Military Units		(3+)	45	11460	7-Unit Steam Freight 64		20
6810	Flat Car with van		(3)	25	11470	7-Unit Steam Freight 64		30
6812	Track Maintenance Car		(3)	25	11480	7-Unit Diesel Freight 64		50
6814	First Aid Medical Car		(3)	30	11490	5-Unit Diesel Passenger 64, 65		100
6816	Flatcar with bulldozer		(4)	100	11500	7-Unit Steam Freight 64-66		30
6816-100	Bulldozer (B&O)		(5)	1000*	11510	7-Unit Steam Freight 64		30
6816-100	Bulldozer (Photo Box*)		(5)	1000*	11520	6-Unit Steam Freight 65, 66		20
6817	Flatcar with scraper		(4)	100	11530	5-Unit Diesel Freight 65, 66		30
6817-100	Scraper (PWB)		(5)	1000*	11540	6-Unit Steam Freight 65, 66		30
6817-100	Scraper (Photo Box)		(5)	1000*	11550	6-Unit Steam Freight 65, 66		30
6819	Flat Car with helicopter		(3+)	30	11560	7-Unit Diesel Freight 65, 66		50
6820	Missile Transport Car		(4)	100	11590	5-Unit Illuminated Passenger Set 66		100
6821	Flat Car with crates		(3+)	25	11600	7-Unit Steam Freight Set 68		300
6822	Nightcrew Searchlight Car		(3)	20	11710	Value Packed Steam Freighter 69		20
6823	Flat Car with missiles		(3)	25	11720	5 Unit Diesel Freighter 69		30
6824	USMC First Aid Medical Car			NOB	11730	6 Unit Diesel Freight 69		40
6824-50	First Aid Medical Car			NOB	11740	7 Unit Diesel Freight 69		40
6825	Flat Car with trestle		(3)	20	11750	7 Unit Steam Freight 69		50
6826	Flat Car with Christmas Trees		(3+)	30	11760	7 Unit Steam Freight 69		30
6827	Flat Car w/P&H Steam Shovel		(3)	45	12502	Prairie-Rider Gift Pack 62		100
6827	Power Shovel		(3)	35	12512	Enforcer Gift Pack 62		100
6828	Flat Car with P&H Crane		(3)	45	12700	7-Unit Steam Freight 64		125
6828	Truck Crane		(3)	35	12710	7-Unit Steam Freight 64-66		125
6830	Flat Car with submarine		(3+)	35	12720	7-Unit Diesel Freight 64		125
6844	Flat Car with missiles		(3)	25	12730	7-Unit Diesel Freight 64-66		125
11201	Fast Starter Steam Freight, 62			20	12740	9-Unit Diesel Freight 64		125
11212	4-Unit Cyclone Diesel Freight 62			40	12750	9-Unit Diesel Freight 64		125
11222	5-Unit Vagabond Steam Freight 62			30	12760	9-Unit Steam Freight 64		125
11232	027 5-Unit Diesel Freight, 62			40	12770	9-Unit Steam Freight 64		125
11242	Trail Blazer Steam Freight 62			20	12780	6-Unit Diesel Passenger 64-66		300
11252	027 7-Unit Diesel Freight 62			50	12800	6-Unit Diesel Freight 65, 66		75
11268	027 6-Unit Diesel Freight 62			100	12820	8-Unit Diesel Freight 65		125
11278	7-Unit Plainsman Steam Freight 62			30	12840	Back by Popular Demand 66		100
11288	7-Unit Orbitor Diesel Freight 62			100	12850	8-Unit Diesel Freight 66		125
11298	7-Unit Vigilant Steam Freight 62			50	13008	6-Unit Champion Steam Freight 62		40
11308	027 6-Unit Diesel Passenger 62			100	13018	6-Unit Starfire Diesel Freight 62		150
11311	Value Packed Steam Freighter 63			20	13028	6-Unit Defender Diesel Freight 62		125
11321	027 5 Unit Diesel Freighter 63			30	13036	6-Unit Plainsman Steam Outfit 62		100
11331	Outdoorsman Steam Freight 63			30	13048	7-Unit Super O Steam Freight 62		100
11341	Space-Prober Diesel Freight 63			150	13058	7-Unit Vanguard Diesel Freight 62		150
11351	Land Rover Steam Freight 63			30	13068	8-Unit Goliath Electric Freight 62		300
11361	Shooting Star Diesel Freight 63			100	13078	5-Unit Presidential Passenger 62		300
11375	Cargomaster Steam Freight 63			75	13088	6-Unit Presidential Passenger 62		300
11385	Space Conqueror Diesel Freight 63			200	13098	Goliath Steam Freight 63		200
11395	Muscleman Steam Freight 63			75	13108	7 Unit Super O Diesel Freight 63		100
11405	027 6 Unit Diesel Passenger 63			100	13118	8 Unit Super O Steam Freight 63		150
11420	4-Unit Steam Freight 64			20	13128	7 Unit Super O Diesel Freight 63		200
11430	5-Unit Steam Freight 64			20	13138	Majestic Electric Freight 63		300
11440	5-Unit Diesel Freight 64			30	13148	Super Chief Passenger 63		300
11450	6-Unit Steam Freight 64			20	13150	9-Unit Super O Steam Freight 64-66		300

POSTWAR

183

Lionel HO, 1957-1966

by Charles Sommer

A combination of diminishing sales in the mid 1950's and a growing interest in the HO scale among the train buying public led The Lionel Corporation to launch an HO line in 1957. Lacking the necessary experience with HO production, Lionel contracted with the Italian firm Rivarossi to furnish them with the cars used in their 1957 line.

In 1958, Athearn made most of Lionel's HO line and in 1959, Lionel manufactured their own line of HO, using tooling purchased from Hobbyline. Starting with the Poultry car in 1959, Lionel introduced a series of HO versions of their O gauge operating cars. While these cars were appealing to kids, they ended any interest HO modelers may have had with Lionel. Lionel discontinued their HO line in 1966.

Today, Lionel HO is drawing interest from collectors because prices are still relatively low and it's still possible to find mint/boxed pieces. In the late 60s, large inventories of Lionel HO were sold in bulk by hobby shops trying to dump the poor-selling line. Many buyers stored the items, waiting for that day when there was enough demand to bring them out. That day is here.

Since very little Lionel HO is purchased to operate, condition is crucial. There is a dramatic drop (50% or more) in price after Mint/boxed. Exceptions would be the very scarce cars that remain in demand no matter what their condition.

Most Lionel HO has a Rarity Rating of 2 or 3. For some of the very scarce variations, we have assigned a Rarity Rating of 4 or 5. Some items have no price because no sales have been reported.

The HO engines and cars made for Lionel by Rivarossi and Athearn were supposed to be stamped with the Lionel "L" trademark.

Rivarossi was vigilant about this policy while Athearn was lax. Only Rivarossi's SP, T&P and C&NW FM units, the 0600 switcher, and the 0610 Consolidation were sold without the "L". Athearn shipped cars without the "L" in Lionel boxes, shipped cars with the "L" in Athearn boxes and some cars have surfaced with the Lionel markings on one side only.

Obviously, for Lionel collectors, the cars with the Lionel "L" trademark, packaged in Lionel boxes, are the most desirable.

1957

Diesels

Fairbanks-Morse Units

None of the FM units supplied by Rivarossi to Lionel's HO line in 1957 were numbered using the assigned catalog number for the unit or with any other number. To distinguish the diesel locomotives supplied to Lionel from its own HO line sold in the US, all units in the Western Pacific, Wabash and Illinois Central road names intended for Lionel were marked with an encircled "L." The prices shown here assumes the presence of this marking for these road names. The Southern Pacific, Texas and Pacific and the Chicago and Northwestern diesels are not known marked in that manner and are priced accordingly. Any of these three roadnames with the Lionel "L" would bring a premium price.

		Ex
0500	Chicago and Northwestern Powered A Unit Green-yellow/orange	120
0501	Texas and Pacific Powered A Unit Light blue-white/white	500
0502	Wabash Powered A Unit Dark blue-gray-white/gold, with L	80
0503	Western Pacific Powered A Unit Gray-orange/black, with L	80
0504	Southern Pacific Powered A Unit Red-gray/black	450
0505	Illinois Central Powered A Unit Brown-orange-yellow/brown, with L	80
0510	Chicago and Northwestern Dummy A Unit Decorated as 0500	100
0511	Texas and Pacific Dummy A Unit Decorated as 0501	430
0512	Wabash Dummy A Unit Decorated as 0502, with L	80
0513	Western Pacific Dummy A Unit Decorated as 0503	70
0514	Southern Pacific Dummy A Unit Decorated as 0504, with L	350
0515	Illinois Central Dummy A Unit Decorated as 0505, with L	80

Lionel HO Assortment

0520	**Chicago and Northwestern Dummy B Unit** decorated as 0500	100
0521	**Texas and Pacific Dummy B Unit** decorated as 0501	200
0522	**Wabash Dummy B Unit** decorated as 0502, with L	50
0523	**Western Pacific Dummy B Unit** decorated as 0503, with L	60
0524	**Southern Pacific Dummy B Unit** decorated as 0504	350
0525	**Illinois Central Dummy B Unit** decorated as 0505, with L	80

Steamers

0600	**Two Axle Shunting Loco** Dockside Switcher, (unnumbered)	90
0610LT	**2-8-0 Consolidation and Tender** 280 on Tender, Black/white, lighted.	

Note that the motor for the consolidation engine was located in the tender and a shaft ran from the motor through the cab to power the drive wheels. Unfortunately, the metal floor of the tender was prone to expansion, cracking the tender and rendering the unit inoperable. This may help explain the extreme scarcity of this engine in any condition grade.

1. Cab has rounded windows and was supplied to Lionel's HO line. No Lionel L. The engine was screw mounted to a wooden frame which served as the "liner" in its Lionel HO box. The box is as scarce as the engine. (5) 400
2. Cab has rectangular windows - believed to be late Rivarossi production and never sold by Lionel. Value about $50 in excellent condition. (2) 50

Rolling Stock
Boxcars

0864-1	**Seaboard** (15412) Brown/white, with L	100
0864-25	**New York Central Pacemaker** (174478) Gray-red/white, with L	100
0864-50	**State of Maine** (2300)	
	1. Red-white-blue/white w/L	60
	2. With Maine Potatoes decal (5)	*
0864-75	**B&O Sentinel** (466464) Silver-blue/blue-white, with L	80
0864-100	**New Haven** (36409) Black/white with orange door, with L	80
0864-125	**Rutland** (104) Yellow-green/green-yellow, with L	90

0864-150	Minneapolis & St. Louis (54652) Red/white with red door, with L	75
0864-175	Timken (646450) Yellow-white/black-blue, with L	80

Cabooses

0819	Pennsylvania Work Caboose (6475) Gray/black, with L	40
0857	Reading Bobber-Type 4-wheel Caboose (90258) Red/white, with L	40

Crane and Miscellaneous Car

0860	Pennsylvania Crane Car (489690) Gray/black, with L	50
0877	Illinois Central Miscellaneous Car (63234) Black/white, with L	40

Flatcars

0811-1	Pennsylvania w/stakes (unnumbered) Gray/black, with L	40
0811-25	Reading w/stakes (91306) Red/white, with L	30

Gondolas

0862-1	Pennsylvania (357843) Tuscan/white, with L	20
0862-25	Michigan Central (15317) Black/white, with L	15

Reefers

0871-1	Fruit Growers Express (39783) Yellow/black, with L	80
0872-25	Illinois Central (51604) Silver/green, with L	70
0872-50	A.T.S.F. (8175) Orange-black/black, with L	50

Stock Cars

0866	MKT Cattle Car (502) Yellow-brown/black, with L	45

1958

While some Rivarossi produced items continued to be listed in the 1958 catalog, the vast majority of Lionel's HO line was produced by Athearn. Since the same cars were often offered under Athearn's name, the encircled Lionel L was again employed to distinguish items intended for sale by Lionel. Despite this, quite a few unmarked Athearn cars were packaged in Lionel boxes. Some cars, such as the 0815 Gulf Chemical Tank Car, are unknown with the identifying encircled L marking. As a result, unmarked cars in a Lionel box are often acceptable, but at a reduced price, when the piece is known to exist with the L trademark.

Diesels
F-7 Units with Belt (Hi-F) Drive

0530	(D&RG) Rio Grande (unnumbered) Silver-orange yellow/black, with L	60
0531	Milwaukee Road Powered A Unit (2376) Gray-red-yellow/yellow, with L	60
0532	B&O Powered A Unit (unnumbered) Dark blue-gray-blue-yellow/yellow	
	1. Without Lionel L but in correct Lionel box	50
	2. With Lionel L	150
0533	NH (New Haven) Powered A Unit (0272) Black-orange-white/orange	
	1. Same size Lionel L each side	50
	2. Different size L symbol each side	70
0540	(D&RG) Rio Grande Dummy B Unit (unnumbered) decorated as 0530	
	1. Without Lionel L, but in correct Lionel box	50
	2. With Lionel L - *does it exist?*	*
0541	Milwaukee Road Dummy B Unit (unnumbered) decorated as 0531, with L	90
	Note: Can be found with the L marking on one side only.	

0542	**B&O Dummy B Unit** (unnumbered) decorated as 0532, with L	90
0543	**NH (New Haven) Dummy B Unit** (unnumbered) decorated as 0533, with L	80
0550	**Rio Grande Dummy A Unit** (unnumbered) decorated as 0530, with L	70
0551	**The Milwaukee Road Dummy A Unit** (2376) decorated as 0531, with L	70
0552	**Baltimore and Ohio Dummy A Unit** (unnumbered) decorated as 0532	
	1. Without Lionel L, but in correct Lionel box	60
	2. With Lionel L	150
0553	**NH (New Haven) Dummy A Unit** (0272) decorated as 0533 with L	70

GP-9 Units with Belt (Hi-F) Drive

0580	**Wabash GP-9** with headlight (452) Dark blue-gray-white with L. In addition to the Lionel L, the unit sold by Lionel has a gray cab while the geep marketed by Athearn had a dark blue cab.	130
0585	**Milwaukee Road GP-9** (unnumbered) Black-orange/black-white, w/headlight, with L	170

Husky Diesel Switchers with Belt (Hi-F) Drive

0560	**Rio Grande Snow Plow Switcher** (unnumbered) with light with L under cab window. Has separate painted orange plastic plow which snaps on to front of the shell, this is often missing.	
	1. Black shell, side of cab painted yellow	185
	2. Black shell, side of cab painted orange like plow	200
0570	**Navy Yard (New York) Switcher** with light (51) Blue/white, with L	100

Electrics

0590	**Virginian Rectifier with Belt (Hi-F) Drive** w/pantograph and headlight (unnumbered). The diesel sold by Lionel had "Built by Lionel" alongside the cab door at the short end. This slogan was absent on the Virginian sold by Athearn. Ironically, the number 0590 appeared either upright or inverted on the unit sold by Athearn and not on the Lionel Rectifier.	120

Steamers

0615 LT	**4-6-2 Pacific** w/tender, headlight, cataloged with Boston and Maine tender. The Athearn company experienced difficulties developing their 4-6-2 Pacific in time to meet the demands of Lionel's HO train line in 1958. Athearn would offer this engine in later years in their own line of HO trains, it was never sold by Lionel. Using modified dies acquired from Hobbyline, Lionel introduced the 0625LT 4-6-2 Southern Pacific in 1959.	NM

Passenger Cars

Note: Add $40 to excellent price if boxed. The New Haven cars do not carry the identifying Lionel L. Since these cars were sold by Athearn in their HO line for years, this poses a problem for the collector in determining which cars were sold by Lionel. The cars supplied to Lionel came from the early production of these units and should have a dark red stripe and a separate, snap in floor without a battery box. Cars with a battery box as part of the floor could not have been sold by Lionel.

0700	**New Haven Baggage** (3406) Silver-dark red/black	12
0701	**New Haven Pullman Coach** (3150) Silver-dark red/black	12
0702	**New Haven Vista Dome** (500) Silver-dark red/black	12
0703	**New Haven Observation** (3246) Silver-dark red/black	12

Rolling Stock
Boxcars

0864-25	**New York Central Pacemaker** (174477) Red-gray/white, with L	60
0864-50	**State of Maine** (5206) Red-white-blue/black-white, with L	
	1. "and" in white section of door	50
	2. "and" absent from white section of door	50
0864-150	**M&St.L** (52673) Red/white, black door, with L	50
0864-175	**Timken** (88) Yellow-white/brown, *Roller Freight* herald, with L	90
0864-200	**Monon** (3029) Brown/white, with L	50
0864-225	**Central of Georgia** (7402) Brown-silver/brown-silver, with L	35
0864-250	**Wabash** (6287) Blue/white, *Wabash* herald, with L	40

Cabooses

0817	**The Milwaukee Road** (01924) Silver/black, with L	30
0817-25	**Virginian** (1217) Dark blue/white, with L	45
0817-50	**(D&RG) Rio Grande** (01439) Silver/black, with L	30

Work Cabooses

0819-1	**Pennsylvania** Cataloged in 1958. *Does it exist?* Cataloged but not pictured in 1958 catalog. Does this car exist with the Lionel L marking and/or does a Lionel HO box exist stamped 0819-1?	*
	Athearn Pennsylvania Gray/black without L	5
0819-25	**U.S. Navy** (1013) Blue/white. This car is not known to have been marked with a Lionel L; however, since Athearn did not market a Navy work caboose in their HO line, the entire production of this item was intended for distribution by Lionel.	50
0819-50	**Wabash** (WAB 615) Blue/white, with L	40
0819-75	**Baltimore and Ohio** (MWC-17) Blue/white, with L	40
0819-100	**Boston and Maine** (MW 24) Reddish blue/white, with L	40

Crane and Miscellaneous Cars

0860-1	**Pennsylvania Derrick Car** Gray/black		
	1. (489711) on side with Lionel L		50
	2. (425500) on side with Lionel L, scarce	(5)	*
0877-1	**Illinois Central Miscellaneous Car** (63210) Black/white, with Lionel L		40
0879	**Union Pacific Wrecker Crane Car** Red/white		
	1. (03043) without Lionel L, but in correct Lionel box		40
	2. (03043) with Lionel L		50
	3. (787) with Lionel L *(Ken Fairchild collection)*	(5)	*

Flatcars

0800	**Nickel Plate Road** w/Airplane (1958) Black/white, with L	
	1. Original Athearn orange plane	60
	2. Original Athearn silver plane	40
0801	**Seaboard** w/Boat (42806) Brown/white, with L	40
0811-25	**Reading** w/Stakes (9440) Brown/white, with L	40
0814	**Evans Four Auto Transport Car**	
	1. NYC (499300) Brown/white, with L	50
	2. Reading (40125) Brown/white, with L	50
0824	**Erie** w/Two Autos (74286) Black/white, with L	40

0830	Flat Car w/Two *Cooper-Jarrett Inc.* Vans	
	1. Reading (40125) Brown/white with L	50
	2. NYC (499300) Brown/white, with L	50

Gondolas

0865	Michigan Central w/five canisters (350623)	
	1. Tuscan body, decorated in white, with L	30
	2. Black body, decorated in white, with L	30

Hoppers

0836	Lehigh Valley (4127) Brown/white, no load	
	1. Without Lionel L, but in correct Lionel box (without the Lionel L) and unboxed is worth under $5	90
	2. With Lionel L - *Does this item exist?*	

Reefers

0872-1	Fruit Growers Express (9253) Yellow-brown/black, with L	80
0872-50	Santa Fe Orange-black/black (cataloged as the El Capitan Reefer Car)	
	1. "El Capitan" on one side, with L	50
	2. "Super Chief " on one side, with L	100

Stock Car

0866-25	AT&SF (50656) Pale green/yellow. w/Lionel L	40

Tank Car

0815	Gulf Chemical Car (2605) Orange-black/black, black frame and dome, does not have Lionel L marking. Not known to have been produced with the Lionel L marking, so it is critical to purchase only with the appropriate Lionel box. Gulf tank car **without** the Lionel box is valued at $5 or less.	50

1959-1966

Lionel Corporation Production 1959-1966
When John English's Hobbyline series of HO trains ceased production in 1959, Lionel acquired several of their dies, including those for the Alco diesel, the Pacific tank engine, the small switcher steam locomotive, and the bodies for the gondola, hopper and boxcar. Some of these were modified, such as the dies for the steam engines which were re-worked to accommodate the Lionel motors. The airplane, boat, auto and canister loads continued to be supplied by Athearn. Athearn passenger car body shells were decorated in both Texas Special and Pennsylvania paint schemes, but, unlike the New Haven cars, carried their Lionel catalog numbers on the side of the car.

Diesels
Alcos

0535	Santa Fe Powered A Unit (0535) Silver-red-yellow/black	60
0535W	Santa Fe Dummy B Unit w/Horn (0535) Silver-red-yellow/black	40
0536	Santa Fe Powered A Unit (0536) Silver-red-yellow/black	75
0537	Santa Fe Powered A Unit Cataloged in 1966. Was it ever produced?	*
0555	Santa Fe Powered A Unit (0555) Silver-red-yellow/black, powered by a Helic drive	70
0556	Santa Fe Powered A Unit (0556) Silver-red-yellow/black, direct gear drive for the rear truck	70
0564	Chesapeake and Ohio Powered A Unit (0564) Blue-yellow/blue-yellow	50
0565	Santa Fe Powered A Unit (0565) Silver-red-yellow/black	45
0566	Texas Special Powered A Unit (0566) Red-white/red	45

0567	**Alaska Railroad Powered A Unit** (0567) Dark blue/yellow	60
0568	**Union Pacific Powered A Unit** (0568) Yellow-gray/red	90
0569P	**Union Pacific Powered A Unit** (0569) Yellow-gray/red	50
0571P	**Pennsylvania Powered A Unit** (0571) Maroon plastic/yellow	200
0575	**Santa Fe Dummy B Unit** (0575) Silver-red-yellow/black	15
0576	**Texas Special Dummy B Unit** (0576) Red-white/red	20
0577	**Alaska Railroad Dummy B Unit** (0577) Dark blue/yellow	30
0586	**Texas Special Dummy A Unit** (0586) Red-white/red	110
0587	**Alaska Railroad Dummy A Unit** (0587) Dark blue/yellow Questions persist as to whether true heat stamped 0587's exist. Known pieces in collections typically resemble a 0567 with the "6" touched up to look like an "8".	75
0595	**Santa Fe Dummy A Unit** (0595) Silver-red-yellow/black	20

Geeps

0592	**Santa Fe Powered GP-9** (0592) Blue/yellow	75
0593P	**Northern Pacific Powered GP-9** (0593) Black-gold/red-white gold	80
0593T	**Northern Pacific Dummy GP-9** (0593) Black-gold/red-white gold	80
0594P	**Santa Fe Powered GP-9** (0594) Blue/yellow	60
0596	**New York Central Powered GP-9** (0596) 2-tone gray/white	70
0597	**Northern Pacific Powered GP-9** (0597) Black-gold/red-white-gold	60
0598	**New York Central Powered GP-7** (0598) 2-tone gray/white	50

Electrics

0581	**Pennsylvania Rectifier** (0581) Tuscan/yellow	140
0591	**New Haven Rectifier** (0591) Black-orange-white/orange-white	140

Husky Locomotive and Powered Units

0050	**Lionel Lines Gang Car** (0050) w/small blue plastic figure		
	1. All orange with white lettering		80
	2. Orange top, gray bottom, white lettering		50
	3. Orange top, gray bottom, bluish-black lettering		50
	4. Gray top, orange bottom, white lettering		50
0054	**Canadian Pacific Husky** Cataloged in 1961. No proof it was produced.		
0055	**Minneapolis and St. Louis** (0055) Red/white		45
0056	**A. E. C. Husky** (0056) White/red		
	1. Normal production		60
	2. Special NBC promotional A.E.C. husky with special billboard (billboard is typically missing)	(5)	1000
0057	**Union Pacific Husky** (0057) Yellow-gray/red		70
0058	**Rock Island Husky** (0058) Black-red/white		50
0059	**U.S. Air Force Husky** (0059) White/blue, Minuteman and Air Force insignia under cab		90
0068	**Executive Inspection Car** (unnumbered) Red/white		100
0545	**Erie Lackawanna GE-44 Switcher** Black/white, headlight, (herald and 0545)		50
0561	**M&St. L Snow Blower** (0561) Red-white/red		150

Steamers

0602(LT)	Pennsylvania 0-6-0 Switcher w/tender, light		60
0605	**0-4-0 Tank Switcher**		
	1. 0605 heat stamped under cab window		60
	2. 0605 and Lionel heat stamped under cab window	(5)	*
0625(LT)	Southern Pacific w/tender, light		50
0626(LT)	Southern Pacific w/tender, light		80
0635(LT)	Southern Pacific w/tender, light, smoke unit		70
0636(LTS)	Southern Pacific w/tender, light, smoke unit		85
0637(LTS)	Southern Pacific w/tender, light, smoke unit, 0637 in white on black paper sticker under cab window		80
0642(LT)	2-4-2 Steam Switcher w/unlettered tender, headlight and combination belt and gear drive		50
0643(LT)	2-4-2 Steam Switcher w/unlettered tender, headlight and Helic drive (set only)		100
0645(LTS)	Southern Pacific w/0645W tender, smoke unit, light		90
0645W	**Plastic Whistle Tender** Long Haul Type w/whistle. This tender's metal six wheel trucks have a tendency towards severe corrosion and even disintegration. Beware of replacements using the more common four wheel trucks utilized for the short Pacific tenders.		25
0646(LTS)	Southern Pacific w/0645W tender, smoke unit, light		95
0647(LTS)	Southern Pacific w/0645W tender, smoke unit, light		
	1. Black paper sticker/white 0647 under cab window		90
	2. Heat stamped 0647 under cab window		100

Passenger Cars

Athearn passenger car body shells were utilized for production of the Texas Special and Pennsylvania series. By 1961 Lionel had developed its own series of streamlined passenger car bodies. These were used for the Santa Fe and the 1963 Pennsylvania series.

0704	**Texas Special Baggage** (0704) Silver-red/red, no battery box in floor	35
0705	**Texas Special Pullman Coach** (0705) Silver-red/red	
	1. Without battery box in floor	30
	2. With battery box in floor	30
0706	**Texas Special Vista Dome** (0706) Silver-red/red	
	1. Without battery box in floor	30
	2. With battery box in floor	30
0707	**Texas Special Observation** (0707) Silver-red/red	
	1. Without battery box in floor	30
	2. With battery box in floor	30
0708	**Pennsylvania Baggage** (0708) Tuscan/yellow	40
0709	**Pennsylvania Vista Dome** (0709) Tuscan/yellow	40
0710	**Pennsylvania Observation** (0710) Tuscan/yellow	40
0711	**Pennsylvania Pullman** (0711) Tuscan/yellow	120
0712	**Santa Fe Baggage Car** (0712) Silver/red	
	1. Red stripe above the windows and illuminated	25
	2. Without red stripe and unlighted	40
0713	**Santa Fe Pullman Coach** (0713) Silver/red	
	1. Red stripe above the windows and illuminated	25
	2. Without red stripe and unlighted	40

POSTWAR

0714	**Santa Fe Vista Dome Car** (0714) Silver/red	
	1. Red stripe above the windows and illuminated	25
	2. Without red strip and unlighted	40
0715	**Santa Fe Observation** (0715) Silver/red	
	1. Red stripe above the windows and illuminated	25
	2. Without red strip and unlighted	40
0723	**Pennsylvania Pullman Coach** (0723) Silver/maroon	
	1. Silver roof (set only)	45
	2. Maroon roof (set only)	60
0725	**Pennsylvania Observation Car** (0725) Silver/maroon	
	1. Silver roof (set only)	50
	2. Maroon roof (set only)	70
0733	**SF Pullman Coach** (0713) Silver/maroon, no stripe, unlighted, numbered 0713 not 0733 in maroon (set only)	25
0735	**SF Observation Car** (0715) Silver/maroon, no stripe, unlighted, numbered 0715 not 0735 in maroon (set only)	25

Rolling Stock
Boxcars

0864-275	**State of Maine** Cataloged in 1962. No proof it was produced.	
0864-285	**State of Maine** Lionel box exists with end flap printed "0864-285 State of Maine Box Car", however no car with that number has been identified.	
0864-300	**The Alaska Railroad** (0864300) Dark blue/yellow	50
0864-325	**Duluth, South Shore & Atlantic** (0864325) Red-black/white	25
0864-350	**State of Maine** (0864350) Red-white-blue/black	40
0864-400	**Boston and Maine** (0864400) Blue-black/white	50
0864-700	**Santa Fe** (0864-400) Red/white	35
0864-900	**New York Central** (0864900) Jade green/black-red	30
0864-935	**New York Central** (0864900) Jade green/black-red, similar to 0864-900 with 0864-935 on box end flap	30
	Note: The previously listed boxcars were all produced by Lionel using dies acquired from Hobbyline. The following boxcars (0874 series) appeared after 1963 and utilized dies developed by Lionel. These cars had a separate floor and an upper body shell of very thin plastic. It is not uncommon to find excellent and even new pieces with cracks in the door guides.	
0874	**New York Central** (0874) Jade green/black-red	30
0874-25	Same as **0874** except box flap is stamped 0874-25	30
0874-60	**Boston and Maine** (0874) Blue/white	60

Cabooses

In 1959, Athearn caboose body shells and floors continued in use for the 0817 series. The AEC, Alaska Railroad, Texas Special, and early New Haven cabooses used a shell with a separate roof walk and a floor with visible metal weight and plastic cross bracing. Beginning in 1960, Lionel developed its own caboose with a roof walk molded to the body and underframe marked "Lionel".

0817-150	**AT&SF** (0817) Red/white	10
0817-200	**Atomic Energy Commission** (0817) White/red	30
0817-225	**Alaska Railroad** (0817) Blue/yellow	50
0817-250	**Texas Special** (0817) Red/white	35
0817-275	**New Haven** (0817) Black/orange-white	
	1. Athearn body shell & floor w/separate cross bracing	30
	2. Lionel caboose body shell w/Lionel name cast into separate floor	25

0817-300	**Southern Pacific** (0817) Maroon/yellow	30
0817-325	**Union Pacific** (0817) Yellow-gray/red	20
0817-350	**Rock Island** (0817) Red-black/white	25
0827	**Safety First** (0827) Illuminated, Red/white	35
0827-50	**A.E.C.** (0827) Illuminated, White/red (set only)	60
0827-75	**AT&SF** (0827) Illuminated, Red/white (set only)	60
0837	**M&St.L** (0837) Red/white	10
0837-110	Same as **0837** with 0837-110 on box end flap	10
0838	**Erie** (E in diamond shaped herald) (0838) Gray/red (set only)	25
0840	**NYC** (0840) Black/white (set only)	20
0841	**Unlettered** but numbered 0841 Red/white	10
0841-50	**Union Pacific** (0841) Yellow-gray/red (set only)	45
0841-85	**AT&SF** (0841) painted Red/white (set only)	10
0841-125	**A.E.C.** (0841) White/red (set only) *Note: The unpainted white plastic shell is prone to discoloration. These are worth less than the values given.*	25
0841-185	**AT&SF** (0841) unpainted red plastic/white, 0841-185 on box end flap	10

Work Cabooses

0819-200	**Boston & Maine** (0819200) Blue/white	30
0819-225	**Santa Fe** (08192255) Gray/yellow-red	30
0819-250	**Northern Pacific** (0819250) Red-black/white-black	30
0819-275	**Chesapeake and Ohio** (0819275) Blue/yellow	15

Crane and Derrick Cars

0860-200	**Pennsylvania Derrick Car** (0860200)	30
0889	**Illinois Central Wrecker Crane Car** (0889) Orange-black green	50

Flatcars

0800-200	**Seaboard Airplane Car** (0800200) Black/white	
	1. Orange top portion of airplane, black undercarriage	50
	2. Silver top portion of airplane, black undercarriage	30
0801-200	**Seaboard Boat Car** (0801200) Black /white, Athearn boats have a white top w/either red or blue hull	30
0806	**Southern Pacific** w/Helicopter (0806) Black/white, helicopter also used for O Gauge 6819, comes both with and without blue "NAVY" heat stamp.	40
0807	**NYC w/"Matchbox Series" Bulldozer** (0807) Tuscan/white. Lesney Caterpillar Bulldozer number 18	120
0808	**NYC w/"Matchbox Series" Tractor** (0808) Tuscan/white. Lesney Tractor number 4	120
0809	**Helium Tank Transport Car** Black (unlettered and unnumbered) Three silver painted wooden cylinders. Black hopper car base.	15
0810	**SP Emergency Transport Generator** (0810) Black/white. Plastic orange generator used on O gauge 3520/3530 generator cars.	40
0813	**Seaboard Mercury Capsule Carrying Car** (0813200) Blue/white. Two soft plastic silver capsules (used on O gauge 3413 Capsule Launching Car)	100

0814-200	**SP Four Auto Transport Car** (0814200) Tuscan/white, four Athearn Autos.	40
0821	**Pipe Transport Car** (unlettered and unnumbered) Three plastic pipes on hopper car underframe. 1. Gray plastic pipes 2. Yellow plastic pipes 3. Gray plastic pipes painted yellow	 15 15 80
0823	**Southern Pacific Twin Missile Carrying Car** (0823) Red/white. Two white missiles as used with O gauge 448 Missile Firing Range.	30
0824-200	**NYC w/Two Autos** (0824200) Black/white, two Athearn autos	30
0842	**Culvert Piper Transport Car** (lettered TLCX, numbered 0842) black tank car underframe. Three metal culvert pipes (also used with O gauge cars and accessories)	20
0861	**Timber Transport Car** (unlettered and unnumbered) Black hopper frame w/three logs	15
0863	**Southern Pacific Rail Trucks Car** (0863) Red/white, w/three trucks	25
0870	**Pennsylvania Maintenance Car** w/Generator (0870) Tuscan/white, gray base and yellow platform. Generator load was produced in both gray and dark gray plastic.	40
0875	**Seaboard Flat Car with Missile** (0875) Black/white, brown carriage load is large missile used on O gauge 6650 flat car. 1. White rocket with blue end 2. Red and white rocket with blue end	 30 30

Gondolas

0862-200	**Michigan Central** (0862200) Black/white 1. With load of scrap metal 2. With red plastic crates (R. Kughn collection) (5)	 30 *
0862-250	**Michigan Central** (0862200) Black/white, similar to 086200 #1 with 862-250 box on end flap	35
0865-200	**Michigan Central** (0865200) Tuscan /gold, five red canisters	50
0865-225	**Michigan Central Gondola** (0865225) load of scrap metal 1. Red plastic body shell with white lettering (set only) 2. Gray plastic body shell with black lettering	 15 20
0865-250	**Michigan Central** (0865250) Red/white, tan plastic crates	15
0865-400	**Michigan Central** (0865250) Blue plastic shell decorated in white. Cataloged as 0865-400 in 1964 as part of sets and then as 0865 in the 1965-66 catalogs. This blue and white gondola was listed as 0865-435 when listed for individual sale. (set only)	5
0865-435	**Michigan Central** (0865-250) Blue/white (see 0865-400 above). Only box end flap stamped 0865-435 when offered for individual sale.	5

Hoppers

0836(1)	**Alaska Hopper** (08361) 1. Black/orange without load 2. Black/orange with load of scrap metal 3. Red plastic/white 4. Painted red on red plastic shell/white 5. Painted red on gray plastic shell/white	 25 30 10 15 30
0836-100	**Alaska Hopper** (08361) Red/white w/nonsprung trucks. The 0836-100 is catalog number only as car still carries 08361.	10
0836-110	**Alaska Hopper** (08361) Red/white w/nonsprung trucks. The 08361-110 appears on end flap of box only. Car is similar to 0836-100 above. Found in sets 14300 and 14310.	10

Operating Cars

0039	**Southern Pacific Track Cleaning Car** (TC-0039) Black-orange/white with track cleaning fluid in plastic bottle used for the O gauge car, abrasive pads and cleansing sponges	45
0300	**TLCX Operating Lumber Car** (0300) Red/white w/three wood logs and dark brown plastic tray. Used with the 0900 unloading platform.	20
0301	**Pennsylvania Operating Coal Dump Car** (0301) Gray/black, black frame w/bag of coal and brown plastic tray. Used with 0900 unloading platform	20
0319	**SP Operating Helicopter Launching Car** (0319) Blue/white, red plastic helicopter (also used with the O-gauge 3619), metal track trip included.	40
0319-110	**Operating Helicopter Launching Car** (0319) Similar to 0319 except nonsprung trucks. Both brake wheel and rear tail support for helicopter are now at the same end of car. 0319-110 is stamped on box end flap.	45
0333	**Southern Pacific Satellite Launching** (0333) Blue/white, with satellite (used on the O gauge satellite car), metal track trip also included.	50
0337	**Animated Circus Giraffe Car** (0337) White/red, with magnet and telltale	30
0349	**Operating Turbo Missile Firing Car** (no numbers or letters) Blue launcher and turbo support w/two turbos. 1. Red plastic car body 2. Maroon plastic car body	 35 90
0357	**Cop and Hobo Car** (0357) Blue/white, black trestle bridge, platform w/no roof is gray plastic. Comes with figures of cop and hobo.	50
0365	**"Minuteman" Missile Launching Car** (0365) White/blue-red w/Strategic Air Command and insignia on left and U.S. Air Force Minuteman on the right, thin blue tipped white missile. The compressed spring launching mechanism often broken. Check even in "Mint/Boxed" cars.	60
0366	**Operating Milk Can Unloading Car** (0366) White/black w/eight metal milk cans. Doors are often broken. Operated w/0900 unloading platform	45
0370	**Animated Sheriff and Outlaw Car** (0370) Red/yellow, sheriff and outlaw alternately appear through cutouts in the car's roof as the car moves.	*
0805	**Illuminated Radioactive Waste Disposal Car** (0805) Black-red/white, single gray plastic waste container lettered in red. 1. Numbered (0805) 2. Numbered (0805200) (4)	 20 *
0834	**Poultry Car** (0834) Red/white, gray painted doors, chickens pictured on plastic inserts, lighted	30
0847	**Exploding Box Car** (0847) Red/white, explodes when bull's-eye target on side is hit by missile	10
0847-100	**Exploding Box Car** same as 0847 except nonsprung trucks and number 0847-100 on end flap of box	15
0850	**U.S. Army Missile Launching Car** (0850) Red missile launcher mounted on gray flat car lettered in black, comes with single small white plastic missile (as used with O gauge 448 Missile Firing Range).	15
0850-110	**U.S. Army Missile Launching Car** (0850) similar to 0850 except nonsprung trucks and 0850-110 on box end flap	15
0873	**Rodeo Car** (0873) w/two bobbing horse heads at each end. 1. Yellowish-orange plastic body w/red lettering 2. Same as 1 but maroon lettering 3. Translucent lemon yellow body w/maroon lettering	 30 75 75
0880	**Pennsylvania Maintenance Car** (0880) with Light yellow platform mounted to gray base which snaps into black flat car lettered in white.	40

POSTWAR

Reefer

0872-200	**Railway Express Reefer** (0872200) Dark green/gold, red-white herald, thin black plastic door, door guides frequently broken and missing doors.	35

Mint Car

0845	**Gold Bullion Transport Car/Fort Knox Reserve** (0845) painted silver on clear plastic/black. Same body shell as 0872-200 REA.	100

Stock Car

0866-200	**Circus Car** (0866-200) White plastic/red w/white painted doors, red painted roof walk. Non-operating version of the 0337 Giraffe car.	25

Tank Cars

0815-50	**Rocket Fuel Tank Car** (0815) White/red tank mounted on black plastic frame with black platform around dome.	30
0815-60	**Rocket Fuel Tank Car** 1. Same as 0815-50 except in box with end flap stamped 0815-60 2. Can be found in sets 14300 and 14310) but without heat stamped 0815 (5)	30 *
0815-75	**Lionel Lines Tank Car** (0815200) Painted tank, Dark orange/black, black plastic platform around dome	40
0815-85	**Lionel Lines Tank Car** (0815200) Orange plastic/black tank, no platform	35
0815-110	**SUNOCO Tank Car** (uncataloged 25064) Black plastic/yellow-white tank with SUNOCO herald and black platform around dome. Can be found in sets 14310 and 14300 in place of 0815-60.	200
0816	**Rocket Fuel Tank Car** (0816) White/red tank, black plastic frame, without platform around dome.	20

0494 Rotary Beacon

Accessories

Note: Several scenic accessories were offered by Lionel and appear to be Life-Like products sold in Lionel HO boxes. These are all rather difficult to find and in demand by the advanced collectors. Prices are given for boxed units only.

0110	**Graduated Trestle Set** with 46 piers, central arch bridge	12
0111	**Trestle Set** 12 "L" piers to be used to extend 0110	10
0114	**Engine House with Horn** horn is often missing	50
0115	**Engine House Kit** kit version of 0117	50
0117	**Engine House** w/skylights in the roof, plastic windows along sides, passageways ends for two tracks	40
0118	**Engine House with Whistle** whistle often missing, 12" wide and 10" high	45
0119	**Landscaped Tunnel** 24 " long	*
0140	**Banjo Signal** operating signal w/0145-200 Contactor Track Section. Smaller version of O gauge accessory, however, not true HO scale	70
0145	**Automatic Gateman** w/0145-200 Contactor Track	40
0197	**Rotating Radar Antenna**	35
0214	**Girder Bridge**	7
0221	**Truss Bridge with Two Trestles**	15
0222	**Deck Bridge with Two Trestles**	15
0224	**Girder Bridge with two Trestles**	15
0282	**Gantry Crane** manually operated, shell is the same as 0889 IC Wrecker Crane but numbered 0282	80
0310	**Billboard Set** w/five plastic frames & five ad posters	25
0430	**Six Tree Assortment** w/pines and flowering shrubs	40
0431	**Landscape Set** w/box of lichen, 3' x 4' grass mat, path mats, 1' x 4' rolls of earth	55
0432	**Tree Assortment** assortment of trees and shrubbery	40
0433	**HO Scenery Set** w/grass mat for a 4' x 6' board, 1' x 4' roll of earth, bag of lichen and nine assorted trees.	65
0470	**Missile Launching Platform** w/Exploding Target Car, same as the O gauge accessory (470) except that the HO 0847 target car replaced the O gauge (6470)	60
480	**Missile Firing Range** w/Camouflage & Target Car w/sealed bag of lichen, four small white plastic missiles and the HO gauge 0847 Target Car	75
0494	**Rotating Beacon**	35
0900	**Unloading Platform**	15

0140 Banjo Signal   *0145 Gateman*

Lionel Plasticville

Note: The only difference between Lionel Plasticville and regular Plasticville is the box. In order to be collectible, the set must be in a Lionel box. When purchasing Lionel Plasticville, make sure the dye lots of the colors match. Sometimes unscrupulous sellers will replace parts of Lionel Plasticville with parts from regular Plasticville. Prices based on far less than normal sampling and are just a very rough estimate as we have very few reports. Prices are based on boxes being in Like New condition.

HO Plasticville

Note: Accessories 0410-0426 were packaged for Lionel in the appropriate Lionel HO boxes by Bachmann Brothers Inc. from their production of the popular Plasticville hobby kits. Prices are given for boxed units only.

0410	Ranch House Set	60
0411	Figure Set	35
0412	Farm Set	45
0413	Railroad Structure Set	50
0414	Village Set	60
0415	Cape Cod Set	10
0416	Station Set	15
0417	Farm Set	20
0418	Industrial Set	35
0419	Rail Junction Set	45
0420	Railroad Set	45
0421	Farm Set	35
0422	Freight Set	40
0425	Figure Set	45
0426	Railroad Station Set	40

O Plasticville

Assorted Lionel Plasticville boxes

951	**Farm Set** Box Type I and Ia, 58	(2)	225
	Truck, tractor, jeep, horses, cows, harrow, plow, wagon and footbridge. Sometimes found with incomplete or broken farm implements.		
952	**Figure Set** Box Type I, 58	(2)	150
	Townspeople, fire plug, fire alarm box and mail boxes. Sometimes confused with the 953 Figure Set. The 952 is harder to find.		
953	**Figure Set** Box Type V, Va & Vb, 59-62	(2)	75
	Same as 952 with paint brush, paint palette and styrene painting fluid and glue. Longest running single item in the series. The difference between a 952 and 953 is a paint brush, paint palette and painting fluid. Bros. instruction sheet for painting.		

954	**Swimming Pool and Playground Set** Box Type V, 59		(2)	**300**
	Playground equipment, patio set, pool, fences and shrubs. Same as Bachmann Playground Equipment Set with a fence and gate added.			
955	**Highway Set** Box Type II, 58		(1)	**300**
	Street signs, telegraph poles, auto and buses			
956	**Stockyard Set** Box Type V, 59		(4+)	**450**
	Corral, cows and railroad signs			
957	**Farm Building & Animal Set** Box Type I & Ia, 58		(1)	**200**
	Farm structures plus a fence, gate, pump, horse, fowl and cat and dog			
958	**Vehicle Set** Autos, fire trucks, bus, ambulance, street signs, fire alarm box, mail box, fire plug and traffic light. There is a rare version included in a Sears uncataloged set 9807. This version came in a white box.			
	1. Box Type III, 58		(1)	**500**
	2. Box Type XII, 64		(5)	**1200▲**
959	**Barn Set** Box Type II & IIa, 58		(2)	**175**
	Dairy barn, horses, fowl and domestic animals			
960	**Barnyard Set** Box Type V & Va, 59-61		(2)	**125**
	Farm buildings, vehicles & equipment, fowl, domestic and farm animals			

Above: 961 School Set box, right: backs of boxes for 987 Town Set and 988 Railroad Structure Set

961	**School Set** Box Type VI, 61		(4+)	**500**
	School, flagpole, busses, street signs, fence, shrubs & benches. Scarce			
962	**Turnpike Set** Box Type IV, 58		(3+)	**600**
	Interchange, stanchions, telegraph poles, street signs, autos, ambulance, bus			
963	**Frontier Set** Box Type VI & VIc, 59, 60		(2)	**250**
	Cabin, windmill, fences, horses, cows and pump. Was not part of the Halloween General Set.			
963-100	**Frontier Set** Box Type VIb, U60		(5)	**750▲**
	Cabin, windmill, fences, horses, cows and pump. This version did come in the Sears' General Halloween Set and is the most desirable and valued of all the Lionel Plasticville line.			
964	**Factory Site Set** Box Type VII, 59		(4)	**750**
	Factory, auto, telegraph poles, and railroad signs. Almost as scarce as the uncataloged Frontier set.			
965	**Farm Set** Box Type VIII, 59		(3)	**300**
	Barn, farm buildings, farm equipment, fowl, dogs, cats and farm animals			

199

964 Factory Site Set box

966	**Firehouse Set** Box Type IV & IVa, 58 Firehouse, fire engines, alarm box, hydrant, ambulance, bus, auto, traffic light, street post and signs, bench, mail box, townspeople, telegraph poles and pine trees	(3)	450
967	**Post Office Set Box Type III & IIIa,** 58 Post office, mail box, townspeople, benches, street signs, street post, traffic light, truck and autos	(3)	500
968	**TV Transmitter Set** Box Type II, 58 TV station, fence, gate, townspeople, mail box, fire plug, jeep, autos and pine trees	(3)	450
969	**Construction Set** Box Type V, 60 House, construction material, workers and autos	(2)	500
980	**Ranch Set** Box Type V, 60 Loading pen, cattle, pigs, sheep, farm implements and vehicles	(2)	450
981	**Freight Yard Set** Box Type VIa, 60 Loading platform with carts, switch tower, telephone poles & RR men	(3)	250
982	**Suburban Split Level Set** Box Type VIIa, 60 Split level house, pine trees, auto, ranch fence, bench and people	(4)	400▲
983	**Farm Set, Box,** Type VIIa, 60, 61 Dairy barn, windmill, colonial house, horse, cows and auto	(4)	450▲
984	**Railroad Set,** Box Type VIa & VId, 61, 62 Switch tower, telegraph poles, loading platform, figures, railroad signs & acc	(3)	250▲
985	**Freight Area Set,** Box Type IX, 61 Water tower, work car, loading platform, switch tower, telegraph poles, autos, watchman's shanty, railroad signs and accessories. Thought to be the most scarce of all Lionel Plasticville.	(5)	550▲
986	**Farmhouse and Barnyard Set,** Box Type X, 62 20 pcs, New England farm house and barn with 18 domestic animals	(3)	450
987	**Town Set,** Box Type XI, 62 24 pcs, church, gas station, auto, 12 street signs, bank, 5 telephone poles and corner store. Hard-to-find and coveted.	(5)	1500▲
988	**Railroad Structure Set,** Box Type XI, 62 Railroad station, crossing gate and shanty, water tank, work car, hobo shacks, bench and figures. Another hard-to-find item.	(5)	1500▲

Lionel In Business

1900 Joshua Lionel Cowen opens up shop in a second-story loft at 24-26 Murray Street in New York City. Cowen's company produces "electric novelties," and is called the Lionel Manufacturing Company. Cowen, along with his friend Harry Grant, designs a small electric motor to power a fan. Response is weak, so Cowen looks for another use for his motor. He scratch builds a wooden train and some track, places four wheels and the fan motor underneath, and sells it to a merchant for $4. The idea is to provide action in the merchant's store window and attract attention. It works…sort of. The merchant sells the trains, not the merchandise. The next day he orders six more train sets. Joshua Lionel Cowen is in the electric train business. The great mass appeal of toy trains, however, is not immediately apparent to Cowen, perhaps because most households do not yet have electricity. But it does not take Cowen long to see the larger marketing possibilities for toy trains. America is bursting with energy and hope as the new century begins. William McKinley is President with Teddy Roosevelt his VP. Engineer Casey Jones, driving engine number 382, dies in a collision with another train, but saves his passengers by staying in the cab to slow the train and minimize impact. Casey Jones will be immortalized in story and song.

Cowen's first train, the Electric Express gondola

1901 Cowen begins to sell his crude "Electric Express" gondola, plus 30 feet of track, for $6. The same car, without the motor, sells for $2.25. The powered unit operates on two-rail track that measures 2-7/8-inches between the rails. The track comes in two bands of steel strips to be inserted into slots carved into the wooden ties. President McKinley is assassinated and Theodore Roosevelt takes over.

1902 It is the Golden Age for electric trolleys. They are the main means of urban transportation in this early part of the 20th Century. Trolleys are also popular toys. Cowen buys a trolley body from Converse, a toy maker in Massachusetts. He adds a motor, and names it "City Hall Park" after the trolleys Cowen sees everyday around his neighborhood. The open-air trolley, with 30 feet of track, sells for $7, and is on the cover of Cowen's third catalog. A suspension bridge in kit form, Lionel's first accessory, is also offered. A New York City carpenter, Le Roy Wait, invents Jell-O. U.S. Congressman Charles Francis Adams says, "Railroads are the most tremendous and far-reaching engine of social change that has ever blessed or cursed mankind."

Lionel's first trolley – City Hall Park.

> **We confess to being copyists – not to makeshift work but to the real thing.**

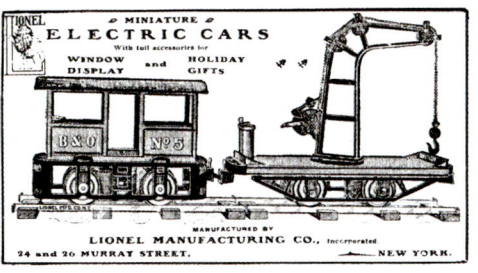

1903 Catalog Cover

1903 Lionel introduces a new engine – the B&O No. 5, patterned after the B&O's electric locomotive used to haul trains through the tunnels of Baltimore. Lionel also produces a motorized crane. Kids can use the hook to lift things and move them about. Cowen quickly realizes children want to do more than just watch trains run around in a circle. From now on, action cars and accessories will always play an important role in the world of Lionel. Henry Ford sells his first Model A for $850. Boston Americans upset Pittsburgh Nationals in the first World Series. Orville Wright flies at Kittyhawk.

1904 Mario Caruso, who later will run the Lionel plant, arrives from Italy and begins to work for Cowen as a solderer. A motorized 800 Boxcar is added along with a matching trailer. Henry Ford sets new speed record at 91.38 mph, Teddy Roosevelt is elected President and Joshua Lionel Cowen marries Cecelia Liberman.

800 Motorized Boxcar, also called the Jail Car by collectors, because of the bars on the windows.

201

1905 Lionel sales at $8000 and climbing. Carlisle & Finch, Howard, Knapp and Voltamp are Cowen's main competitors. The catalog refers to the trains as "Lionel" for the first time, and, also for the first time, contains the aggressive, combative text that will become standard for Lionel catalogs. Cowen accuses his "unscrupulous" competitors of copying and selling for a lower price. If you want the best, "YOU MUST GET A LIONEL!" shouts the catalog. The 1000 Passenger Car, which resembles a trolley, is new, and comes with a matching 1050 Trailer. A special display set, featuring a No. 5 Electric, trailer gondola and elevated posts, sells for $30. Cowen still thinks animated displays will be a major part of his business. William Hafner introduces a line of cast-iron locomotives with a wind-up motor. On the real railroads, electric lighting is added to the Union Pacific's Overland Express. Passengers are now able to light up their compartments with a flick of a switch. Before, they made do with gas lamps. What will they think of next?

A fact: If you want a miniature electric car to work satisfactorily as a toy or for window display, YOU MUST GET A LIONEL.

Carlisle & Finch Mining Train

Unscrupulous manufacturers have endeavored to duplicate our outfits and sell the goods at lower prices.

Lionel Introduces Standard Gauge

The Early Period

1906 Catalog Cover

1906 Cowen introduces a new line of trains and a new fixed track – Standard gauge. No more loose ties with slots and bands of steel. No more clumsy looking trains. In their place is the beginning of a new style of toy train that will improve and change over the next 50 years, just as the real railroads will improve and change. These new toy trains will provide fun, and they will teach, and they will become important in a young man's life. This is Joshua Lionel Cowen's vision. This is what he passionately believes, and this is what he will accomplish. Cowen's new line features three trolleys (including a No. 3, which is available in three different colors – cream, olive green and orange), two steamers (Lionel's first), passenger cars, and seven new freight cars. It is early in the new Century and America is growing rapidly. So is Lionel. Both will share in the boom times and the bad times that lie ahead. A devastating earthquake rocks San Francisco. Coca-Cola replaces cocaine with caffeine, and the forward pass is legalized in college football.

No. 3 Trolley

1907 Hafner convinces William Ogden Coleman to become a partner, and eventually they name the company after one of their sets: American Flyer. Lionel sales pass $20,000 and Joshua and Cecelia have a son, Lawrence, who will become the Lionel poster boy in the teens and '20s, and eventually president of the company in 1945. First metered taxis arrive in New York City, and first interurban electric operates between Cedarburg and Milwaukee, Wisconsin.

No. 5 Special

1909 Cowen coins "Standard of the World" phrase and names his track Standard Gauge. "Pay as You Enter" trolleys are introduced. Leo H. Baekeland, Belgian-born chemist, invents a new plastic material made from phenol and formaldehyde. He calls it Bakelite. Lionel will use Bakelite to make their Irvington passenger cars in the '40s and '50s.

No. 8 Trolley

1910
U.S. population now at 92 million. Lionel uses mass production techniques for the first time, and sales continue to climb. The Ives Company of Bridgeport, Connecticut, producers of a large line of toys, introduces a line of No. 1 gauge trains to compete with Lionel. Cowen moves manufacturing to New Haven, Connecticut. Mario Caruso takes over plant operations. This is the peak year for trolleys. 13 are offered. Top-of-the-line trolley sells for $17 (with twin motors). Catalog also offers a No. 10 Interurban, three steamers, including the brass No. 7, and an S-type electric locomotive is introduced. Kids in New York are more familiar with electric locomotives than they are with steamers because New York has an ordinance, still in effect today, which prohibits steam locomotives from operating in Manhattan or in tunnels under the Hudson River. So, the S-type cab electrics were familiar sights to the boys in Lionel's primary marketing area. Biggest of these S-type electrics is the 1912. Sales reach $57,000. A set of 12 miniature figures, to sit in the open air trolleys, sells for 60 cents. The Boy Scouts are founded, and Haley's Comet reaches nearest point to the earth.

Voltamp 2115 Interurban

Brass No. 7

No. 10 Interurban

1912 Special in brass, modeled after NYC's S-type electric

1911 A 1912 Special is offered. It is the same as the regular 1912, except it is made of brass. The 1912 Special, along with the 7 brass steamer, are the two most desirable engines from this era, which is referred to as the Early Period. Pitcher Cy Young retires with 509 victories. Over the next 89 years, no other pitcher will ever win more than 325 games. That's why they call it the Cy Young Award.

1912 The Lionel Racing Automobiles – the first slot cars – are new. Trolley sales fall as real trolleys begin to give way to commuter trains. The unsinkable Titanic sinks. Al Berry is the first man to ever jump from an airplane with a parachute. The chute opens at the last second. Al says, "Never again." Woodrow Wilson defeats Teddy Roosevelt for President.

Lionel Announces O Gauge

Millions of happy users the world over.

O gauge S-type electric locomotive.

1915 Lionel introduces a smaller size train (O gauge –1-1/4 inches between the outside rails) to supplement their popular line of Standard gauge trains. Sales, pumped by government contracts, jump to $355,000. Hafner splits from Coleman to start the Hafner Manufacturing Company, and, along with the help of his son, John, would continue to produce a line of clockwork trains until 1951. Red Sox sign Babe Ruth as a pitcher, and Charlie Chaplin charms the nation with his soulful eyes and funny walk. A German U-boat sinks the Lusitania. Frank Lloyd Wright's son, John, invents Lincoln Logs.

203

U.S. Declares War on Germany

1917 Congress declares war on April 6, 1917, and George M. Cohan writes *Over There* on the same day. Cowen converts to war production and lands lucrative government contracts. Lionel is allowed to continue train production on a limited scale. Trolleys are discontinued, and the real railroads prove vital to the war effort. Automatic train control is patented, Lionel brings out the 203 Armored Loco and moves production to new factory in Irvington, New Jersey. The Post Office's new airmail service gets off to a bumpy start. Lt. George Boyle takes off from Washington headed for Philadelphia; follows the wrong set of railroad tracks; misses Philadelphia, and crashes.

203 Armored locomotive

1918 The Great War ends as Germans sign armistice agreement in France. The Lionel Manufacturing Company becomes the Lionel Corporation, with Joshua Lionel Cowen its president. American Flyer introduces a new line of O gauge electric trains. The Pullman Deluxe set heads Lionel's fleet. This spectacular set consists of a polished brass and nickel 54 twin-motored electric engine, and three illuminated passenger cars: the 18, 19 and 190. List is $62.50. Josh's son, Larry, becomes Lionel's poster boy. Either his photo or his likeness becomes part of Lionel's advertising, packaging, and dealer displays.

Poster boy Larry Cowen.

1919 A printer's strike prevents Lionel from printing a new catalog, but doesn't prevent Cowen from getting word out to his loyal customers. Instead of a catalog, boys all around the country receive a printed apology from the man who makes Lionel trains. Sir Barton becomes the first horse to win the Triple Crown, and the Chicago White Sox throw the World Series to the Cincinnati Red Stockings.

54 in brass and with nickel trim.

The Roaring Twenties

1920 It is a bullish time – the Jazz Age – for America and toy trains, but by the end of the decade, the economic bottom will fall out. The '20s will see the full development of Lionel's aggressive "pitch product" advertising style. Lionel expands its ad campaigns to include newspapers, magazines, and becomes the first toy train company to advertise in the comic section of Sunday newspapers. The exclamation point becomes a staple of the Lionel catalog, as in, "Oh, Boy!" and Lionel dealers get flashy point-of-purchase displays. But the heart of Lionel is their catalog – big, bold and colorful. It aggressively proclaims Lionel trains are the best (Cowen never lets the facts stand in the way of persuasive ad copy), and blazes a permanent trail in every boy's memory. Lionel sales top one million for the first time, and the accessory line expands dramatically – RR crossing signs, telegraph posts, street lamps, and operating semaphores are added. Also new is the Lionel City Station and steel tunnels. Prohibition begins, the

122 Lionel City Station

New York Yankees buy Babe Ruth for $20,000, and women win the right to vote. New Cadillac is $2,885 and bread costs 12 cents a loaf. Warren Harding is elected President, and the Dow-Jones goes over 100 for the first time.

A Challenge to the Toy World!

Our goods should not be confused with any other on the market – they are in a class by themselves. Every line is carried out to the proper proportions. All parts are enameled and lettered in harmonious colors. They are so strong and well constructed that they may be used year after year.

1921 Cowen hires a new salesman, Arthur Raphael, who will develop into a brilliant merchandiser and establish ties with the largest retailers in America. Wally Anderson and Eddy Ingram open first White Castle hamburger stand. Eskimo Pies, Wrigley Chewing gum, and the Lincoln automobile all appear for the first time.

1923 The catalog cover shows a father and son playing with trains. This idyllic family scene – a father playing with his son – will become the cornerstone of Lionel's marketing strategy. Big 402 Electric with two motors is new. Babe Ruth celebrates opening of Yankee Stadium by hitting a home run. Harding dies and Calvin Coolidge becomes President.

402 Electric

256 Electric

1924 Lionel surpasses Ives in sales for the first time, and will never be second again. Frank Pettit is hired. He will go on to invent many of Lionel's most popular accessories. Ives beats the competition by developing first mass-produced, sequence reverse unit for toy trains. Until now, direction of the train had to be changed by hand. This is a major innovation, and pumps new life into Ives. Lionel counters by introducing modern-style electrics headed by the twin-motored O gauge 256. The 402 leads Lionel's Standard gauge fleet and Dorfan joins the toy train hunt by introducing a line of O and Standard gauge trains.

Lionel's 25th Anniversary

1925 Lionel celebrates its Silver Anniversary with record-breaking sales of $2,168,307 and a net profit of $248,553. American Flyer announces a line of Standard gauge trains. They call them Wide Gauge because Lionel has copyrighted Standard gauge. Advertisers spend $1 billion in an attempt to convince Americans to buy, buy, buy. Cowen advertises in magazines with a combined readership of 17 million. Dow Jones passes 150, and doughnuts cost 19 cents a dozen.

Artist's fanciful rendition of the Lionel factory.

The new Lionel 100% Electrically Controlled Railroad. As if by magic. The world's supreme line. Look boys. It's a Lionel!

1926 Catalog cover shows a boy, his dog, and Lionel trains. Distance Control and automatic reverse units are introduced, but the reverse unit has no neutral. When current is broken (intentionally or unintentionally), the train starts going in the opposite direction. Cowen covets the Ives sequential reverse. The brightly painted 200 series freights, with brass and nickel trim, replace the 10 series as the top-of-the-line freight cars.

The Classic Period

Collectors consider Lionel trains made between 1923 and 1942 to belong to the Classic Period. The first Classic Period electric was the 402, introduced in 1923. Classic Period trains are characterized by brighter colors, more detailing, and brass and nickel trim.

1927 The new 408E is similar to the 402, but with four running lights, large operating pantographs, and handrails on the roof. The 408E heads the four-car "Lionel Twin-Super Motor De-Luxe Special" set, which is depicted in a three-page fold out. This giant set sells for $82.50. Lionel is emerging as the dominant toy train company due to superior marketing, not superior trains. Although Lionel trains are as good, they are not any better than the trains made by Ives and American Flyer. Both can match Cowen's trains, but neither can match Cowen's marketing genius. Lionel also introduces a smaller line of Standard gauge freight cars, the 500 series. A&W Root Beer and Movietone News are new, and Charles Lindberg flies solo, non-stop, from New York to Paris. William Paley starts CBS radio, television is seen for the first time, and Babe Ruth swats 60.

ALL ABOARD!

Lionel Trains are Superior Electrically and Mechanically. All aboard!

517 Caboose

4U Build-a-Loco

MORE THAN A TOY — AN ELECTRIC ACHIEVEMENT!

840 Power Station

1928 Ives files bankruptcy. Cowen joins with Coleman to take over Ives. The line is continued, but not for long. Lionel introduces a steel replica of the Hellgate Bridge, which spans New York's East River, and a huge 840 Power Station that houses two transformers. Lionel's world expands with crossing signals, boulevard lamps, sheds, light towers, and toy houses. Trains and accessories are selling as fast as Lionel can produce them. The new Bild-a-Loco is an engine in kit form that has to be assembled. "No boy can build a 'Bild-a-Loco' without getting a better understanding of electricity and mechanics," touts the catalog. Cowen preaches the "Lionel trains are fun and educational" gospel constantly in both print ads and in his catalog. American Flyer brings out a gorgeous President's Special passenger set. Enameled in two shades of Rolls Royce blue, this beautifully proportioned set represents a high-level of the toy train maker's art. It is considered by many to be the most beautiful toy train set ever made. Herbert Hoover, promising a chicken in every pot and a car in every garage, is elected President. 24 million cars on are the road. Dow-Jones is at 300, and Mickey Mouse debuts in *Steamboat Willie*.

1929 Cowen buys out Coleman and becomes the sole owner of Ives. In the deal, Cowen also obtains the rights to the Ives sequential reverse mechanism, which he has been lusting after since its introduction. First Classic Period Standard gauge steamer – the 390E – debuts. Ives, American Flyer, and the others are making die-cast steamers. Cowen designs his steamer differently. He makes the frames from pot metal and the boilers from stamped metal. Brass and copper trim, and some red paint, add highlights.

Don't get stung. Many a boy has been mighty sorry that he got a cheap train and track that wouldn't last anywhere near as long as the Lionel.

390E Steamer

The grandest trains of all-time are being produced – American Flyer's dazzling chrome Mayflower, the Ives Olympian, and Lionel's massive Transcontinental Limited – nine-feet long, headed by the new 381 Electric, and featuring four cars named after states – California, Colorado, New York and Illinois. The set sells for $110, and will become known as the State Set – Lionel's most prized set of the Classic Period. Stock market reaches 381, and toy train manufacturers anticipate the best Christmas season ever. It never happens.

American Flyer Mayflower Set and two-tone blue President's Special

Black Tuesday
October 29, 1929

Stock market plummets. 19 million shares are sold.
Lionel, like the rest of the nation, is in shock.

The stock market collapse begins a shaky period for Lionel, although, of course, no pessimism is apparent in the catalogs. But there is a subtle change in emphasis from the high-priced sets to lower-priced items, a concession to the hard times. The economy will gradually improve, and Lionel is first to parallel the real railroads' leap into streamlining. By the end of the decade, the great scale Hudson will be produced and the future will look optimistic, but there will come a great war that will halt train production completely.

1930 Sales drop from $2,278,000 in 1929 to $1,932,000, and the net falls $281,000 to $84,000. Cowen closes the Ives plant in Bridgeport, and manufacturing of Ives Trains is moved to Irvington. The Lionel stove invites little girls to "learn the art of cookery." Not many takers at $29.95, about the same price as a real stove. Store clerks earn $5-$10 per week. Lone Ranger debuts on radio, and the U.S. population hits 120 million. The beautiful two-tone *Blue Comet* passenger set is introduced. The set is named after the Central of New Jersey's train, which runs from New York to Atlantic City. Lionel introduces O gauge steamers. The 260 is the biggest, and has a red light under the boiler. Hostess Twinkies and the Snickers bar go on sale for the first time.

1931 Despite the deepening Depression, Lionel brings out 400E - the Big Daddy of Lionel's steam fleet. A two-tone blue version replaces the 390E, and heads the *Blue Comet* set. A two-toned brown 408E now heads a four-car state set with a price tag of $97.50. Lionel loses over $200,000, and in an effort to offer a line of low-priced trains, introduces Winner Lines consisting of Ives wind-up trains painted in new colors. The *Stephen Girard*, the smallest of Lionel "name" sets, also debuts in Standard gauge. Almost five million are jobless as the Empire State Building, the world's tallest structure, and a symbol of American confidence despite hard times, opens.

400E Blue Comet

408E Two-tone brown

Boy, oh boy! What dashing beauty and realism! The greatest achievement in model railroading – beauty, speed and service that has never been surpassed.

1035 Winner Lines Steamer

1932 Another year of over $200,000 in losses. Winner Line fails to generate enough sales, and is dropped. Roundhouse sections are introduced. Franklin Delano Roosevelt is elected President. Zippo lighters are new, along with Frito corn chips. Dow-Jones is at 88.

Lionel 260E Steamer

1933 New line of clockwork trains, and low-priced electric sets called Lionel/Ives. These sets are the forerunners of the Lionel Jr. series, which later becomes Lionel's O-27 line. Century of Progress Expo opens in Chicago, Prohibition is repealed, and unemployment reaches 15 million. Lionel sales down again. Dow-Jones is at 108.

1934 In May, the diesel-powered Burlington Zephyr captivates the nation as it streaks from Denver to Chicago in 13 hours and five minutes. The UP follows with the articulated M10000, and the Streamline Era begins. Leading industrial designers like Raymond Loewy, Henry Dreyfuss, and Otto Kuhler are hired by the railroads to spiff up their steam engines to better compete with the emerging airline and automobile industries. The result is some of the most beautiful steam engines ever built: the New York Central's Dreyfuss, Commodore Vanderbilt, and Empire State Express; the Pennsy's K-4 Pacific and the

Hiawatha Prototype

Collector Dave Garrigues comments on Lionel tinplate steam locomotives: "They look weird. For example, look at the 260 series. The drivers are way too small. They used the same drivers for a little 258, as they do for the big 260. The drivers look fine on the 258 but ridiculous on the 260s. The earlier steamers like the 5, 6 and 7 looked like the American steam locomotives of the era, but Classic Period steamers looked more European than American. Ives and American Flyer steamers were much better looking than Lionel's. The Lionel electric-type engines were beautiful, but their steamers just looked weird."

S-1 Duplex; the Milwaukee Road's Hiawatha; the SP's Daylight; and the Norfolk & Western Js. For the first time, O gauge trains – the M10000 Streamliner and a 260 steamer – are featured on the cover of the Lionel catalog. The M10000 is the first tinplate diesel to be offered by any toy train manufacturer, but Lionel still loses over $200,000 for the third consecutive year. With cash reserves depleted, and creditors banging at the door, Lionel enters into receivership on May 7. Cowen is able to stave off the creditors, but still needs a small miracle, which he gets in the shape of a mouse – the Mickey Mouse Handcar. 253,000 handcars are sold for $1.00 each at retail. Figuring the profit at 40 cents per handcar, those sales generate about $100,000 in much needed cash.

1935 Lionel's new steam whistle and streamline trains helps propel Lionel to their first profitable year since 1929. Lionel is able to pay $296,197 to creditors and has $400,000 left over. The catalog offers an impressive lineup – the UP M10000, Flying Yankee, Hiawatha, Pennsy Torpedo, and a Commodore Vanderbilt. While streamlining on the real railroads only prolonged the inevitable demise of passenger service, streamlining proves a bonanza for Lionel. The sleek and colorful trains are eagerly snapped up by the buying public, who are feeling better about things as the Dow-Jones continues to climb (144 is the high for the year). The Mickey Mouse Circus Train also sells well, and the automatic Gateman, the longest running accessory Lionel will ever make, is new. The Rural Electrification Act, which Cowen had lobbied for because it will mean more customers, is finally passed.

Harry Spalding was six years old in 1929. He had two older brothers and the Spaulding family lived in a large brownstone in New York City. "We had this huge Standard gauge layout on the third floor," recalls Harry, who now lives in Maryland horse country. "I remember it clearly. There was nothing else in the room and the track was laid right on the wood floor. The trains were so heavy. I couldn't even lift the engines. I'd play with that crane car for hours. Lift up lead soldiers and drop them in a gondola, then tell my brother 'She's all loaded,' and watch it whiz around the track. My favorite thing to do was turn the lights out, put my head on the floor as close to the track as I dare, and watch the train, headlight blazing, flash by. Then the Depression hit. My dad lost everything and we moved in with my mom's parents. I have no idea what happened to all the trains, but a few year ago I found an old box that had somehow survived about ten moves. In it were my dad's Lionel, Ives, and American Flyer catalogs from the '20s. He had marked everything he purchased with an 'x'. There was an 'x' next to the huge Lionel 408E set from 1928, the Ives *Olympian*, and the *Fast Freight Senior*. We had the Hellgate Bridge, the Power Station, City Station and Terrace, and just about every signal Lionel made. There was a photograph of all of us sitting around the layout. We all look very happy. I love that photograph."

1936 Lionel's model of the Pennsy Torpedo, one of the most popular of the new streamline steamers, is on the cover of the catalog. Cowen, never one to miss any trend, also cashes in on the nation's fascination with airplanes by introducing the Lionel remote control electric airplane. The O gauge Blue Comet is new, and sales continue to increase. The Santa Fe's Super Chief goes from Los Angeles to Chicago in under 40 hours, and Roosevelt is re-elected in a landslide. Dow is now at 182. *Gangbusters* and *The Shadow* debut on radio, and first knock-knock jokes are heard.

Catalog art.

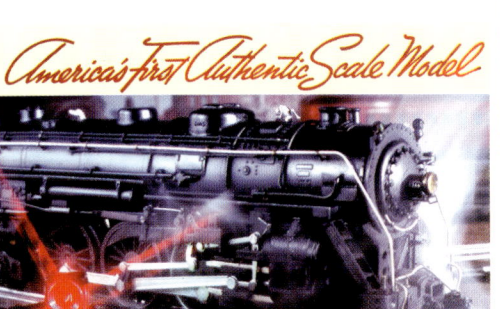

Graced with meticulous detail, the scale Hudson was the finest locomotive ever made by Lionel.

"I guess the fascination started with the catalogs," says Tom Kelly, of Manhattan. "I'd look at them for hours. Study every page. I'd dream about having that Santa Fe diesel or one of the big steamers. They just looked so great. And the accessories. Oh my. I never even knew anyone who had a Bascule Bridge or the Magnetic Crane, but I felt I owned them because I dreamed about them so much."

1937 In response to the growing trend towards model railroading, Lionel introduces the scale Hudson (1/48th actual size), an engine that combines scale model accuracy with mass production performance and economy. "It was the most beautiful thing my eyes ever beheld," Cowen will say years later. The Hudson sells for $75 and aims at the growing adult model train market. With all economic signs pointing up, Lionel goes public and generates almost a million dollars. The money is used to replace outdated machinery and pay off loans. The success of the die-cast Hudson will lead to a new line of highly detailed die-cast locomotives, which will sell for far less than the Hudson, but have far more detail than their sheet-metal predecessors. San Francisco's Golden Gate Bridge opens, and Howard Hughes flies from Los Angeles to Newark, in a record seven and one-half hours. Joe Louis knocks out Jimmy Braddock and is the new heavyweight champion of the world.

1938 Lionel introduces a Hudson in OO gauge (1/76th actual size). With people moving to the cities, living space shrinks. HO gauge (half the size of O gauge) emerges as the gauge of choice for the serious modeler. Lionel's entry into OO gauge is an attempt to offer an alternative. It never catches on, and Lionel gives up on it. Some say that if Lionel would have continued the OO line after the war, they would have created a buffer against the eventual decline in O gauge by offering a viable alternative to HO. Realism is in and the toy train look is out. Lionel introduces its second scale item – a fine model of the Pennsy's B-6 0-6-0 switcher. Three other die-cast steamers are new: the 226E, 225E and 224E. The 226E will become the smoothest-running Lionel steam engine ever made. The 97 Coal Loader is introduced. A. C. Gilbert buys the rights to manufacture American Flyer trains from William Coleman, and moves the company to New Haven, Connecticut. Gilbert quickly develops a line of scale trains, feeling that Lionel's scale and semi-scale trains are aimed at the adult hobbyist. Gilbert believes kids should also have realistic scale trains and at affordable prices. Thus, the stage is set for the Postwar battle between the two companies. The Reds' John Vander Meer throws consecutive no-hitters, and Action Comics No. 1 stars Superman. Disney's *Snow White and the Seven Dwarfs* makes the nation smile, and *The Green Hornet* is the hot new radio show.

LIONEL LEADS THE WORLD!

Upon seeing a movie studio for the first time, Orson Wells remarked, "This is the biggest electric train set any boy ever had."

1940 "Electrified action – all at the touch of a button." is the theme of the 1940 catalog. The new 313 Bascule Bridge stops the approaching train as the bridge slowly rises, then lowers; then the train lurches forward to continue on its journey. "Amazing! Thrills! Excitement!" Also new is the 164 Log Loader. Scale and semi-scale freight cars are introduced to go with the scale and semi-scale Hudsons and switchers. Sales climb to $3.5 million, but Lionel has their eyes towards war production, not toy trains. German troops are in Paris and FDR is elected for a third term. Population is at 130 million. The Bears beat the Redskins 73 to 0, and Tex Avery creates Bugs Bunny. Gas costs 16 cents a gallon, and a glass of beer is a nickel.

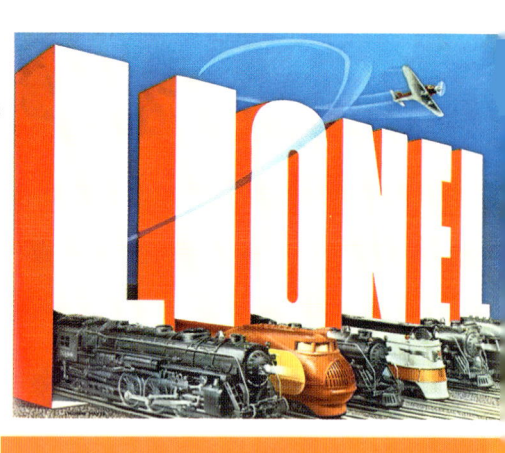

Oh boy! Have the fun of your life with Lionel electric trains and accessories.

Lionel 'OO' Gauge Models

1939 Germany invades Poland. War is inevitable, and Lionel begins seeking war contracts rather than designing new trains. Standard gauge is cataloged for the last time and American Flyer introduces a line of 3/16th-inch scale O-gauge trains. *Gone With the Wind*, Disney's *Pinocchio*, and *The Wizard of Oz* lead the movie parade, and Americans spend $25 million to go see them, while *The Shadow* and *Capt. Midnight* are radio favorites. Edward R. Murrow starts broadcasting nightly reports from Europe.

"You were either a Lionel guy or a Flyer guy," recalls Jim Bowden, who grew up in Pittsburgh right after the war. "Flyer guys thought Lionel made short, stubby trains, had way over-sized accessories, and that the Lionel three-rail track was goofy. We made fun of Flyer's link couplers, their smaller, light weight trains, and the reverse loop problem. You couldn't set up a Flyer layout on the floor on a rainy Saturday afternoon and have a reverse loop. Kids were very brand name conscious - just like now. Today they argue over the merits of Nike or Converse sneakers, and Sega, Sony and Nintendo video games. In my day, the first line brands were Schwinn bikes, Wilson gloves and Lionel trains. The second bananas were JC Higgins bikes, Spalding gloves and American Flyer trains. That's just the way it was. Like Beta and VHS. In Postwar America, Flyer was Beta."

Japan Attacks Pearl Harbor

1941 Accessories emerge as a major part (40%) of Lionel's business, and "Remote Control" becomes the buzzword of a generation. Cranes turn and lift, logs dump and are picked up and loaded into another car, coal is dumped and loaded, cars shoot out boxes and uncouple – all at the touch of a button. Lionel offers about as much excitement as a ten-year-old heart can stand. Joe DiMaggio, who will become a spokesman for Lionel in the '50s, hits safely in 56 straight games. *Dumbo, The Maltese Falcon,* and *Citizen Kane* are big hits. On December 7th, the Japanese launch a surprise attack on Pearl Harbor and America declares war on Japan. Lionel already has $5 million in government contracts, and switches immediately to war production. Rationing begins.

1942 Lionel catalog

1942 The last Prewar catalog is printed. Appropriately, the 700E scale Hudson is on the cover. The few items that are produced use a glossy gray paint instead of silver (silver paint requires metal). War rages on two fronts, and the real railroads become the life line of the nation, carrying troops and supplies from coast-to-coast. Jimmy Cagney wins an Oscar for *Yankee Doodle Dandy,* and Glenn Miller's *Chattanooga Choo Choo* becomes the first gold record, selling over one million copies.

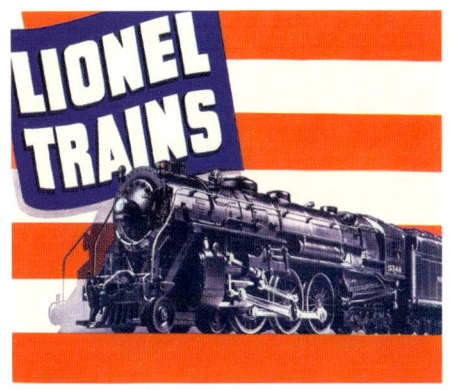

1943 Lionel produces a Paper Train so their young customers won't forget. The war is very profitable for Lionel. Sales reach $7.3 million. "Use it up, wear it out, make it do, or do without" are the words Americans live by. *Casablanca* wins the Academy Award for best picture.

The Lionel Paper Train

DEVELOPING NEW ACCESSORIES WAS ALWAYS A HIGH PRIORITY AT LIONEL. COWEN ONCE SAID, "CHILDREN WANT TO PARTICIPATE. THEY WANT MOVEMENT AND ACTION. THEY DON'T JUST WANT TO WATCH A TRAIN GO AROUND AND AROUND. A FEW MINUTES OF THAT, AND THE LITTLE NIPPERS WILL WANDER OFF AND SQUEEZE OUT SOME TOOTHPASTE OR SET FIRE TO THE CURTAINS. THEY'VE GOT TO GET IN ON THE ACTION."

1944 D-Day! Allied troops storm the beaches of Normandy. Germans are driven from Paris. MacArthur returns to the Philippines. The great Postwar boom is just ahead. Mario Caruso, after 40 years of helping Joshua Cowen build Lionel, resigns. Lots of babies on the way.

Germany and Japan Surrender

1945 16 million babies are born during the year, and it is clear that the demand for toy trains will be immense during the early 1950s. New technology developed for the war effort is now utilized for peacetime production. Plastic emerges as a viable alternative to tin. Plastic costs less, and more detail can be applied. The Postwar

"Prewar Lionel is what toy trains should look like," says Paul Fox of Seattle. "Bright colors, cheerful, made of tin and sheet metal. It thrills me to think of these trains being made in the '30s and some kid playing with them and loving them and now, many years later, I am able to pick them up. It's like holding history in your hands."

> To a boy growing up in the forties or fifties, the Lionel catalog was a treasure to be savored and saved. The illustrations were pleasantly deceptive, drawn by artists who used angles, settings, and proportions that made the trains look larger and more detailed than they really were. But no one was disappointed. Somehow, reality lived up to fantasy.

boom begins. People are weary of war and ready for fun. Toy trains will be high on everyone's list, right after a new house, new car, new appliances, new furniture, and a TV. Lionel is the first toy train company to catalog a Postwar line of trains. It doesn't matter that only one freight set, headed by a carry-over 224 steamer, is offered. What matters is that toy trains are back and happy days are here again. Lost in the excitement is the one major innovation – the automatic knuckle coupler – a giant improvement over the Prewar box coupler.

1946 If the 1946 Lionel line at Toy Fair was a Broadway play, it would have been a smash hit. Everything sells. The new Pennsy Turbine with smoke tops the list, followed by new scale-detailed freight cars, the 726 with Irvington cars, accessories, track, and switches. Smoke is the big news, the best toy train innovation ever. Talk to someone who had trains as a kid. Invariably, he will recall the little white pellets he dropped in the smokestack. A paper shortage curtails the print run on both Lionel and American Flyer catalogs. Lionel out-maneuvers Flyer by buying 16 color pages in *Liberty Magazine*. The pages contain Lionel's complete catalog, and are seen by 8.5 million readers. The Norman Rockwell-like cover depicts an upset son glowering at his father who has taken over the kid's train set. The track is three-rail, and the train looks like a Lionel. This brilliant promotional move captures the attention of many first-time, Postwar train buyers, and they become lifelong Lionel customers. Also new is the amazing 38 Water Tower, which seems to pump real water and is the brain child of Josh Cowen. Sales over $10 million for the first time. American Flyer introduces a fine line of smaller S gauge (1/64th scale to O gauge's 1/48th) trains featuring two-rail track and steam engines with "Smoke and Choo Choo." Many feel the American Flyer trains, with two-rail track and a more realistic appearance, are superior to Lionel's. It is a hot debate and it rages in neighborhoods across America. Lionel, with superior marketing, wins the sales race, outselling American Flyer about three to one. However, those fierce loyalties are permanently forged and even 50 years later, American Flyer enthusiasts still insist they have the best trains.

671 Turbine

Thrill Packed Engineering!

> "We'd always go downtown to Marshall Fields right after Thanksgiving. They had a huge Lionel display layout," says Roger Whittingham, who now lives in Los Angeles. "The shelves behind the layout were stacked with those gorgeous orange and blue boxes. I would get the new catalog and make a wish list. Then, on Christmas morning, I'd race down to the living room. Dad had set everything up during the night. I remember the tunnel he made using the empty boxes. I just stood there with my mouth open. Mom and dad were watching me, smiling. Nobody said anything. Then I started running the trains. Blew the whistle. Stopped, went in reverse, then forward again. Ohmigosh, it smokes! Made the cars uncouple. Operated the Milk Car. It was just the best time. I will never forget it."

1947 The Automatic Milk Car is new and it will become the most popular operating car ever. Next to the Santa Fe diesel and smoke, it is the item most thought of when Lionel is mentioned. Lionel also brings out a model of the Raymond Loewy designed GG-1. This is a fine model of the famous Pennsy locomotive, but it does not receive the hype that an important new engine would normally receive. The following year it does. The two-page spread shows a beaming boy looking down on two

212

Illustration depicting GG-1 in 1948 catalog.

1948 A very good year for both Lionel and America. Railroads switch to diesel power, and the most popular new diesel is EMD's F-3. Lionel introduces two models of the F-3. A red and silver Santa Fe and a handsome two-tone gray New York Central. The Santa Fe will run for 18 years and become the best-selling engine Lionel ever produces. It is the engine most people think of when you mention Lionel. Other important new items include the Cattle Car, Diesel Coal Loader, Conveyor Lumber Loader, and the Lionel Electronic Control Railroad. Priced at $200, this set is strictly for rich kids. The transformer of everyone's dreams is unveiled – the ZW. Two handles, brutish, just like controlling real trains. To show off all these new products, Lionel builds a new layout for their showroom at 15 East 26th Street, in Manhattan. The layout measures 16x32' and will stay forever in the memories of those kids lucky enough to see it. Frank Sinatra, who will later build a layout reminiscent of the new showroom layout, drops in to buy a set for a friend. Sales increase to over $15 million and Lionel acquires Airex, producers of fishing equipment. John Houston wins best director for *Treasure of the Sierra Madre*. *The Texaco Star Theater,* starring Milton Berle, premiers and a *Chicago Tribune* headline declares: "Dewey Defeats Truman". A Buick Roadmaster sells for $2,900, the Dow-Jones hits 193, and McDonalds sells its first franchise.

GG-1 sets. One is emerging from a tunnel. The angle of sight is low and the GG-1 appears massive, shiny, and irresistible. It is one of the best illustrations ever to appear in a Lionel catalog and, presumably, sells a lot of GG-1s. A new line of low-priced sets are called Scout, perhaps after Tonto's horse. Sales at $12.1 million. Jackie Robinson breaks the color line in baseball, and the Yankees-Dodger World Series is the first to be televised.

Santa Fe F-3 illustration in 1952 catalog.

New York Central F-3

1949 A model of GMs NW-2 switcher is produced with a mechanical ringing bell and a new rail-gripping invention called Magne-Traction. Magne-Traction will not be officially announced until 1950, but the new GM switcher comes equipped with it. The Cattle Car is new. It becomes, after the Milk Car, Lionel's best-selling operating car. For the first time, mom and sis make the catalog cover. Before, only sons and dads appeared. Lionel decides that in Postwar America, the women of the family are a force to be recognized. Sales at $15.5 million. Arthur Miller's *Death of a Salesman* opens on Broadway. Nat King Cole's *Mona Lisa* tops the pop charts, and Casey Stengel is named to manage the New York Yankees. Dow-Jones is over 200 for first time since 1929, and the Polaroid Land Camera goes on sale for $89.75.

Magnificent realism and Super-power

213

1950 Lionel celebrates its 50th birthday by bringing back the Hudson – not the highly detailed scale masterpiece, but a good model none-the-less. A new O-27 UP Alco leads three yellow streamline passenger cars in a set that will eventually be referred to by collectors as the Anniversary Set. Magne-Traction is announced, and promises "more speed, more pull, more climb and more control." The 456 Operating Coal Ramp is new, along with the Oil Derrick, and a Lift Bridge that is pictured in the catalog, but never made. Lionel sales reach $21.5 million as a survey shows the Lionel name ranks right behind Cadillac and Sears in terms of acceptance and perception of quality. Roy Campenella, the great Dodger catcher, is interviewed by Edward R. Murrow on *Person-to-Person*. During the interview, Campenella shows off his large Lionel layout in his basement. One million Lionel catalogs are distributed. American Flyer introduces two diesels – a beautiful model of an Alco PA and the GM GP-7. *Your Hit Parade* and *Beat the Clock* premier. A comic strip, *Charlie Brown*, appears for the first time.

The thrill of power, beauty and speed.

"I specialize in the Lionel trains made between 1946 and 1952," says Jim Noonan, of Dallas. "After 1952 they started cheapening the line. The changes were subtle. Little things, like the wire mesh in the vents of the F-3s were removed. So were the handrails. The Alcos and NW-2 switchers were cheapened. Lionel had to cut costs in the face of declining profits, and the quality was never again up to the trains they made between '46 and '52. Funny thing is, the more they cut costs, the more sales dropped. Maybe there was a connection."

1951 Truce in Korea. The happy family of 1949 returns to the cover of the catalog. Because of the Korean war, Lionel is unable to obtain magnets, so only diesels come equipped with Magne-Traction. Even though not one new train or accessory is produced, sales are at $19 million. The only change has to do with the UP Alco. It is now painted silver, rather than yellow. George Reeves is Superman, and Johnny Ray sings *The Little White Cloud That Cried*. Dow is at 276 and going up.

1952 Best catalog cover ever. It shows a kid in an engineer's hat, smiling, above a stone arch bridge. "Lionel" is etched in powerful, three-dimensional block letters on the side of the bridge. Under the bridge is a six-track mainline packed with engines – all with the headlights blazing. "The men of tomorrow choose Lionel today," says the catalog, still pitching the educational aspect of toy trains. New diesels include a Western Pacific F-3, blue and yellow C&O switcher, and a Rock Island Alco. The top set is the Lionel Super Speedliner – AA Santa Fe F-3s with four new aluminum streamline cars. Lionel finally catches up with Kusan, which has had a line of aluminum passenger streamline cars since 1949. Even Flyer had streamline cars to go with their new Alco in 1950. Streamlined passenger cars is one area where Lionel lagged behind the rest. 180,000 Milk Cars are sold, which help sales rocket to $28,159,463. The Barrel Loader and Operating Switch Tower are new accessories. Eisenhower is elected President, Mad Comics No. 1 is released, and the Yankees beat the Dodgers in the World Series. Gary Cooper wins an Oscar for *High Noon*. *Dragnet* is the top TV show. *The Jackie Gleason Show* premiers, along with *The Adventures of Ozzie and Harriet*.

Engineered for a lifetime of real railroad operation.

These two O27 switchers love yard work.

214

1953 Catalog cover

Lionel '027' Diesels with Magne-Traction

1953 Lionel sales peak at $32.9 million. Everything sells and Lionel is the largest toy company in the world. American Flyer also has their best year, with sales of $16 million. Flyer's knuckle coupler, introduced in 1952, is a big hit and contributes to the record sales year. 1953 to 1958 will be the Golden Age for American Flyer. Many gorgeous passenger trains will be made, and all are highly prized today. The 497 Coaling Station, and the 6464-Series Boxcars are introduced. Despite the banner year, there are some ominous signs. Rail travel continues its decline as more and more people travel by air, and Lionel's President Larry Cowen, always looking to diversify, brings out the Linex Stereo camera but forgets to develop any film for his new camera. It will serve only to drain energy and resources. *From Here to Eternity* wins the Oscar, and an ad for L&M cigarettes states, "Just what the doctor ordered."

1954 A Seaboard is added to the NW-2 switcher line-up, and a gorgeous red and white Texas Special, along with a gray and green Southern, are added to the F-3s. A new diesel, the Lackawanna FM Trainmaster, with two motors, is the largest single unit ever built by Postwar Lionel. The 50 Gang Car, the first of many popular motorized units, is new, and more 6464-Boxcars are offered. Lionel, in an attempt to boost sales in the spring and summer, adds the Airex line of fishing gear to the catalog. Airex, like all other Lionel non-train projects, will fail. It seems people trust the Lionel name for trains, but nothing else. Dow-Jones jumps to a high of 404.

LIONEL . . . .
THE WORLD'S FINEST TRAINS
1900-1955

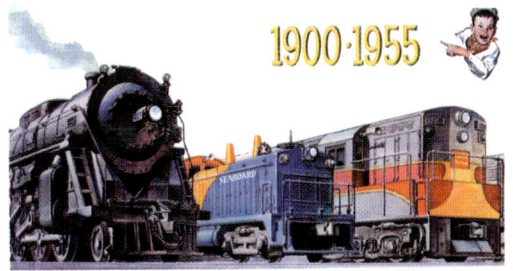

Lionel promotional material.

"Dad — they're a Million Miles ahead of everything — these LIONEL Trains"

1955 Wabash and Illinois Central are new F-3s, a Virginian FM is added, along with a red and yellow reversible Trolley and a U.S. Army switcher. New accessories include the Diesel Fueling Station, Ice Depot, and the Piggyback Transportation Set. The Congressional Set, headed by a Tuscan GG-1, retails for $49.95. Kids are dancing to Bill Haley's *Rock Around the Clock*, Disneyland opens, and James Dean, 24, is killed in his Porsche Spyder. Sales are down 38% from the 1953 peak as the number of Lionel's core market, eight-to-ten-year-old boys, begins to level off. The country is booming, but dark clouds are forming on Lionel's horizon.

1956 Lionel decides to fight back with an impressive line-up of new trains and accessories, their first wrap-around catalog cover, and a new mascot: the Lionel Lion. A Jersey Central FM, Budd RDC Car, and New Haven EP-5 Electric are new, along with Milwaukee Road and Baltimore & Ohio F-3s. New operating cars include the Searchlight Extension Car, GM Generator Car, Brakeman Car, and Burro Crane. The Sound Dispatching Station and Lumber Mill are top new accessories. Lionel sales are down to $22 million. 54 million tune in to *The Ed Sullivan Show* to see Elvis Presley sing *Heartbreak Hotel* and *Don't Be Cruel*. Ike wins a second term and Don Larsen throws a perfect game against the Brooklyn Dodgers. Dow-Jones is over 500.

1956 Catalog cover.

FROM PERKY GADABOUTS TO MASSIVE BRUISERS. ALL THE EXCITEMENT OF REAL-LIFE RAILROADING.

215

1957 America's fascination turns skyward. For the first time, airplanes carry more passengers than trains. Sputnik is launched. Lionel tries to keep pace by introducing a line of space and military toys, but they never catch on. Kids are playing with slot cars, space toys, and robots. HO trains, half the size of O Gauge, dominate model train sales. Lionel introduces a line of HO trains and a new showroom layout is designed to introduce Lionel's new Super O track. A misguided marketing decision leads to a Girl's Train, which features a pink engine and freight cars in pastel colors. A giant flop at the time, the Girl's Train goes on to become a valuable collector's item. The Canadian Pacific F-3 passenger set, Milwaukee Road EP-5 Electric, and a Norfolk & Western J are new. It's a big year for accessories. New are the Culvert Loader and Unloader, Operating Fork Lift Platform, Dispatching Board, Animated Newsstand, and Transfer Table. Sales fall to under $19 million, but Lionel manages to make a profit, the last profitable year of the Postwar era. *American Bandstand* makes it's TV debut on ABC; Brooklyn weeps as the Dodgers move West. So do the New York Giants. *Chances Are, All Shook Up, Jailhouse Rock* and *All the Way* are hit records. Average salary is $4,200.

The Lionel Lion first appeared in 1956.

The rails hum! Glowing headlights swing into view around the curve...and your midnight freight sweeps past.

Milwaukee Road EP-5

1958 The nation is in a defensive mood in the wake of the successful launch of Sputnik by the U.S.S.R. In an attempt to turn around the downward trend of sales, Lionel goes even more Space Age and military with rocket launchers, rocket-carrying flat cars, and trains with military loads including anti-aircraft guns, an amphibious duck, and radar units. The 68 Executive Inspection Car and Ballast Tamper are new motorized units, and Pennsylvania and Virginian are new electrics. Sales fall to $14.4 million, and the company shows a loss of $469,000, the first since the Depression. Americans are wild for Hoola Hoops, and Joshua Lionel Cowen retires.

1959 More military trains. A US Army Rocket Launcher, AEC Switcher, Helicopter Launching Car, Radar Car, IRBM Launcher, and a Flat Car with Missiles. The General, a fine model of the 4-4-0 American-type steam locomotive from the Civil War period, is also new. Cowen sells his remaining Lionel shares to Roy Cohn, former chief investigator for Senator Joseph McCarthy. Cowen's son, Lawrence, the poster boy from the '20s, also sells out to Cohn. This will be the first in a series of power shifts and take-overs that will plague Lionel for the next ten years. Lionel loses $1.2 million on sales of $15.7 million. Lionel's HO line acquires dies from Hobbyline. Three rock stars, Buddy Holly, Richie Valens, and J.P. "Big Bopper" Richardson, die in a plane crash. Barbie Doll is new and a new Oldsmobile sells for $2,933. Green Bay Packers name Vince Lombardi coach.

216

1960 Weak catalog. Bad color. Bad art. A retired Army Major General, John B. Maderis, becomes Lionel's president. Cohn thinks Maderis will be able to obtain government contracts to offset the downward trend of toy train sales. Cohn orders sweeping cutbacks, and sells off equipment for cash. Sales plummet. Lionel produces the "Father/Son" set, made up of matching O and HO equipment. This will become one of the most sought-after sets of the Postwar era, mainly because so few are sold. The same holds true for a number of other items that sold poorly, and have since become highly desirable 25 years later. John F. Kennedy becomes the youngest man ever elected President, and we enter the tumultuous '60s.

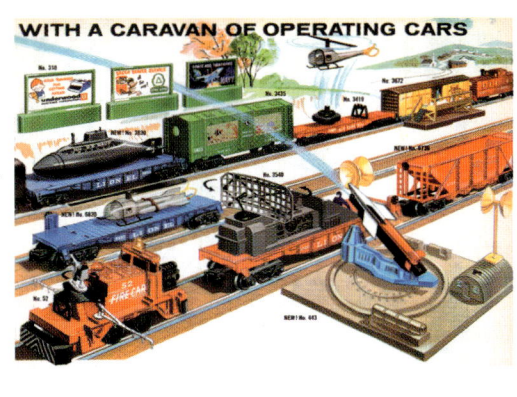

Americans Are In Space

1961 Management searches for other products to increase sales, as train sales continue to fall. Most of the first 21 pages of the catalog are filled with science sets, chemistry sets, the Famous Inventor series, weather stations, plastic engineering sets, and toy tool kits. The train line is a mixture of military and space items, gift sets, and action and operating cars. The top-of-the-line Super Chief sells for $100, and consists of AA Santa Fe's with four red-stripe aluminum passenger cars. Few are sold, but it will have made a good investment (if you don't play with it). Forty years later, this set (in mint condition) will sell at auction for $12,000. Other future hot collector items include the Great Northern Rotary Snowplow, a solid-striped GG-1, Flat Cars with a Crane and Power Shovel, a motorized Fire Car, Maintenance Car, Minuteman Missile Launching Car, Animated Sheriff and Outlaw Car, Satellite Launching Car, Auto Loader, Boat Loader, Submarine Car, and the Aquarium Car. The 452 Gantry Signal and 161 Mail Pick-up Set are two mediocre accessories that don't sell, but become very collectible. That can be said about the entire 1961 line. A bad year for business, but a great year for future collectors. Cohn continues his shell game by acquiring Dale Electronics, and Pacific Western and Sterling Power. Maris hits 61 home runs, the Dow is at 734, and you can see a Broadway play for $8.60. The *Lucy Show* debuts, and *The Apartment* wins the Academy Award.

1962 John Glenn orbits the earth three times in Friendship 7, and we go deeper into the Space Age. Lionel prints it's biggest catalog ever (100 pages), but only half is devoted to trains. The rest is a potpourri of stuff carried over from last year, with Scalextric Racing Cars and a Talking Teddy added. Trains are a mixture of action cars with a space theme (like the Operating Satellite Launching Car and the Turbo Missile Firing Car) and traditional items. Top-of-the-line Santa Fe set now has gold stripe aluminum cars and is called the Presidential Special. The Maderis experiment fails, and he is booted upstairs. Year-end loss is at $4.8 million. The first James Bond film, *Dr. No*, is released, and Johnny Carson debuts as host of *The Tonight Show*. The Dow is at 767.

217

1963 Catalog cover is color but trains are in black and white against a weak red background, Santa Fe F-3, 736 steamer, and solid stripe GG-1 return, plus space and military cars and sets – all carry-overs. Losses hit $6.5 million. Cohn sells out to Victor Muscat, who sells out to Hotel Corporation of America. Lionel is blowin' in the wind, which is the title of Bob Dylan's hit song. Zip codes are introduced, the Pepsi Generation arrives, and *The Fugitive* premiers. President Kennedy is assassinated.

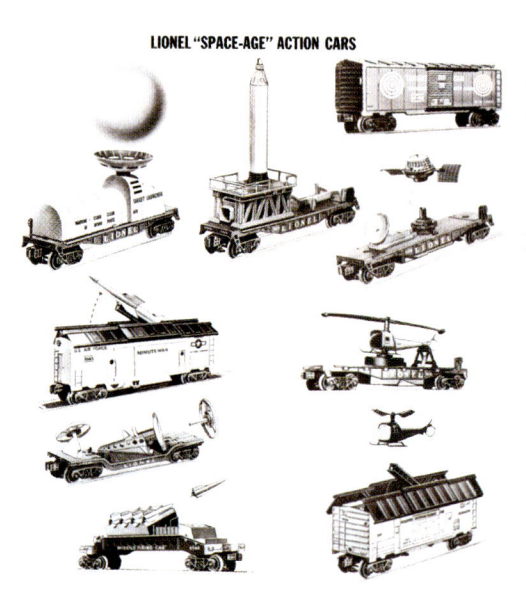

1965 On September 8, Joshua Lionel Cowen dies at the age of 85. A Virginian FM is resurrected, and the 736, Santa Fe F-3 AA, and Hudson continue. Catalog is black and white, with a bizarre cover. The Dodgers beat the Twins in the World Series and the Sony home video tape recorder is new. Dow is up to 969.

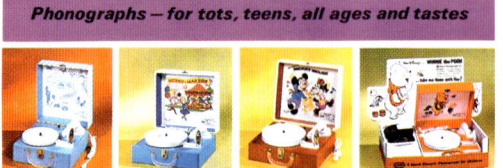

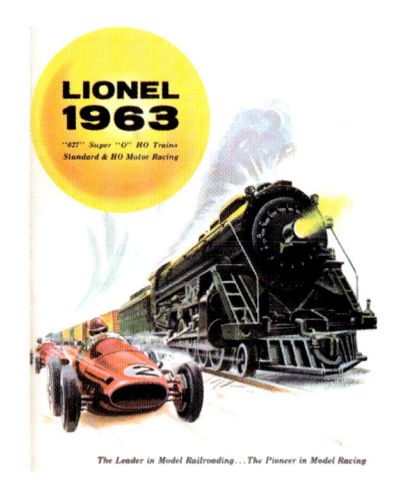

1964 Now even the cover is no longer in full color. Lionel re-issues the 773 Hudson, with a Pennsy-style tender, heading a seven-car freight set for $200. 736 and Santa Fe F-3 continue as other top items. Robert Wolfe is now president of Lionel. Beatles invade America, and Dow-Jones is at 891. New Oldsmobile is $3,495, LBJ defeats Barry Goldwater in a landslide, *Jeopardy* premiers, and *My Fair Lady* is best picture.

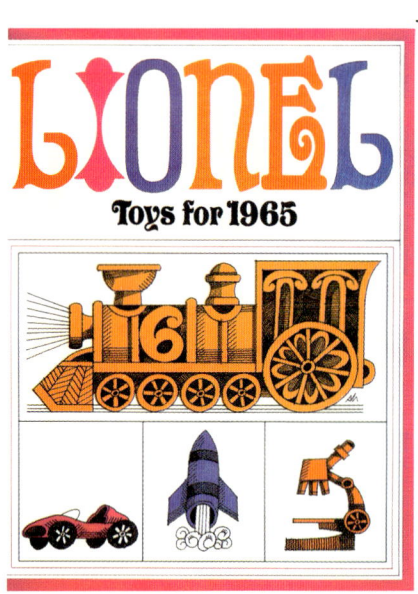

1966 Cowen's death the previous year goes unnoticed in the Lionel catalog. Last year the 773 Hudson is produced, and the rest of the line is all carry-overs. Lionel's President, Robert Wolfe, writes in the catalog, "Here at Lionel we've been making toys that are good, clean fun for almost 60 years." Actually, Lionel had been making toys for almost 70 years. This carelessness is an indication of the casual attitude Lionel's top man has about the company. No fire. No passion. Would Joshua Lionel Cowen ever understate anything? Not surprisingly, sales continue to fall, and losses continue to mount. This is the last year of any significant production from Postwar Lionel. HO trains and Super O track (the tooling for which has since been destroyed) appear for the last time. The Dow hits 950. An American Flyer bicycle (no relation) sells for $110, Simon and Garfunkle sing the *Sounds of Silence*, Adam West is Batman, and *A Man for all Seasons* wins best picture.

1967 For the first time since 1946, no catalog is printed. The few dealers left are told to use the 1966 catalog. Lionel buys American Flyer for $150,000, a surprising purchase given Lionel's financial condition and the demand for toy trains. Lionel moves its manufacturing to one of its subsidiaries: the Porter-Spear Company of Hagerstown, Maryland. The Green Bay Packers defeat Kansas City Chiefs in first Super Bowl, folks are buzzing about *The Graduate,* starring Dustin Hoffman, and the Cards beat the Red Sox in the World Series.

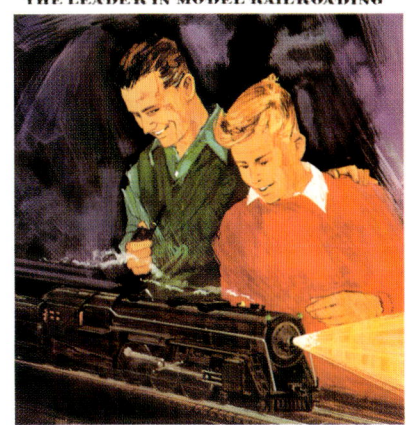

1966 Lionel catalog.

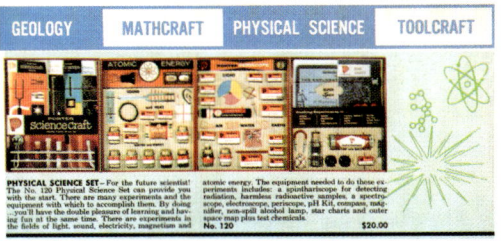

1968 Some Lionel trains and parts are produced in Japan for the first time. Ronald Saypole, a corporate gadabout with a penchant for $200 lunches, becomes Lionel's president. Sales fall to under $2 million. Pie ala mode is 50 cents, and a hot dog with the works is 25 cents. Nixon squeaks out a victory over Hubert Humphrey, and the Beatles top the charts with *Lady Madonna.*

AMERICA PUTS MAN ON THE MOON
"THE EAGLE HAS LANDED."

1969 All motors and E-units are manufactured in Japan. On April 24, 1969, the Lionel Corporation gets out of the train business and enters into licensing agreement with General Mills. MPC, a toy division of General Mills, purchases the molds, tools, and dies and moves them from the Hillside, New Jersey plant to a 97,000 square-foot building in Mt. Clemens, Michigan. In April, 1970, production of Lionel trains resumes, and a new era begins. The Dow peaks at 962, John Wayne wins best actor for *True Grit,* Neil Armstrong sets foot on the moon, and Joe Namath guarantees a Super Bowl win and delivers on the boast.

1968 Lionel catalog.

The end of an era.

219

Item #	Page #	Item #	Page #	Item #	Page #
1/2 0C	22, 156	46	9, 28, 60	92	13, 28, 158
1/2 OS	22, 156	47	9, 28, 60	93	13, 28, 143
1	59, 77	47-73	152	94	13, 28
2	9, 59, 77	48	156	95	26
3	59, 77	48W	9	96	13
4	35, 59	49	9, 157	96C	26, 158
4U	35	0050	190	97	13, 28, 48, 143, 172
5	65	50	9, 62, 90, 172	98	13
5/F	156	51	10, 65, 90, 172	99	13
6	65	52	10, 90, 172	99N	13
7	65	53	10, 62, 63, 91, 172	100	13, 78, 79
8	61, 78	0054	190	100-104	13
8E	61	54	10, 63, 91, 172	101	13, 78
9	61, 78	0055	190	102	13
9E	61	55	10, 91, 172	103	13
9U	61	55-150	152	104	13
10	61, 78	0056	190	105	14
10E	61	56	10, 91, 143, 172	105-110	14
11	22, 72	0057	190	106	14
12	22, 72	57	10, 91, 172	108	14
13	23, 72	0058	190	109	14
14	60, 72	58	10, 91, 143, 172	0110	197
15	60, 72	0059	190	110	14, 143
16	60, 72	59	10, 91, 172	110-85	172
17	60, 72	60	10, 28, 91, 172	0111	197
20	23, 24	60N	10	111	14, 143
20X	24	61	10	111-50	152
21	23, 24	62	11	111-100	153
22	23, 25	63	11	112	14, 73, 157
23	9	63W	172	113	14, 73
23-65	25	64	11, 143	0114	197
23-65N	9	64-15	152	114	14, 73, 143, 172
24	60	65	11, 26, 91, 172	0115	197
25	9, 60	66	11, 26	115	14, 143, 172
25-50	25	67	11, 26	116	14, 73
25-50N	9	0068	190	0117	197
27	60	68	11, 92, 172	117	14, 73
27N	9	69	11, 92, 172	0118	197
28	152	69N	11	118	14, 144, 172
29	67	70	11, 143	118L	14
30	22, 143, 172	71	11, 28, 143	0119	197
31	22, 156	71N	11	119	14
32	22, 156	74	60	119L	14
33	22	75	60, 143	120	14, 157
33	61, 62, 156	76	11, 28, 143	120L	14
34	22, 62, 156	77	11, 60	121	14
35	9, 28, 143	77N	11	122	14, 153
35-30	152	78	11	123	14, 153
36	156	79	12	123-60	153
37	156	80	12	124	14
38	62, 143, 156, 172	80N	12	125	14, 144
0039	195	81	12, 26	126	15
39-3	152	82	12	127	15
40	152	82N	12	128	15, 144, 172
40-25	152	83	12	129	15
40-40	152	84	12	130	15, 157
41	22, 90, 172	85	12, 28	130L	15
42	23, 62, 90, 172	86	12, 28	131	15
43	9, 156	87	12	132	15, 144, 172
44	9, 60, 90, 172	88	26, 158	133	15, 144, 172
44-80	152	89	12, 143, 172	134	15
45	9, 60, 90, 143, 172	90	13, 158	135	15
45N	9, 28, 143	91	26, 158	136	15

Item #	Page #	Item #	Page #	Item #	Page #
37	15, 28	194W	48	222R	25
38	144, 172	195	18, 147	223	25
0140	197	195-75	153	223L	25
40	144	196	18, 153	223P	173
40L	16	0197	197	223R	25
42	157	197	147, 172	0224	197
42-125	157	197-75	153	224	40, 81, 95, 173
42-150	157	198	18	224C	173
44	48	199	18, 147	224E	40
44E	48	200	18, 77, 79	224P	173
0145	197	201	44	225	25, 81, 173
45	144	202	78, 80, 172	225	40
45C	158	203	37, 44	225E	40
46W	48	204	40, 80	226	81, 173
47	158	204P	172	226E	40
48	144	205	18, 80	227	44, 81, 173
148-100	158	205P	172	228	44, 81, 173
150	35, 36, 145, 172	205T	172	229	40, 81
151	145	206	153	229C	173
152	16, 28, 36, 145	207	153	229E	40
152-33	153	208	18, 29, 80	229P	173
153	16, 28, 36, 145	208P	172	230	44, 81, 173
153-23	153	208T	172	231	44, 81, 173
153C	22, 158	209	18, 80, 153	232	44, 81, 173
154	16, 28, 36, 145	209P	172	233	44, 96, 173
155	16, 145	209T	172	233W	173
156	16, 28, 36, 145	210	25, 80	234	96
156X	36	210L	25	234E	48
157	17, 145	210P	172	235	96, 173
158	17, 36	210R	25	236	96, 173
159	22	210T	172	237	96, 173
160	153	211	74, 80	238	40, 97, 173
161	17, 145	211P	172	238E	40
162	17	211T	172	239	97, 173
163	17, 146	212	74, 80, 172	240	97, 173
164	17, 28, 146, 172	212P	172	241	97, 173
164-64	153	212T	80, 172	241E	48
165	17, 29	213	74, 80, 147	242	97, 173
165-53	153	213P	172	242T	173
167	26, 158	213T	172	243	97, 173
167X	26	0214	197	243W	173
168	26	214	74, 147	244	97, 173
169	26	214R	74	244T	173
170	26	215	74, 80, 172	245	97, 173
171	26	216	75, 80, 153, 172	246	97
172	26	216P	172	246E	49
175	146, 172	217	75, 80	247	97, 173
175-50	153	217C	173	247T	173
182	146, 172	217P	172	248	37, 97, 173
182-22	153	218	75, 80	249	43, 97, 173
182E	48	218C	173	249E	43
184	17	218P	173	250	37, 97, 173
185	17	218T	173	250E	41
186	17, 59	219	75, 81, 173	250T	173
186W	48	220	25, 75, 81	251	37, 97, 173
187	17	220P	173	251E	37
188	59	0221	197	252	37, 147
189	17	221	81, 95, 173	252E	37
190W	48	221T	173	253	37. 148
191	17	221W	173	253E	37
192	17, 146, 172	0222	197	254	38
193	17, 146, 172	222	25, 81, 173	254E	38
194	17	222L	25	255E	39

Item #	Page #	Item #	Page #	Item #	Page #	Item #	Page #
256	38, 148, 173	342	149, 173	430	69
257	43, 148, 173	345	149, 173	0431	197
258	43	346	149, 173	431	68
259	43	347	149, 173	0432	197
255E	39	348	149, 173	0433	197
260	157	0349	195	435	19
260E	39	350	149, 173	436	19
261	43	350-50	149, 173	437	19
261E	44	352	149, 173	438	19
262	44, 148	352-55	153	439	20
262E	44	353	149	440	20
263E	40	356	150	440C	20
264	148, 173	356-35	153	440N	20, 29
264-150	153	0357	195	441	20
264E	41	362	150, 173	442	20
265E	41	362-78	153	443	150, 173
267	49	364	150, 173	444	20
268	49	364C	158	445	150, 173
270	18	0365	195	448	151, 173
271	18	365	150, 173	450	38, 151
272	18	0366	195	450L	153
276W	49	0370	195	452	151, 173
279E	51	375	150, 173	455	120, 51, 173
280	18	380	63	456	151, 173
280X	18	380E	63	460	151, 173
281	18	381	63	460-150	154
0282	197	381E	63	460P	151, 173
282	18, 148, 173	381U	63	461	151, 173
282R	148, 173	384	65	462	151, 173
283W	49	384E	65	463W	159
289E	41	385E	65	464	151, 173
298W	49	390	66	464-150	154
299	148, 173	390C	158	465	151, 173
0300	195	390E	66	0470	197
300	18, 77, 79	392E	66	470	151, 173
0301	195	394	150	0480	197
303	78	395	150	480-25	154
308	18, 148	397	150, 173	480-32	154
309	70, 79, 148	394-37	153	490	68
0310	197	400	79, 82, 173	0494	197
310	70, 148	400E	66	494	151
312	70	402	64	497	151, 173
313	18, 29, 148, 173	402E	64	0500	184
314	18, 29, 148	404	82, 173	500	79
315	19, 29, 148	408E	64	0501	184
316	19, 29, 148	410	150	0502	184
317	148	412	68	0503	184
318	63	413	68, 158	0504	184
318E	63	414	68	0505	184
0319	195	415	150, 173	0510	184
319	70	416	68	0511	184
0319-110	195	418	68	511	76
320	71	419	68, 150, 173	0512	184
321	148	420	69	512	76
322	71	421	69	0513	184
332	71, 149	422	69	513	76
0333	195	424	69	0514	184
334	149, 173	425	69	514	76
0337	195	426	69	514R	29, 76
337	71	427	69	0515	184
338	71	428	69	515	76
339	71	429	69	516	76
341	71	0430	197	517	76

Item #	Page #	Item #	Page #	Item #	Page #
0520	185	601	86, 174	700	39
520	76, 88, 173	0602	191	700E	42
0521	185	602	86, 174	700EWX	42
0522	185	603	45	700K	42
0523	185	0605	191	0701	187
0524	185	0610	185	701	39, 44
0525	185	610	86, 174	0702	187
0530	186	611	86, 174	0703	187
0531	186	613	86, 174	703	39
0532	186	614	86, 174	703-10	154
0533	186	0615	187	0704	191
0535	189	616	87, 174	0705	191
0535W	189	617	87, 174	0706	191
0536	189	620	29, 52	706	39
0537	189	621	87, 174	0707	191
0540	186	622	87, 174	0708	191
0541	186	623	87, 174	0709	191
0542	187	624	87, 174	709W	49
0543	187	0625	191	0710	191
0545	190	625	85, 174	0711	191
0550	187	0626	191	711	23
550	20	626	85, 174	711L	23
0551	187	627	85, 174	711R	23
551	20	628	85, 174	0712	191
0552	187	629	85, 174	0713	191
552	20	633	87, 174	0714	192
0553	187	634	87, 174	714	58
553	20	0635	191	714K	58
554	20	635	87, 174	0715	192
0555	189	0636	191	715	58
555	20	0637	191	715K	58
0556	189	637	95, 174	716	58
556	20	638-2361	105	716K	58
0560	187	0642	191	717	58
0561	190	0643	191	717K	58
0564	189	0645	191	720	23
0565	189	645	87, 174	721	23
0566	189	0645W	191	721L	23
0567	190	0646	191	721R	23
0568	190	646	94, 174	0723	192
0569P	190	646-25	174	0725	192
0570	187	0647	191	726	92, 174
0571P	190	651	52	726RR	174
0575	190	652	52	726S	154
0576	190	653	52	728	39
0577	190	654	29, 52	730	24
0580	187	655	52	731	24
0581	190	656	52	731L	24
0585	187	657	52	731R	24
0586	190	659	52	732	39
0587	190	665	94, 174	0733	192
0590	187	671	99, 174	0735	192
0591	190	671-75	154	736	92, 174
0592	190	671R	99, 174	736W	174
0593P	190	671RR	99	746	93, 174
0593T	190	671S	154	746W	174
0594P	190	671W	174	746WX	174
0595	190	675	94, 95, 174	748W	49
0596	190	681	99, 174	755W	50
0597	190	682	99, 174	760	23, 157
0598	190	685	94, 174	761	23
0600	185	0700	187	762	24
600	45, 79, 86, 174			762S	24

223

Item #	Page #	Item #	Page #	Item #	Page #
763E	42	818	59	0864-225	188
766W	50	0819	186	0864-250	188
768W	50	0819-1	188	0864-275	192
771	24	0819-25	188	0864-285	192
772	24	0819-50	188	0864-300	192
772S	24	0819-75	188	0864-325	192
773	24, 94, 174	0819-100	188	0864-350	192
773W	174	0819-200	193	0864-400	192
0800	188	0819-225	193	0864-700	192
800	53, 79	0819-250	193	0864-900	192
0800-200	193	0819-275	193	0864-935	192
0801	188	820	55	0865	189
801	53, 59	0821	194	0865-200	194
0801-200	193	821	55	0865-225	194
801X	59	822	55	0865-250	194
802	53, 59	0823	194	0865-400	194
802X	59	0824	188	0865-435	194
803	53	0824-200	194	0866	186
804	53	0827	193	0866-25	189
0805	195	0827-50	193	0866-200	196
805	53	0827-75	193	0870	194
0806	193	0830	189	0871-1	186
806	53	831	55	0872-1	189
0807	193	0834	195	0872-25	186
807	53	0836	189	0872-50	186, 189
0808	193	0836-1	194	0872-200	196
808	59	0836-100	194	0873	195
0809	193	0836-110	194	0874	192
809	53	0837	193	0874-25	192
0810	193	0837-110	193	0874-60	192
810	53	0838	193	0875	194
811	53	0840	193	0877	186
0811-1	186	840	20	0877-1	188
0811-25	186, 188	0841	193	0879	188
812	54	0841-50	193	0880	195
812T	20	0841-85	193	0889	193
0813	193	0841-125	193	890W	50
813	54	0841-185	193	0900	197
0814	188	0842	194	900	55, 79
814	54	0845	196	901	55
0814-200	194	0847	195	902	55, 151
814R	54	0847-100	195	908	151
0815	189	0850	195	909	154
815	55	0850-110	195	910	20, 151
0815-50	196	0857	186	911	21
0815-60	196	0860	186	912	21
0815-75	196	0860-1	188	913	21
0815-85	196	0860-200	193	914	21
0815-110	196	0861	194	915	21
0816	196	0862-1	186	916	21
816	55	0862-25	186	917	21
0817	188	0862-200	194	918	21
817	55	0862-250	194	919	21, 154
0817-25	188	0863	194	920	21, 151, 174
0817-50	188	0864-1	185	920-2	151
0817-150	192	0864-25	185, 188	920-3	154
0817-200	192	0864-50	185, 188	920-4	154
0817-225	192	0864-75	185	920-5	154
0817-250	192	0864-100	185	920-8	154
0817-275	192	0864-125	185	921	21
0817-300	193	0864-150	186, 188	921C	21
0817-325	193	0864-175	186, 188	922	21
0817-350	193	0864-200	188	923	21

Item #	Page #	Item #	Page #	Item #	Page #
924	22	1050	79, 97, 174	1431W	160, 175
925	22, 154	1050T	174	1432	160, 175
926	154	1053	158	1432W	160, 175
927	22, 155	1053E	32	1433	160, 175
928	155	1055	81, 174	1433W	160, 175
943	132, 152	1057E	32	1434WS	160, 175
958	174	1060	50, 98	1435WS	160, 175
963-100	174	1061	59, 98	1437WS	160, 175
970	152, 174	1062	98	1439WS	160, 175
986	174	1063	158	1441WS	161, 175
987	174	1065	81, 174	1443WS	161, 175
988	174	1066	81, 174	1445WS	161, 175
1000	78, 79	1066E	32	1447WS	161, 175
1000W	159, 174	1073	158	1449WS	161, 175
1001	97, 159, 174	1100	27, 78	1451WS	161, 175
1002	128	1101	98	1453WS	161, 175
1004	105	1103	27	1455WS	161, 175
1005	140	1105	27	1457B	161, 175
1007	116	1107	27	1459WS	161, 175
1008	157	1110	98	1461S	161, 175
1008-50	157	1111	159, 174	1463W	161, 175
1009	157	1112	159, 174	1463WS	161, 175
1010	34, 78, 158	1113	159, 174	1464W	161, 175
1011	34, 158	1115	159, 174	1465	161, 175
1012	26, 158	1117	159, 174	1467W	161, 175
1013	23, 157	1119	159, 174	1469WS	161, 175
1014	158	1120	98	1471WS	161, 175
1015	34, 158	1121	23, 157	1473WS	161, 175
1016	158	1122	157	1475WS	161, 175
1017	26, 32	1122E	157	1477S	161, 175
1018	23, 157	1122LH	157	1479WS	161, 175
1019	23, 157	1122RH	157	1481WS	161, 175
1020	157	1130	98	1483WS	161, 175
1021	23	1130T	174	1484WS	161, 175
1022	22, 157	1229	27	1485WS	161, 175
1023	22, 157	1230	27	1500	22, 161, 175
1024	23, 157	1239	27	1501S	161, 175
1024L	23	1400	159, 174	1502WS	161, 175
1024R	23	1400W	159, 174	1503WS	161, 175
1025	23, 157, 158	1401	159, 174	1505WS	162, 175
1026	158	1401W	159, 174	1506	28
1027	26	1402	159, 174	1506L	28
1028	26	1402W	159, 174	1507WS	162, 175
1029	26	1403	159, 174	1508	28
1030	26, 34	1403W	159, 174	1509WS	162, 175
1032	158	1405	159, 174	1511	28
1033	158	1405W	159, 174	1511S	162, 175
1034	158	1407B	160, 174	1512	29, 34
1035	34	1409	160, 174	1513S	162, 175
1037	26, 158	1409W	160, 174	1514	29, 34
1038	27	1411W	160, 174	1515	29
1039	27	1413WS	160, 174	1515WS	162, 175
1040	27	1415WS	160, 174	1516WS	162, 175
1041	27, 158	1417WS	160, 174	1517	30, 34
1042	158	1419WS	160, 174	1517W	162, 175
1043	158	1421WS	160, 174	1519WS	162, 175
1044	158	1423W	160, 174	1520W	162, 175
1045	22, 29, 152	1425B	160, 174	1521WS	162, 175
1047	152, 174	1426WS	160, 174	1523	162, 175
1048	50	1427WS	160, 174	1527	162, 175
1048X	50	1429WS	160, 174	1529	162, 175
1049	59	1430WS	160, 175	1531W	162, 175
1049X	59	1431	160, 175	1533WS	162, 175

225

Item #	Page #	Item #	Page #	Item #	Page #
1534W	162, 175	1625T	176	1800	164, 176
1536	27	1625WS	164, 176	1805	164, 176
1536W	162, 175	1626W	164, 176	1809	164, 176
1537WS	162, 175	1627S	164, 176	1810	164, 176
1538WS	162, 175	1629	164, 176	1811	34
1539W	162, 175	1630	29	1812	34
1541WS	162, 175	1631	29	1813	34
1542	162, 175	1631WS	164, 176	1835E	66
1543	162, 175	1633	164, 176	1862	93, 176
1545	162, 175	1635WS	164, 176	1862T	176
1547S	162, 175	1637W	164, 176	1865	100, 101, 176
1549S	162, 175	1639WS	164, 176	1866	100, 101, 176
1551S	162, 175	1640-100	155, 176	1872	93, 176
1552	162, 175	1640W	164, 176	1872T	176
1553W	162, 175	1641	164, 176	1875	100, 101, 176
1555WS	162, 175	1642	164, 176	1875W	100, 101, 176
1557W	162, 175	1643	164, 176	1876	100, 101, 176
1559W	162, 175	1644	164, 176	1877	123, 176
1560	22	1645	164, 176	1882	93, 176
1561WS	162, 175	1646	164, 176	1885	100, 101, 176
1562W	162, 175	1647	164, 176	1887	123, 176
1563W	162, 175	1648	164, 176	1910	64, 67
1565W	162, 175	1649	164, 176	1911	64
1567W	162, 175	1650	164, 176	1912	64
1569	22, 162, 175	1651	32, 39, 164, 176	2016	95, 176
1571	163, 175	1654	98	2018	95, 176
1573	163, 175	1655	98	2020	99, 176
1575	163, 175	1656	98, 176	2020W	176
1576	50	1661E	32	2023	81
1577	59	1662	44	2024	81, 176
1577S	163, 175	1663	44	2025	95, 176
1578S	163, 175	1664	41	2026	95, 96, 177
1579S	163, 175	1664E	41	2026X	95, 177
1581	163, 176	1665	98, 176	2028	87, 177
1583WS	163, 176	1666	41, 95, 176	2029	96, 177
1585W	163, 176	1666E	41	2031	81
1586	163, 176	1668	42	2032	82
1587S	163, 176	1668E	42	2033	82
1588	28	1677	30, 32	2034	98, 177
1589WS	163, 176	1678	32	2035	95, 177
1590	163, 176	1679	30	2036	96, 177
1591	163, 176	1679X	30	2037	96, 177
1593	163, 176	1680	30	2037-500	96
1595	163, 176	1680X	30	2041	82, 177
1597S	163, 176	1681	32	2046	94, 177
1599	163, 176	1681E	33	2046W	177
1600	163, 176	1682	30	2046WX	177
1601W	163, 176	1682X	30	2055	94, 177
1603WS	163, 176	1684	42	2056	94, 177
1605W	163, 176	1688	42	2065	94, 177
1607W	163, 176	1688E	42	2100	164, 177
1608W	163, 176	1689E	42	2100W	164, 177
1609	163, 176	1700	33	2101	164, 177
1611	163, 176	1700E	33	2101W	164, 177
1612	163, 176	1717	31	2103W	165, 177
1613S	163	1717X	31	2105WS	165, 177
1615	98, 163, 176	1719	31	2110WS	165, 177
1615T	176	1719X	32	2111WS	165, 177
1617S	163, 176	1722	32	2113WS	165, 177
1619W	164, 176	1722X	32	2114WS	165, 177
1621WS	164, 176	1766	71	2115WS	165, 177
1623W	164, 176	1767	71	2120S	165, 177
1625	98, 176	1768	71	2120WS	165, 177

Item #	Page #	Item #	Page #	Item #	Page #
2121S	165, 177	2235W	167, 178	2338	87, 178
2121WS	165, 177	2237WS	167, 178	2339	87, 178
2123WS	165, 177	2239W	167, 178	2340-1	178
2124W	165, 177	2240	83	2340-25	178
2125WS	165, 177	2240C	178	2341	85, 178
2126WS	165, 177	2240P	178	2343	83
2127WS	165, 177	2241WS	167, 178	2343C	83, 178
2129WS	165, 177	2242	83	2343P	178
2131WS	165, 177	2242C	178	2343T	178
2133W	165, 177	2242P	178	2344	83
2135WS	165, 177	2243	83	2344C	83, 178
2136WS	165, 177	2243C	83, 178	2344P	178
2137WS	165, 177	2243P	178	2344T	178
2139W	165, 177	2243W	167, 178	2345	83
2140WS	165, 177	2244W	167, 178	2345P	178
2141WS	165, 177	2245	83	2345T	178
2143WS	165, 177	2245C	178	2346	87, 178
2144W	165, 177	2245P	178	2347	87, 178
2145WS	165, 177	2245WS	167, 178	2348	87, 178
2146WS	165, 177	2247W	167, 178	2349	87, 178
2147WS	165, 177	2249WS	167, 178	2350	88, 179
2148WS	165, 177	2251W	167, 178	2351	88, 179
2149B	165, 177	2253W	167, 178	2352	88, 179
2150WS	165, 177	2254W	167, 178	2353	83
2151W	165, 177	2255W	167, 178	2353P	179
2153WS	165, 177	2257	116	2353T	179
2155WS	166, 177	2257WS	167, 178	2354	83
2159W	166, 177	2259W	167, 178	2354P	179
2161W	166, 177	2261WS	167, 178	2354T	179
2163WS	166, 177	2263W	167, 178	2355	83
2165WS	166, 177	2265SW	167, 178	2355P	179
2167WS	166, 177	2267W	167, 178	2355T	179
2169WS	166, 177	2269W	167, 178	2356	83
2171W	166, 177	2270W	167, 178	2356C	83, 179
2173WS	166, 177	2271W	167, 178	2356P	179
2175W	166, 177	2273W	167, 178	2356T	179
2177WS	166, 177	2274W	167, 178	2357	116
2179WS	166, 177	2275W	167, 178	2358	88, 179
2183WS	166, 177	2276W	167, 178	2359	88, 179
2185W	166, 177	2277SW	167, 178	2360-1	90, 179
2187WS	166, 177	2279W	167, 178	2360-25	178
2189WS	166, 177	2281W	167, 178	2363	83
2190W	166, 177	2283WS	168, 178	2363C	179
2191W	166, 177	2285W	168, 178	2363P	179
2193W	166, 177	2287W	168, 178	2365	88, 179
2200	78	2289WS	168, 178	2367	83
2201WS	166, 177	2291W	168, 178	2367C	179
2203WS	166, 177	2292WS	168, 178	2367P	179
2205WS	166, 177	2293W	168, 178	2368	84
2207W	166, 177	2295WS	168, 178	2368C	179
2209W	166, 177	2296W	168, 178	2368P	179
2211WS	166, 177	2297SW	168, 178	2373	84
2213WS	166, 178	2321	84, 178	2373P	179
2217WS	166, 178	2322	84, 178	2373T	179
2219W	166, 178	2328	87, 178	2378	84
2221WS	166, 178	2329	88, 178	2378C	179
2222WS	166, 178	2330	89, 178	2378P	179
2223W	166, 178	2331	84, 178	2379	84
2225WS	167, 178	2332	89, 178	2379C	179
2227W	167, 178	2333	83	2379P	179
2229W	167, 178	2333P	178	2383	84
2231W	167, 178	2333T	178	2383P	179
2234W	167, 178	2337	87, 178	2383T	179

Item #	Page #	Item #	Page #	Item #	Page #
2400	179	2523	102, 180	2659	56
2401	179	2523W	168, 179	2660	56
2402	179	2525WS	168, 179	2671W	180
2403B	179	2526W	168, 180	2671WX	180
2404	179	2527	168, 180	2672	58
2405	179	2528WS	168, 180	2677	30
2406	179	2529W	168, 180	2679	30
2408	179	2530	102, 180	2680	31
2409	179	2531	102, 180	2682	31
2410	179	2531WS	168, 180	2682X	31
2411	123	2532	102, 180	2717	32
2412	179	2533	102, 180	2719	32
2414	179	2533W	168, 180	2722	32
2416	179	2534	102, 180	2755	29, 58, 140, 180
2419	120, 179	2535WS	169, 180	2757	58
2420	120, 179	2537W	169, 180	2757X	59
2421	179	2539WS	169, 180	2758	59, 105, 180
2422	179	2541	103, 180	2810	56
2423	179	2541W	169, 180	2811	56
2429	179	2542	103, 180	2812	56
2430	100, 101, 179	2543	103, 180	2812X	56
2431	100, 101, 179	2543WS	169, 180	2813	56
2432	179	2544	103, 180	2814	56
2434	179	2544W	169, 180	2814R	57
2435	179	2545WS	169, 180	2815	57
2436	179	2547WS	169, 180	2816	57
2440	100, 101, 179	2549W	169, 180	2817	57
2441	100, 101, 179	2550	82, 180	2820	57
2442	100, 101, 102, 179	2551	103, 180	2855	140, 180
2443	100, 101, 179	2551W	169, 180	2954	59
2444	102, 179	2552	103, 180	2955	29, 59
2445	102, 179	2553	103, 180	2956	59
2446	102, 179	2553WS	169, 180	2957	59
2452	128	2554	103, 180	3300	78
2452X	128	2555	140, 180	3309	132
2454	179	2555W	169, 180	3330	132, 180
2456	130	2559	82, 180	3330-100	132, 155, 180
2457	115	2560	121, 180	3349	133, 180
2460	121, 179	2561	103, 180	3356	139, 180
2461	122, 179	2562	103, 180	3356-2	155, 180
2465	140	2563	103, 180	3356-150	155, 180
2466T	179	2570	169, 180	3357	104, 180
2466W	179	2571	169, 180	3357-27	155
2466WX	179	2572	169, 180	3359-55	121, 180
2472	115	2573	169, 180	3360	92, 180
2481	102, 179	2574	169, 180	3361-55	123
2482	102, 179	2575	169, 180	3362	123
2483	102, 179	2576	169, 180	3364	123
2501W	168, 179	2620	29, 55	3366	139, 180
2502W	168, 179	2625	103, 180	3366-100	155
2503WS	168, 179	2627	103, 180	3370	104, 180
2505W	168, 179	2628	103, 180	3376	104, 180
2507W	168, 179	2630	29	3376-160	180
2509WS	168, 179	2631	29	3386	104, 180
2511W	168, 179	2642	29	3409	133, 180
2513W	168, 179	2643	29	3410	133, 180
2515WS	168, 179	2651	55	3413	133, 180
2517W	168, 179	2652	56	3419	133, 180
2518W	168, 179	2653	56	3424	104, 180
2519W	168, 179	2654	29, 56	3424-50	155
2521	102, 179	2655	56	3424-100	155
2521WS	168, 179	2656	56	3428	105, 180
2522	102, 179	2657	56	3429	134, 180

228

Item #	Page #	Item #	Page #	Item #	Page #
3434	104, 180	3859	58	6112	129
3435	104, 180	3927	92, 181	6112-25	155
3444	105, 180	3927-50	155	6119	120, 181
3451	123	3927-75	155	6119-25	120, 181
3454	105, 180	4109WS	169, 181	6119-50	120, 181
3454-51	155	4110WS	169, 181	6119-75	120
3456	130	4357	116, 181	6119-100	120, 181
3459	121	4452	128, 181	6119-125	120, 121, 181
3460	124, 180	4454	107, 181	6120	120
3461	124	4457	115, 181	6130	120
3462	137	4460	121	6142	129
3462-70	155	4681	99	6149	157
3462P	155	5159	155	6151	124, 181
3464	106	5459	121, 181	6157-125	117
3469	121	6002	128	6162	129
3470	134, 180	6004	107	6162-60	129, 181
3472	137	6007	116	6162-110	129, 181
3474	106, 180	6009	157	6167	118
3482	137	6012	129	6167-25	118
3484	106, 180	6014	107, 181	6167-50	118
3484-25	106, 180	6014-60	181	6167-85	118
3494-1	107, 180	6014-85	107	6167-100	118
3494-150	107, 180	6014-100	181	6167-125	118
3494-275	107, 180	6014-150	181	6167-150	118
3494-550	107, 180	6014-335	107	6175	134, 181
3494-625	107, 180	6014-410	181	6176	130
3509	134, 180	6015	140	6176-100	130
3510	134, 180	6017	116	6176-1967	131
3512	124, 180	6017-50	116, 181	6219	120
3519	134, 181	6017-85	116, 181	6220	87, 181
3520	138	6017-100	117, 181	6250	87, 181
3530	138, 181	6017-185	117	6257	119
3530-50	155	6017-200	117, 181	6257X	119, 181
3535	134, 181	6017-225	117	6262	124, 181
3540	134, 181	6019	157	6264	124, 181
3545	124, 181	6020W	181	6311	125, 181
3559	121	6024	108	6315	141, 181
3562	128	6024-60	108, 181	6315-60	141
3562-1	181	6025	140	6342	130
3562-25	181	6026T	181	6343	125, 181
3562-50	181	6026W	181	6346-56	131, 181
3562-75	181	6027	117, 181	6352-1	108
3619	134, 181	6029	157	6352-25	155, 181
3620	138	6032	129	6356	181
3650	138	6034	108	6356-1	139
3651	57	6035	140	6357	119
3652	57	6037	117	6357-50	181
3656	139	6042	129	6361	125
3656-34	155	6044	108	6362	181
3656-150	155	6044-1X	108, 181	6362-55	125
3659	57	6045	140, 141	6376	139, 181
3662-1	137	6047	117	6401	181
3662-79	155	6050	108, 181	6401-1	125
3665	134, 181	6057	117	6402	125
3666	134, 181	6057-50	117	6402-25	125
3672	137, 181	6058	117	6403B	181
3672-79	155	6059	117	6404	125
3672P	155	6059-50	117	6405	125, 181
3811	57	6062	129	6406	125, 181
3814	57	6062-50	129	6407	125, 134, 181
3820	134, 181	6067	117	6408	125, 181
3830	134, 181	6076	130	6409	181
3854	107, 181	6110	98	6409-25	125, 181

229

Item #	Page #	Item #	Page #	Item #	Page #
6411	125, 181	6464-200	111, 182	6556	139, 182
6413	135, 181	6464-225	111, 182	6557	119, 182
6414	125, 181	6464-250	111, 142, 182	6560	122, 182
6414-25	155, 181	6464-275	111, 182	6560-25	122, 182
6414-85	181	6464-300	111, 182	6561	123, 182
6415	141	6464-325	111, 182	6562	130
6416	126, 181	6464-350	112, 182	6572	137, 182
6417	116, 181	6464-375	112, 142, 182	6630	135, 182
6417-25	116	6464-400	112, 182	6636	132
6417-50	116, 181	6464-425	112, 182	6640	135, 182
6418	123, 181	6464-450	112, 182	6646	139
6419	120	6464-475	112, 142, 182	6650	135, 182
6419-25	120	6464-500	113, 182	6650-80	156
6419-50	120	6464-510	113, 182	6651	135, 182
6419-75	120	6464-515	113, 182	6656	139
6419-100	120, 181	6464-525	113, 142, 182	6657	119, 182
6420	120, 181	6464-650	113, 142, 182	6660	127, 182
6424	126	6464-700	113, 142, 182	6670	127, 182
6424-110	181	6464-725	113, 182	6672	138, 182
6425	141	6464-735	142	6736	132, 182
6427	116	6464-825	114, 182	6800	127, 182
6427-60	116, 181	6464-900	114, 142, 182	6800-60	156, 182
6427-500	116, 181	6464-1965	142	6801	127, 182
6428	108	6464-1965X	142	6801-50	182
6429	121, 181	6465	141, 142	6801-60	156
6430	126, 181	6465-60	142	6801-75	182
6431	126, 181	6466W	182	6802	127, 182
6434	139, 181	6466WX	182	6803	135, 182
6436	181	6467	126, 182	6804	135, 182
6436-1	131	6468	182	6805	135, 182
6436-25	131, 181	6468-1	114	6806	135, 182
6436-110	131, 181	6468-25	114	6807	135, 182
6436-500	131, 181	6468X	114, 182	6808	135, 182
6436-1969	131	6469	126, 182	6809	135, 183
6437	116	6470	135	6810	127, 183
6440	100, 101, 126, 181	6472	137	6812	127, 183
6441	100, 101, 181	6473	105, 139	6814	121, 136, 183
6442	100, 101, 181	6475	142, 182	6816	128, 183
6443	100, 101, 181	6476	132	6816-100	156, 183
6445	136, 181	6476-1	132	6817	128, 183
6446	181	6476-125	132	6817-100	156, 183
6446-1	131	6476-135	132	6818	128
6446-25	131, 181	6477	126, 182	6819	136, 183
6446-60	181	6480	135, 182	6820	136, 183
6447	116, 181	6482	137	6821	128, 183
6448	135, 182	6500	126, 182	6822	138, 183
6452	130	6501	126, 182	6823	136, 183
6454	108, 109, 155, 182	6502	126, 182	6824	121, 183
6456	131	6502-50	126, 182	6824-50	121, 183
6457	119	6502-75	126, 182	6825	128, 183
6460	121, 182	6511	127, 182	6826	128, 183
6461	123, 182	6511-24	155	6827	128, 183
6462	130	6512	127, 135, 182	6827-100	156
6462-500	130, 182	6517	115, 182	6828	128, 183
6463	135, 141, 182	6517-75	115, 182	6828-100	156
6464-1	109, 182	6517-1966	115, 142	6830	136, 183
6464-25	109	6518	123, 182	6844	136, 183
6464-50	110, 182	6519	127, 182	11201	169, 183
6464-75	110, 182	6520	138, 182	11212	169, 183
6464-100	110, 182	6530	114, 182	11222	169, 183
6464-125	110, 182	6536	132	11232	169, 183
6464-150	110, 182	6544	135, 182	11242	169, 183
6464-175	111, 182	6555	142	11252	169, 183

230

Item #	Page #	Item #	Page #	Item #	Page #
11268	169, 183	12850	171, 183	OCS	156
11278	169, 183	13008	171, 183	OO-31	24
11288	169, 183	13018	171, 183	OO-32	24
11298	169, 183	13028	171, 183	OO-34	24
11308	170, 183	13036	171, 183	OO-51	24
11311	170, 183	13048	171, 183	OO-52	24
11321	170, 183	13058	171, 183	OO-54	24
11331	170, 183	13068	171, 183	OO-61	24
11341	170, 183	13078	171, 183	OO-62	24
11351	170, 183	13088	171, 183	OO-63	24
11361	170, 183	13098	171, 183	OO-64	24
11375	170, 183	13108	172, 183	OO-65	24
11385	170, 183	13118	172, 183	OO-66	24
11395	170, 183	13128	172, 183	OO-70	24
11405	170, 183	13138	172, 183	OO-72	24
11420	170, 183	13148	172, 183	OO-72L	24
11430	170, 183	13150	172, 183	OO-72R	24
11440	170, 183	A	25	OO1KW	59
11450	170, 183	B	25	OO44K	60
11460	170, 183	B909	152	OO45K	60
11470	170, 183	C	25	OO47K	60
11480	170, 183	ECU-1	157, 172	OO81K	59
11490	170, 183	F	25	OS	22, 156
11500	170, 183	H	25	OSS	22, 156
11510	170, 183	J	25	OTC	22, 156
11520	170, 183	K	25	Q	25, 157
11530	170, 183	KW	157	R	25, 157
11540	170, 183	L	25	RCS	22, 156
11550	170, 183	L363	152	RW	157
11560	170, 183	L461	152	S	24, 157
11590	170, 183	LW	157	SC	24
11600	170, 183	N	25	SW	157
11710	171, 183	O11L	22	SP	152
11720	171, 183	O11R	22	T	25
11730	171, 183	O12L	22	TO20	156
11740	171, 183	O12R	22	TOC	156
11750	171, 183	O20	156	TOS	156
11760	171, 183	O20X	23, 156	TW	157
12502	171, 183	O21L	23	U	25
12512	171, 183	O21R	23	UCS	156
12700	171, 183	O22	156	UTC	22
12710	171, 183	O22A	156	V	25, 158
12720	171, 183	O22L	23	VW	158
12730	171, 183	O22LH	156	W	25
12740	171, 183	O22R	23	X2454	105
12750	171, 183	O22RH	156	X2458	105
12760	171, 183	O25	156	X3464	106
12770	171, 183	O26	156	X6014	107
12780	171, 183	O42	156	X6454	109
12800	171, 183	O42L	23	Z	25, 158
12820	171, 183	O42R	23	ZW	158, 172
12840	171, 183	OC	22, 156		

Quick Reference

Prewar

Accessories	9
Track	22
Transformers	25
Clockwork Trains	27
Gray Years	28
Lithographed Cars	29
1600-2600 Freight	30
1700-2700 Freight	31
Lionel-Ives	32
Lionel Jr.	32
Winner Lines	34

O Gauge
Electrics	35
Steamers	39
Passenger Cars	48
Passenger Sets	52
Rolling Stock	
600 Series	52
800 Series	53
2600 Series	55
2800 Series	56
Scale, Semi Scale	58
Rolling Stock Outfits	59

OO Gauge	59

Standard Gauge
Electrics	61
Steamers	65
Passenger Cars	67

Rolling Stock
10 Series	72
100 Series	73
200 Series	74
500 Series	76
Trolleys	77

2 7/8" Gauge	79

Postwar

Diesels
Alcos	80
Budd Cars	82
F-3 Units	83
FM Units	84
GE-44 Tonners	85
GM Switchers	86
GP-7s & GP-9s	87

Electrics
EP-5s	88
GG-1s	89
Powered Units	90
Steamers	92

Passenger Cars	100

Rolling Stock
Action & Animation	104
Boxcars	105
6464 Boxcars	109
Cabooses	115
Coal Dump	121
Crane Cars	121
Depressed Center Flatcar	122
Flatcars	123
Gondolas	128
Hoppers	130
Military & Space	132
Mint Car	136
Refrigerator Cars	137
Searchlight Cars	138
Stock Cars	139
Tank Cars	140
TCA Conv. Cars	142
Vat Cars	142

Accessories	143
Replacement Acc.	152
Track	156
Transformers	157
Sets	159
Boxes	172
HO	184
Plasticville	198
Index	220

232